RUNNING PRESS

CYCLOPEDIA

THE ULTIMATE VISUAL REFERENCE TOOL

Fourth Edition

The Diagram Group

RUNNING PRESS
PHILADELPHIA • LONDON

Originally published by HarperCollins Publishers under the title
Collins Gem Encyclopedia

Copyright © Diagram Visual Information 2006

Printed in Hong Kong

9 8 7 6 5 4 3 2 1
Digit on the right indicates the number of this printing.

ISBN-13: 978-0-7624-2679-9
ISBN-10: 0–7624–2679–9

Library of Congress Cataloging-in-Publication number
2005934333

Cover design by Bill Jones

This book may be ordered by mail from your publisher. Please
include $2.50 for postage and handling.
But try your bookstore first!

Running Press Book Publishers
125 South Twenty-second Street
Philadelphia, Pennsylvania 19103–4399

The *Running Press Cyclopedia* provides a wealth of information presented in a concise and innovative manner.

The *Running Press Cyclopedia* is a digest of the basic subjects contained within a single-volume encyclopedia. The style of presentation is thematic, allowing all the topics included to be examined in context rather than with the fragmented viewpoint typical of an alphabetically organized encyclopedia. The contents pages (pages 6–11) show how the *Cyclopedia* has been structured with six major parts, each of which is divided into a series of sections. The sections are numbered 1 through 21 and each is identified by a different color. Within each section are groups of self-contained pages and two-page units. Wherever possible within these units, the information is further subdivided into headed paragraphs, captions, charts, tables, and structured diagrams.

The information in each of the sections is presented in a way that is appropriate for the subject concerned. For example, a tabular style has been used for "Countries of the World;" "History" is displayed as a series of timecharts; and explanatory text and labeled diagrams illustrate the intricacies of machinery and technology in "How Things Work."

As information can be more clearly presented with the aid of diagrams and charts, much of the *Cyclopedia* has been extensively illustrated with simple line drawings. They readily reveal the pattern of information, whether it relates to the world distribution of religious faiths, the groups of chemical elements, the orders of classical architecture, or an explanation of how an airplane flies.

Additional colors have been employed to facilitate access to information and to help clarify the subject.

HOW TO USE THE *CYCLOPEDIA*

The *Running Press Cyclopedia* is organized so that information can be found in a number of ways. The four methods by which you can find the information that you need are described here.

1 THE CONTENTS PAGES

Pages 6–11 list all the parts, sections, and major subsections of the book. The six main parts are:

The World (pages 12–131) covers the physical structure of the Earth, the weather, the environment, world population, and religions of the world.

Countries of the World (pages 132–79) gives statistical and geographical information for countries.

History (pages 180–253) details key events within timecharts of specific periods in world history.

Science (pages 254–533) contains major sections on astronomy, mathematics, physics, chemistry, biology, and the human body, including explanations of key principles. In addition, there is a chronology of inventions and a section explaining how things work.

The Arts (pages 534–81) combines timecharts of the major developments in the visual arts, music, theater, and literature, with illustrated explanations of particular aspects of these topics.

By adopting a visual approach to the presentation of information, the *Running Press Cyclopedia* offers a stimulating and refreshing approach to understanding key information on all the major areas of study.

The United States (pages 582–612) gives political, geographical, and historical information about the United States of America.

2 THE TOP OF EACH PAGE
You can quickly locate information by glancing at the top of each page. The part titles appear on the left-hand pages, and the section titles appear on the right-hand ones.

3 THE SIDE OF EACH PAGE
You can also locate information using color coding. The color designated for each section (as shown in the contents pages) appears on a band across the outside edge of each page, and the section number appears in a break on the color band.

4 THE INDEX
A comprehensive, fully cross-referenced alphabetical index of the subject areas covered appears at the back of the *Cyclopedia*.

CONTENTS

THE WORLD

SECTION 1: THE EARTH

SECTION 2: MAPPING

SECTION 3: THE WEATHER

SECTION 4: THE ENVIRONMENT

SECTION 5: WORLD POPULATION

SECTION 6: RELIGIONS

COUNTRIES OF THE WORLD

SECTION 7: POPULATION AND WEALTH

SECTION 8: COUNTRIES

HISTORY

SECTION 9: HISTORY

SCIENCE

SECTION 17: HOW THINGS WORK

THE ARTS

SECTION 18: ARTS CHRONOLOGIES

SECTION 19: VISUAL ARTS

SECTION 20: PERFORMING ARTS

THE UNITED STATES

SECTION 21: THE UNITED STATES

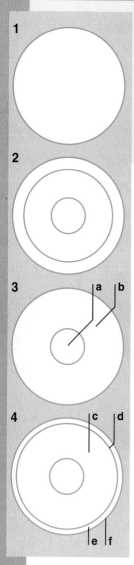

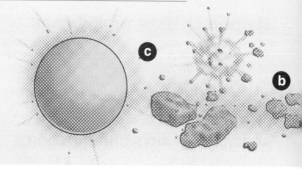

ORIGINS
How the Earth formed

The Earth began to form about 4600 million years ago from particles of dust, swirling gases, and tiny forming planets. The force of gravity compressed or tightly squeezed these elements together. This created intense heat and pressure inside the swirling mass.

At the same time, the pull of gravity was drawing the heavier elements in this mass toward the centre. Lighter elements and compounds, including gases, gathered near the surface.

The young Earth was surrounded by poisonous gases which were eventually replaced by air. The outer layer of the Earth cooled and hardened, although the centre remained liquid.

1 A cloud of moving dust particles, gases, and chemical compounds

2 The heavier particles were drawn toward the centre of the cloud

3 The earliest form of Earth, with a metal core (**a**) and meteorite-like matter around the core (**b**)

4 Outer rocks melted, forming the mantle (**c**) and the crust (**d**), and chemicals from the Earth's interior rose to form the oceans (**e**) and the early atmosphere (**f**)

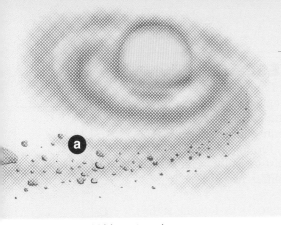

The space material **(a)** accretes and **(b)** collides to form larger clumps which formed **(c)** planets

Evolving continents

1 200 million years ago the Earth had only one large landmass called Pangaea. This mass was just beginning to break up, the start of continental drift.

2 135 million years ago the pieces of Pangaea broke into a northern landmass called Laurasia. India formed a separate, unattached area. A southern landmass was called Gondwana.

3 65 million years ago the landmasses began forming today's continents with their recognizable shapes. They were moving toward their present positions. India had not yet joined Asia.

4 Today the Earth's continents are Asia, Africa, North America, South America, Australia, Europe, and Antarctica.

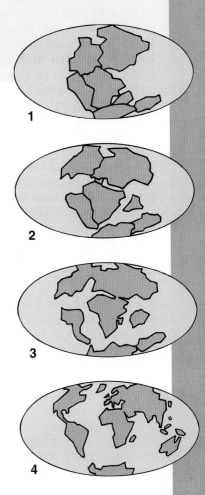

GEOLOGICAL TIMESCALE

The Earth's history is recorded in the rocks of the Earth's crust. Rocks have been forming, eroding, and re-forming from the beginning of the Earth's existence. Pieces of rocks which have worn away are called sediments. They accumulate in layers or strata, forming new rock. Strata hold clues about the Earth's history as they contain varied elements and settle in different ways.

Earth's ancient history

Geologists explain the clues in rocks by looking at the processes shaping the Earth's surface today. They believe these processes have always been the same. Many rocks contain fossils revealing the history of life on Earth. Fossils help geologists discover the age of rock strata and when a plant or animal lived. However, rocks do not provide a complete history of the Earth, as many rocks are destroyed by weathering and erosion or changed by heat and pressure deep in the Earth's crust. Geological clues in rocks only give a picture of Earth at the time the rock was formed. Geologists have pieced together clues from rocks of different ages but the complete history of the Earth will never be known.

Dividing geological time

The known history of the world is divided into three periods of time called eras: Paleozoic, Mesozoic, and Cenozoic.

Eras are divided into periods, which in turn are divided into epochs. Before this was the Precambrian time about which much less is known. These divisions are based on various stages in the development of life shown by fossils. The lengths of eras, periods, and epochs are not equal. A chart showing the Earth's history by using the different time divisions is called a geological timescale. The Earth's earliest history is shown at the bottom and the most recent at the top. This pattern resembles how rock strata are formed, with the youngest uppermost.

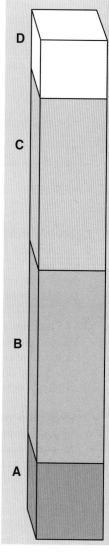

The four Eons – major time periods of Earth's existence	**Era** millions of years ago	**Period**	**Epoch**
D Phanerozoic eon (543 million years ago to today)	**Cenozoic** 65-present	**Quaternary** 1.8-present	**Holocene** 0.01-present
			Pleistocene 1.8-0.01
		Tertiary 65-1.8	**Pliocene** 5.3-1.8
			Miocene 23.8-5.3
C Proterozoic eon (2.5 billion–543 million years ago)			**Oligocene** 34-23.8
			Eocene 55-34
			Paleocene 65-55
	Mesozoic 248-65	**Cretaceous** 144-65	
		Jurassic 206-144	
		Triassic 248-208	
	Paleozoic 543-248	**Permian** 290-248	
B Archean eon (4–2.5 billion years ago)		**Carboniferous** 354-290 Mississippian and Pennsylvanian periods in N. America	
		Devonian 417-354	
		Silurian 443-417	
		Ordovician 490-443	
A Hadean eon (4.5–4 billion years ago)		**Cambrian** 543-490	
	Precambrian time before 540		

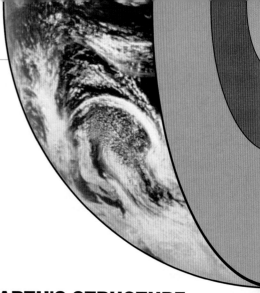

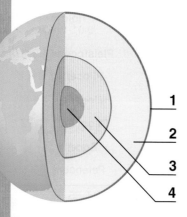

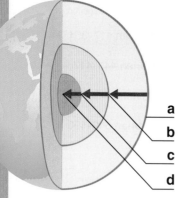

EARTH'S STRUCTURE

The Earth consists of four layers. The crust (**1**) is the outermost layer. It is made of rock and it carries the land and the oceans. The mantle (**2**) lies under the crust and consists of liquid rock. The outer core (**3**) is liquid iron and the inner core (**4**) is solid iron.

Earth's measurements
Mass
6586 million million million tons (5976 million million million tonnes)
Surface area
196,935 million sq mi (510,066 sq km)
Polar circumference
24,859.7 mi (40,008 km)
Equatorial circumference
24,901.5 mi (40,075 km)
Distance from Earth's crust
a 13 mi (21 km)   **c** 3065 mi (4935 km)
b 1823 mi (2935 km) **d** 3907 mi (6291 km)

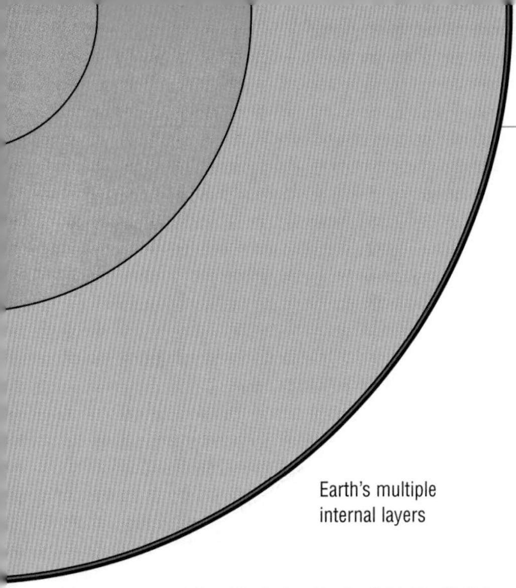

Earth's multiple
internal layers

EARTH'S COMPOSITION

The Earth is made up of elements and minerals. There are 93 naturally occurring elements. Nine of these make up 99 per cent of the mass of the Earth's crust. Two non-metals, oxygen and silicon, make up three-quarters of the mass. The rest consists of seven metals: aluminium, iron, calcium, sodium, potassium, magnesium, and titanium.

Inside the crust, most elements are present as minerals, of which there are around 2000 types. Some, like gold, exist as just one element. However, a majority consist of two or more elements joined together to form compounds. The most abundant minerals are silicates. These are minerals which contain silicon and oxygen. They make up four-fifths of our planet's volume.

Composition
of the Earth

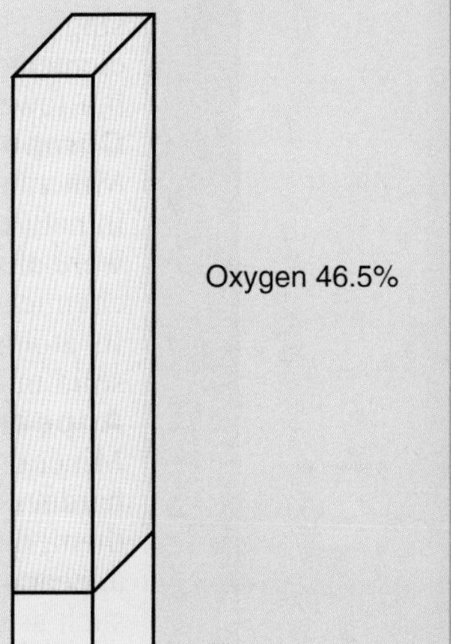

Oxygen 46.5%

Silicon 27.72%

Aluminium 8.13%

Iron 5%

Calcium 3.63%

Sodium 2.83%

Potassium 2.59%

Magnesium 2.09%

Titanium 0.4%

Other elements
1.01%

MINERALS

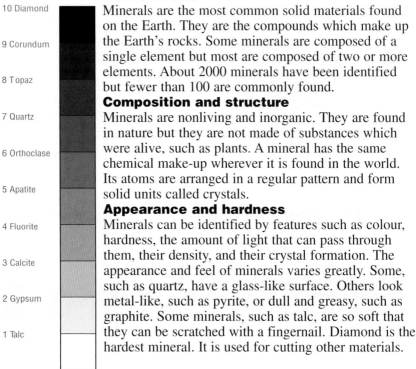

10 Diamond

9 Corundum

8 Topaz

7 Quartz

6 Orthoclase

5 Apatite

4 Fluorite

3 Calcite

2 Gypsum

1 Talc

Minerals are the most common solid materials found on the Earth. They are the compounds which make up the Earth's rocks. Some minerals are composed of a single element but most are composed of two or more elements. About 2000 minerals have been identified but fewer than 100 are commonly found.

Composition and structure

Minerals are nonliving and inorganic. They are found in nature but they are not made of substances which were alive, such as plants. A mineral has the same chemical make-up wherever it is found in the world. Its atoms are arranged in a regular pattern and form solid units called crystals.

Appearance and hardness

Minerals can be identified by features such as colour, hardness, the amount of light that can pass through them, their density, and their crystal formation. The appearance and feel of minerals varies greatly. Some, such as quartz, have a glass-like surface. Others look metal-like, such as pyrite, or dull and greasy, such as graphite. Some minerals, such as talc, are so soft that they can be scratched with a fingernail. Diamond is the hardest mineral. It is used for cutting other materials.

MOHS' SCALE

Mohs' scale is used to measure the relative hardness of minerals. The framework uses the 10 minerals – talc to diamond – shown in the scale. Each of these minerals is assigned a numerical value from 1 to 10: the higher the number, the harder the mineral.

Order is determined by the ability of a mineral to scratch all those that have a lower number and to be scratched by those with a higher number. Once this is established, it is possible to place all other minerals on the scale by means of the same scratching procedure.

CRYSTALS

In the Earth's crust most elements occur as minerals. Most minerals contain two or more elements joined together as compounds. For example, silicates contain the elements silicon and oxygen.

Many minerals exist in the form of crystals. The reason for this is that most minerals are made when hot. Liquid rocks cool down to form solids. When this happens crystals are formed.

The diagrams show some common crystal shapes, and give examples of minerals that are made of them.

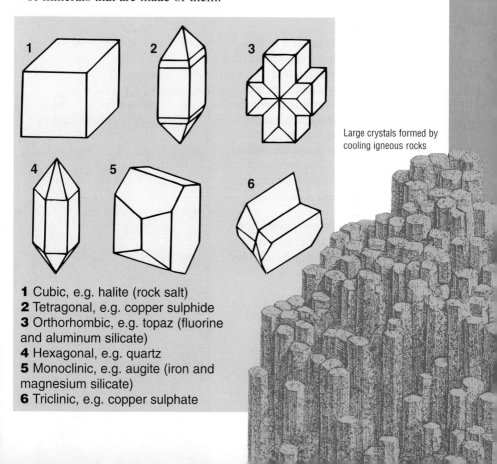

Large crystals formed by cooling igneous rocks

1 Cubic, e.g. halite (rock salt)
2 Tetragonal, e.g. copper sulphide
3 Orthorhombic, e.g. topaz (fluorine and aluminum silicate)
4 Hexagonal, e.g. quartz
5 Monoclinic, e.g. augite (iron and magnesium silicate)
6 Triclinic, e.g. copper sulphate

ROCK CYCLE

The rock cycle is a continuous round of erosion, deposition, and heat.

1 Igneous (volcanic) rocks are formed when magma (liquid rock) is forced to the surface under pressure and erupts through a volcano. As the magma reaches the surface it solidifies and becomes igneous rock.

2 The rock is now exposed to the elements, and over a long period of time begins to be eroded and weathered. The rock particles are carried by rivers, wind, and rain to the oceans and seas. The particles build up into layers which over many thousands of years are buried deeper and deeper. The weight of layers presses the lowest layers into a solid; this is called sedimentary rock.

3 The constant pressure pushes the sedimentary rock further and further down, where it begins to be affected by heat from the Earth's core. This heat causes the structure of the rock to change or metamorphose, and it now becomes known as metamorphic rock. If it remains under high pressure and constant heat, the rock will eventually become magma, which may rise to the surface under pressure and erupt again as a volcano.

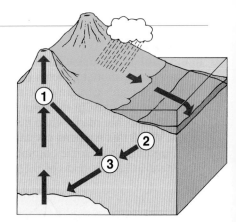

ROCK TYPES

Igneous rocks are formed when magma or molten rock from the inside of the Earth rises to the surface and cools down to harden. The size of the crystals in the rock shows the speed at which the magma cooled. Granite and basalt are igneous rocks.

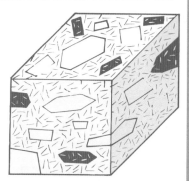

The hard igneous rocks of Mt. Rushmore make ideal material for carving

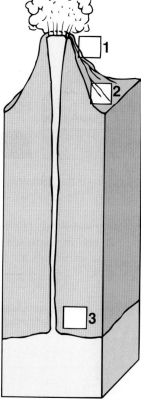

1 Pumice is made by gases bubbling through lava. It is very light.

2 Basalt hardens quickly above the surface. The rock crystals are small because they have not had much time to form and grow.

3 Granite hardens slowly below the surface and so the crystals in the rock are large.

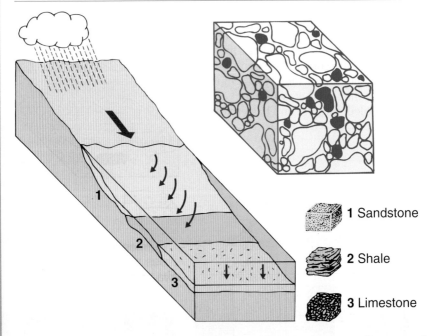

1 Sandstone

2 Shale

3 Limestone

Sedimentary rocks are mainly made from the remains, or sediments, of older rocks which have been worn away. These are washed into rivers and out to sea.

Fragments settle near the shore forming sandstone (**1**). Further offshore rock deposits collect to form shale (**2**), and in warm seas deposits collect to form limestone (**3**). On the seabed the sediments are squeezed together, eventually becoming solid rock.

Coal and limestone are both forms of sedimentary rock

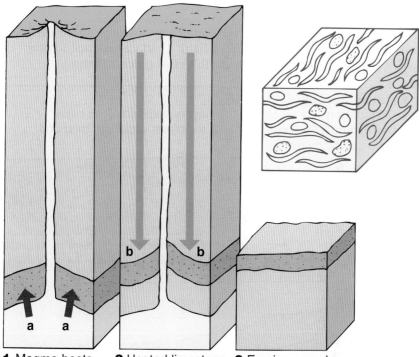

1 Magma heats (**a**) limestone

2 Heated limestone is compressed (**b**)

3 Erosion reveals marble

Metamorphic rocks are formed from other rocks which have been heated or placed under pressure. These factors change the rock. Metamorphic rocks such as marble or slate tend to have crystals in bands, or layers.

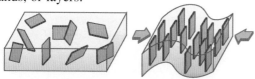

Heat and pressure force the particles of rock into flat bands or layers such as those found in marble or slate

PHYSICAL FORCES

Forces that produce changes to the Earth's physical appearance are of two types. Those that operate on the Earth's surface (external forces) and those that operate within the Earth's crust (internal forces).

External forces
1 Denudation The erosion of rock layers, exposing rock below
2 Deposition The accumulation of sediment, especially mud and sand carried by rivers

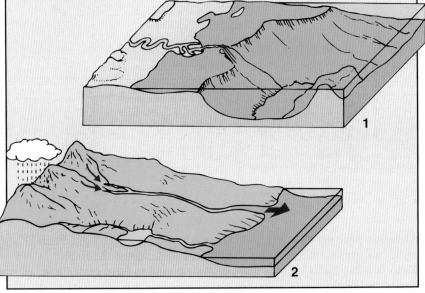

Internal forces

3 Earth movement Faults that produce changes in the elevation of rocks, e.g. horsts (**a**), escarpments (**b**), and basins (**c**). Movements sideways causing folding or fractures to the surface, e.g. rift valleys (**d**)

4 Volcanic eruptions The external features produced by lava flow and geysers, e.g. volcanic cones (**e**), lava plains (**f**), and geyser ponds (**g**). The internal pressures from volcanoes produce dykes, sills, batholiths, and laccoliths

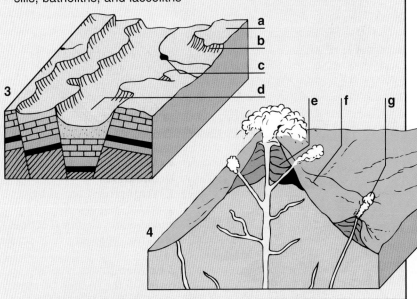

Cross section through the Alps

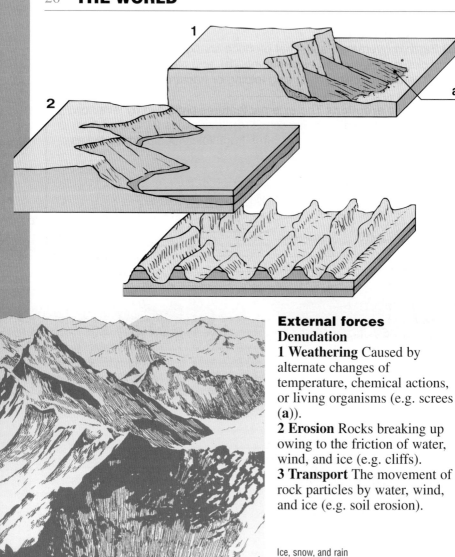

External forces
Denudation
1 Weathering Caused by
alternate changes of
temperature, chemical actions,
or living organisms (e.g. screes
(**a**)).
2 Erosion Rocks breaking up
owing to the friction of water,
wind, and ice (e.g. cliffs).
3 Transport The movement of
rock particles by water, wind,
and ice (e.g. soil erosion).

Ice, snow, and rain
shape mountains

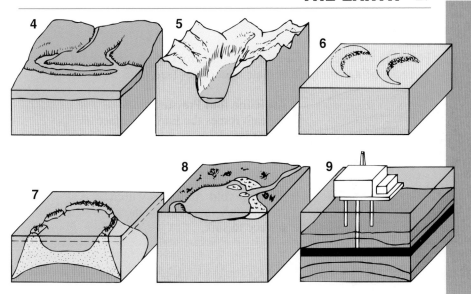

Deposition

4 By water The movement by seas or rivers (e.g. spits).

5 Ice The movement of particles by ice flows (e.g. glaciers).

6 Wind The transportation of particles by wind (e.g. sand dunes).

7 Living particles Atolls formed by coral (e.g. lagoon).

8 Evaporation and precipitation Heat drying up sea water to leave salt deposits (e.g. salt marsh).

9 Organic matter Fossil fuel deposits formed from plants and marine creatures (e.g. coal).

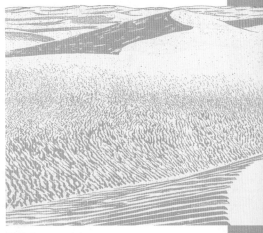

Wind shapes sand dunes and transports sand

Internal forces
Folds
Folds are the buckling of once horizontal rock strata, frequently caused by rocks being crumpled at plate boundaries (see page 30).

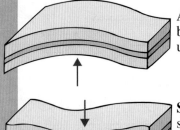

Anticline fold Pressure from beneath forces the Earth's surface upwards.

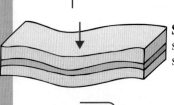

Syncline fold Activities within sedimentary layers allow the surface to sink.

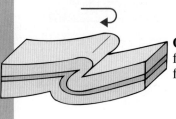

Over fold Sideways pressures force the surface to buckle and fold over itself.

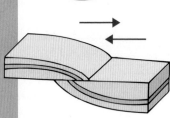

Nappe fold Extreme overfolding shears rocks which ride over subterranean layers.

Folded layers
of rock

Faults

Faults are fractures in the Earth's crust either side of which rocks have been moved relative to each other.

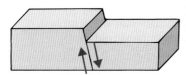

Normal fault Stretching surfaces cause rocks to move upwards and downwards to reveal an escarpment (exposed new surface).

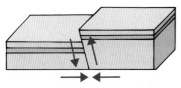

Reverse fault Compression of an area causes rocks to ride up over others to produce an overhang.

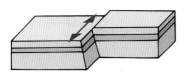

Tear fault Sideways-moving plates which produce earthquakes.

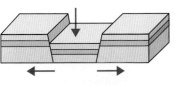

Graben A long narrow area which sinks between two parallel faults.

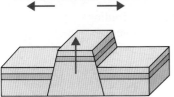

Horst A horizontal block raised between two normal faults.

Rocks dissected by many faults

PLATE TECTONICS

The Earth's surface consists of large pieces, or plates, which fit together rather like a jigsaw. They form the lithosphere, or the Earth's outer shell. The plates are constantly moving. Plate tectonics is the study of how they move. When plates slide past each other, they cause fractures or faults. If the rock bends instead of breaking, it creates folds.

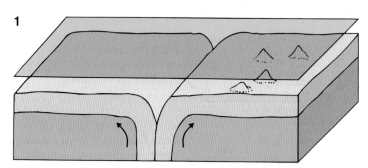

1 Spreading
Two plates spreading apart form ocean floors and underwater volcanoes

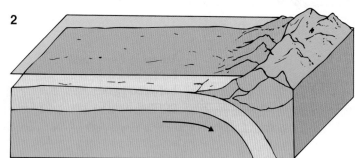

2 Subduction
Plates which push against each other and bend downward are called subduction zones

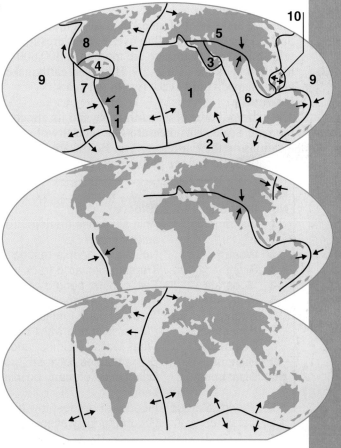

Lithospheric plates

1 African plate
2 Antarctic plate
3 Arabian plate
4 Caribbean plate
5 Eurasian plate
6 Indo-Australian plate
7 Nazca plate
8 North American plate
9 Pacific plate
10 Philippines plate
11 South American plate

Lithospheric plates

There are eleven major plates whose edges either part or sink into the Earth's interior.

Subduction zones

The two major subduction zones are on the west coast of South America and across the lower part of Asia and South Asia.

Spreading

The three main spreading regions are Mid-Atlantic, Eastern Pacific and on the edge of the South Indian ocean.

EARTHQUAKES

Earthquakes are sudden movements in the ground which occur when parts of the Earth's crust move or fracture. Most earthquakes happen when the plates forming the Earth's crust push against each other or when one plate moves under another. Some earthquakes occur when molten rock rises from beneath the Earth's crust, pushing the plates apart.

Magnitude

The size and extent of an earthquake is measured in units on the Richter Scale. This scale, from 0 to over 8, measures the amount of energy released. Every year there are more than 300,000 Earth tremors which have a magnitude of 2 to 2.9. However, earthquakes measuring 8.5 or higher happen only every five to ten years.

Intensity

The extreme force of an earthquake and its effects are measured on the Mercalli Scale. This measures the intensity of an earthquake at particular locations on the Earth's surface. Below are listed the numbers on the Mercalli Scale and the physical characteristics of earthquakes.

Mercalli Scale

No.	Intensity	Effects
1	Instrumental	Animals sense tremors; tremors recorded on seismograph
2	Weak	Noticed by people resting
3	Slight	Tremors similar to truck vibrations
4	Moderate	Felt indoors; parked cars shake
5	Fairly strong	Tremors felt generally and waken sleepers
6	Strong	Trees shaken; furniture falls over
7	Very strong	Plaster falls and walls crack
8	Destructive	Weak walls, columns, and chimneys fall
9	Ruinous	Some houses collapse; ground cracks
10	Disastrous	Destruction of many buildings; railway lines bend
11	Very disastrous	Floods, landslides; few buildings left standing
12	Catastrophic	Ground forms waves; overall destruction

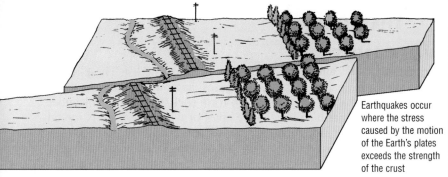

Earthquakes occur where the stress caused by the motion of the Earth's plates exceeds the strength of the crust

Most powerful earthquakes
1 Sumatra, Indonesia 2004 (9.3)
2 Gansu, China 1920 (8.6)
3 Nanshan, China 1927 (8.3)
4 Kwanto, Japan 1923 (8.3)
5 Tangshan, China 1976 (8.2)
6 Shensi, China 1556 ★
7 Calcutta, India 1737 ★
8 Antioch, Turkey 526 ★
9 Hokkaido, Japan 1730 ★

★ denotes too early to be recorded on Richter Scale

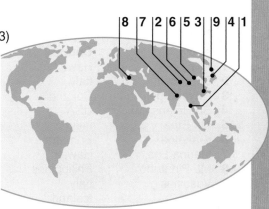

Deaths from earthquakes
6 Shensi, China 830,000
7 Calcutta, India 300,000
1 Sumatra, Indonesia 283,000
8 Antioch, Turkey 250,000
5 Tangshan, China 242,000
3 Nanshan, China 200,000
2 Gansu, China 180,000
4 Kwanto, Japan 143,000
9 Hokkaido, Japan 137,000

1

VOLCANOES

Sometimes holes and cracks appear in the Earth's crust. These release hot liquid rock, called magma, ash, gases, and other matter. As the magma and ash cool, they harden to form rock. Generally, volcanoes erupt when the Earth's plates move apart or when one plate is forced beneath another. Throughout the world there are 500 to 800 active volcanoes. However, during a year only 30 might erupt on land. An inactive, or dormant, volcano is still capable of erupting. An extinct volcano is dead and cannot erupt.

Selected active volcanoes

Volcano	Country	Major periods of eruption
1 Kilauea	Hawaii	1823–present
2 Stromboli	Italy	1768–1989
3 Nevado del Ruiz	Colombia	1985
4 St. Helens, Mt.	USA	1800–87, 1989
5 Mt. Etna	Italy	1947–present
6 Krakatoa	Sumatra	1680–1972
7 Mauna Loa	Hawaii	1859–1987
8 Mt. Pinatubo	Philippines	1380–1991
9 Vesuvius	Italy	AD 79–1944
10 Hekla	Iceland	1693–1970

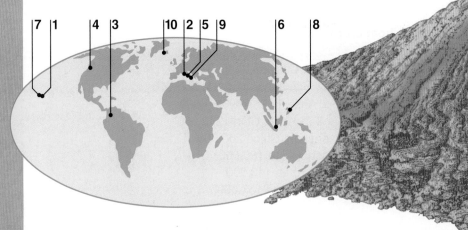

Anatomy of a volcano

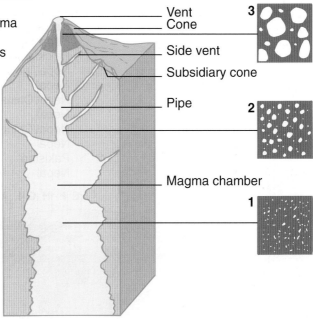

Gases in the magma escape and form expanding bubbles (**1, 2, 3**). These gases push magma out of the volcano.

Vent
Cone
Side vent
Subsidiary cone
Pipe
Magma chamber

3
2
1

Undersea volcanoes can form islands such as Iceland and Hawaii

Major volcanic areas

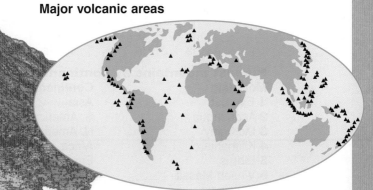

MOUNTAINS
Highest mountains in the world

Mountain	Range	ft
A Mount Everest	Nepal/China	29,028
B K2	Pakistan	28,250
C Kanchenjunga	Nepal/India	28,208
D Lhotse	Nepal	27,890
E Makalu I	Nepal/China	27,824
F Dhaulagiri	Nepal	26,810
G Cho Oyu	Nepal/China	26,750
H Manaslu I	Nepal	26,760
I Nanga Parbat	Pakistan	26,660
J Annapurna I	Nepal	26,504

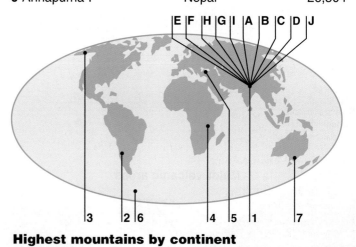

Highest mountains by continent

Mountain	Continent	ft
1 Everest	Asia	29,028
2 Aconcagua	S. America	22,834
3 McKinley	N. America	20,320
4 Kilimanjaro	Africa	19,340
5 Elbrus	Europe	18,481
6 Vinson Massif	Antarctica	16,863
7 Kosciusko	Australia	7316

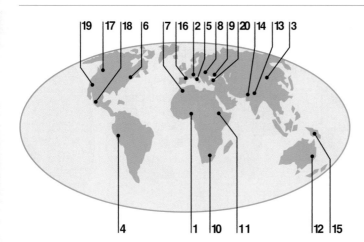

Major mountain ranges

1 **Adamawa Highlands** Central West Africa
2 **Alps** Central Europe
3 **Altai** Siberia
4 **Andes** West South America
5 **Apennines** South Europe
6 **Appalachians** East North America
7 **Atlas** Northwest Africa
8 **Carpathians** East Europe
9 **Caucasus** Southwest Russia
10 **Drakensberg** South Africa
11 **Ethiopian Highlands** East Africa
12 **Great Dividing Range** East Australia
13 **Himalayas** South Central Asia
14 **Hindu Kush** South Central Asia
15 **Maoke/Central Range** New Guinea
16 **Pyrenees** West Europe
17 **Rockies** West North America
18 **Sierra Madre** Central America
19 **Sierra Nevada** West North America
20 **Taurus** Asia Minor

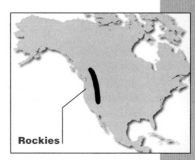

Rockies

The Rockies are 3750 miles long

LONGEST RIVERS

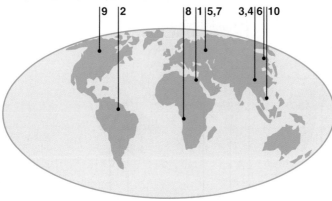

River	Continent	mi
1 Nile	N. and E. Africa	4160
2 Amazon	S. America	4000
3 Chang Jiang (Yangtze)	China	3964
4 Huang He	China	3395
5 Ob-Irtysh	Russian Fed.	3362
6 Amur	Northeast Asia	2744
7 Lena	Russian Fed.	2734
8 Congo	Central Africa	2718
9 Mackenzie	Canada	2635
10 Mekong	Southeast Asia	2600

If the Nile ran north in a straight line from its source it would reach to within 100 miles of the North Pole.

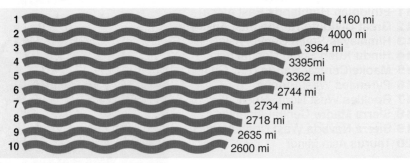

1 4160 mi
2 4000 mi
3 3964 mi
4 3395mi
5 3362 mi
6 2744 mi
7 2734 mi
8 2718 mi
9 2635 mi
10 2600 mi

LARGEST WATERFALLS

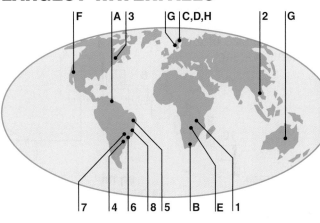

By height

Waterfall	Country	ft
A Angel	Venezuela	3212
B Tugela	South Africa	2800
C Utigård	Norway	2625
D Monge	Norway	2540
E Mutarazi	Zimbabwe	2499
F Yosemite	USA	2425
G Pieman	Australia	2346
H Espelands	Norway	2307

By volume

Waterfall	Country	cu ft/s	cu m/s
1 Boyoma (Stanley)	Dem.Rep.Congo	600,000	16,980
2 Khône	Laos	410,000	11,605
3 Niagara	Canada/USA	212,000	6000
4 Grande	Uruguay	160,000	4530
5 Paulo Afonso	Brazil	100,000	2830
6 Urubu-pungá	Brazil	97,000	2745
7 Cataratas del Iguazú	Brazil/Argentina	61,660	1745
8 Patos-Maribondo	Brazil	53,000	1500

LARGEST OCEANS AND SEAS

The Pacific Ocean is the largest of the Earth's oceans. It is twice the size of the Atlantic Ocean.

Ocean/sea	sq mi	sq km
1 Pacific	64,000,000	165,760,000
2 Atlantic	31,500,000	81,585,000
3 Indian	28,400,000	73,556,000
4 Arctic	5,440,000	14,100,000
5 South China Sea	1,063,000	2,975,000
6 Caribbean	1,049,500	2,718,200
7 Mediterranean	970,000	2,512,300
8 Bering Sea	878,000	2,275,000
9 Gulf of Mexico	695,000	1,800,000
10 Sea of Okhotsk	613,838	1,589,840

70 per cent of the Earth's surface is covered by water

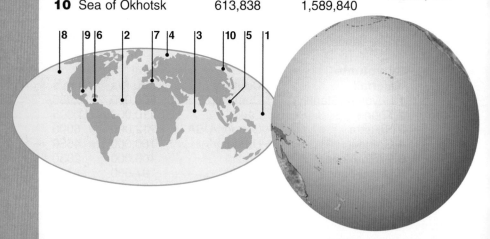

LARGEST ISLANDS

The world's largest island, Greenland, is three times the size of Texas.

Island	sq mi	sq km
1 Greenland	840,000	2,176,000
2 New Guinea	316,856	820,657
3 Borneo	286,967	743,254
4 Madagascar	227,000	587,930
5 Baffin (Canada)	183,810	476,068
6 Sumatra	182,866	473,623
7 Honshu (Japan)	88,930	230,329
8 Great Britain	88,756	229,878
9 Victoria (Canada)	82,119	212,688
10 Ellesmere (Canada)	81,930	212,199

Only 30 per cent of the Earth's surface is covered by land

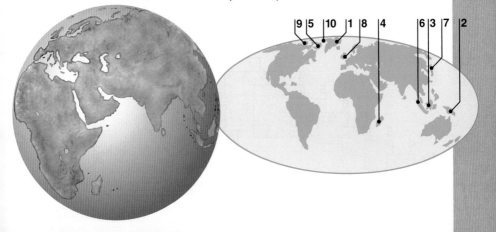

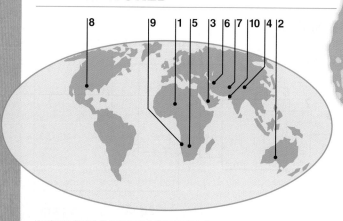

LARGEST DESERTS

Desert	Continent	sq mi	sq km
1 Sahara	Africa	3,242,000	8,397,000
2 Australian	Australia	598,000	1,549,000
3 Arabian	Asia	502,000	1,300,000
4 Gobi	Asia	401,000	1,039,000
5 Kalahari	Africa	201,000	521,000
6 Turkestan	Asia	139,000	360,000
7 Takla Makan	Asia	124,000	321,000
8 Sonoran	N. America	120,000	311,000
9 Namib	Africa	120,000	311,000
10 Thar	Asia	100,000	259,000

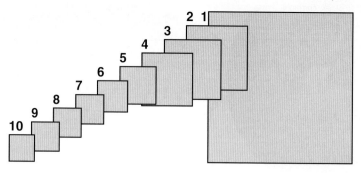

FORESTS
Tropical

Tropical forests grow near the Equator, where the climate is warm and wet all year round. They have the greatest variety of trees of any type of forest. Tropical seasonal forests grow in parts of the tropics and subtropics. These areas have a wet and a dry season and are cooler than tropical rainforests.

Degrees of dryness

- very arid
- arid
- semi-arid

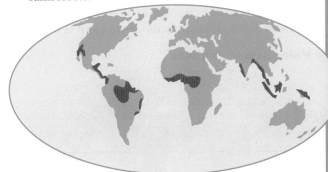

Coniferous and broadleaf

Coniferous forests consist of trees that have long narrow needle-like leaves and that are cone-bearing. Broadleaf forests have trees with broad, flat leaves and are found in temperate areas of the world with mild climates. Most broadleaf trees shed their leaves in autumn.

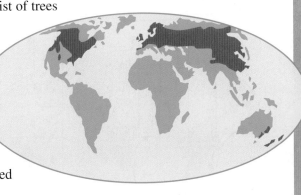

OCEAN CURRENTS

Ocean currents are the movements of the surface water of an ocean. The most important causes of these movements are the prevailing winds and differences in water density due to temperature or salinity. The shape of the continents and the rotation of the Earth can also influence the direction of currents. Ocean currents caused by prevailing winds are called drift currents, the best known being the Gulf Stream. Between the Equator and the temperate regions in the northern hemisphere (**1**), the circulation of ocean currents is clockwise, whereas in the southern hemisphere (**2**) it is anticlockwise.

Polar ocean regions

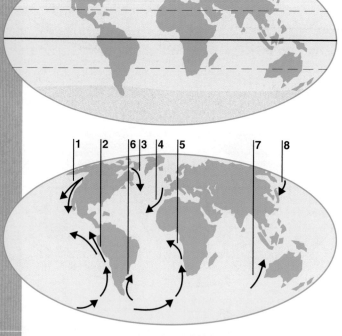

Major cold currents
1 California
2 Humboldt
3 Labrador
4 Canaries
5 Benguela
6 Falkland
7 West Australian
8 Okhotsk

The areas around the North & South regions are the cold polar seas. The areas either side of the Equator are tropical seas. The regions between the cold and warm are temperate zones.

In Equatorial regions, the currents move in opposite directions, those in the north moving left to right, and those in the south from right to left (**3**). Currents moving north and south from Equatorial regions carry warm water and those moving south and north from Polar regions carry cold water.

Tropical ocean regions

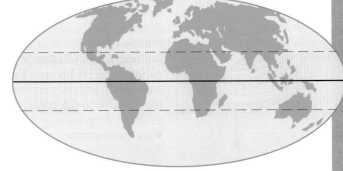

Major warm currents
1 North Atlantic (Gulf Stream)
2 South Atlantic
3 South Indian Ocean
4 South Pacific
5 North Pacific
6 Monsoons

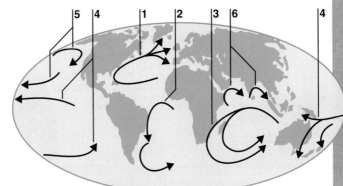

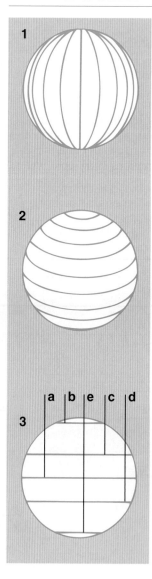

LONGITUDE AND LATITUDE

Longitude

On a map or a globe, longitude is marked by vertical lines which run from north to south (**1**). Lines of longitude are also called meridians. Longitude is measured east or west of the prime meridian, which lies at 0 degrees longitude (0°) and passes through Greenwich, England. Each degree (°) of longitude is divided into 60 minutes ('). Each minute is divided into 60 seconds (").

Latitude

Latitude is a position on a map or globe shown by a horizontal line (**2**). This marks a position north (N) or south (S) of the Equator, the imaginary line around the middle of the Earth (**a**). The Equator is at 0° latitude. Lines of latitude are sometimes called parallels because they run parallel to each other and they are evenly spaced from the Equator to the poles. Latitudes are also given in degrees, minutes, and seconds.

Key latitudes

Key lines of latitude (**3**) are the Equator at 0° (**a**), the Arctic Circle at 66° 30'N (**b**), the tropic of Cancer at 23° 27'N (**c**), the tropic of Capricorn at 23° 27'S (**d**), and the Antarctic Circle at 66° 30'S (**e**).

Locating a point on a globe

Locating a spot on a map or a globe, for example Washington DC, is done by finding its latitude and longitude. Globes and maps do not show every line of latitude or longitude. They usually only show lines spaced 15° apart. If the longitude lines are combined with the latitude lines they form a grid pattern which can be used to find a location (**1**).

The co-ordinates of a particular place will tell you how far north or south the place is and whether it is east or west of the prime meridian. The exact location of Washington DC is 38° 55'N and 77°W. To find it, first measure 38° 55' north of the equator to find the latitude (**2**).

To find the longitude, locate the position 77° west of the prime meridian (**3**).

The Earth's axis is an imaginary line that runs from the North Pole to the South Pole. It is tilted, as the Earth lies at an angle. This is called the angle of inclination and is 23.5 degrees (**4**).

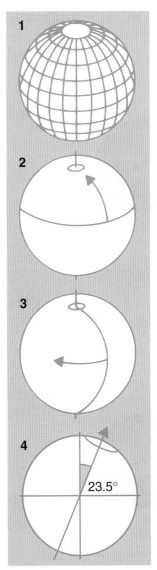

MAP PROJECTIONS

A globe is a scale model of the Earth showing land shape and distance in their true proportions. There are many ways to project, or transfer, the shapes on a round globe onto flat paper. Each projection gives a map which shows a particular view of the world. Each projection distorts size or shape.

The azimuthal projection

This shows either the whole of the northern or southern hemispheres. It shows areas in their proper proportions but distorts the shapes of countries.

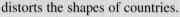

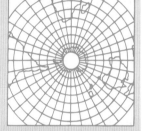

The cylindrical projection

This is made as if a sheet of paper were wrapped around a globe to produce a cylinder or tube shape. This projection is best for navigating at sea because it gives the best compass readings. Areas close to the Equator have land shapes accurately shown but land sizes are badly distorted the nearer they are to the poles. The Mercator projection is a well-known example.

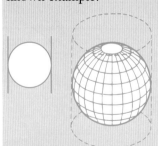
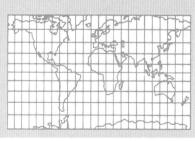

The conic projection

This is made as if a cone of paper were wrapped around a globe so that one or two lines of latitude touched the paper. This projection is used mainly to show parts of the world in the middle latitudes which run east to west. This map shows the shape of limited areas accurately but distorts size from one area to another.

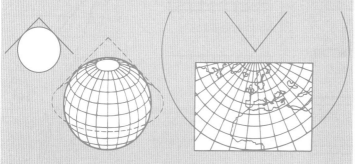

The mathematical projection

This is called an Interrupted-Homolosine map. Oceans and continents are shown with little distortion in shape or size. In order to show this, each continent or ocean is centred on its own central meridian. This may involve interruption, or breaks, in the projection.

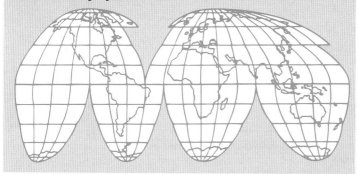

MAP SYMBOLS

How to read a relief map

Most relief maps are provided with keys to show meanings of symbols. Shown below are examples of the types of symbol used on maps.

Roads

Primary road

Secondary road

Other road, surfaced

Unsurfaced road

Relief

Index contour

Supplementary contour

.8463
Spot elevation

Intermediate contour

Railways

Main-line track

Single track

Cutting

Embankment

Boundaries

National boundary

State boundary

County/Parish boundary

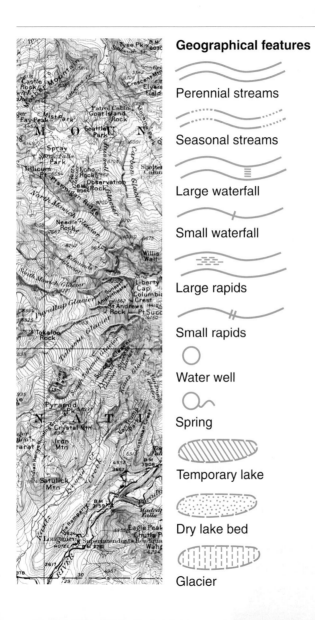

Geographical features

Perennial streams

Seasonal streams

Large waterfall

Small waterfall

Large rapids

Small rapids

Water well

Spring

Temporary lake

Dry lake bed

Glacier

Vegetation

Marsh or swamp

Woods

Vineyard

Orchard

Scrubland

Other features

Urban area

Viewpoint

Quarry

Landmark

THE ATMOSPHERE

The atmosphere is a layer of mixed gases surrounding the Earth. It stretches from the Earth's surface into outer space (about 100 mi from the surface). The atmosphere exerts pressure on us all the time. This is caused by the weight of the air at the top of the atmosphere pressing down on air below. The atmosphere is divided into layers which merge. The temperature, composition, and properties of each layer vary.

The atmosphere of the Earth is concentrated in the troposphere. Its composition is given below.

In addition there are smaller traces of hydrogen, ozone, and xenon. The atmosphere also contains variable quantities of water vapor, and particles such as dust and industrial pollutants.

Gas	% by volume
nitrogen	78.08
oxygen	20.95
argon	0.93
carbon dioxide	0.03
neon	0.0018
helium	0.0005
methane	0.0002
krypton	0.0001

The Earth's atmosphere is proportionately no thicker than the skin of an apple

The layers of the atmosphere

The troposphere (1) A shallow layer extending up to 5 mi at the poles and 10 mi at the Equator. It is the first layer of the atmosphere around the Earth. It contains 80 per cent of the total mass of the atmosphere, all the Earth's weather, and all life on Earth. Temperature falls with height at a rate of about 18 °F for every 0.66 mile.

The stratosphere (2) This extends from 5 mi to 30 mi. Military aircraft fly in it. The temperature is fairly constant in the lower stratosphere and then increases to around 32 °F at the stratopause, its outer limit. The stratosphere contains the ozone layer (see page 76), between approximately 15 mi and 25 mi.

The mesosphere (3) This extends from 18.64 mi to 31.06 mi. The highest weather balloons reach the mesosphere. The temperature becomes lower, reaching around –148 °F at the mesopause, its outer limit. Trails of hot gases left by meteors can be seen in this layer.

The thermosphere (4) This extends from 50 mi to around 310 mi. The density of the atmosphere at the thermopause, its outer limit, averages less than a billionth of that at sea level. It contains the ionosphere layers, which reflect radio waves back to Earth. Meteors and aurorae appear in the thermosphere.

The exosphere (5) This extends from around 310 mi to outer space. Molecules of atmospheric gases are so rare they hardly ever collide.

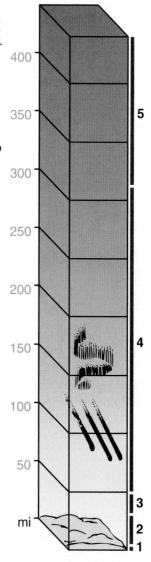

GLOBAL WEATHER PATTERNS

The weather we experience is made up of three elements: the Sun, air, and water. The energy needed to create weather movement over the face of the Earth comes from the Sun. The surface of the Earth is curved. This means the Sun's rays are concentrated near the Equator and are more spread out over the poles. This uneven heating effect creates energy, like a machine, to drive the weather. Warm air, which is lighter than cool air, rises and cold air flows beneath it, making a low pressure zone. Air moving like this creates wind. North and south of the Equator, air cools and sinks again. Air pressing down on the surface produces zones of high pressure. At about 30° north and south of the Equator, this air creates no wind in areas called the horse latitudes. Wind always blows from high-pressure areas to low-pressure areas. Air flows back to the Equator in the trade winds and into the temperate regions in the westerlies. Polar easterlies blow from the polar high-pressure areas. These main winds carry our weather around the world.

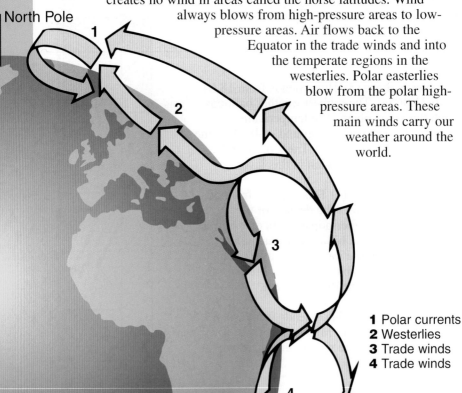

North Pole

1 Polar currents
2 Westerlies
3 Trade winds
4 Trade winds

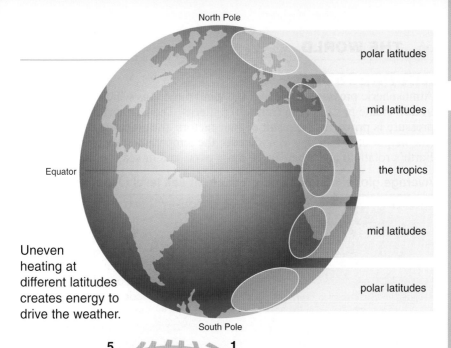

polar latitudes

mid latitudes

the tropics

mid latitudes

polar latitudes

North Pole

Equator

South Pole

Uneven heating at different latitudes creates energy to drive the weather.

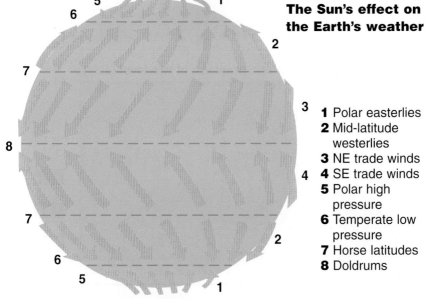

The Sun's effect on the Earth's weather

1 Polar easterlies
2 Mid-latitude westerlies
3 NE trade winds
4 SE trade winds
5 Polar high pressure
6 Temperate low pressure
7 Horse latitudes
8 Doldrums

AIR PRESSURE

Atmospheric pressure influences the wind directions which in turn create precipitation (rainfall) patterns. The Earth's air pressure is primarily the result of four factors: the altitude (the height of the air above sea level); the temperature; the Earth's rotation; and whether the air is over land or sea.

Average global atmospheric pressure at sea level (January)

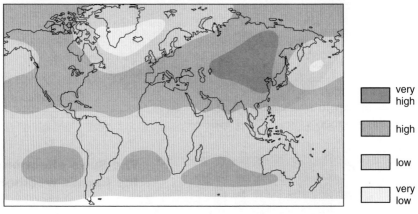

very high

high

low

very low

Average global atmospheric pressure at sea level (July)

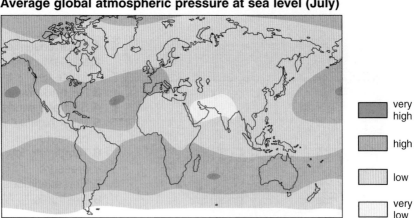

very high

high

low

very low

**January
high-pressure
areas**

High-pressure areas
dominate northern
hemisphere land areas
in winter

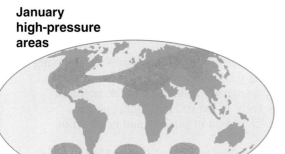

**January
low-pressure areas**

**July
high-pressure
areas**

**July
low-pressure
areas**

WIND

Prevailing winds create patterns which are very different in January and July.

North America and Asia High pressure in winter causes out-blowing winds. Low pressure in summer causes in-blowing winds.

Westerly winds blow more persistently in January in the northern hemisphere. They blow constantly in the southern hemisphere.

Monsoon winds blow south from Asia in January and north from Australia in July.

Doldrums are windless regions in the equatorial areas of the Pacific, Atlantic, and Indian oceans.

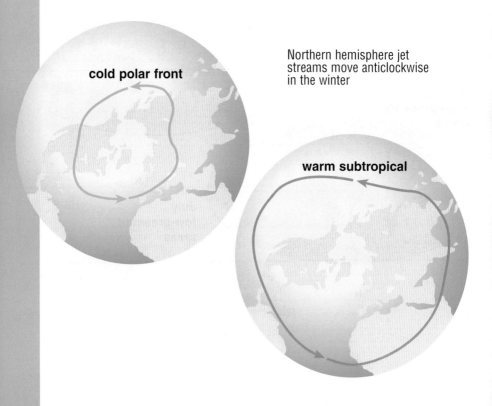

cold polar front

Northern hemisphere jet streams move anticlockwise in the winter

warm subtropical

3

January monsoons

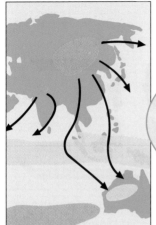

January wind pattern

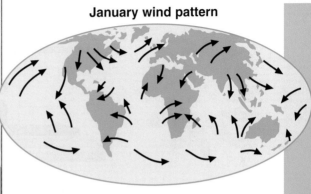

July monsoons

July wind pattern

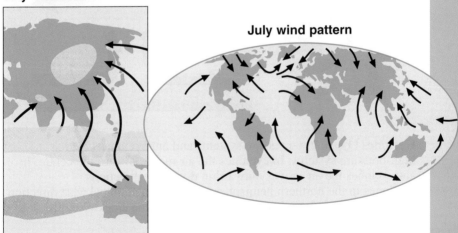

High pressure   Low pressure   Monsoon winds

CYCLONES

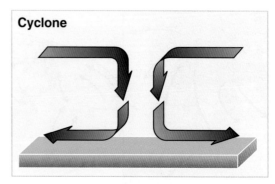

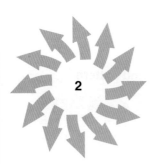

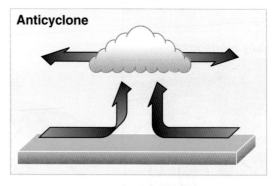

Cyclones (**1**) are low-pressure systems and anticyclones (**2**) are high-pressure systems. In cyclones the air moves toward the centre. In anticyclones the air moves outward in divergent directions.

Cyclones in the northern hemisphere move in an anticlockwise direction (**3**) and in the southern hemisphere they move in a clockwise direction (**4**). They bring disturbed weather.

Anticyclones in the northern hemisphere move in a clockwise direction (**5**) and in the southern hemisphere they move in an anticlockwise direction (**6**). They bring settled weather.

3

**Northern
Hemisphere**

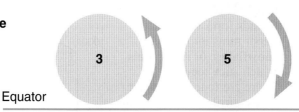

Equator

**Southern
Hemisphere**

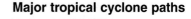

Cyclonic paths

As well as revolving and circulating warm and cold air, cyclones move over the surface of the Earth carrying cold or warm fronts. They follow fairly predictable paths caused by the influences of the seasons, the changing wind currents and the landmasses over which they pass. In America, cyclones are called hurricanes, and in the Far East, typhoons.

Major tropical cyclone paths

Tornadoes

Tornadoes are small, intense cyclones in which the air is spiralling inwards and upwards at a very high speed.

CLOUD TYPES

Clouds form when water vapor turns into droplets, snowflakes, or ice crystals which stick together.

There are four main cloud types: cirrus (wispy); stratus (layered); cumulus (heaped); nimbus (rain-bearing).

1 Cirrus White or gray.

2 Cirrostratus High, nearly transparent layer.

3 Cirrocumulus Thin, white ribbed layer.

4 Altocumulus White or gray heaped cloud.

5 Cumulonimbus Towering cloud with anvil head that brings thunderstorms.

6 Altostratus White or gray sheets, less dense than stratus.

7 Nimbostratus Dark thick layer that brings rain or snow.

8 Cumulus Individual clouds with dark even bases and white fluffy tops that bring rain.

9 Stratocumulus White layers with wave-like patterns.

10 Stratus Low layer that brings rain or snow.

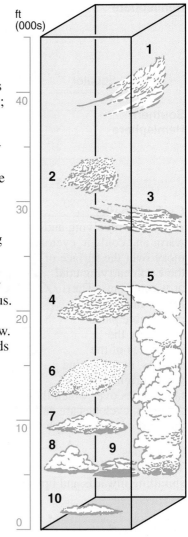

ft (000s)

40

30

20

10

0

WEATHER FRONTS

The weather in the temperate regions of the world is controlled by lows, or depressions. These are swirling wheels of air hundreds of miles across. They form where cold polar air meets warm moist subtropical air. The boundary between them is called the polar front. Lows bring both warm and cold fronts.

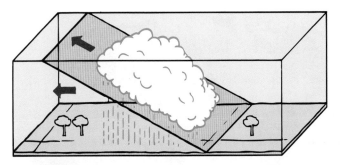

Warm fronts occur when warm moist air rises above cold air, forming a blanket-like layer of cloud which brings light rain or snow.

Cold fronts occur after a warm front. Cold air cuts under the warm air, moving in from behind. This can result in towering cumulonimbus clouds which give heavy showers of rain or snow.

RAINFALL

Rainfall is unevenly distributed over the surface of the Earth. Westerly winds carry abundant rain to the western parts of Europe and North America and trade winds carry rain to the Amazon rainforest.

Annual rainfall

Less than 8 in.

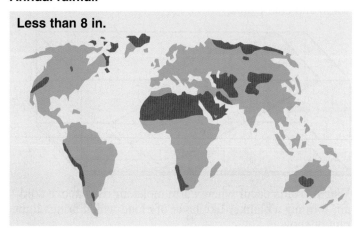

8–20 in.

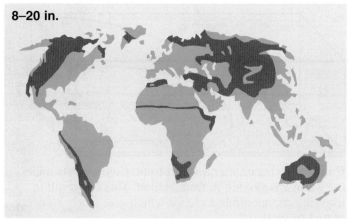

Deserts receive little or no rain as they often lie downwind of mountain ranges and by the time the air has reached them it has lost all its moisture crossing the high ground.

3

20–60 in.

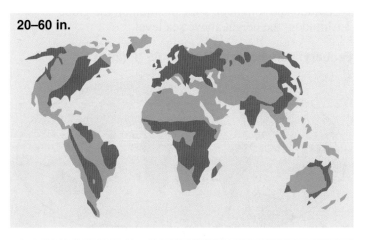

More than 60 in.

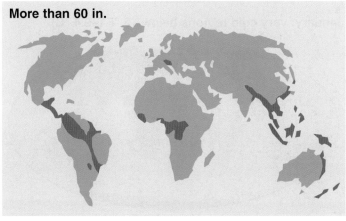

TEMPERATURE

The Earth's atmosphere is warmed indirectly by heat
radiated from the Sun. This radiation passes through the air
and strikes the Earth, warming its surface. Heat is then radiated back from the surface.

The temperature of any place is influenced by
1 Latitude and longitude – the position on the globe
2 Altitude – the height above sea level

January: very hot regions over 85 °F (29 °C)

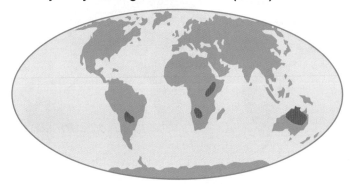

January: very cold regions below 15 °F (–9.4 °C)

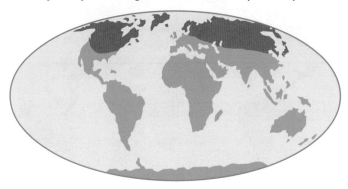

3 Regional location – distance from the sea
4 Aspect – whether the Earth's surface is facing or oblique to the Sun's rays
5 Sky cover – cloud, smoke, or dust
6 Ocean currents – which bring cold or warm water to a region
7 Prevailing winds – which circulate the air
8 The season of the year

July: very hot regions over 85 °F (29 °C)

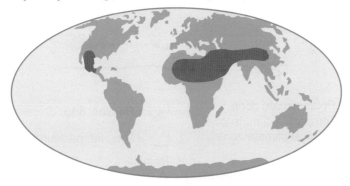

July: cool regions below 50 °F (10 °C)

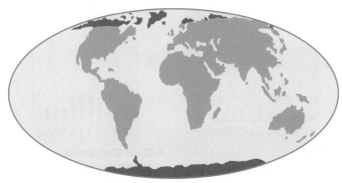

CLIMATE

The climate of a region is primarily the result of location (latitude and longitude); altitude (height above sea level); the air pressure; the wind patterns; and the rainfall.

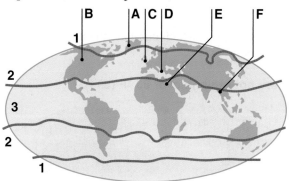

1 Polar climate zone
2 Temperate climate zone
3 Tropical climate zone

▮▮ = Rainfall (in.)

◸◹ = Max. temperatures (°F)

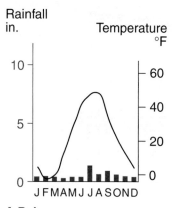

A Polar
Thule (Greenland)

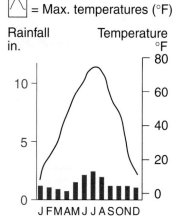

B Cold temperate (continental)
Peace River (Canada)

3

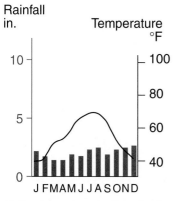

C Cool temperate (marine)
London (UK)

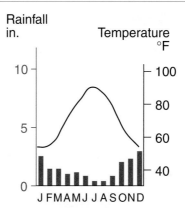

D Warm temperate
Athens (Greece)

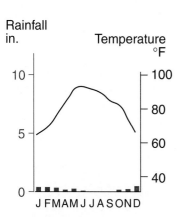

E Tropical (desert)
Cairo (Egypt)

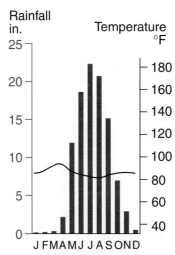

F Tropical (monsoon)
Yangon (Myanmar)

WEATHER MAP SYMBOLS

Wind direction and speed

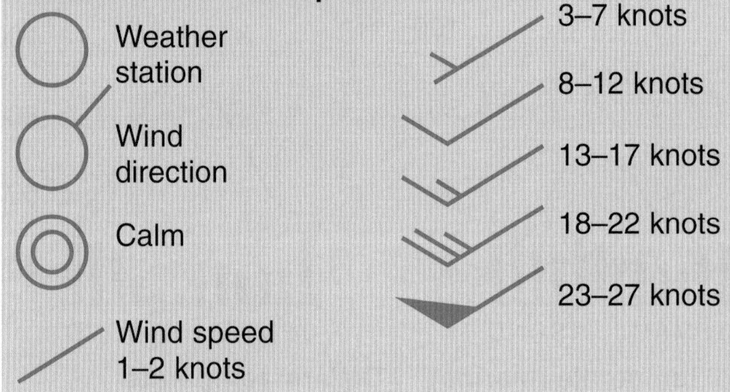

Weather station

Wind direction

Calm

Wind speed 1–2 knots

3–7 knots

8–12 knots

13–17 knots

18–22 knots

23–27 knots

Cloud types

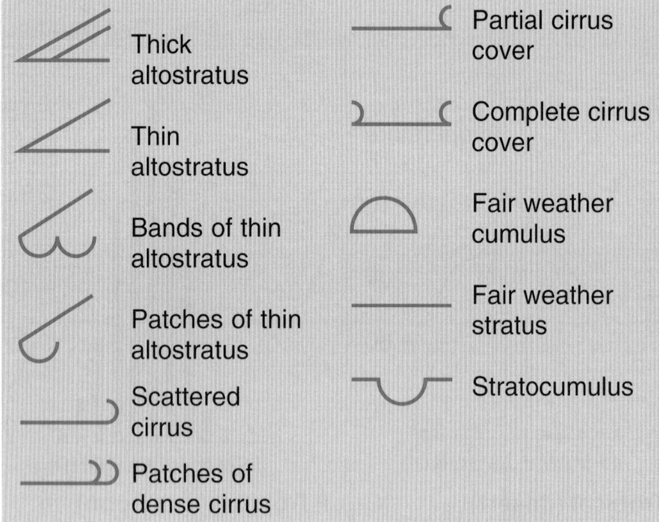

Thick altostratus

Thin altostratus

Bands of thin altostratus

Patches of thin altostratus

Scattered cirrus

Patches of dense cirrus

Partial cirrus cover

Complete cirrus cover

Fair weather cumulus

Fair weather stratus

Stratocumulus

3

Cloud cover

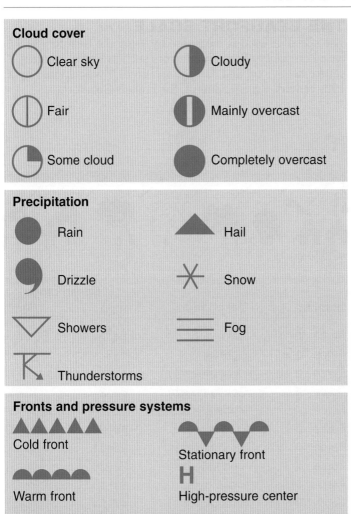

Clear sky

Cloudy

Fair

Mainly overcast

Some cloud

Completely overcast

Precipitation

Rain

Hail

Drizzle

Snow

Showers

Fog

Thunderstorms

Fronts and pressure systems

Cold front

Stationary front

Warm front

H
High-pressure center

Occluded front

L
Low-pressure center

THE BEAUFORT SCALE

The speed of wind is measured by using the Beaufort Scale, based on easily observable factors such as tree movement, smoke behaviour, and damage incurred. It was devised by a 19th-century British admiral, Sir Francis Beaufort.

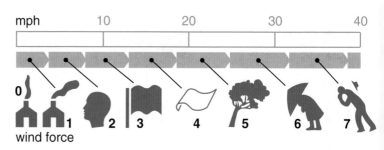

wind force

		Speed range	
Number	**Description**	**mph**	**km/h**
Force 0	Calm	Below 1	Below 1
Force 1	Light air	1–3	1–5
Force 2	Light breeze	4–7	6–12
Force 3	Gentle breeze	8–12	13–20
Force 4	Moderate breeze	13–18	21–29
Force 5	Fresh breeze	19–24	30–39
Force 6	Strong breeze	25–31	40–50
Force 7	Moderate gale	32–38	51–61
Force 8	Fresh gale	39–46	62–74
Force 9	Strong gale	47–54	75–87
Force 10	Whole gale	55–63	88–102
Force 11	Storm	64–75	103–120
Force 12	Hurricane	Over 75	Over 120

3

As air moves across the surface of the Earth, its direction is determined by such factors as the Earth's rotation, variations in temperature, air pressure, and land features such as mountains. Listed below are examples showing the effects of wind as measured on the Beaufort Scale, the variety of winds that are measured, and the range of speeds to which they apply.

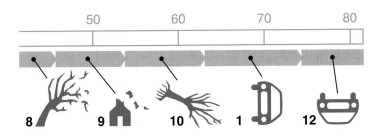

Number	Characteristics
Force 0	Smoke rises straight up
Force 1	Smoke shows wind direction
Force 2	Wind felt on face
Force 3	Flag extends
Force 4	Dust and paper blow in wind
Force 5	Small trees sway in wind
Force 6	Umbrellas are difficult to use
Force 7	Difficult to stand up in wind
Force 8	Twigs break off trees
Force 9	Chimney pots and tiles are dislodged
Force 10	Trees are uprooted
Force 11	Extensive damage
Force 12	Extremely violent

AIR POLLUTION

Air pollutants from sources including road vehicles, power stations, industry and domestic activity now affect Europe, the USA and South America, and many parts of Asia. Air pollution is especially bad in the cities, causing a dramatic rise in the incidence of respiratory problems among inhabitants.

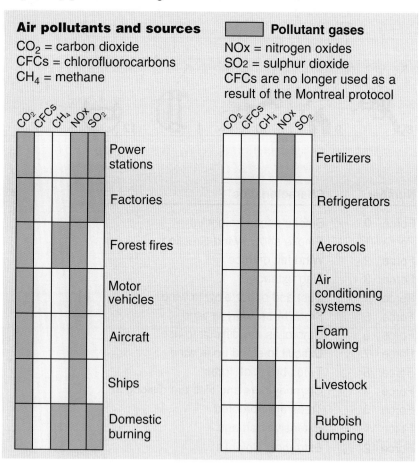

Air pollutants and sources

CO_2 = carbon dioxide
CFCs = chlorofluorocarbons
CH_4 = methane

| | Pollutant gases

NOx = nitrogen oxides
SO_2 = sulphur dioxide
CFCs are no longer used as a result of the Montreal protocol

Power stations
Factories
Forest fires
Motor vehicles
Aircraft
Ships
Domestic burning

Fertilizers
Refrigerators
Aerosols
Air conditioning systems
Foam blowing
Livestock
Rubbish dumping

4

Acid rain

1 Source Acid rain is produced by smoke and gases from factories, power stations, and cars. They all emit sulphur dioxide and nitrogen oxides which mix with water in the air to form clouds, making acid.

2 Transportation The acid clouds are blown across the sky by winds and are sometimes carried far from the source of pollution.

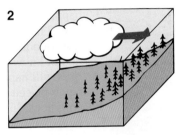

3 Rain When rain falls from the sky, the acid falls to the ground. This is acid rain.

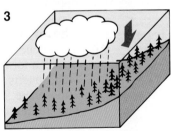

4 Seepage The rain falls on lakes and rivers, killing the fish. The rain is also absorbed into the ground and seeps into lakes and rivers. The acid kills trees, plants, and fish.

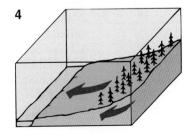

CLIMATIC CHANGES
The greenhouse effect

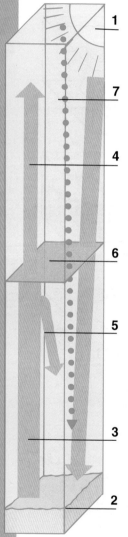

Heat from the Sun (**1**) enters the atmosphere and heats the Earth (**2**). The heat is reflected by the Earth's surface (**3**) and some heat escapes into space (**4**). In large quantities, certain gases, such as carbon dioxide, build up in the atmosphere and trap some of the heat (**5**). If this happened some of the polar icecaps would melt and sea levels would rise, flooding some land. Scientists do not know if these temperature rises will happen. Limits are now being placed on carbon dioxide emissions. In the mid-21st century temperatures could rise as shown opposite.

The ozone layer

The ozone layer (**6**) contains ozone, a form of oxygen, in the stratospheric layer of the Earth's atmosphere. It filters out the Sun's harmful ultraviolet rays (**7**) which can cause skin cancer. At present the ozone layer is being depleted as a result of chemical reactions started by chlorofluorocarbons (CFCs). Since the mid-1980s the use of CFCs in aerosols and refrigerators has been reduced. In spite of this, the ozone hole over Antarctica reached the size of North America in 1993.

1979

1986

1991

1996

Change in the size of the ozone hole over Antarctica

Since 1979 the protective layer of ozone gasses has been thinning over the South Pole. A hole is believed to be caused by the emission of industrial gasses. To recover the layer and maintain the Earth's protection, international co-operation should be intensified to prevent temperature rises.

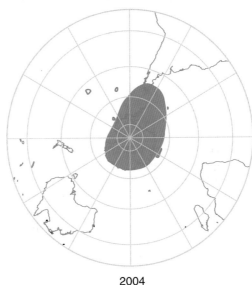

2004

Possible rises in temperature by 2050

14–15 °F   7–14 °F   4–7 °F

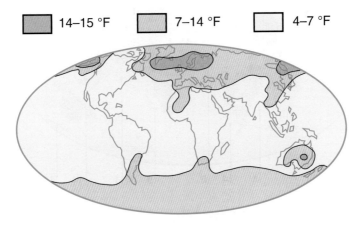

MARINE POLLUTION

The world's seas and oceans have always been regarded as legitimate dumping grounds for waste. However, the volume of pollutants is now so great that harmful pollution, once confined to coastal waters, is spreading to the open oceans.

Sources of marine pollution include dumping, pollution from rivers, contamination from air pollution, and shipping activities. The table (opposite) lists the pollution sources for each of the affected seas and oceans marked on the map below.

Contaminated seas and oceans

1 Southeast Pacific Ocean
2 North American areas
3 Caribbean Sea
4 Southwest Atlantic Ocean
5 West African areas
6 North Sea
7 Baltic Sea
8 Mediterranean Sea
9 South African areas
10 Persian Gulf
11 Indian Ocean
12 Southeast Asian areas
13 Japanese areas
14 Australian areas
15 New Zealand areas
16 Aral Sea

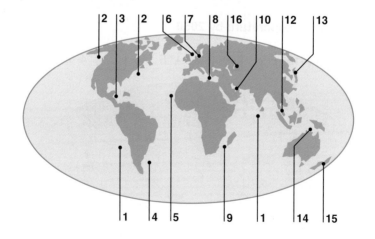

Sources of pollution

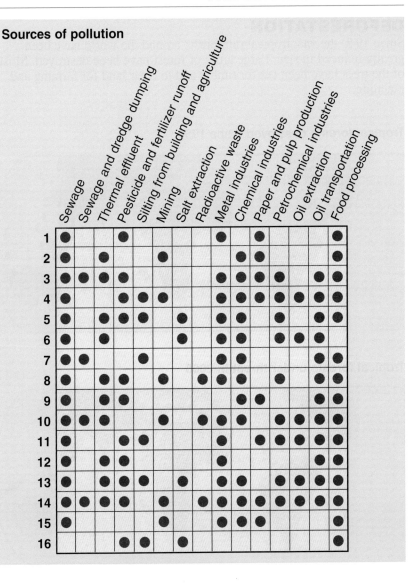

DEFORESTATION

Since 1940 the vast tropical rainforests around the world have been greatly reduced in size. Large areas of forest have been destroyed. Most of the trees have been cut for timber and to clear land for farming and ranching.

Tropical forests destroyed since 1950

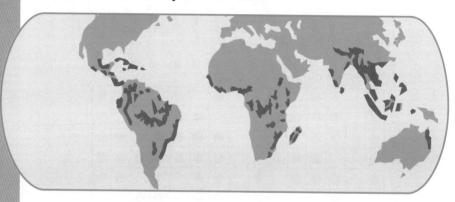

Tropical forests under threat in 2005

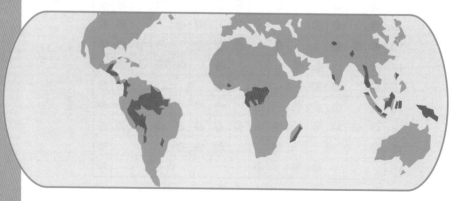

DESERTIFICATION

Deforestation, overgrazing, and intensive farming cause desertification. If the soil is dry, it is left exposed to the wind and rain, which strip away the topsoil. Agricultural lands which were once productive become infertile and lose their vegetation. The desert then extends and takes over the land.

4

Areas of land threatened by desertification

		million hectares
1	Africa	739
2	Asia	365
3	China and Mongolia	216
4	South America and Mexico	206
5	Former USSR (in Asia)	164
6	North America	163
7	Australia	111
8	Mediterranean Europe	22

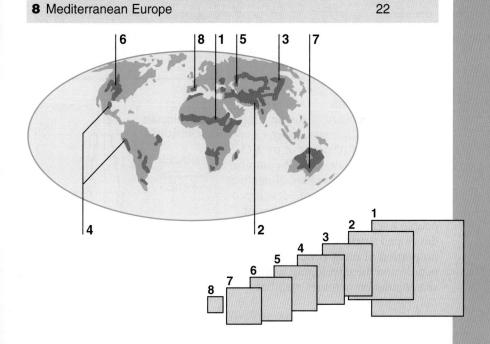

POPULATION STRUCTURE

The population pyramid for Equatorial Guinea (**1**), a developing country, has a wide base (many births), reducing steadily to a narrow point (few old people). In contrast, the pyramid for France (**2**), a developed country, has a narrow base and a wide middle, denoting a low birth rate and many middle-aged people.

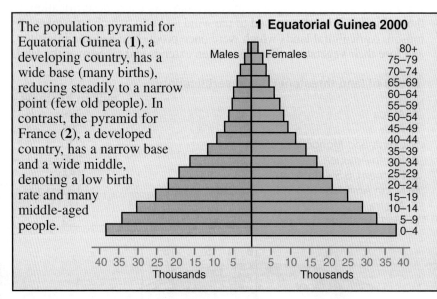

1 Equatorial Guinea 2000

Future patterns

In 1985, 22 per cent of the developed world's population was under 13 and 11 per cent was 65 years or over (**1**). In the developing world (**2**), the number of children under 15 years of age was almost double that for the developed world, and only a small number of people lived to old age. By 2025, the developed world will have a larger proportion of older people than young people and the developing world will see population numbers stabilize.

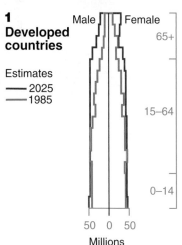

**1
Developed
countries**

Estimates
— 2025
— 1985

5

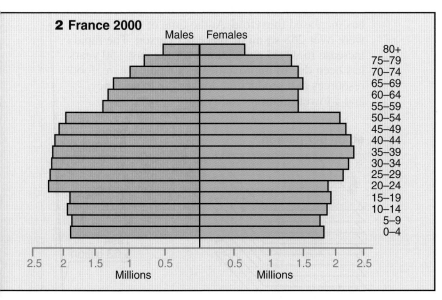

2 France 2000

Males Females

80+
75–79
70–74
65–69
60–64
55–59
50–54
45–49
40–44
35–39
30–34
25–29
20–24
15–19
10–14
5–9
0–4

2.5 2 1.5 1 0.5 0.5 1 1.5 2 2.5
Millions   Millions

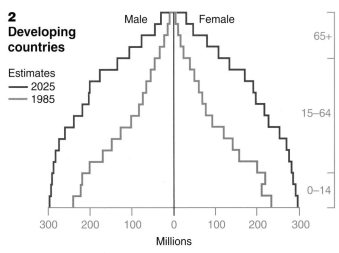

2 Developing countries

Male Female

Estimates
— 2025
— 1985

65+

15–64

0–14

300 200 100 0 100 200 300
Millions

POPULATION GROWTH

Over the past 2000 years the population of the world has increased thirtyfold. At the time of Christ there were over 255 sq mi of space per person. The rapid increase in world population over the past 150 years has been due to improvements in medical care, food resources and production, longer life expectancy, and a lower infant mortality rate.

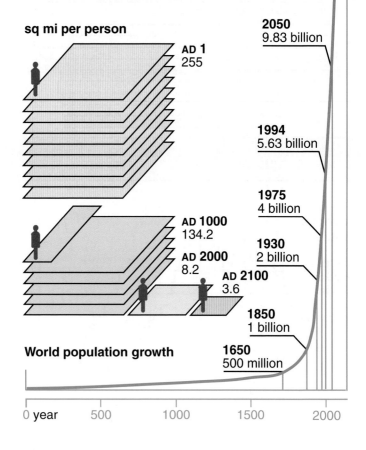

sq mi per person

AD 1
255

AD 1000
134.2

AD 2000
8.2

AD 2100
3.6

World population growth

2050
9.83 billion

1994
5.63 billion

1975
4 billion

1930
2 billion

1850
1 billion

1650
500 million

0 year   500   1000   1500   2000

POPULATION DISTRIBUTION

Between 2005 and 2050 it is estimated that the world's
population will increase by more than a third. The largest
growth in population will occur in Africa. It is thought the
percentage of the world's population will decrease in
Europe, Asia, and North America during this period.

5

Population distribution (%)

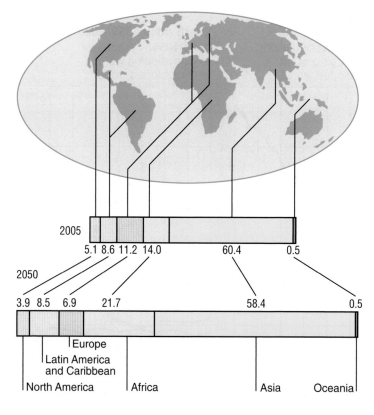

BIRTHS AND DEATHS

Birth rates are affected by such factors as nutrition, the availability of contraception and, to a certain extent, culture. Death rates tend to fall with improved health care and nutrition. There is a significant difference in the birth and death rates between the developed and the developing worlds. The graphs below show that birth and death rates for developing countries look set to continue rising into the 21st century. In developed countries, the rise in birth rate should slow down, and the death rate could remain static.

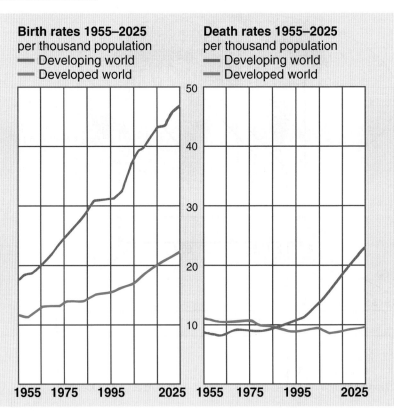

Birth rates 1955–2025
per thousand population
━━ Developing world
━━ Developed world

Death rates 1955–2025
per thousand population
━━ Developing world
━━ Developed world

LIFE EXPECTANCY

People in developed countries have a longer life expectancy on average than those in the developing world, with women living longer than men. Figures shown are from years 1981–2004.

5

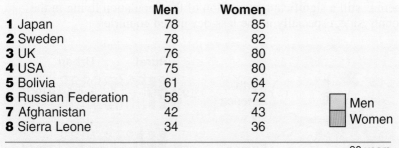

		Men	Women
1	Japan	78	85
2	Sweden	78	82
3	UK	76	80
4	USA	75	80
5	Bolivia	61	64
6	Russian Federation	58	72
7	Afghanistan	42	43
8	Sierra Leone	34	36

Men
Women

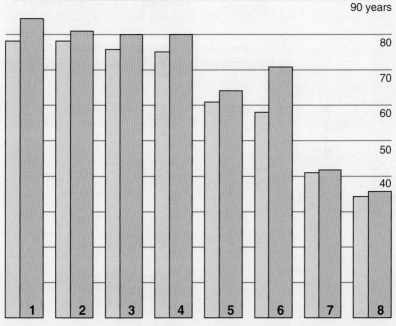

URBAN AND RURAL POPULATIONS

In many parts of the world, people are packed into cities. Growing urban populations bring problems, including poor sanitation, poverty, and lack of health care. Growing cities also mean encroachment on land previously used for agriculture. While the trend is toward living in cities, there is still a significant proportion of the population living in the countryside, especially in the less-developed countries.

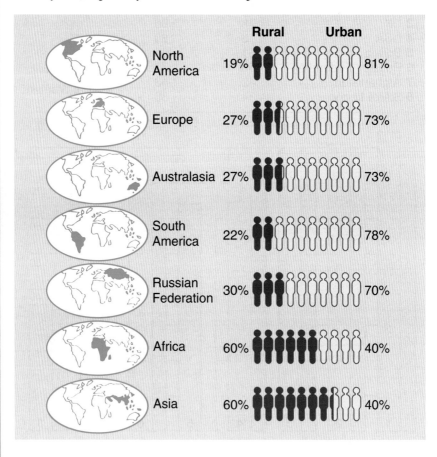

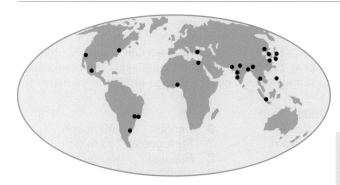

5

Population of selected large cities (in millions)

London
1970	10.4
1980	10
1990	9.2
2005	7.1

New York
1970	16.2
1980	15.7
1990	14.6
2005	13.6

São Paulo
1970	8
1980	16
1990	18
2005	20

Mexico City
1970	9
1980	17.5
1990	20.2
2005	22.7

Cities predicted to have 10 million population by 2015
(projected population in millions)

Tokyo 26.4
Mumbai (Bombay) 26.1
Mexico City 24
Lagos 23.2
Dhaka 21.1
São Paulo 20.4
Karachi 19.2
New York 17.4
Jakarta 17.3
Kolkata (Calcutta) 17.3
Delhi 16.8
Metro Manila 14.8
Shanghai 14.6
Los Angeles 14.1
Buenos Aires 14.1
Cairo 13.8
Istanbul 12.5
Beijing 12.3
Rio de Janeiro 11.9
Osaka 11.0
Tianjin 10.7
Hyderabad 10.5
Bangkok 10.1

Since 1970 cities in the developed world have seen a fall in population, which is predicted to continue. By comparison, cities in the developing world are expanding at a fast rate.

LANGUAGES

Chinese is spoken by the largest number of people in the world. English, however, is more widespread as it is spoken in several countries (up to 600 million people speak English as a second language). Most languages can be grouped into families. Each covers a range of languages native to one area.

Native speakers (2005)

1	Chinese	1300 million	**6**	Bengali	200 million
2	Arabic	420 million	**7**	Portuguese	200 million
3	Hindi	360 million	**8**	Russian	160 million
4	English	340 million	**9**	Japanese	120 million
5	Spanish	320 million	**10**	German	100 million

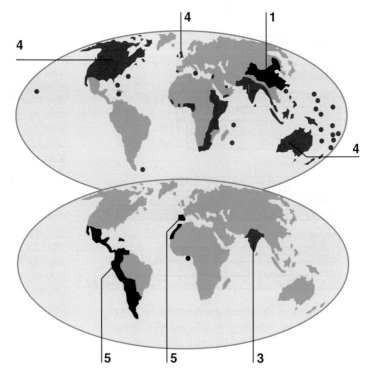

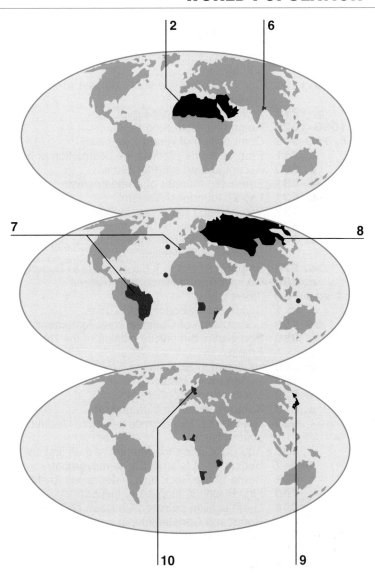

CHRONOLOGY OF RELIGIONS

c. 2000–1400 BC	Jewish patriarchs Abraham, Isaac, Jacob, Joseph, and Moses
1500–1200	Composition of the *Vedas*, earliest scriptures of Hinduism
c. 1275	Jewish exodus from Egypt
c. 1050–1020	Reign of Jewish King Saul
c. 700–500	Composition of Hindu *Upanishads*
751	Prophet Amos predicts the destruction of Israel
c. 660	Accepted start-date for Shinto
c. 628–c. 551	Zoroaster, founder of Zoroastrianism
c. 604–c. 531	Lao Zi, founder of Taoism
599–527	Vardhamana Mahavira, founder of Jainism
c. 551–c. 479	Kongzi, founder of Confucianism
c. 528	Siddhartha Gautama becomes the Buddha, founding of Buddhism
c. 270	Emperor Asoka of India converts to Buddhism
c. 200	Composition of Hindu *Bhagavadgita*
c. 4 BC–AD 30	Jesus Christ
c. AD 1	Buddhism introduced into China
50–150	Composition of Christian New Testament
380	Christianity the official religion of the Roman Empire
c. 380	Hinduism in SE Asia
c. 550	Buddhism in Japan
c. 570–632	Mohammed, prophet of Islam
c. 610	Koran revealed to Mohammed
622	The Hegira, Mohammed's flight to Medina, official start of Islam
632	Abu Bakr succeeds Mohammed as first caliph
685–7	Beginning of Islamic Shi'ite movement
691	Dome of the Rock built in Jerusalem by Muslims
700	First Buddhist monastery in Tibet
1054	Great schism between Christian churches of Rome and Constantinople
1096–1215	First persecution of Jews in Europe
1135–1204	Moses Maimonides, Jewish religious philosopher
1469–1539	Nanak, founder of Sikhism

6

1492	Jews expelled from Spain
1517	Martin Luther issues his 95 theses against Papal indulgences, beginning of Reformation
1534	Church of England established, with Monarch as head
1541	Calvinism in Geneva
1604	Sikh *Guru Granth Sahib* completed
1606	Completion of Sikh Golden Temple at Amritsar
1609	Baptist Church founded
1647	First unitarian tract published
1648	Society of Friends (Quakers) founded
1654	First Jews arrive in America
1699	Founding of Sikh Khalsa Path
1703–91	John Wesley, founder of Methodism
1805–1844	Joseph Smith, founder of Mormons
1863	Bahaism founded
1865	Salvation Army established by William Booth
1866	Christian Science founded
1897	First Zionist Congress
c. 1920	Rastafarianism established in Jamaica
1948	Israel becomes Jewish national home
1954	Unification Church founded by Sun Myung Moon
1965	Hare Krishna movement founded by Bhaktivedanta Swami Prabhupada
1974	First women priests ordained in the Episcopalian Church of the USA
1989	Death of Ayattolah Khomeini, Iran
1992	Muslims riot in India after Hindu fundamentalists destroy a mosque at Ayodhya: 1500 killed
2003	Anglican Church in America elect an openly gay bishop
2005	Death of Pope John Paul II succeeded by Pope Benedict XVI
2005	On the 60th Anniversary of the Hiroshima Nagasaki bombs the World Council of Churches calls for the banning of nuclear weapons

BAHAI FAITH

Founded 1863 in Persia (present-day Iran) by Mirza Hosein Ali (1817–92), known as Baha'ullah or "Glory of God".

Traditions Bahais believe that God has sent a series of prophets to teach eternal moral truths. The most recent of these was Baha'ullah.

Organization There are no clergy or sacraments. The community is organized by elected bodies (Spiritual Assemblies) at local, national, and international levels. There are ceremonies for marriage, naming babies, and funerals, and some shrines and temples.

Beliefs

1 Absolute oneness of God
2 The unification of all faiths
3 Harmony of all people
4 Equality of the sexes
5 Universal education
6 Obedience to government

Practices

1 Membership open to all who profess faith in Baha'ullah and his teachings.
2 Obligation to pray daily and to fast 19 days a year.
3 Abstention from narcotics and alcohol.
4 To practice monogamy.
5 To attend 19th Day Feast each month.

Sacred texts

1 *Kitab al-Aqdas* (*The Most Holy Book*) – Baha'ullah's laws.
2 *Ketab e Iqan* (*The Book of Certitude*) – teachings on the nature of God and religion.
3 *The Seven Valleys* – mystic treatise.

1 Shrine of Baha'ullah
2 Bahai house of worship, New Delhi

2

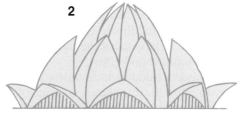

1

6

Calendar of events

The Bahai year is divided into 19 months of 19 days each.

Month	Festival
March 21	New Year; a holy day
April 21, 29	Baha'ullah's declaration of his mission
November 12	Birth of Baha'ullah
May 29	Passing of Baha'ullah

Major centres of Bahai faith

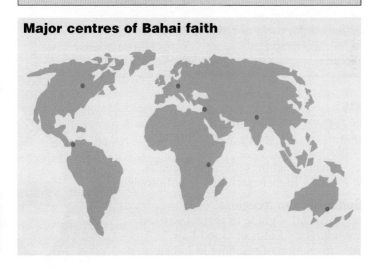

BUDDHISM
Founded c. 528 BC in India by Prince Siddhartha Gautama (c. 563– 483 BC), known as Buddha ("the enlightened").
Two traditions
1 Theravada Buddhism. Close to Buddha's original teachings. Believes that the only road to salvation is one of strict discipline and effort.
2 Mahayana Buddhism. Later tradition. Teaches salvation is possible for all. Introduced doctrine of Bodhisattva ("enlightened being"). Zen Buddhism, a Japanese branch.
Organization Monastic system, involving meditation, personal discipline, and spiritual exercises. Pilgrimages also of spiritual value.

Buddha's four noble truths	Eightfold Path
1 Suffering is always present in life	1 Right understanding
2 Desire causes suffering	2 Right thought
3 Suffering ends when desire is overcome	3 Right speech
	4 Right action
4 Freedom from life achieved by nirvana (release from cycle of birth, death, rebirth). Eightfold Path leads to nirvana	5 Right livelihood
	6 Right effort
	7 Right awareness
	8 Right concentration

Sacred texts
Pali Canon or *Tripitaka*, comprising:
1 *Vinaya Pitaka* – rules governing way of life of Buddhist monks and nuns.
2 *Sutta Pitaka* – oldest teachings given by Buddha.
3 *Abhidamma Pitaka* – higher teachings or philosophy.

Mahayana Buddhists also recognize:
1 *Prajnaparamita Sutras* – guide to perfect wisdom.
2 *Saddharmapundarika* – Lotus of Good Law.
3 *Lankavatara* – revelation of teaching in Lanka.

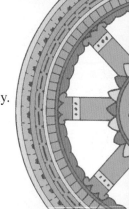

Objects associated with prayer and meditation

1 Mandala – symbolic diagram
2 Wheel of Law symbol
(depicting Eightfold Path)
3 Mantra – meditation chant

4 Chorten or bell of wisdom
5 Tibetan hand prayer wheel
6 Prayer beads (27 beads)

1   2   3   4 5   6

6

Calendar of events

Month		Festival
April	Japan	Hana Matsuri (birth of Buddha)
April–May	Tibet	Saga dawa (Buddha's first sermon)
May–June	Thailand	Festival of Wesak (celebrating Buddha's birth and enlightenment)
July	China	Summer Retreat (time of prayer and study)
Dec–Jan	Sri Lanka	Anniversary of arrival of Sanghamitta

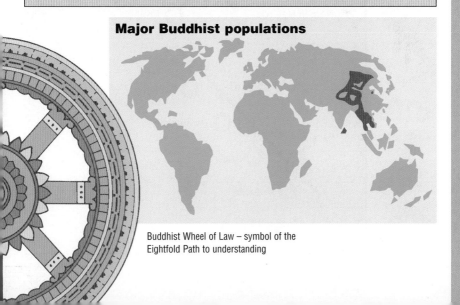

Major Buddhist populations

Buddhist Wheel of Law – symbol of the
Eightfold Path to understanding

Symbols
of the 12
Apostles

CHRISTIANITY

Founded 1st century AD by Jesus Christ, the "Messiah"
(c. 4 BC – AD 30). 12 disciples (Peter, Andrew, James, John,
Philip, Bartholomew, Thomas, Matthew, James son of
Alphaeus, Simon the Canaanite or "Zealot", Thaddeus/Judas
or James, and Judas Iscariot) became defined body, the
Church, which quickly spread through the evangelism of the
Apostles and their successors. By AD 380, Christianity was
the official religion of the Roman Empire, and became the
basis of European civilization in the Middle Ages.

Peter

Andrew

Thomas

James

John

Jude

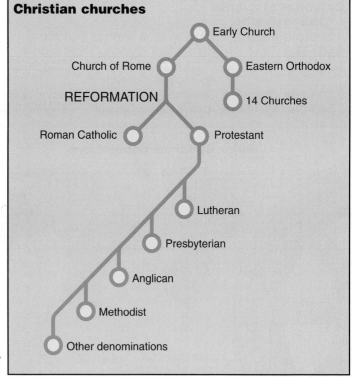

Christian churches

Early Church

Church of Rome

Eastern Orthodox

REFORMATION

14 Churches

Roman Catholic

Protestant

Lutheran

Presbyterian

Anglican

Methodist

Other denominations

Main teachings

1 Love of God and of one's neighbour, unselfishness, and compassion
2 Divinity of Jesus, and his resurrection (coming to life again) after his death from crucifixion
3 That Christ (Messiah or Saviour) will return to inaugurate "Kingdom of God"
4 Concept of Trinity, according to which God is made known as Father (in Heaven), Son (Jesus), and Holy Spirit (God's continuing presence in the world)

Objects associated with prayer

1 Icon (religious painting) of Christ or Mary (Orthodox)
2 Crucifix; statuette of Christ crucified on a cross
3 Rosary beads (one for each prayer) with crucifix and Mary medallion (Roman Catholic)

Calendar of events

Month	Festival
December	Advent
December/January	Christmastide (celebration of the birth of Jesus)
January/February	Epiphany
February/March	Lent (40 days)
March/April	Holy Week
April/May	Eastertide
May	Ascension
May/June	Pentecost

Matthew

6

Matthias

Bartholomew

Philip

James

Simon

Sacred texts
Holy Bible, consisting of:

1 Old Testament 39 books: Genesis, Exodus, Leviticus, Numbers, Deuteronomy, Joshua, Judges, Ruth, 1 Samuel, 2 Samuel, 1 Kings, 2 Kings, 1 Chronicles, 2 Chronicles, Ezra, Nehemiah, Esther, Job, Psalms, Proverbs, Ecclesiastes, Song of Solomon, Isaiah, Jeremiah, Lamentations, Ezekiel, Daniel, Hosea, Joel, Amos, Obadiah, Jonah, Micah, Nahum, Habakkuk, Zephaniah, Haggai, Zechariah, Malachi.

2 New Testament 27 books: Matthew, Mark, Luke, John, Acts of the Apostles, Romans, 1 Corinthians, 2 Corinthians, Galatians, Ephesians, Philippians, Colossians, 1 Thessalonians, 2 Thessalonians, 1 Timothy, 2 Timothy, Titus, Philemon, Hebrews, James, 1 Peter, 2 Peter, 1 John, 2 John, 3 John, Jude, Revelation.

3 Apocrypha 15 books: 1 Esdras, 2 Esdras, Tobit, Judith, Additions to Esther, Wisdom of Solomon, Ecclesiasticus, Baruch, Letter of Jeremiah, Prayer of Azariah and the Song of the Three Young Men, Susanna, Bel and the Dragon, Prayer of Manasseh, 1 Maccabees, 2 Maccabees.

The four Evangelists

Matthew

Mark

Luke

John

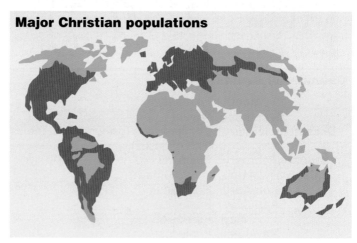
Major Christian populations

Christianity includes many denominations and styles of worship. Some of the most important are described below.

Orthodox Churches
Founded As a result of the schism of 1054, when the Pope excommunicated the Patriarch of Constantinople.
Traditions As the name implies, Orthodox Churches regard themselves as maintaining the truth of Christianity. While Roman Catholics focus mainly on the sacrifice of the crucifixion, Orthodox Churches concentrate on the miracle of the resurrection. Priests may marry, but bishops may not.
Organization There are 14 self-governing Churches, each under its Patriarch. Each Church is divided into dioceses and parishes. Parishes are led by priests, with deacons to assist.

Roman Catholic Church
Founded Traditionally founded by St. Peter, a disciple of Jesus. He arrived in Rome c. AD 50.
Traditions Doctrine of the Church set out in Apostles' Creed and Nicene Creed. The Bible is accepted as the word of God, as are all the teachings of Christ. The Pope is regarded as the supreme head of the Church. Seven sacraments: anointing the sick, baptism, holy orders, confirmation, marriage, holy eucharist, and penance. Veneration of Mary as the Mother of Christ. Celibacy of priesthood.
Organization The Pope is the head of the Church. The College of Cardinals elects him. Priests are not allowed to marry. There are many monastic orders. It is the most widespread Christian Church.

Protestant Churches
Baptists
Founded In Amsterdam in 1609 by John Smythe and in London in 1612 by Thomas Helwys.
Traditions Baptists believe that the Bible is the highest authority, and that everyone can find personal salvation.

Baptism takes place in adulthood. Complete immersion at baptism symbolizes the washing away of sin.

Organization Each church is autonomous and functions in a highly democratic way in governing its own affairs.

Church of England (C of E)

Founded 1534 as a result of Henry VIII's break with Rome.

Traditions Doctrines are set out in the 39 Articles, its forms of service in the *Book of Common Prayer* and the *Alternative Service Book*. Some sections of the Church of England emphasize the Catholic tradition while others stress Protestantism (High and Low Church).

Organization The C of E comprises two provinces, Canterbury and York, with the Archbishop of Canterbury the Primate of All England. The reigning monarch is the official head. Dioceses are governed by bishops, parishes are under the care of clergy. The church parliament is the General Synod, made up of bishops, clergy, and lay people. The Anglican Communion is the name given to all Churches that adhere to the basic teaching of the C of E. Each Church is independent but recognizes the Archbishop of Canterbury as its leader.

Protestants destroying Catholic imagery

Churches of Christ

Founded In the USA in the 19th century by Thomas Campbell, his son Alexander, and Barton Stone.

Traditions Stress on restoring New Testament Christianity, recognizing Christ as the founder, head, and saviour of the Church. The New Testament is the sole source of doctrine and practice. Baptism and confession are keys to salvation.

Organization There are around 20,000 separate groups, mostly in the USA, governed by a system of elders.

Episcopal Church

Founded In Jamestown, USA, in 1789, as successor to the

Church of England in America; the Episcopal Church is also the name of the Anglican Church in Scotland.

Traditions Doctrine is similar to that of the C of E.

Organization Parishes and missions are grouped into dioceses, governed by bishops.

Lutheran Church

Founded 1530 by Martin Luther and Philipp Melanchthon, after split with Rome.

Traditions Lutherans believe that death is overcome by the forgiveness and mercy of God. Individuals are responsible to God for their conduct. There are two sacraments, baptism and Holy Communion. Great stress is laid on the importance of education.

Organization Services are conducted by a pastor, churches are grouped into synods or districts.

Martin Luther

Methodism

Founded In England in 1729 by John Wesley, originally as an evangelical movement within the Church of England, after 1791 as a separate church. The name derives from the systematic approach which characterizes the Church.

Traditions Direct personal experience of salvation through Christ is stressed. The scriptures are recognized as the supreme authority. Members make public declarations of their faith. Salvation is achieved through faith, personal morality and evangelism.

Organization An Annual Conference directs policy and, in partnership with local churches, appoints ministers. Local churches are grouped into Circuits and Districts. Ministry by lay or "local" preachers is strongly encouraged.

John Wesley

Pentecostal Churches (Charismatic Renewal)

Founded In the USA in the early years of the 20th century.

Traditions Pentecostalism is inspired by the visitation of the Holy Spirit to the Apostles at the first Pentecost (Whit Sunday), which enabled them to speak in tongues. The core belief is that the Holy Spirit can come into the life of anyone, and that healing, speaking in tongues, and making prophecies bear witness to this. The Bible is taken as the literal word of God.

Organization Worship is informal, with strong emphasis on singing and spontaneous exclamations of praise.

Presbyterian Churches
Founded 1530s in Geneva by John Calvin.

Traditions Doctrine of predestination and irresistible Grace of God. Good works cannot "earn" salvation, which is pre-determined. Success in the world may be a "sign" of being elected by God. The two sacraments are baptism and the Lord's Supper.

Organization Elected board of elders and ministers govern each church. The General Assembly is made up of equal numbers of ministers and laity. The Church of Scotland is a Presbyterian Church.

Salvation Army
Founded In 1865 by William Booth, a former Methodist minister.

Traditions Sacraments are not essential. The Army's chief aim is to rehabilitate the poor and needy. Holiness of life, discipline, and loyalty are the key virtues. Music plays an important part. Alcohol and smoking are prohibited.

Organization A military-type hierarchy, with elected Generals, and Soldiers who sign "articles of war".

George Fox

Society of Friends (Quakers)
Founded George Fox in England in the 17th century. The name was originally intended to be insulting, after Fox instructed his followers to "quake" at the word of God.

Traditions The faith is built on a belief in immediate contact with the divinity (the "inner light"). There are no sacraments because the whole of life is considered sacramental.

Organization At meetings, the Friends sit in silence until moved by the Spirit to speak. Alternatively, there may be led prayers and discussion. At community business meetings, a "clerk" leads the discussion.

Churches with Christian-derived beliefs
Christian Science
Founded 1866 by Mary Baker Eddy.

6

Traditions Adherents believe that evil and disease can be overcome by the individual's awareness of spiritual truth. Emphasizes spiritual healing and the unreality of matter.
Organization Headquarters in Boston, USA, is known as the "Mother Church." Its affairs are ordered by a five-member board of directors.

Jehovah's Witnesses
Founded 19th century in the USA by Charles Taze Russell.
Traditions The Bible is interpreted literally and the Holy Trinity rejected. Witnesses believe that Armageddon is imminent and that 144,000 will be selected to rule with Christ. All other Churches are rejected and only God's war will rid the earth of evil.
Organization Witnesses reject blood transfusions and non-medical use of drugs, refuse military service, and do not recognize earthly institutions. Members are actively evangelical.

Unitarianism
Founded First tract published in 1647. Church founded in 1770s as secession from Church of England.
Traditions God is one. Rejects the deity of Jesus Christ and the Holy Trinity. Christ was a religious teacher. Denial of everlasting hell, believing that all people can be saved. Emphasis on brotherhood.
Organization Self-governing congregations. Use of Christian sacraments of baptism and Lord's Supper, and of preaching and lecture groups.

CONFUCIANISM

Founded 6th century BC in China by Kongzi (Confucius)
(c. 551–c. 479 BC).

Two traditions

1 Associated with Confucius and Xunzi (c. 298–c. 238 BC) which
says: follow traditional codes of behaviour for their own sake.
2 Associated with Mencius (Mengzi, c. 372–c. 289 BC) which
says: we ought to do as our moral natures dictate.

Organization No church or clergy; it is not an institution.
No teaching on the worship of God or gods, or life after
death. Confucianism in its broadest sense can be seen
more as a philosophy of ideas which influenced
Chinese government, education, and attitudes
toward correct personal behaviour and the
individual's duty to society. Social life is
ritualized, and weddings and funerals follow a
tradition handed down by scholars. The colour
and patterns of clothes have a sacred meaning.

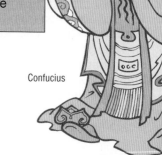

Confucius

Some Confucian truths

1 Sincerity in public and private conduct
2 Orderly social life
3 Moral character
4 Respect for elders and ancestors
5 Respect for the ruler
6 Study and practice self-examination
7 Become "superior man" through learning and devotion to moral ideals
8 Importance of the family

Sacred texts

1 The *Analects*, the teachings of Confucius
– basic scriptures.
2 *I Ching*, the book of changes.
3 *Mengzi*, book of second sage Mencius.

Objects associated with prayer and meditation
1 Confucius studied patterns such as this symbolizing good and evil
2 The Temple of Heaven in Beijing is the largest temple ever built for ancestral worship
3 The Temple of Confucius, 12th century
4 An ancestral tablet

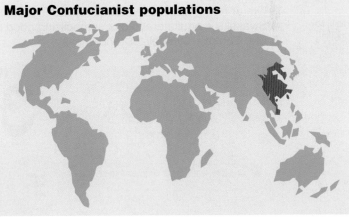

6

Major Confucianist populations

HINDUISM

Founded c. 1500 BC by Aryan invaders of India.

Traditions Hinduism stresses the right way of living (dharma). There are diverse beliefs and practices. There are many gods and many sects. Important beliefs are the samsara cycle of birth and rebirth, and karma, the law by which the consequences of our actions in this life are carried over into the next.

Organization Hinduism varies in nature from region to region. Complex rituals supervised by Brahman priest or teacher.

Practices Temple, domestic, and congregational worship. The most performed ceremony is prayer (puja).

Sacred texts

1 *Vedas* – revealed scriptures including songs, hymns, sayings, and teachings.

2 *Smriti* – traditional scriptures including the *Ramayana, Mahabharata,* and the *Bhagavadgita.*

Symbols associated with prayer and meditation

1 Brahma, the Hindu creator god

2 Vishnu, the god of love, appears in 10 forms, or incarnations

3 Om or Aum – sacred symbol of spiritual goodness

4 Swastika – equilateral cross symbolizing good luck

5 Shri Yantra – symbolizes wholeness

Hindu boy praying

6

Calendar of events

The 12 Hindu months overlap months in the Julian calendar, e.g. Magha runs mid-January to mid-February, and so on.

Month	Festival
Magha	winter solstice and time for peacemaking
Phalguna	great Shiva night and spring dedication to goddess of music, Saraswati
Chaitra	spring festival; regional new year festivals
Vaisakha	Ram Navami – birthday of god Rama, an incarnation of Vishnu
Ashadha	Ratha Yatra celebration of Krishna, Lord of the Universe
Bhadrapada	Raksha Bandhan holiday for brothers and sisters
Asvina	Navaratri Dussehra Durga Puja, marks Rama's victory over his enemy Ravana
Karttika	Diwali new year festival and festival of lights

Major Hindu populations

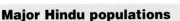

Siva Nataraja –
Lord of Dance

ISLAM

Founded 7th century AD as a result of revelation to Mohammed (c. 570–632) the Prophet.

Three traditions

1 The Sunni form the majority and more orthodox group. They recognize the succession from Mohammed to Abu Bakr to the next three caliphs (rulers of the Islamic world).

2 The Shi'ites, followers of Ali, Mohammed's nephew and son-in-law. They believe in 12 imams (teachers) who guide the faithful to paradise.

3 Three other subsects exist: the Sufis, the Ismailis, and the Wahhabis.

Organization No one priesthood, though great respect is given to descendants of Mohammed, holy men, scholars, and teachers (mullahs and ayatollahs). Sharia, Islamic law, applies to every aspect of life and conduct. Religious life centres on the mosque and the family.

Central beliefs

1 God is creator of the whole universe

2 Absolute unity and power resides in God

3 God is just and merciful

4 Mohammed was last of the great prophets. The Jewish prophets and Jesus were his predecessors

5 The *Koran* forbids representation of human and animal figures. It denounces usury, games of chance, the consumption of alcohol, and pork

6 Life on earth is a test and only a preparation for the life to come

7 The good and obedient will go to heaven

8 Pride is a cardinal sin

Sacred texts

1 The *Koran* – the word of God as revealed to Mohammed.

2 The *Hadith* – what Mohammed the Prophet said and did.

3 The *Sunnah* – rules and regulations of Muslim life.

DAWN

NOON

NOON

SUNSET

Five daily prayer times of Islam

FAJR

Five pillars of faith

1 Profession of faith – there is no God but Allah, and Mohammed is his prophet.
2 Prayer – five prayers a day.
3 Zakat – giving a proportion of one's wealth to the needy.
4 Fasting – between dawn and dusk during Ramadan.
5 The Hajj – pilgrimage to Mecca.

6

ZUHR

Calendar of events

Muslim calendar based on lunar calendar, which is shorter than the Julian, so festivals fall earlier each year.

Month	Festival
Muharram 1	Mohammed's departure from Mecca
Rabi I 12	Birthday of Mohammed the Prophet
Rajab 27	Night Mohammed ascended to heaven
Ramadan 1	Month of fasting
Ramadan 27	Revelation of *Koran* to Mohammed
Shawwal 1	Festival of breaking the fast (Id al-Fitr)
Dhu-i-Hijja 8–13	Month of great pilgrimage
Dhu-i-Hijja 10	Feast of sacrifice (Id al-Adha)

'ASR

MAGHRIB

Major Islamic populations

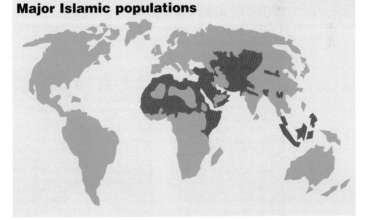

'ISHA

JAINISM

Founded 6th century BC in India by Vardhamana Mahavira (599–527 BC), sometimes considered an offshoot of Hinduism.

Two traditions

1 The Svetambara ("white-robed") follow a canon of scripture containing the sermons and dialogues of Mahavira.
2 The Digambara ("sky-clad" or "naked") believe original teachings have been lost but the original message is preserved. Monks and nuns vow nudity.

Organization Monastic system, followers dedicated to life of the ascetic. Some temple rituals. There are a series of vows and religious practices for lay people to follow.

Member of the Svetambara sect

Member of the Digambara sect

Vows of Jainist monk

1 No harming any living thing (ahimsa)
2 No stealing
3 No lying
4 No sexual activity
5 No possession of property
6 Devotion of whole life to task (Moksha)

Objects associated with prayer

1 Offerings of flowers, fruit, perfumes, and lamps to idols
2 Pillars surmounted by elephants
3 Wheel of law

1

2

3

Sacred texts

1 *Agama* – believed by the Svetambara to be the dialogues and discourses of Mahavira written down and collected together by his disciples. There are a total of 45 texts, 11 parts.
2 *Cheda-sutras* – the rules of asceticism.
3 *Culika-sutras* – texts concentrating on the nature of the mind and knowledge.

Indra enlightens
Mahavira

6

Calendar of events

Month	Festival
August–September	Pajjusana – a period of forgiving, giving to the poor, and confession of sins
March–April	Oli – a period of nine days spent fasting
September–October	Oli – a period of fasting and of mythical celestial worship of Jina images
October–November	Commemoration of the Nirvana of Mahavira by lighting lamps

Major Jainist populations

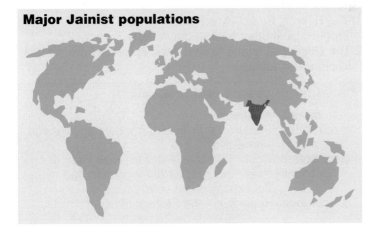

The 12 tribes of Israel

Judah

Zebulun

The Torah

Issachar

Reuben

JUDAISM

Founded c. 2000 BC, consolidated by Abraham and Moses.

Three traditions

1 Orthodox Judaism. Strict adherence to laws and traditions.
2 Conservative Judaism. Recognizes law and tradition but holds that revelation is open to many interpretations.
3 Reform Judaism. Each generation can accept, reject, and modify traditions.

Organization Synagogue is house of worship and centre of Jewish education and communal affairs. Rabbi is spiritual leader, teacher, and interpreter of Jewish law. Each congregation chooses its own rabbi. There is no world leader and no ruling body with authority over practice.

Central beliefs

1 Faith in one God
2 God created man in his own image
3 Abraham, father of the Jewish people, made a covenant with God
4 Moses superior to all other prophets
5 Believe a Messiah will come one day to redeem mankind

Sacred texts

1 The Hebrew *Bible* – which includes the Torah, the Prophets, and other books (known as writings).
2 The *Talmud* – a guide to civil laws, religious laws, and the teachings of Judaism.

Calendar of events and festivals

Month	Festival
March–April	Passover – festival of freedom and exodus from Egypt
September	Rosh Hashanah – Jewish New Year
October	Yom Kippur – Day of Atonement, the holiest day of the year
December	Hanukkah – the Festival of Light

Objects associated with prayer and devotion

1 Mezuzah – a wood, metal, and glass case containing parchments inscribed with 15 verses from the Bible; reminder of God's presence everywhere

2 Tefillin – containing parchments with four passages from the Bible

3 Menorah – a candlestick with seven branches.

Gad

6

Simeon

Ephraim

Benjamin

Menasseh

Dan

Asher

Napthali

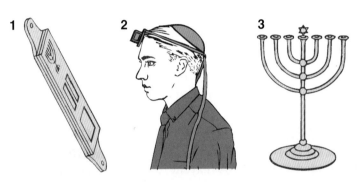

Major Jewish populations

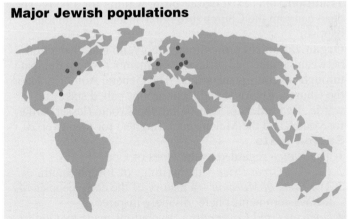

UNIFICATION CHURCH

Founded 1954 in Korea by Rev. Sun Myung Moon.

Tradition Religious sect who believe the Messiah has come and that he heads the family of perfect children. Jesus offered spiritual salvation, not physical. Mass wedding ceremonies are held at intervals with most partners chosen by the leader.

Organization Members are required to spend time raising money for the organization. They live in community centres, practice celibacy outside marriage, and follow no other formal rituals, only a weekly pledge.

Sacred texts

1 The *Bible* – Old and New Testaments.

2 *Divine Principle* – additional revelations told to the Rev. Sun Myung Moon.

CHURCH OF JESUS CHRIST OF LATTER-DAY SAINTS (MORMONS)

Founded 1830 in USA (Fayette, NY) by Joseph Smith (1805–44).

Tradition Souls exist before birth, waiting for a body. The dead can join the Church through a special posthumous baptism.

Joseph Smith

Organization No professional clergy, no real distinction between laymen and officials. All members can participate through several organizations. The General Authority leads the Church. Regional and local groups called stakes or wards. Two orders of priesthood: the Aronic (lesser) order for youths and the Melchizedek (higher) for men over 20.

Sacred texts

1 The *Bible*– regarded as the word of God.

2 *Pearl of Great Price* – the writings of Joseph Smith.

3 The *Book of Mormon* – a history of the early peoples of the Western hemisphere; divinely inspired.

4 *Doctrines and Covenants* – revelations made by God to Joseph Smith.

RASTAFARIANISM

Founded In Jamaica during the 1920s. Inspired by Marcus Garvey's "back to Africa" movement.

Tradition Named after Ras Tafari, who became Emperor Haile Selassie I of Ethiopia in 1930, and believed to be Jah (God) as prophesied. Strong links with Christianity and Judaism. Guided by the culture and traditions of Ethiopia and unity and pride in African heritage.

6

Organization More a way of life than a religion. Followers meet weekly to discuss community business and spirituality. No church. Song, prayer, and music are important.

Sacred texts

The *Bible* – All 39 books of Old Testament.

Calendar of events	
Month	**Festival**
January 7	Ethiopian Christmas
July 16	Ethiopian Constitution Day
July 23	Haile Selassie's Birthday
August 17	Marcus Garvey's Birthday
September 11	Ethiopian New Year

Mormons, Rastafarians and Unification Church

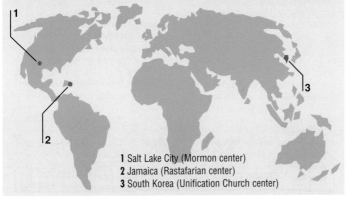

1 Salt Lake City (Mormon center)
2 Jamaica (Rastafarian center)
3 South Korea (Unification Church center)

SHINTOISM

Founded c. 660 BC in Japan.

Two main traditions

1 Shrine Shinto (Jinga). Japanese state cult and national religion until 1945.

2 Sectarian (Kyoko). Follows the teachings of a particular leader or group.

Organization Shinto shrines are visited at a person's convenience, but some may go on the first or 15th of each month. Shinto priests perform ceremonies.

Sacred texts

1 The *Kojiki* – records of ancient matters AD 712.

2 The *Nihon Shoki* – the chronicles of Japan AD 720.

Religious objects

1 Tori, the sacred gates of shrines

2 Three sacred treasures – the mirror, sword, and jewels.

3 Grand Shrine of Ise, the most respected shrine

4 Jino Stone, placed in the garden in a thatched hut to honour Jino, the god who looks after property

5 The Sakaki, the holy tree

Shinto myth – creation of land

Shinto myth – creation of day

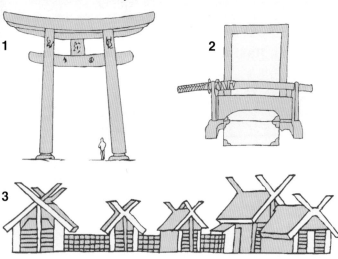

4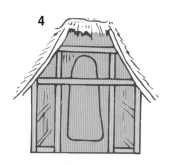
5

6

Calendar of events

Month	Festival
Spring Festival	Prayer for good harvest
Autumn Festival	Shinto thanksgiving
Animal Festival	Divine Procession – miniature shrines are carried by the faithful
November 15	Shichi-go-san Festival – children of three, five, and seven visit shrines
January 15	Adults' Day

Japanese paper kites flown at spring festivals

Major Shinto populations

Guru Nanak

SIKHISM

Founded 15th century in India by Guru Nanak (1469–1539).

Tradition Sikh means "disciple". Sikhs are the disciples of their 10 Gurus (religious teachers). Gurus teach the way to truth and how to find it. Meditation is a source of Sikh expression.

Organization No priestly caste. Worship is performed in temples where hymns of praise are sung and morning prayers said. A guru guides followers to Moksa (release).

Sacred texts

1 *Guru Granth Sahib* – three versions, 6000 hymns by the first five gurus.

2 *Vars* – heroic ballads.

3 *Janam-Sakhis* or "life stories" written 50 to 80 years after Nanak's death.

Objects associated with worship

1 Chauri – fan

2 *Guru Granth Sahib* – a sacred object of worship

3 Channani – awning

4 Manji sahib – stool

5 Romalla – cloth coverings

6 Takht – platform

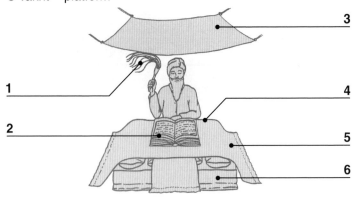

Sikh symbols – the five Ks

1 Kesa – hair must be retained unshorn

2 Kangha – the "comb"

3 Kachh – shorts worn under clothes

4 Kirpan – sabre

5 Kara – bracelet of steel worn on the right arm. Boys add Singh (lion) to their surname and girls Kaur (princess)

The Five Ks

6

Calendar of events

The 12 Sikh months overlap months in the Gregorian calendar, e.g. Phagan runs mid-February to mid-March.

Month	Festival
Phagan	Hola Mohalla (Day of Military Power)
Vasakh	Baisakhi (birthday of Khalsa). New Year
Asun	Installation of Guru Granth Nanak. Birthday of Guru Ram
Katik	Birthday of Guru Nanak, Diwali (release of Guru Har Gobind)
Magar	Martyrdom of Guru Tegh Bahardur

Major Sikh populations

TAOISM

Founded By tradition in the 6th century BC by Lao Zi.
Traditions Tao means the way or course of life. It stresses the integral unity of mankind and the natural order.
1 Spirit Cloud Taoists. Masters of methods or Headed Taoists. Concentrate on meditation not ritual.
2 Orthodox – Tao masters and Black Headed Taoists. Stress importance of rituals, cosmic renewal, and controlling spirits.
Organization Priesthood and monastic system. Multitude of sacred texts. Personal and metaphysical preoccupations.

Philosopher Lao Zi riding a water buffalo

Taoist philosophy

1 All is in flux except Tao
2 Yin balances Yang
3 Belief in meditation and simplicity
4 Te (virtue) and Ch'i (energy) the power of effortless action
5 Quest for immortality
6 Heaven rules earth, earth rules man, Tao rules heaven
7 Tao produces and sustains all things
8 All move in harmony

The Three Pure Ones (San-tsing)

1 Yüan Shih T'ien Tsun (Creator and source of all truth)
2 T'ai Shang Tao-chun (who looks after learning)
3 Lao Zi (who became a god after death)

1

2

3

6

Sacred texts
1 *Dao De Jing* (*Tao te-ching*) – "the way and its power".
2 The writings of Zhuang Zi (369 – 286 BC).

Object associated with prayer and meditation
Incense burner essential to every rite.

Symbols and signs
1 The Tai Chi, the supreme ultimate, which expresses the production of Yin and Yang, complementary and interacting forces of nature – such as male and female, light and dark – to achieve perfect harmony.

2 Lao Zi's divine seal, used in Taoist magic

3 Priest's robe with applied symbols of Tai Chi and the eight mystic trigrams

1

2

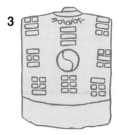
3

Major Taoist populations

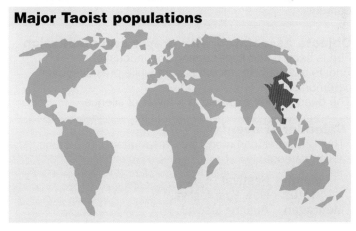

ZOROASTRIANISM

Founded In 6th century BC by Persian prophet Zoroaster.

Tradition Before Islam it is thought that Zoroastrianism was the official religion of three major world empires.

Organization Priesthood led by Dastûr, a type of bishop, who directs and administers temples. Priesthood is hereditary. Ceremony of initiation in which a child receives a shirt and the Girdle (Kusti) which are worn for life. The Parsis in W India practice a form of Zoroastrianism.

Ahura Mazda

Sacred texts

1 *Avesta* – the holy book consisting of prayers, hymns, rituals, instruction, practice, and law.
2 *Gathas* – hymns attributed to Zoroaster.
3 *Pahlavi* – literature.

Zoroastrian beliefs

Two principles – good and evil. Ahura Mazda the supreme deity, creator of all things good. Ahriman the destructive principle of greed, anger, and darkness

1 Good will triumph
2 The dead will be resurrected
3 There will be paradise on earth

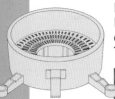

Objects associated with prayer and meditation

Fire is sacred and kept burning continuously.
Priests always wear mouth covers while presiding over ceremonies.
The dead are left exposed in a tower of silence

Tower of silence where the dead are exposed to the elements

Calendar of events

The 12 Zoroastrian months correspond to those of the Julian calendar.

Month	Festival
Noruz	New Year festival
Mehragan	Autumn festival

CALENDAR OF WORLD RELIGIONS
Winter

Christian Festival of Christmas
Jewish Festival of Light (Hanukkah)
Sikhs Celebrate birthday of Guru Gobind Singh
Hindu Winter solstice festival (Maker Sankrakanti Lohri)
Orthodox Christians celebrate St Basil's Day
Christian Epiphany
Hindu Spring festival (Saraswati Puja)
Christian Ash Wednesday

Birth of Christ

6

Spring

Orthodox Christian Annunciation
Christian Easter (movable between March and April)
Festival of **Buddha's** birth, enlightenment, and death
Sikh Festival of Baisakhi (April/May)
Jewish Passover
Shinto Spring festival

Summer

Christian Pentecost
Sikhs commemorate martyrdom of Guru Arjan
Buddhist Summer Retreat (China)
Hindu Celebration of Krishna as Lord of the Universe (Ram Navami)
Rastafarian Celebration of Marcus Garvey's Birthday
Orthodox Christian Feast of Transfiguration

Passover table

Autumn

Jewish New Year (Rosh Hashanah)
Jewish Day of Atonement (Yom Kippur)
Christian Nativity of Blessed Virgin
Hindu New Year (Diwali)
Sikhs celebrate birthday of Guru Nanak
Christian All Saints' Day

Islamic festivals

The **Islamic** calendar is based on cycles of the moon, so the year is shorter. This means that Islamic festivals such as Ramadan occur at a different time each year.

Jagannatha festival

GODS OF ANCIENT CULTURES

Egyptian gods

God	Influence
1 Anubis	death
2 Bastet	pleasure
3 Hathor	love
4 Horus	light
5 Maat	truth
6 Osiris	underworld
7 Ra	sun
8 Thoth	scholarship

Anubis weighs the soul

Thoth records a life

Ammit devours a sinner

Norse gods and goddesses

God	Influence
1 Woden	death, poetry, victory
2 Thor	thunder and war
3 Tyr	war
4 Loki	evil and fire
5 Balder	light or beauty
6 Frey	sun or fertility
7 Idun	eternal youth

6

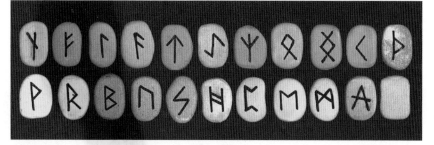

Ancient Nordic runes have the seals of different spirits carved as symbols – one blank stone representing fate is also used

Greek gods and goddesses

God		Roman equivalent	Position
1	Apollo	Apollo	God of sun and youth
2	Ares	Mars	God of war
3	Cronus	Saturn	God of time
4	Dionysus	Bacchus	God of wine
5	Eros	Cupid	God of love
6	Hades	Pluto	God of the underworld
7	Hephaestus	Vulcan	Blacksmith of the gods
8	Hermes	Mercury	Messenger of the gods
9	Poseidon	Neptune	God of the sea
10	Zeus	Jupiter	King of the gods

Goddess	Roman equivalent	Position
1 Aphrodite	Venus	Goddess of love
2 Artemis	Diana	Goddess of the moon
3 Athena	Minerva	Goddess of wisdom
4 Demeter	Ceres	Goddess of agriculture
5 Hera	Juno	Queen of the Gods
6 Hestia	Vesta	Goddess of the home
7 Tychea	Fortuna	Goddess of fate
8 Rhea	Ops	Goddess of plenty, and harvests
9 Eirene	Pax	Goddess of peace
10 Elpis	Spes	Goddess of hope

6

Mythical creatures

Animals	Appearance
1 Basilisk	dragon's body with serpent's tail
2 Cerberus	dog's body with serpent's tail and three heads
3 Dragon	serpent's body, bat's wings, tiger's claws
4 Griffin	lion's body, bird's wings, eagle's head
5 Hippocampus	horse's body with fish's tail
6 Pegasus	horse's body with bird's wings
7 Phoenix	eagle-like bird reborn in fire
8 Unicorn	horse's body with spiral horn on forehead

Female	Appearance
9 Harpy	bird with female head
10 Mermaid	female body with fish's tail
11 Siren	female body with bird's legs and sometimes wings
12 Sphinx	lion's body with female head

Male	Appearance
13 Centaur	male torso with horse's legs
14 Triton	male sea creature with human head and body, fish's tail, and horse's forelegs
15 Satyr	head and torso of man, legs of goat
16 Cyclops	hairy giant with one eye in center of forehead

6

Largest countries sq mi

1 The Russian Federation 6,592,735
2 Canada 3,855,081
3 USA 3,717,792
4 China 3,705,386
5 Brazil 3,286,470
6 Australia 2,967,893
7 India 1,269,338
8 Argentina 1,068,296
9 Kazakhstan 1,049,150
10 Sudan 967,493

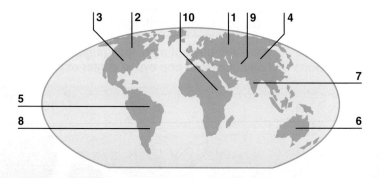

Smallest countries sq mi

1 Vatican City 0.2
2 Monaco 0.75
3 Nauru 8
4 Tuvalu 10
5 Bermuda 21
6 San Marino 24
7 Anguilla 37
8 Montserrat 39
9 British Virgin Islands 59
10 Liechtenstein 62

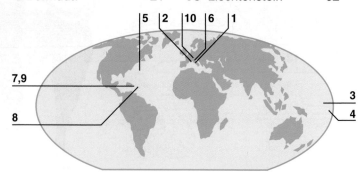

Largest populations 2005 (000s)

1	China	1,306,313	**6**	Pakistan	162,419
2	India	1,080,264	**7**	Bangladesh	144,319
3	USA	295,734	**8**	The Russian	
4	Indonesia	241,973		Federation	143,420
5	Brazil	186,112	**9**	Nigeria	128,771
			10	Japan	127,417

7

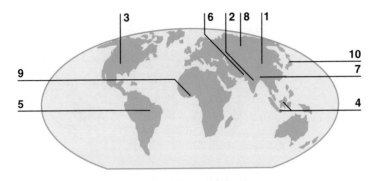

Smallest populations 2005 (000s)

1	Vatican City	0.9	**6**	Palau	20
2	Nauru	8	**7**	Turks & Caicos Is.	20
3	Montserrat	9	**8**	British Virgin Islands	22
4	Tuvalu	10	**9**	San Marino	24
5	Anguilla	13	**10**	St Kitts and Nevis	38

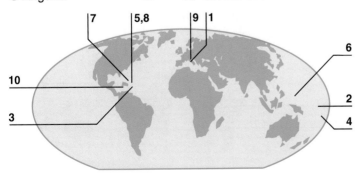

Highest per capita GNI (2003 US$)

1	Luxembourg	45,740	**6**	Denmark	33,570
2	Norway	43,400	**7**	Iceland	30,910
3	Switzerland	40,680	**8**	Sweden	28,910
4	USA	37,780	**9**	United Kingdom	28,320
5	Japan	34,180	**10**	Finland	27,060

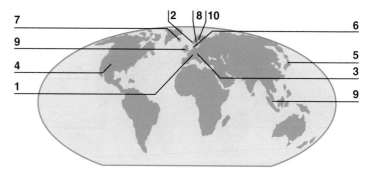

Lowest per capita GNI (2003 US$)

1	Burundi	90	**6**	Sierra Leone	150
2	Ethiopia	90	**7**	Malawi	180
3	Dem Rep. of Congo	100	**8**	Eritrea	190
4	Liberia	110	**9**	Niger	200
5	Guinea-Biseau	140	**10**	Mozambique	210

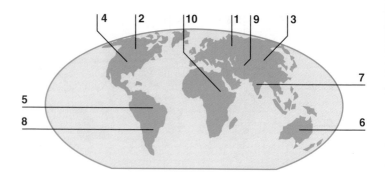

Highest population densities per sq mi (2005)

1 Monaco	43,046	**6** Maldives	3014
2 Singapore	21,230	**7** Bahrain	2681
3 Vatican City	5362	**8** Bangladesh	2596
4 Malta	3266	**9** Barbados	1678
5 Bermuda	3176	**10** Taiwan	1648

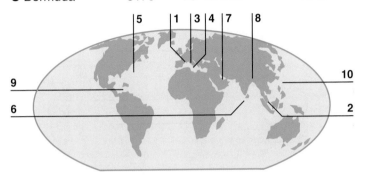

7

Lowest population densities per sq mi (2005)

1 Western Sahara	3	**6** Botswana	7
2 Mongolia	5	**7** Iceland	7
3 French Guiana	6	**8** Suriname	7
4 Namibia	6	**9** Libya	8
5 Australia	7	**10** Mauritania	8

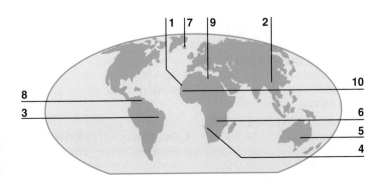

NORTHERN EUROPE

Denmark

Finland

Iceland

Norway

Sweden

Countries by size

		sq mi
1	Sweden	173,731
2	Finland	130,127
3	Norway	125,181
4	Iceland	39,768
5	Denmark	16,639

Populations

2005 (000s)

1 Sweden	9001	4 Norway	4593
2 Denmark	5432	5 Iceland	296
3 Finland	5223		

Densities (people per sq mi)

1 Denmark	326	4 Norway	37
2 Sweden	52	5 Iceland	7
3 Finland	40		

Per capita GNI (2003 US$)

1 Norway	43,400	4 Sweden	28,910
2 Denmark	33,570	5 Finland	27,060
3 Iceland	30,910		

COUNTRY	CAPITAL	LANGUAGE	CURRENCY
Denmark (Kongeriget Danmark)			
	Copenhagen	Danish	Danish krone
Finland (Suomen Tasavalta)			
	Helsinki	Finnish	Euro
		Swedish	
Iceland (Lýdveldid Island)			
	Reykjavik	Icelandic	Krona
Norway (Kongeriket Norge)			
	Oslo	Norwegian	Krone
Sweden (Konungariket Sverige)			
	Stockholm	Swedish	Krona

EASTERN EUROPE

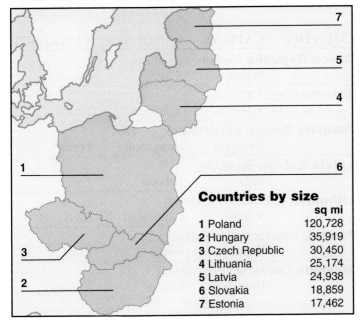

Czech Republic

Estonia

Hungary

8

Countries by size

		sq mi
1	Poland	120,728
2	Hungary	35,919
3	Czech Republic	30,450
4	Lithuania	25,174
5	Latvia	24,938
6	Slovakia	18,859
7	Estonia	17,462

Latvia

Lithuania

Poland

Slovakia

Populations

2005 (000s)

1 Poland	38,635	**5** Lithuania	3596
2 Czech Republic	10,241	**6** Latvia	2290
3 Hungary	10,006	**7** Estonia	1332
4 Slovakia	5431		

Densities (people per sq mi)

1 Czech Republic	336	**5** Lithuania	143
2 Poland	320	**6** Latvia	92
3 Slovakia	288	**7** Estonia	76
4 Hungary	279		

Per capita GNI (2003 US$)

1 Czech Republic	7150	**5** Slovakia	4940
2 Hungary	6350	**6** Lithuania	4500
3 Estonia	5380	**7** Latvia	4400
4 Poland	5280		

COUNTRY	CAPITAL	LANGUAGE	CURRENCY
Czech Republic (Česka Federativní)			
	Prague	Czech	Koruna
Estonia (Eesti Vabariik)			
	Tallinn	Estonian	Kroon
Hungary (Magyar Köztársaság)			
	Budapest	Hungarian	Forint
Latvia (Latvijas Republika)			
	Riga	Latvian	Lat
Lithuania (Lietuvos Respublika)			
	Vilnius	Lithuanian	Litas
Poland (Rzeczpospolita Polska)			
	Warsaw	Polish	Zloty
Slovakia (Slovenska Federativní)			
	Bratislava	Slovak	Koruna

SOUTHERN EUROPE

Populations

2005 (000s)

1	Turkey	69,660	**10**	Bosnia-Herzegovina	4025
2	Italy	58,103	**11**	Albania	3563
3	Spain	40,341	**12**	Macedonia	2045
4	Romania	22,329	**13**	Slovenia	2011
5	Serbia and Montenegro	10,829	**14**	Malta	398
6	Greece	10,668	**15**	Andorra	70
7	Portugal	10,566	**16**	San Marino	28
8	Bulgaria	7450	**17**	Vatican City	0.9
9	Croatia	4495			

Densities (people per sq mi)

1	Vatican City	5362	**10**	Romania	244
2	Malta	3266	**11**	Turkey	231
3	San Marino	1222	**12**	Greece	209
4	Italy	500	**13**	Macedonia	209
5	Andorra	390	**14**	Spain	207
6	Albania	321	**15**	Croatia	206
7	Portugal	296	**17**	Bosnia-Herzegovina	204
8	Serbia and Montenegro	274	**18**	Bulgaria	174
9	Slovenia	257			

Per capita GNI (2003 US$)

1	Italy	21,570	**11**	Macedonia	1980
2	Spain	17,040	**12**	Serbia and Montenegro	1910
3	Greece	13,230	**13**	Albania	1740
4	Slovenia	11,920	**14**	Bosnia-Herzegovina	1530
5	Portugal	11,800	**15**	Andorra	-
6	Malta	10,780	**16**	San Marino	-
7	Croatia	5370	**17**	Vatican City	-
8	Turkey	2800			
9	Romania	2260			
10	Bulgaria	2130			

Albania

Andorra

8

Bosnia-Herzegovina

Bulgaria

Croatia

Greece

Italy

Macedonia

Malta

Portugal

Romania

San Marino

Countries by size

	sq mi			sq mi
1 Turkey	301,382		**10** Bosnia-	
2 Spain	194,896		Herzegovina	19,741
3 Italy	116,305		**11** Albania	11,100
4 Romania	91,699		**12** Macedonia	9928
5 Greece	50,942		**13** Slovenia	7827
6 Bulgaria	42,822		**14** Andorra	181
7 Serbia and			**15** Malta	122
Montenegro	39,517		**16** San Marino	24
8 Portugal	35,672		**16** Vatican City	0.2
9 Croatia	21,831			

COUNTRY	CAPITAL	LANGUAGE	CURRENCY
Albania (Republika e Shqipërisë)			
	Tirana	Albanian	Lek
		Greek	
Andorra (Principat d'Andorra)			
	Andorra la Vella	Catalan Spanish French	Euro
Bosnia-Herzegovina (Republika Bosna i Hercegovina)			
	Sarajevo	Bosnian	Marka
Bulgaria (Narodna Republika Bulgaria)			
	Sofia	Bulgarian Turkish	Lev

COUNTRY	CAPITAL	LANGUAGE	CURRENCY
Bulgaria (Narodna Republika Bulgaria)			
	Sofia	Bulgarian Turkish	Lev
Croatia (Republika Hrvatska)			
	Zagreb	Croatian	Kuna
Greece (Elliniki Dimokratia)			
	Athens	Greek	Euro
Italy (Repubblica Italiana)			
	Rome	Italian	Euro
Macedonia (Republika Makedonija)			
	Skopje	Macedonian	Denar
Malta (Malta)			
	Valletta	Maltese, English	Maltese Lira
Portugal (República Portuguesa)			
	Lisbon	Portuguese	Euro
Romania (Republica Popularâ România)			
	Bucharest	Romanian	Leu
San Marino (Repubblica di San Marino)			
	San Marino	Italian	Euro
Serbia and Montenegro			
	Belgrade	Serbian	Serbian dinar
Slovenia (Republika Slovenija)			
	Ljubljana	Slovene	Tolar
Spain (España)			
	Madrid	Spanish, Catalan Basque, Galician	Euro
Turkey (Türkiye Cumhuriyeti)			
	Ankara	Turkish	Turkish lira
Vatican City (Stato della Città del Vaticano)			
	Vatican City	Italian Latin	Euro Papal coinage

Serbia and Montenegro

Slovenia

8

Spain

Turkey

Vatican City

WESTERN EUROPE

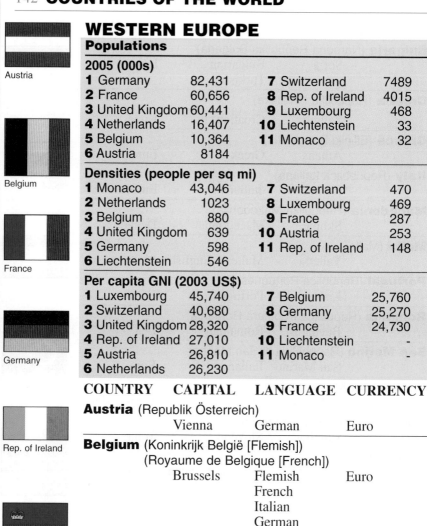

Populations

2005 (000s)

1 Germany	82,431	**7** Switzerland	7489
2 France	60,656	**8** Rep. of Ireland	4015
3 United Kingdom	60,441	**9** Luxembourg	468
4 Netherlands	16,407	**10** Liechtenstein	33
5 Belgium	10,364	**11** Monaco	32
6 Austria	8184		

Densities (people per sq mi)

1 Monaco	43,046	**7** Switzerland	470
2 Netherlands	1023	**8** Luxembourg	469
3 Belgium	880	**9** France	287
4 United Kingdom	639	**10** Austria	253
5 Germany	598	**11** Rep. of Ireland	148
6 Liechtenstein	546		

Per capita GNI (2003 US$)

1 Luxembourg	45,740	**7** Belgium	25,760
2 Switzerland	40,680	**8** Germany	25,270
3 United Kingdom	28,320	**9** France	24,730
4 Rep. of Ireland	27,010	**10** Liechtenstein	-
5 Austria	26,810	**11** Monaco	-
6 Netherlands	26,230		

COUNTRY	CAPITAL	LANGUAGE	CURRENCY
Austria (Republik Österreich)			
	Vienna	German	Euro
Belgium (Koninkrijk België [Flemish]) (Royaume de Belgique [French])			
	Brussels	Flemish French Italian German	Euro
France (République Française)			
	Paris	French	Euro

Austria

Belgium

France

Germany

Rep. of Ireland

Liechtenstein

Countries by size

		sq mi			sq mi
1	France	211,208	7	Switzerland	15,942
2	Germany	137,846	8	Belgium	11,780
3	United Kingdom	94,525	9	Luxembourg	998
4	Austria	32,378	10	Liechtenstein	62
5	Rep. of Ireland	27,135	11	Monaco	0.75
6	Netherlands	16,033			

Luxembourg

Monaco

Netherlands

Switzerland

United Kingdom

8

COUNTRY	CAPITAL	LANGUAGE	CURRENCY
Germany (Bundesrepublik Deutschland)			
	Berlin	German	Euro
Republic of Ireland (Eire)			
	Dublin	English	Euro
		Gaelic	
Liechtenstein (Fürstentum Liechtenstein)			
	Vaduz	German	Swiss franc/Euro
Luxembourg (Grand-Duché de Luxembourg)			
	Luxembourg-	French	
	Ville		Euro
Monaco (Principality of Monaco)			
	Monaco-Ville	French	Euro
Netherlands (Koninkrijk der Nederlanden)			
	Amsterdam	Dutch	Euro
Switzerland (Swiss Confederation)			
	Berne	German	Swiss franc
		French	
		Italian	
UK (United Kingdom of Great Britain and Northern Ireland)			
	London	English	Sterling

CENTRAL ASIA

Populations

2005 (000s)

Armenia

1 The Russian		**7** Tajikistan	7163
Federation	143,420	**8** Kyrgyzstan	5146
2 Ukraine	47,425	**9** Turkmenistan	4952
3 Uzbekistan	26,851	**10** Georgia	4677
4 Kazakhstan	15,185	**11** Moldova	4455
5 Belarus	10,300	**12** Armenia	2982
6 Azerbaijan	7911		

Azerbaijan

Densities (people per sq mi)

1	Moldova	341	**8**	Belarus	129
2	Armenia	259	**9**	Kyrgyzstan	67
3	Azerbaijan	237	**10**	Turkmenistan	26
4	Ukraine	203	**11**	The Russian	
5	Georgia	174		Federation	22
6	Uzbekistan	155	**12**	Kazakhstan	14
7	Tajikistan	130			

Per capita GNI (2003 US$)

1	The Russian		**7**	Azerbaijan	820
	Federation	2610	**8**	Georgia	770
2	Kazakhstan	1780	**9**	Moldova	590
3	Belarus	1600	**10**	Uzbekistan	420
4	Turkmenistan	1120	**11**	Kyrgyzstan	340
5	Ukraine	970	**12**	Tajikistan	210
6	Armenia	950			

COUNTRY	CAPITAL	LANGUAGE	CURRENCY
Armenia (Haikakan Hanrapetoutioun)			
	Yerevan	Armenian	Dram
Azerbaijan (Azerbaijchan Respublikasy)			
	Baku	Azeri	Manat
		Armenian	
		Russian	
Belarus (Respublika Belarus)			
	Minsk	Belarusian	Rouble
Georgia (Sakartvelos Respublica)			
	Tbilisi	Georgian	Coupon
Kazakhstan (Kazak Respublikasy)			
	Alma-Ata	Kazakh	Tenge
Kyrgyzstan (Republika Kirguizstan)			
	Bishkek	Kyrgyz	Som
Moldova (Republica Moldoveneasca)			
	Kishinev	Romanian	Leu

Belarus

Georgia

8

Kazakhstan

Kyrgyzstan

Moldova

The Russian
Federation

Tajikistan

Turkmenistan

Ukraine

Uzbekistan

Countries by size

	sq mi		sq mi
1 The Russian Federation	6,592,735	7 Kyrgyzstan	76,641
2 Kazakhstan	1,049,150	8 Tajikistan	55,251
3 Ukraine	233,089	9 Azerbaijan	33,436
4 Turkmenistan	188,455	10 Georgia	26,911
5 Uzbekistan	172,741	11 Moldova	13,067
6 Belarus	80,154	12 Armenia	11,506

COUNTRY	CAPITAL	LANGUAGE	CURRENCY
The Russian Federation (Rossiyskaya Federatsiya)			
	Moscow	Russian	Rouble
Tajikistan (Respubliki Tajikistan)			
	Dushanbe	Tajik	Rouble
Turkmenistan (Turkmenistan)			
	Ashkhabad	Turkmen Russian Uzbek	Manat

COUNTRY	CAPITAL	LANGUAGE	CURRENCY
Ukraine (Ukrayina)			
	Kiev	Ukrainian	Karbovanets
Uzbekistan (Ozbekistan Respublikasy)			
	Tashkent	Uzbek	Som

SOUTHERN ASIA

Countries by size

		sq mi
1	India	1,269,338
2	Pakistan	310,401
3	Afghanistan	250,000
4	Bangladesh	55,598
5	Nepal	54,363
6	Sri Lanka	25,332
7	Bhutan	18,147
8	Maldives	116

Afghanistan

Bangladesh

Populations

2005 (000s)

1 India	1,080,264	5 Nepal	27,676
2 Pakistan	162,419	6 Sri Lanka	20,064
3 Bangladesh	144,319	7 Bhutan	2232
4 Afghanistan	29,928	8 Maldives	349

Densities (people per sq mi)

1 Maldives	3014	5 Pakistan	523
2 Bangladesh	2596	6 Nepal	509
3 India	851	7 Bhutan	123
4 Sri Lanka	792	8 Afghanistan	120

Per capita GNI (2003 US$)

1 Maldives	2350	5 Pakistan	520
2 Sri Lanka	930	6 Bangladesh	400
3 Bhutan	630	7 Nepal	240
4 India	540	8 Afghanistan	-

Bhutan

India

Maldives

8

Nepal

Pakistan

Sri Lanka

COUNTRY	CAPITAL	LANGUAGE	CURRENCY
Afghanistan (De Afghanistan Jamhuriat)			
	Kabul	Pushtu	Afghani
		Dari	
Bangladesh (Gama Prajàtantrï Bangladesh)			
	Dhaka	Bengali	Taka
Bhutan (Druk-Yul)			
	Thimphu	Dzongkha	Ngultrum
India (Bharat)			
	New Delhi	Hindi	Rupee
		English	
Maldives (Divehi Jumhuriya)			
	Malé	Dhivehi	Rufiyaa
Nepal (Sri Nepala Sarkar)			
	Katmandu	Nepali	Nepalese rupee
Pakistan (Islam-i Jamhuriya-e Pakistan)			
	Islamabad	Urdu	Pakistani rupee
Sri Lanka (Sri Lanka Prajathanthrika Samajavadi Janarajaya)			
	Colombo	Sinhala	Sri Lankan
		Tamil	rupee

SOUTHEASTERN ASIA
Populations

Brunei
Darussalam

2005 (000s)

1 Indonesia	241,973		**7** Cambodia	13,607
2 The Philippines	87,857		**8** Laos	6217
3 Vietnam	83,535		**9** Singapore	4425
4 Thailand	65,444		**10** East Timor	1040
5 Myanmar	42,909		**11** Brunei Darussalam	372
6 Malaysia	23,953			

Densities (people per sq mi)

1	Singapore	16,548	**7**	Malaysia	188
2	The Philippines	759	**8**	East Timor	180
3	Vietnam	657	**9**	Brunei Darussalam	167
4	Thailand	330	**10**	Myanmar	164
5	Indonesia	327	**11**	Laos	68
6	Cambodia	195			

Per capita GNI (2003 US$)

1	Singapore	21,230	**7**	East Timor	460
2	Malaysia	3880	**8**	Laos	340
3	Thailand	2190	**9**	Cambodia	300
4	The Philippines	1080	**10**	Brunei Darussalam	-
5	Indonesia	810	**11**	Myanmar	-
6	Vietnam	480			

Countries by size

		sq mi			sq mi
1	Indonesia	741,096	**4**	Malaysia	127,316
2	Myanmar	261,969	**5**	Vietnam	127,243
3	Thailand	198,455	**6**	The Philippines	115,830
			7	Laos	91,428
			8	Cambodia	69,900
			9	East Timor	5794
			10	Brunei Darussalam	2228
			11	Singapore	267

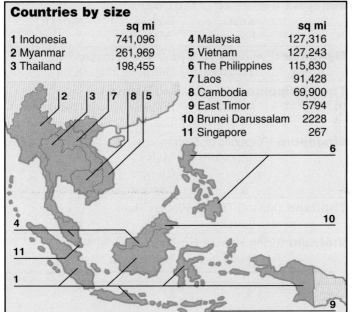

Cambodia

East Timor

8

Indonesia

Laos

Malaysia

Myanmar

The Philippines

Singapore

Thailand

Vietnam

COUNTRY	CAPITAL	LANGUAGE	CURRENCY
Brunei Darussalam (Negara Brunei Darussalam)			
	Bandar Seri Begawan	Malay English	Brunei dollar
Cambodia (State of Cambodia)			
	Phnom Penh	Khmer	Riel
East Timor	Dili	Tetum, Portuguese	US dollar
Indonesia (Republik Indonesia)			
	Jakarta	Bahasa Indonesian	Rupiah
Laos (Sathalanalat Paxathipatai Paxaxôn Lao)			
	Vientiane	Lao	Kip
Malaysia (Federation of Malaysia)			
	Kuala Lumpur	Bahasa Malaysian	Ringgit
Myanmar (Pyeidaungzu Myanma Naingngandaw)			
	Yangon	Burmese	Kyat
The Philippines (Republika ng Pilipinas)			
	Manila	Pilipino English	Philippine peso
Singapore (Republic of Singapore)			
	Singapore	Malay Chinese English	Singapore dollar
Thailand (Muang Thai or Prathet Thai)			
	Bangkok	Thai	Baht
Vietnam (Công Hòa Xã Hôi Chu Ngĩa Viêt Nam)			
	Hanoi	Vietnamese	Dong

Countries by size

		sq mi			sq mi
1	China	3,705,386	**4**	North Korea	46,540
2	Mongolia	604,247	**5**	South Korea	38,023
3	Japan	145,882	**6**	Taiwan	13,892

EASTERN ASIA

Populations

2005 (000s)

1	China	1,306,313	**4**	North Korea	22,912
2	Japan	127,417	**5**	Taiwan	22,894
3	South Korea	48,422	**6**	Mongolia	2791

Densities (people per sq mi)

1	Taiwan	1648	**4**	North Korea	492
2	South Korea	1274	**5**	China	353
3	Japan	873	**6**	Mongolia	5

Per capita GNI (2003 US$)

1	Japan	34,180	**4**	Mongolia	480
2	South Korea	12,030	**5**	North Korea	-
3	China	1100	**6**	Taiwan	-

8

China

Japan

Mongolia

	COUNTRY	CAPITAL	LANGUAGE	CURRENCY
North Korea	**China** (Zhonghua Renmin Gonghe Guo)			
		Beijing	Mandarin Chinese	Yuan
	Japan (Nippon)			
		Tokyo	Japanese	Yen
South Korea	**Mongolia** (Bügd Nayramdakh Mongol Ard Uls)			
		Ulan Bator	Mongolian	Tugrik
	North Korea (Chosun Minchu-chui Inmin Konghwa-guk)			
		Pyongyang	Korean	North Korean won
Taiwan	**South Korea** (Taehan Min'guk)			
		Seoul	Korean	South Korean won
	Taiwan (Chung-hua Min-kuo)			
		Taipei	Mandarin Chinese	Taiwan dollar

AUSTRALASIA
Populations

2005 (000s)

1 Australia	20,090		**8** Tonga	112
2 Papua New Guinea	5545		**9** Micronesia	108
			10 Kiribati	103
3 New Zealand	4035		**11** Marshall Islands	59
4 Fiji	893		**12** Palau	20
5 Solomon Islands	538		**13** Nauru	13
6 Vanuatu	205		**14** Tuvalu	11
7 Samoa	177			

North Korea

South Korea

Taiwan

Australia

Fiji

Countries by size

		sq mi			sq mi
1	Australia	2,967,893	8	Kiribati	313
2	Papua New Guinea	178,703	9	Tonga	289
3	New Zealand	103,737	10	Micronesia	271
4	Solomon Islands	10,985	11	Palau	177
5	Fiji	7054	12	Marshall Islands	70
6	Vanuatu	4710	13	Tuvalu	10
7	Samoa	1137	14	Nauru	8

Kiribati

Marshall Islands

8

Micronesia

Nauru

Densities (people per sq mi)

1	Nauru	1609	8	Fiji	127
2	Tuvalu	1159	9	Palau	115
3	Marshall Islands	844	10	Solomon Islands	49
4	Micronesia	399	11	Vanuatu	44
5	Tonga	389	12	New Zealand	39
6	Kiribati	329	13	Papua New Guinea	31
7	Samoa	156	14	Australia	7

Per capita GNI (2003 US$)

1	Australia	21,950	3	Palau	6500
2	New Zealand	15,530	4	Marshall Islands	2710

New Zealand

Palau

Papua New
Guinea

Per capita GNI (2003 US$) (continued)

5 Fiji	2240	**11** Solomon Islands	560
6 Micronesia	2070	**12** Papua New Guinea	500
7 Tonga	1490	**13** Nauru	n.a.
8 Samoa	1440	**14** Tuvalu	n.a.
9 Vanuatu	1180		
10 Kiribati	860		

Samoa

COUNTRY	CAPITAL	LANGUAGE	CURRENCY
Australia (Commonwealth of Australia)			
	Canberra	English	Australian dollar
Fiji (Republic of Fiji)			
	Suva	Fijian English	Fiji dollar
Kiribati (Republic of Kiribati)			
	Tarawa	Gilbertese English	Australian dollar
Marshall Islands (Marshall Islands)			
	Majuro	English	US dollar
Micronesia (Federated States of Micronesia)			
	Palikir	English	US dollar
Nauru (Naoero)			
	Yaren	Nauruan English	Australian dollar
New Zealand (New Zealand)			
	Wellington	English	New Zealand dollar
Palau (Republic of Palau)			
	Koror	English	US dollar
Papua New Guinea (Papua New Guinea)			
	Port Moresby	English	Kina

Solomon
Islands

Tonga

Tuvalu

Vanuatu

COUNTRY	CAPITAL	LANGUAGE	CURRENCY
Samoa (Malotuto'atasi o Samoa i Sisifo)			
	Apia	Samoan English	Tala
Solomon Islands (Solomon Islands)			
	Honiara	English	Solomon Islands dollar
Tonga (Pule 'anga Tonga)			
	Nuku'alofa	Tongan English	Pa'anga
Tuvalu (Tuvalu)			
	Funafuti	Tuvaluan English	Australian dollar
Vanuatu (Ripablik Blong Vanuatu)			
	Port-Vila	Bislama English French	Vatu

8

NORTH AMERICA
Populations

2005 (000s)

1 USA	295,734	**3** Canada	32,805
2 Mexico	106,202		

Densities (people per sq mi)

1 Mexico	139	**3** Canada	9
2 USA	80		

Per capita GNI (2003 US$)

1 USA	37,870	**3** Mexico	6230
2 Canada	24,470		

Canada

Mexico

COUNTRY	CAPITAL	LANGUAGE	CURRENCY
Canada (Canada)			
	Ottawa	English French	Canadian dollar

USA

COUNTRY	CAPITAL	LANGUAGE	CURRENCY
Mexico (Estados Unidos Mexicanos)			
	Mexico City	Spanish	Mexican peso
USA (United States of America)			
	Washington DC	English	US dollar

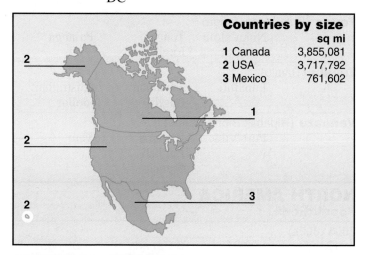

Countries by size

sq mi

1 Canada   3,855,081
2 USA   3,717,792
3 Mexico   761,602

CENTRAL AMERICA
Populations

2005 (000s)

1 Guatemala	14,655	**5** Costa Rica	4016
2 Honduras	6975	**6** Panama	3039
3 El Salvador	6704	**7** Belize	279
4 Nicaragua	5465		

Densities (people per sq mi)

1 El Salvador	825	**5** Nicaragua	109
2 Guatemala	349	**6** Panama	101
3 Costa Rica	204	**7** Belize	32
4 Honduras	161		

Belize

Costa Rica

Per capita GNI (2003 US$)

1 Costa Rica	4300	**5** Guatemala	1910
2 Panama	4060	**6** Honduras	970
3 Belize	3370	**7** Nicaragua	740
4 El Salvador	2340		

El Salvador

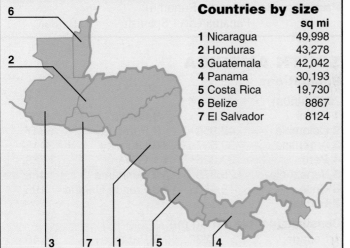

Countries by size

		sq mi
1	Nicaragua	49,998
2	Honduras	43,278
3	Guatemala	42,042
4	Panama	30,193
5	Costa Rica	19,730
6	Belize	8867
7	El Salvador	8124

Guatemala

8

Honduras

Nicaragua

COUNTRY	CAPITAL	LANGUAGE	CURRENCY
Belize (Belize)			
	Belmopan	English	Belizean dollar
Costa Rica (República de Costa Rica)			
	San José	Spanish	Costa Rican colón
El Salvador (República de El Salvador)			
	San Salvador	Spanish	El Salvador colón
Guatemala (República de Guatemala)			
	Guatemala City	Spanish	Quetzal

Panama

COUNTRY	CAPITAL	LANGUAGE	CURRENCY
Honduras (República de Honduras)			
	Tegucigalpa	Spanish	Lempira
Nicaragua (República de Nicaragua)			
	Managua	Spanish	Córdoba
Panama (República de Panamá)			
	Panama City	Spanish	Balboa

SOUTH AMERICA

Populations

2005 (000s)

Argentina

1 Brazil	186,112	8 Bolivia	8857
2 Colombia	42,954	9 Paraguay	6347
3 Argentina	39,537	10 Uruguay	3415
4 Peru	27,925	11 Guyana	765
5 Venezuela	25,375	12 Suriname	438
6 Chile	15,980	13 French Guiana	195
7 Ecuador	13,363		

Bolivia

Densities (people per sq mi)

1 Ecuador	122	8 Paraguay	40
2 Colombia	98	9 Argentina	39
3 Venezuela	72	10 Bolivia	21
4 Brazil	57	11 Guyana	9
5 Peru	56	12 Suriname	7
6 Chile	55	13 French Guiana	6
7 Uruguay	50		

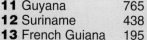
Brazil

Per capita GNI (2003 US$)

1 Chile	4360	8 Ecuador	1830
2 Uruguay	3810	9 Colombia	1810
3 Argentina	3810	10 Paraguay	1110
4 Venezuela	3490	11 Bolivia	900
5 Brazil	2720	12 Guyana	900
6 Suriname	3710	13 French Guiana	-
7 Peru	2140		

Chile

Countries by size

		sq mi			sq mi
1	Brazil	3,286,470	**8** Paraguay		157,046
2	Argentina	1,068,296	**9** Ecuador		109,483
3	Peru	496,223	**10** Guyana		83,000
4	Colombia	439,733	**11** Uruguay		68,039
5	Bolivia	424,162	**12** Suriname		63,039
6	Venezuela	352,143	**13** French Guiana		35,135
7	Chile	292,258			

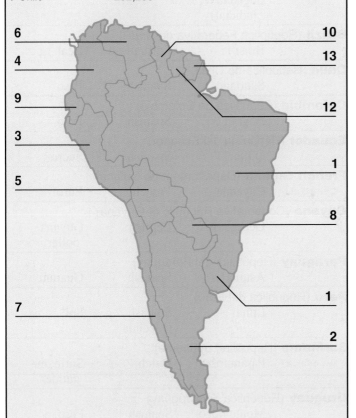

Colombia

Ecuador

8

French Guiana

Guyana

Paraguay

Peru

Suriname

Uruguay

Venezuela

COUNTRY	CAPITAL	LANGUAGE	CURRENCY
Argentina (República de Argentina)			
	Buenos Aires	Spanish	Peso
Bolivia (República de Bolivia)			
	La Paz (administrative)	Spanish Aymara	Boliviano
	Sucre (legislative, judicial)	Quechua	
Brazil (República Federativa do Brasil)			
	Brasilia	Portuguese	Real
Chile (República de Chile)			
	Santiago	Spanish	Peso
Colombia (República de Colombia)			
	Bogotá	Spanish	Peso
Ecuador (República del Ecuador)			
	Quito	Spanish	Sucre
French Guiana (Département de Guiana)			
	Cayenne	French	Euro
Guyana (Cooperative Republic of Guyana)			
	Georgetown	English	Guyana dollar
Paraguay (República del Paraguay)			
	Asunción	Spanish	Guarani
Peru (República del Perú)			
	Lima	Spanish Quechua	Sol
Suriname (Republiek Suriname)			
	Paramaribo	Dutch	Suriname guilder
Uruguay (República del Uruguay)			
	Montevideo	Spanish	Peso

COUNTRY   CAPITAL   LANGUAGE   CURRENCY

Venezuela (República de Venezuela)

        Caracas   Spanish   Bolívar

CARIBBEAN

Countries by size

	sq mi			sq mi
1 Cuba	42,803		**14** Barbados	166
2 Dominican			**15** Turks and Caicos	
Republic	18,815		Islands	166
3 Haiti	10,714		**16** St. Vincent and the	
4 The Bahamas	5382		Grenadines	150
5 Jamaica	4244		**17** US Virgin Islands	136
6 Puerto Rico	3515		**18** Grenada	133
7 Trinidad and Tobago	1980		**19** Cayman Islands	101
8 Guadeloupe	687		**20** St. Kitts and Nevis	101
9 Martinique	425		**21** British Virgin Isles	59
10 Netherlands Antilles	371		**22** Anguilla	39
11 Dominica	291		**23** Montserrat	39
12 St. Lucia	238		**24** Bermuda (not shown)	21
13 Antigua and Barbuda	171			

8

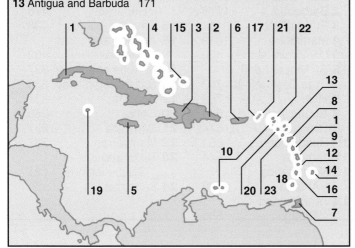

Anguilla

The Bahamas

Barbados

Bermuda

British Virgin
Isles

Cayman Islands

Populations

2005 (000s)

1 Cuba	11,346	**13** St. Vincent and	
2 Dominican		the Grenadines	117
Republic	8950	**14** US Virgin Islands	108
3 Haiti	8121	**15** Grenada	89
4 Puerto Rico	3916	**16** Dominica	69
5 Jamaica	2731	**17** Antigua and	
6 Trinidad and		Barbuda	68
Tobago	1088	**18** Bermuda	65
7 Guadeloupe	448	**19** St. Kitts and Nevis	38
8 Martinique	432	**20** Cayman Islands	44
9 Bahamas	301	**21** British Virgin Isles	22
10 Barbados	279	**22** Turks and	
11 Netherlands		Caicos Islands	20
Antilles	219	**23** Anguilla	13
12 St. Lucia	166	**24** Montserrat	9

Cuba

Densities (people per sq mi)

1 Bermuda	3176	**14** Dominican	
2 Barbados	1678	Republic	476
3 Puerto Rico	1114	**15** Cayman Islands	438
4 Martinique	1019	**16** Antigua and	
5 US Virgin Islands	800	Barbuda	402
6 St. Vincent and		**17** St. Kitts and Nevis	387
the Grenadines	783	**18** British Virgin Isles	383
7 Haiti	758	**19** Anguilla	337
8 St. Lucia	699	**20** Cuba	265
9 Grenada	674	**21** Dominica	237
10 Guadeloupe	653	**22** Montserrat	237
11 Jamaica	644	**23** Turks and	
12 Netherlands		Caicos Islands	124
Antilles	593	**24** Bahamas	56
13 Trinidad and			
Tobago	550		

Dominica

Dominican Republic

Grenada

Haiti

Per capita GNI (2003 US$)

1 Barbados	9260	**12** Anguilla	-
2 Antigua and Barbuda	9160	**13** Bahamas	-
		14 Bermuda	-
3 Trinidad and Tobago	7790	**15** British Virgin Islands	-
		16 Cayman Islands	-
4 St. Kitts and Nevis	6630	**17** Cuba	-
		18 Guadeloupe	-
5 St. Lucia	4050	**19** Martinique	-
6 Grenada	3710	**20** Montserrat	-
7 Dominica	3330	**21** Netherlands Antilles	-
8 St. Vincent and the Grenadines	3310	**22** Puerto Rico	-
9 Jamaica	2980	**23** Turks and Caicos Islands	-
10 Dominican Republic	2130	**24** US Virgin Islands	-
11 Haiti	400		

Jamaica

Montserrat

8

Netherlands Antilles

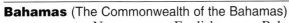

COUNTRY	CAPITAL	LANGUAGE	CURRENCY
Anguilla (The Commonwealth of the Bahamas)			
	The Valley	English	East Caribbean dollar
Antigua and Barbuda (Antigua and Barbuda)			
	St. John's	English	East Caribbean dollar
Bahamas (The Commonwealth of the Bahamas)			
	Nassau	English	Bahamian dollar
Barbados (Barbados)			
	Bridgetown	English	Barbados dollar
Bermuda (Bermuda)			
	Hamilton	English	Bermuda dollar

Puerto Rico

St. Kitts and Nevis

St. Lucia

St. Vincent and
the Grenadines

Trinidad and
Tobago

Turks and
Caicos Islands

US Virgin
Islands

COUNTRY	CAPITAL	LANGUAGE	CURRENCY
British Virgin Isles (British Virgin Isles)			
	Road Town	English	US dollar
Cayman Islands (Cayman Islands)			
	Georgetown	English	Cayman Islands dollar
Cuba (República de Cuba)			
	Havana	Spanish	Cuban peso
Dominica (Commonwealth of Dominica)			
	Roseau	English	East Caribbean dollar
Dominican Republic (República Dominicana)			
	Santo Domingo	Spanish	Peso
Grenada (Grenada)			
	St George's	English	East Caribbean dollar
Guadeloupe (Guadeloupe)			
	Basse-Terre	French	Franc
Haiti (République d'Haiti)			
	Port-au-Prince	French Creole	Gourde
Jamaica (Jamaica)			
	Kingston	English	Jamaican dollar
Martinique (Martinique)			
	Fort-de-France	French	French franc
Montserrat (Montserrat)			
	Plymouth	English	East Caribbean dollar
Netherlands Antilles (Nedelandse Antillen)			
	Willemstad	Dutch Spanish	Netherlands Antilles guilder

COUNTRY	CAPITAL	LANGUAGE	CURRENCY

Puerto Rico (Estado Libre Asociado de Puerto Rico)

	San Juan	Spanish	Dollar

St. Kitts and Nevis (Federation of St. Kitts and Nevis)

	Basseterre	English	East Caribbean dollar

St. Lucia (St. Lucia)

	Castries	English	East Caribbean dollar

St. Vincent and the Grenadines

	Kingstown	English	East Caribbean dollar

Trinidad and Tobago (Republic of Trinidad and Tobago)

	Port of Spain	English	Dollar

Turks and Caicos Islands (Turks and Caicos Islands)

	Grand Turk	English	US dollar

US Virgin Islands (Virgin Islands of the United States)

	Charlotte Amalie	English	US dollar

NORTHERN AFRICA

Populations

2005 (000s)

1 Egypt	77,505	**5** Tunisia	10,074
2 Sudan	40,187	**6** Libya	5765
3 Morocco	32,725	**7** Western Sahara	273
4 Algeria	32,531		

Densities (people per sq mi)

1 Egypt	200	**3** Tunisia	159
2 Morocco	190	**4** Sudan	42

Algeria

Egypt

Libya

Morocco

Sudan

Tunisia

Western Sahara

Countries by size

		sq mi			sq mi
1	Sudan	967,493	**5** Morocco		
2	Algeria	919,590	(including W. Sahara)		275,116
3	Libya	679,358	(without W. Sahara)		172,413
4	Egypt	386,660	**6** Western Sahara		102,703
			7 Tunisia		63,170

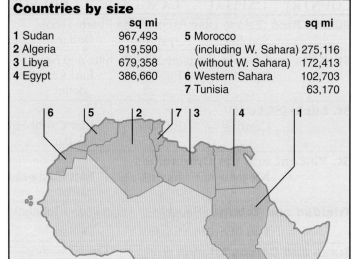

Densities (people per sq mi) (continued)

5 Algeria	35	**7** Western Sahara	3
6 Libya	8		

Per capita GNI (2003 US$)

1 Tunisia	2240	**5** Sudan	460
2 Algeria	1930	**6** Libya	-
3 Egypt	1390	**7** Western Sahara	-
4 Morocco	1310		

COUNTRY	CAPITAL	LANGUAGE	CURRENCY
Algeria (al-Jumhuriya al-Jazairiya ad-Dimuqratiya Ash-Shabiya)			
	Algiers	Arabic	Algerian dinar
Egypt (Jumhuriyah Misr al-Arabiya)			
	Cairo	Arabic	Egyptian pound

COUNTRY	CAPITAL	LANGUAGE	CURRENCY
Libya (al-Jamahiriyah al-Arabiya al-Libya al-Shabiya al-Ishtirakiya)			
	Tripoli	Arabic	Libyan dinar
Morocco (al-Mamlaka al-Maghrebia)			
	Rabat	Arabic	Dirham
Sudan (Jamhuryat as-Sudan)			
	Khartoum	Arabic	Sudanese dinar
Tunisia (al-Jumhuriyah at-Tunisiyah)			
	Tunis	Arabic	Tunisian dinar
Western Sahara			
	Laâyoune	Arabic	Peseta

8

CENTRAL AFRICA

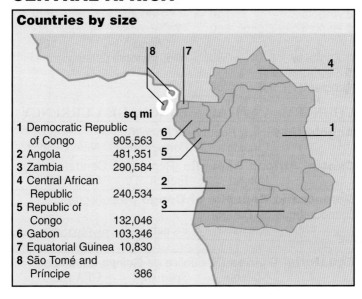

Countries by size

		sq mi
1	Democratic Republic of Congo	905,563
2	Angola	481,351
3	Zambia	290,584
4	Central African Republic	240,534
5	Republic of Congo	132,046
6	Gabon	103,346
7	Equatorial Guinea	10,830
8	São Tomé and Príncipe	386

Angola

Central African Republic

Dem. Republic of Congo

Equatorial
Guinea

Gabon

São Tomé and
Príncipe

Zambia

Populations

2005 (000s)

1 Democratic Republic of Congo	60,085	**5** Republic of Congo	3039
2 Zambia	11,261	**6** Gabon	1389
3 Angola	11,190	**7** Equatorial Guinea	535
4 Central African Republic	3799	**8** São Tomé and Príncipe	187

Densities (people per sq mi)

1 São Tomé and Príncipe	485	**5** Angola	23
2 Democratic Republic of Congo	66	**6** Republic of Congo	23
3 Equatorial Guinea	49	**7** Central African Republic	16
4 Zambia	39	**8** Gabon	13

Per capita GN1 (2003 US$)

1 Gabon	3340	**6** Central African Republic	260
2 Angola	740	**7** Democratic Republic of Congo	100
3 Republic of Congo	650	**8** Equatorial Guinea	-
4 Zambia	380		
5 São Tomé and Príncipe	300		

COUNTRY	CAPITAL	LANGUAGE	CURRENCY
Angola (República Popular de Angola)			
	Luanda	Portuguese	New kwanza
Central African Republic (République Centrafricaine)			
	Bangui	French	CFA franc
Democratic Republic of Congo (République Democratique du Congo)			
	Kinshasa	French	Congolese franc
Equatorial Guinea (República de Guinea Ecuatorial)			
	Malabo	Spanish	CFA franc

COUNTRY	CAPITAL	LANGUAGE	CURRENCY
Gabon (République Gabonaise)			
	Libreville	French	CFA franc
Republic of Congo (République Populaire du Congo)			
	Brazzaville	French	CFA franc
São Tomé and Príncipe (República Democrática de São Tomé e Príncipe)			
	São Tomé	Portuguese	Dobra
Zambia (Republic of Zambia)			
	Lusaka	English	Kwacha

SOUTHERN AFRICA

Countries by size

		sq mi
1	South Africa	471,008
2	Namibia	318,694
3	Mozambique	309,494
4	Botswana	231,804
5	Madagascar	226,656
6	Zimbabwe	150,803
7	Lesotho	11,720
8	Swaziland	6704
9	Réunion	972
10	Comoros	838
11	Mauritius	788

Populations

2005 (000s)

1	South Africa	44,344	7	Botswana	1640
2	Mozambique	19,406	8	Mauritius	1230
3	Madagascar	18,040	9	Swaziland	1173
4	Zimbabwe	12,746	10	Réunion	776
5	Lesotho	1867	11	Comoros	671
6	Namibia	2030			

8

Botswana

Comoros

Lesotho

Mauritius

Mozambique

Namibia

South Africa

Swaziland

Zimbabwe

Densities (people per sq mi)

#	Country	Density	#	Country	Density
1	Mauritius	1562	7	Zimbabwe	85
2	Comoros	801	8	Madagascar	80
3	Réunion	799	9	Mozambique	63
4	Swaziland	175	10	Botswana	7
5	Lesotho	159	11	Namibia	6
6	South Africa	94			

Per capita GNI (2003 US$)

#	Country	GNI	#	Country	GNI
1	Mauritius	4100	7	Comoros	450
2	Botswana	3530	8	Madagascar	290
3	South Africa	2750	9	Mozambique	210
4	Namibia	1930	10	Réunion	-
5	Swaziland	1350	11	Zimbabwe	-
6	Lesotho	610			

COUNTRY	CAPITAL	LANGUAGE	CURRENCY
Botswana (Republic of Botswana)			
	Gaborone	English	Pula
Comoros (Jumhuriyat al-Qumur al-Itthadiyah al-Islamiyah)			
	Moroni	Arabic	Comoro franc
Lesotho (Kingdom of Lesotho)			
	Maseru	English Sotho	Loti
Madagascar (Repoblika Demokratika Malagasy)			
	Antananarivo	Malagasy	Malagasy franc
Mauritius (State of Mauritius)			
	Port Louis	English	Mauritian rupee
Mozambique (República Popular de Moçambique)			
	Maputo	Portuguese	Metical
Namibia (Namibia)			
	Windhoek	Afrikaans English	Namibian dollar

COUNTRY	CAPITAL	LANGUAGE	CURRENCY
Réunion (Département de Réunion)			
	St. Denis	French	Euro
South Africa (Republic of South Africa)			
	Pretoria (administrative)	Afrikaans English	Rand
	Cape Town (legislative)	Xhosa Zulu	
	Bloemfontein (judicial)		
Swaziland (Kingdom of Swaziland)			
	Mbabane	Swazi English	Lilangeni
Zimbabwe (Republic of Zimbabwe)			
	Harare	English	Zimbabwe dollar

8

EASTERN AFRICA

Countries by size

		sq mi
1	Ethiopia	435,184
2	Tanzania	364,898
3	Somalia	246,199
4	Kenya	224,961
5	Uganda	91,135
6.	Eritrea	46,842
7	Malawi	45,745
8	Burundi	10,745
9	Rwanda	10,169
10	Djibouti	8880
11	Seychelles	176

Burundi

Djibouti

Eritrea

Ethiopia

Kenya

Malawi

Rwanda

Seychelles

Somalia

Populations

2005 (000s)

1 Ethiopia	73,053	**7** Rwanda	8440
2 Tanzania	36,766	**8** Burundi	6370
3 Kenya	33,829	**9** Eritrea	4561
4 Uganda	27,269	**10** Djibouti	476
5 Malawi	12,158	**11** Seychelles	81
6 Somalia	8591		

Densities (people per sq mi)

1 Rwanda	830	**7** Kenya	150
2 Burundi	593	**8** Tanzania	101
3 Seychelles	462	**9** Eritrea	97
4 Uganda	299	**10** Djibouti	54
5 Malawi	266	**11** Somalia	35
6 Ethiopia	168		

Per capita GNI (2003 US$)

1 Seychelles	7490	**7** Eritrea	190
2 Djibouti	910	**8** Malawi	180
3 Kenya	400	**9** Burundi	90
4 Tanzania	300	**10** Ethiopia	90
5 Uganda	250	**11** Somalia	-
6 Rwanda	220		

COUNTRY	CAPITAL	LANGUAGE	CURRENCY
Burundi (Republika y'Uburundi)			
	Bujumbura	French	Burundi
		Kirundi	franc
Djibouti (Jumhouriyya Djibouti)			
	Djibouti	French	Djibouti
		Arabic	franc
Eritrea (State of Enitrea)			
	Asmera	Tigrinya	Birr
Ethiopia (Ityo'pia)			
	Addis Ababa	Amharic	Birr

COUNTRY	CAPITAL	LANGUAGE	CURRENCY
Kenya (Jamhuriya Kenya)	Nairobi	Swahili	Kenyan shilling
Malawi (Republic of Malawi)	Lilongwe	English Chewa	Kwacha
Rwanda (Republika y'u Rwanda)	Kigali	Kinyarwanda French	Rwanda franc
Seychelles (Republic of Seychelles)	Victoria	English French	Seychelles rupee
Somalia (Jamhuriyadda Dimugradiga Somaliya)	Mogadishu	Somali Arabic	Somali shilling
Tanzania (Jamhuriya Mwungano wa Tanzania)	Dodoma	Swahili English	Tanzanian shilling
Uganda (Republic of Uganda)	Kampala	English	Ugandan shilling

Tanzania

Uganda

8

WESTERN AFRICA
Populations

2005 (000s)

1 Nigeria	128,771	**10** Guinea	9467
2 Ghana	21,029	**11** Benin	7460
3 Cote d'Ivoire	17,298	**12** Sierra Leone	6017
4 Cameroon	16,380	**13** Togo	5681
5 Burkina Faso	13,925	**14** Liberia	3482
6 Mali	12,291	**15** Mauritania	3086
7 Niger	11,665	**16** The Gambia	1593
8 Senegal	11,126	**17** Guinea-Bissau	1416
9 Chad	9826	**18** Cape Verde	418

Benin

Burkina Faso

Cameroon

Cape Verde

Densities (people per sq mi)

1 The Gambia	365	**10** Burkina Faso	132
2 Nigeria	361	**11** Guinea-Bissau	102
3 Cape Verde	269	**12** Guinea	100
4 Togo	259	**13** Cameroon	89
5 Ghana	227	**14** Liberia	81
6 Sierra Leone	217	**15** Mali	26
7 Benin	172	**16** Niger	24
8 Senegal	147	**17** Chad	20
9 Cote d'Ivoire	139	**18** Mauritania	8

Per capita GNI (2003 US$)

1 Cape Verde	1440	**10** Togo	310
2 Cote d'Ivoire	660	**11** Burkina Faso	300
3 Cameroon	630	**12** Mali	290
4 Senegal	540	**13** The Gambia	270
5 Benin	440	**14** Chad	240
6 Guinea	430	**15** Niger	200
7 Mauritania	400	**16** Sierra Leone	150
8 Nigeria	350	**17** Guinea-Bissau	140
9 Ghana	320	**18** Liberia	110

Chad

Cote d'Ivoire

The Gambia

Guinea

COUNTRY	CAPITAL	LANGUAGE	CURRENCY
Benin (République du Benin)			
	Porto-Novo	French	CFA franc
Burkina Faso (République du Burkina Faso)			
	Ouagadougou	French	CFA franc
Cameroon (Republic of Cameroon)			
	Yaounde	English French	CFA franc
Cape Verde (República de Cabo Verde)			
	Praia	Portuguese	Escudo
Chad (République du Tchad)			
	N'djamena	French Arabic	CFA franc

Countries by size

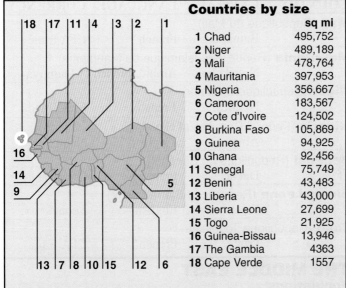

	sq mi
1 Chad	495,752
2 Niger	489,189
3 Mali	478,764
4 Mauritania	397,953
5 Nigeria	356,667
6 Cameroon	183,567
7 Cote d'Ivoire	124,502
8 Burkina Faso	105,869
9 Guinea	94,925
10 Ghana	92,456
11 Senegal	75,749
12 Benin	43,483
13 Liberia	43,000
14 Sierra Leone	27,699
15 Togo	21,925
16 Guinea-Bissau	13,946
17 The Gambia	4363
18 Cape Verde	1557

8

COUNTRY	CAPITAL	LANGUAGE	CURRENCY

Cote d'Ivoire (République de la Côte d'Ivoire)
| | Yamoussoukro | French | CFA franc |

The Gambia (Republic of the Gambia)
| | Banjul | English | Dalasi |

Ghana (Republic of Ghana)
| | Accra | English | Cedi |

Guinea (République de Guinée)
| | Conakry | French | Guinea franc |

Guinea-Bissau (República da Guiné-Bissau)
| | Bissau | Portuguese | CFA franc |

Liberia (Republic of Liberia)
| | Monrovia | English | Liberian dollar |

Guinea-Bissau

Liberia

Mali

Mauritania

Niger

Nigeria

Senegal

Sierra Leone

Togo

COUNTRY	CAPITAL	LANGUAGE	CURRENCY
Mali (République du Mali)			
	Bamako	French	CFA franc
Mauritania (République Islamique de Mauritanie)			
	Nouakchott	Arabic, French	Ouguiya
Niger (République du Niger)			
	Niamey	French	CFA franc
Nigeria (Federal Republic of Nigeria)			
	Abuja	English	Naira
Senegal (République du Sénégal)			
	Dakar	French	CFA franc
Sierra Leone (Republic of Sierra Leone)			
	Freetown	English	Leone
Togo (République Togolaise)			
	Lomé	French	CFA franc

THE MIDDLE EAST

Populations

Bahrain

Cyprus

Iran

2005 (000s)

1	Iran	68,017	**9**	Oman	3001
2	Saudi Arabia	26,417	**10**	United Arab	
3	Iraq	26,074		Emirates	2563
4	Yemen	20,727	**11**	Kuwait	2335
5	Syria	18,448	**12**	Qatar	863
6	Israel	6276	**13**	Cyprus	780
7	Jordan	5759	**14**	Bahrain	688
8	Lebanon	3826			

Densities (people per sq mi)

1	Bahrain	2681	**9**	Iraq	155
2	Lebanon	953	**10**	Iran	107
3	Israel	783	**11**	Yemen	102
4	Kuwait	339	**12**	United Arab	
5	Syria	258		Emirates	80
6	Cyprus	218	**13**	Oman	37
7	Qatar	195	**14**	Saudi Arabia	35
8	Jordan	162			

Countries by size

	sq mi			sq mi
1 Saudi Arabia	756,981		8 United Arab Emirates	32,000
2 Iran	636,293		9 Israel	8019
3 Yemen	203,849		10 Kuwait	6880
4 Iraq	168,753		11 Qatar	4416
5 Oman	82,031		12 Lebanon	4015
6 Syria	71,498		13 Cyprus	3571
7 Jordan	35,637		14 Bahrain	257

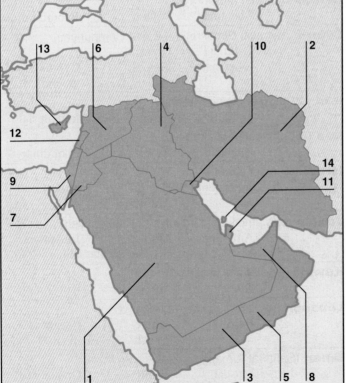

8

Iraq

Israel

Jordan

Kuwait

Lebanon

Qatar

Saudi Arabia

Syria

Per capita GNI (2003 US$)			
1 Kuwait	17,960	**8** Yemen	520
2 Israel	16,240	**9** Bahrain	-
3 Saudi Arabia	9240	**10** Cyprus	-
4 Lebanon	4040	**11** Iraq	-
5 Iran	2010	**12** Oman	-
6 Jordan	1850	**13** Qatar	-
7 Syria	1160	**14** United Arab Emirates-	

COUNTRY	CAPITAL	LANGUAGE	CURRENCY
Bahrain (Dawlat al-Bahrayn)			
	Manama	Arabic	Bahraini dinar
Cyprus (Kypriaki Dimokratia – Kibris Cumhuriyeti)			
	Lefkosia	Greek	
	(Nicosia)	Turkish	Cyprus pound
Iran (Jomhori-e-Islami-e-Iran)			
	Tehran	Farsi	Iranian rial
Iraq (al Jumhouriya al 'Iraqia)			
	Baghdad	Arabic	Iraqi dinar
Israel (Medinat Israel)			
	Jerusalem	Hebrew Arabic	Shekel
Jordan (al Mamlaka al Urduniya al Hashemiyah)			
	Amman	Arabic	Jordanian dinar
Kuwait (Dowlat al-Kuwait)			
	Kuwait City	Arabic	Kuwaiti dinar
Lebanon (al-Jumhouriya al-Lubnaniya)			
	Beirut	Arabic French	Lebanese pound
Oman (Saltanat 'Uman)			
	Muscat	Arabic	Omani riyal

United Arab Emirates

Yemen

COUNTRY	CAPITAL	LANGUAGE	CURRENCY
Qatar (Dawlet al-Qatar)			
	Doha	Arabic	Qatari riyal
Saudi Arabia (al-Mamlaka al-'Arabiya as-Sa'udiya)			
	Riyadh	Arabic	Saudi riyal
Syria (al-Jumhuriyah al-Arabiyah)			
	Damascus	Arabic	Syrian pound
United Arab Emirates (Ittih-ad al-Imarat al-Arabiyah)			
	Abu Dhabi	Arabic	UAE dirham
Yemen (al-Jumh-urïyah al-Yamani-yah)			
	San'a	Arabic	Yemeni riyal

8

EARLY MAN 3 MILLION–3000 BC

Neanderthal burial

3 million–c. 10,000 Palaeolithic (Old Stone Age)

c. 400,000–360,000 Middle Pleistocene Period. Peking man in Asia, Africa, southern Europe. Makes tools, uses fire, hunts, gathers berries, grains, nuts. Practices burial

c. 120,000–75,000 Neanderthal man (*Homo sapiens neanderthalensis*) in Africa, Europe, and Asia. Improves hunting skills, cares for the old

c. 60,000 Neanderthal man includes flowers in burial rites (Near East)

c. 50,000 Last Ice Age ends. Neanderthal man reaches Australia

c. 40,000–20,000 *Homo sapiens sapiens* develops. Controls fire, improves tools, hunts, fishes, collects honey, fruit, and nuts

c. 36,000 *Homo sapiens* reaches Americas from Asia

c. 35,000 Cave paintings in France and Spain

c. 33,000 *Homo sapiens* dominant species; Neanderthal man declines

c. 28,000 Seafarers reach New Guinea and Japan from Asian mainland

c. 13,500 Northern ice sheet melts, causing flooding

c. 12,000 Dogs domesticated (Near East)

c. 10,000–8000 Mesolithic (Middle Stone Age)

c. 10,000 Goats domesticated (Near East)

c. 8000–3500 Neolithic (New Stone Age)

c. 7500 Sheep domesticated (Greece)

c. 7000 Wheat and barley cultivated, walled settlements develop (Near East)

c. 6500 Wheel developed by Sumerians

c. 6000 Pottery evolved. Bread made, fruit and vegetables preserved by drying (Switzerland)

c. 5500 Copper smelted (Persia)

c. 5000 Irrigation canals and ditches built in Nile area

c. 4000 Horses domesticated (Europe). Fruit cultivated, wine made (Pakistan)

c. 3500 Bronze made (south-west Asia). Wheeled vehicles and oar-propelled ships developed by Sumerians

c. 3000 Cuneiform writing developed by Sumerians

THE MIDDLE EAST 3000–500 BC

c. 2800	**Menes of Upper Egypt first pharaoh of first dynasty**	**841**	Philistines, unites Israel
c. 2700	Gilgamesh builds walls around Uruk	**750**	Assyrians conquer Syria
c. 2600	Third Egyptian dynasty; step pyramid built	**732–29**	Nubians conquer Egypt Assyrians annex Babylon and Damascus
c. 2550	Fourth Egyptian dynasty; **Great Pyramid at Giza**, Great Sphinx	**724–21**	Assyria annexes Israel
c. 2500	First civilization at Troy	**708**	Empire of Medes founded
c. 2400	Akkad dynasty in Mesopotamia	**669–63**	**Assyrians conquer Egypt**
c. 2300	Guti tribesmen destroy Mesopotamian empire		Second Babylonian empire established. Collapse of Assyrian empire
c. 2200	Egypt fragments with dynasties in rival capitals	**614**	Medes sack Assur
c. 2000	Middle kingdom reunites Egypt	**612**	Babylonians and Medes sack Nineveh
c. 1900	Start of first Babylonian empire	**610**	Babylonians annihilate Assyrian army; end of Assyrian state
c. 1800	Babylon supreme: **Hammurabi's legal code**	**605**	King Nebuchadnezzar of Babylon defeats Egyptians
c. 1500	Hittites sack Aleppo and Babylon; establish Hittite old kingdom	**598**	Nebuchadnezzar takes Jerusalem
c. 1375-1350	Pharaoh Akhenaton attempts to introduce monotheistic religion	**550**	Cyrus of Persia defeats Medes
c.1300	**Exodus of Jews from Egypt**	**539**	Cyrus annexes Babylonia; Persian empire supreme
c. 1250–1200	Israelites conquer Palestine, replacing Canaanites	**525**	Egypt conquered by Persians
c. 1200	Hittite empire overthrown by Phrygians	**521**	Darius usurps Persian throne
c. 1005	King David of Judea defeats	**516**	Darius campaigns against Syths; annexes Indus Valley

Assyrians conquer Egypt

9

Great Pyramid at Giza

ASIA 3000 BC – AD 1

c. 3000	Harappan culture in Indus Valley
2200	Xia dynasty in China
c. 1800	Indus Valley invaded by Aryans
c. 1200	Cambodia settled
c. 1100	Zhou dynasty in China overthrows Shang
c. 770	Nomads invade Zhou capital Hao
c. 720	Warring feudal states claim independence in China
c. 660	Jimmu Tenno emperor in Japan
605–520	**Lao Zi, Chinese philosopher, founder of Taoism**
563–483	**Siddhartha Gautama, the Buddha**
551–479	Confucius (Kongzi), Chinese founder of Confucianism
c. 510	Persians annex Indus Valley
c. 500	Mons and Tibetan peoples enter Burma. **Magadha kingdom on Ganges**
c. 364	Nanda dynasty usurps Magadha throne
330	Viet kingdom in lower Yangtse Valley destroyed
329–25	Alexander the Great campaigns in North India
321	Mauryan dynasty of Magadha
316	Chinese destroy An Lac kingdom
305	Alexander's general Seleucus attempts to invade India
c. 300	China invaded by Huns (Xiongnu)
273	Ashoka becomes Mauryan emperor
258	Second kingdom of An Lac
c. 250	Korean Yaoi people in Japan
232	Ashoka dies; kingdom divided between grandsons
220–10	**Great Wall of China built to keep out Xiongnu**
206	Han dynasty in China as last Qin emperor dies; independent feudal states incorporated into territory
c. 200	Tamils invade Ceylon
c. 174–60	Yueh-Chi enter India from China
160–40	Xiongnu fight Han dynasty
133–19	Renewed conflict between Xiongnu and Han dynasty
111	Vietnam conquered by China
108	West Korea conquered by China
104–2	Xiongnu fail to follow up military success against Han troops
c. 100	Andhra dynasty in South India
58–51	Xiongnu revert to nomadism
c. 50	Satavahana dynasty in South India
c. 10	Langkasuka kingdom in Malaysia

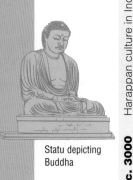

Statu depicting Buddha

HELLENISTIC WORLD 2000 BC – AD 1

Trojan War

Persian soldiers

9

Socrates

Alexander the Great

c. 2000–1800 BC	Bronze Age: Athens, Argos, Thebes founded
1800–1700	**Minoan culture in Crete**
1580	Mycenaean civilization begins
1450–1375	Minoan culture destroyed
1350	Corinth founded
1300–1200	Mycenaean king mainland overlord
c. 1200	**Trojan war; Greece defeats Troy**
1200–1100	Iron Age. North Greeks (Dorians) conquer Mycenaeans
1100–1000	Sparta founded
776	**Olympic Games founded**
700–650	Greeks settle Anatolia and Syria
508	Democratic constitution in Athens
499–494	Ionian Greeks rebel against Persia; suppressed
490	**Persians, under Darius, invade Greece; defeated at Marathon**
480	Persians invade under Xerxes; Athens burned
479	**Greeks defeat Persians at Salamis and Plataea**
477	League of Delos establishes Athenian democracy
443–29	Athens under Pericles
431–4	**Peloponnesian War:** Sparta defeats Athens
415–13	Athenian expedition to Syracuse
408	Rhodes founded
398	**Socrates condemned to death in Athens**
387	Sparta makes treaty with Persia
385	Plato (Socrates' pupil) founds Academy in Athens
378	Athens allies with Thebes
382	Thebes defeated by Sparta
359	Philip II becomes king of Macedon
356	Birth of Alexander the Great
343	Aristotle appointed Alexander's tutor
338–36	Philip II of Macedon defeats Athenians and Thebans, then is assassinated
334–26	**Alexander the Great conquers Persian empire; founds Alexandria**
280	Pharos of Alexandria and Colossus of Rhodes built
211	Romans sack Syracuse
197	Romans defeat Philip V of Macedon
171–68	Rome conquers Macedon
148–46	**Rome annexes Greece**

THE ROMAN WORLD 750 BC – AD 500

Horace

Ovid

Augustus

753 BC	**City of Rome founded**
c. 338	Earliest Roman coins
312	Emperor Appius Claudius completes Appian aqueduct and begins Appian Way
264–41	**First Punic War between Rome and Carthage**
218–1	Second Punic War. Hannibal defeated by Fabius Maximus in Crete
215	Roman armies in Spain
172–68	War between Rome and Macedon. Beginning of Roman world domination
170	Earliest known paved streets in Rome
149–46	**Third Punic War. The destruction of Carthage**
82–79	Dictatorship of Sulla
70–19	Virgil, Roman poet
73–71	Slaves' rebellion led by gladiator Spartacus
65–8	Horace, Roman poet
60	First Triumvirate between Julius Caesar, Pompey, and Crassus
59–51	**Caesar conquers all of Gaul**
49	Caesar crosses the Rubicon, an action which begins civil war
47–44	Dictatorship of Caesar. Assassination of Caesar
46	Julian calendar adopted; introduction of leap year
43–AD 18	Ovid, Roman poet
43–36	Second Triumvirate between Mark Antony, Octavian Caesar, and Lepidus
40	**Herod appointed king of Judea**
39–31	Mark Antony allies with Cleopatra of Egypt. They are defeated by Octavian (Augustus) at Battle of Actium. Construction of Roman Pantheon begins
27	**Augustus proclaimed emperor**
AD 14	Augustus succeeded by Tiberius
37	Caligula succeeds Tiberius
41	Caligula assassinated. Succeeded by Claudius
43	**Roman invasion of Britain under Claudius**
54	Claudius murdered by his wife. Succeeded by Nero
60–61	Revolt of Queen Boudicca

THE ROMAN WORLD 750 BC – AD 500

64	Great fire of Rome. **First persecution of Christians**
65–70	Jewish revolt crushed. Destruction of Jerusalem
69	Year of Four Emperors; Vespasian gains throne
78	Titus proclaimed emperor
79	Eruption of Mount Vesuvius
81–96	Titus succeeded by his brother, Domitian
98	Domitian succeeded by Trajan
98–117	**Roman empire reaches its greatest geographical extent under Trajan**
116	Second Jewish revolt led by Bar Kokhba
121–32	Construction of Hadrian's Wall from Solway to Tyne
161–80	Reign of Marcus Aurelius
164–80	Plague sweeps Roman empire
192–3	Severus emperor
c. 190	Galen establishes medical practices that last 1500 years
257	Goths invade Black Sea area
248	**Rome celebrates 1000th anniversary**
c. 250–70	Increased persecution of Christians under Decius
268	Goths sack Athens, Corinth, and Sparta
270–75	Aurelian emperors launch reconquest
284	Diocletian proclaimed emperor
303–11	Renewed persecution of Christians
305	Diocletian abdicates in the East
306	Constantine proclaimed emperor
337	Constantine converts to Christianity on deathbed
363	**Roman empire splits into West and East**
375–78	Visigoths invade Roman territory
383	Romans begin evacuation of Britain
406	Vandals invade Gaul
408	**Visigoths, under Alaric, invade Italy**
409–39	Vandals invade Spain and cross into North Africa (Carthage)
410	**Alaric captures and sacks Rome**
436	Last Roman troops leave Britain
451	Attila leads Hun invasion of Gaul
455	**Vandals sack Rome**
460	Vandals destroy Roman fleet

Boudicca

9

Trajan

THE DARK AGES 500–1000

Justinian I

511	Clovis, king of Franks, dies
526	Theodoric the Great, king of the Ostrogoths, dies
527	Justinian I, east Roman emperor
535–40	Belisarius conquers Sicily and enters Rome
552	Narses reconquers Italy
558	Chlotar, son of Clovis, reunites kingdom of Franks
572	Emperor Justin at war with Persia
610	Heraclius, east Roman emperor
613	Frankish kingdom reunited by Chlotar's grandson, Chlotar
629	Byzantines expelled from Spain by Visigoths
640–42	Byzantines defeated by Arabs
687	Pepin II, mayor of Franks
732	**Charles Martel defeats Arabs at Poitiers**
751	Pepin the Short becomes king of Franks
779	Offa becomes Anglo-Saxon overlord in England
800	Charlemagne emperor of West
828	Egbert, king of Wessex, becomes Anglo-Saxon overlord
843	Charlemagne's empire partitioned
844	Picts and Scots united under Kenneth MacAlpine
845–46	Normans pillage Paris. Arabs pillage Rome
865–74	Vikings conquer northeast England
871	Alfred (the Great) king of Wessex
880	Treaty between Alfred and Viking leader Guthrum partitions England
894–96	Byzantium at war with Bulgars
895	Magyars migrate to Hungary
896	France recognizes dukedom of Normandy
927	Athelstan established as first king of all England
962	Otto I crowned emperor of West (Holy Roman Emperor)
965	Danish king accepts Christianity
979	Ethelred (the Unready) becomes king of England
980–82	Renewed Danish raids on southern England
989	Vladimir, great prince of Kiev, accepts Christianity
991	Danes raiding East Anglia bought off (Danegeld)
1000	Sveyn of Denmark kills Olaf of Norway. Venetians conquer Istria

THE ISLAMIC WORLD 500–1500

570	Mohammed born in Mecca
610	Mohammed preaches first sermon
622	**Flight to Medina (Hegira); start of Islamic calendar**
630	Mecca submits to Mohammed
632	Mohammed dies; father-in-law Abu Bakr elected successor (caliph)
636–41	Arab expansion begins
634	Abu Bakr succeeded by Omar
644	Omar succeeded by Othman
656	Othman assassinated; succeeded by last Suni caliph, Ali
651	**Umayyad dynasty founded in Damascus**
680	Origin of Shi'ites, supporters of the Prophet's son-in-law, Ali
694	Umayyads take Carthage
711	Umayyads invade Spain
750	Abbasids overthrow Umayyads
786	Harun al Rashid caliph of Baghdad
874	Samanid dynasty in Samarkand
962	Samanids conquer Afghanistan
969	Fatimids from Morocco conquer Egypt
999	Ghaznevids overthrow Samanids
1009	Caliph al Hakim orders destruction of Holy Sepulchre in Jerusalem
c. 1020	Origin of Druzes, a sect venerating the Fatimid caliph al-Hakim, proclaimed God incarnate in 1017
1037–39	Seljuk revolt against Ghaznevids
1071	Seljuks take Anatolia
1099	Seljuks lose Jerusalem to Crusaders
1145	Almohades, a Berber dynasty, cross to Spain
1174	Saladin sultan of Egypt
1187	Saladin conquers Jerusalem
1191	Saladin defeated by Crusaders
1212	Almohade rule in Spain ends
1236	Almohade empire starts to fragment
1258	Mongols take Baghdad
1291	Mamluks of Egypt take Acre
1356	Ottomans cross into Europe
1363	Timur begins conquests in Asia
1390	Ottoman sultan Beyazit annexes five Turkish emirates in Anatolia
1402	Timur invades Anatolia
1453	Ottomans take Constantinople. As Istanbul, it becomes capital of Ottoman (Turkish) empire
1456	Turks besiege Belgrade; repulsed
1492	Granada, last Muslim emirate in Spain, falls. Forced conversion of Spanish Muslims to Christianity

Muslims invade Spain

9

Saladin

Mehemmed, leader of the Ottomans

THE GOTHIC WORLD 1000–1500

Christian
knights of the
Crusades

Battle for
Jerusalem

Year	Event
1001	St. Stephen of Hungary crowned
1002	Danish settlers in England massacred. Ethelred (the Unready) buys peace (Danegeld)
1013	**Danes invade England. Sveyn takes throne from Ethelred**
1014	Sveyn succeeded by Canute
1031	Muslim Spain fragments, with Christian kingdoms in north. Canute dies; Danish empire fragments
1042	Edward (the Confessor), king of England
1054	**Schism between Orthodox and Catholic churches final**
1059–61	Normans in southern Italy and Sicily
1066	**Battle of Hastings; William of Normandy defeats King Harold**
1077	German Emperor Henry IV does penance at Canossa
1086	**Domesday Book (census) compiled in England**
1092	Moroccan Almoravides aid Muslims in Spain
1094	Roderigo Diaz (El Cid), in service of
1096	**First Crusade to take Muslim Jerusalem begins**
1099	Crusaders take Jerusalem. El Cid defeated at Cuenca; dies
1122	Concordat of Worms, on relations between papacy and secular government, signed by papal legate and emperor Henry V
1129	Roger II of Sicily takes over mainland Norman territories
1140	Roger II of Sicily captures Pope Innocent II
1146	Almohades take Morocco from Almoravides and cross into Spain
1147	Second Crusade sets out
1155	Frederick I (Barbarossa) German emperor
1163	Lombard League formed by Italian cities Padua, Verona, and Vicenza
1167	Oxford University founded
1170	**Thomas Becket, archbishop of Canterbury, murdered**
1176	Lombard League defeats Barbarossa
1182	Jews banished from France

Alfonso I of Castile, defeats Almoravides

THE GOTHIC WORLD 1000–1500

1187	Jerusalem kingdom falls to Muslims under Saladin
1190	**Third Crusade led by Richard I (the Lionheart), Philip II of France, and Barbarossa**
1192	Richard I held for ransom in Austria
1199	Richard I succeeded by John
1201	Fourth Crusade sets out
1204	Crusaders sack Constantinople; Latin empire set up
1209	King John excommunicated
1212	Almohade rule in Spain ends
1215	**John concedes charter of rights (Magna Carta)**
1237	Lombard League defeated by German Frederick II
1263–65	**Civil war in England between Henry III and barons led by Simon de Montfort**
1271–96	Marco Polo's voyage to China
1290	Jews expelled from England
1337	Edward III of England claims France; Hundred Years' War begins
1346	Edward defeats French at Battle of Crécy
1346–49	**Black Death ravages Europe**
1356	Edward, Prince of Wales (Black Prince), wins Battle of Poitiers
1380	Byzantine empire subject to Ottoman (Turkish) sultan
1381	Peasants' Revolt in England, led by Wat Tyler
1415	**Henry V of England invades France; wins Battle of Agincourt**
1420	Hussite Wars in Bohemia against Holy Roman Empire
1428	English besiege Orléans
1429	Joan of Arc raises siege of Orléans
1431	**Joan of Arc burned at stake**
1434	Medici dynasty controls Florence
1436	End of Hussite Wars in Bohemia
1453	English lose France, except Calais, after battles at Bordeaux and Castillon. **Hundred Years' War ends**
1455	Civil war in England between Yorkists and Lancastrians begins (Wars of the Roses)
1485	Richard III killed at Bosworth; Henry VII succeeds
1492	Last Muslim state in Spain falls. Columbus discovers New World
1498	Vasco da Gama reaches India

Richard I (the Lionheart)

9

King John

Joan of Arc

ASIA AD 1–1500

Year	Event
AD 9–23	Usurpation of Han throne by Wang Man; Chinese influence in north Korea wanes
40–42	**Vietnam rebellion against China, led by Trong sisters**
57	Japan sends embassy to China
c. 100	Kushan empire in Turkestan, Afghanistan, and Punjab. Funan empire in Mekong Delta, Cambodia
220	Han empire falls. Replaced by Wei, Wu, and Shu-Han kingdoms
280	China reunited under Wei dynasty. Jin annexes Wu kingdom
308	China divided into northern (Xiong-nu) and southern (Jin) empires
320	Gupta empire of north India founded by Chandra Gupta I
c. 340	**Yamato state emerges in Japan.** Champa kingdom in central Vietnam
c. 425	Funan empire in Cambodia declines
470	Gupta kingdom disintegrates as White Huns attack
552	Turks of central Asia control steppes
562	**Japanese driven out of north Korea**
581	Sui dynasty reunites China
c. 600	Independent Tibetan kingdom established
605–10	**Grand Canal links Yangtse and Yellow rivers**
612	Harsha conquers upper India
618	Tang dynasty founded in China
639	Chinese protectorate established over central Asia
645	Japan begins to model government on Chinese lines
655	Empress Wu is virtual Tang ruler
661	China at war with Korea
668	Silla kingdom unites Korea, with China as overlord
678	Tibetans defeat Chinese armies. China withdraws from Korea
684	Manavamura dynasty in Ceylon
690	Empress Wu seizes Tang throne
705	Arabs invade Turkestan. Anarchy in Cambodia
712	Arabs invade India
c. 750	Arabs defeat Chinese armies in central Asia
755–57	An Lushan rebellion in China weakens Tang dynasty
c. 790	**China abandons attempt to**

Empress Wu

ASIA AD 1–1500

794	Heian period in Japan
c. 800	**Khmer kingdom established in Cambodia**
c. 840	Sanjaya dynasty conquers Srivijaya kingdom in Java
842	Tibetan kingdom collapses; rule passes to Buddhist clergy
849	Pyu kingdom in Burma collapses
857–58	Fujiwara clan controls Japan
879–80	Huang Chao rebellion in China
892	Korean kingdom of Koryo claims independence from China
c. 900	Khmer capital Angkor founded
907	Tang dynasty collapses and is succeeded by 5 dynasties in northern Vietnam
947–48	Khitan Mongols sack Yellow River towns, establish capital at Beijing
960	Song dynasty in China founded
979	Song complete reunification of China except Mongol territory
986	Khitan Mongols defeat Song dynasty
993–4	**Delhi founded**
1086	Shenzong emperor in China. State interference leads to

	disorganization
1115	Jin state founded in northern China
1175	Muhammed of Ghor invades India
1186–93	Kamakura era in Japan
1187	Muhammed of Ghor conquers Punjab
1206	Islamic sultanate established in Delhi
1211	Genghis Khan invades China
1271	Kublai Khan founds Yuan dynasty in China
1271–95	Marco Polo's journey to China
1274	Kublai Khan fails to conquer Japan
1279–	
1368	Yuan dynasty ruling in China
1355	Iliyas Shah founds kingdom in Bengal
1363	**Timur the Great begins conquest of Asia**
1398	Timur conquers Delhi
1405	Timur succeeded by Shah Rokh. Beijing established as Chinese capital
1447	India, Persia, and Afghanistan independent as Timur's empire breaks up

Yarimoto, ruler of the Kamukura dynasty

9

Kutub minar: Islam in Delhi

Kublai Khan

THE RENAISSANCE 1400–1600

Early printing press

Illustration from the *Divine Comedy*

1400	Rise of Medici family in Florence.
1403	*Chronicles* by Jean Froissart
	Lorenzo Ghiberti begins work on *Gates of Paradise* for Baptistry in Florence
1405	Pisa bought by Florence; Florence gains direct access to sea
1406	Venice seizes Padua after break-up of Visconti territories
1408	Statue of David by Donatello
1412	Filippo Brunelleschi's *Rules of Perspective*. Donatello's statues of St. Peter, St. George, and St. Mark
1414	Thomas à Kempis' *Imitatio Christi*. Medici become bankers to the papacy
1416–18	First Venetian–Turkish War
1420	Brunelleschi's cupola of Florence cathedral
1425–30	Second Venetian–Turkish War
1429	Joan of Arc takes Orléans from English
1431	Universities of Poitiers and Caen founded
1434–64	Cosimo de' Medici rules in Florence
1436	**Gutenberg invents moveable type for printing**
1447	University of Palermo founded
1450	Pope Nicholas V founds Vatican Library
	Florence under the Medici becomes centre of the Renaissance and Humanism
1450–66	Francesco Sforza, duke of Milan
1452	Ghiberti completes *Gates of Paradise* at Florence Baptistry. Metal plates are used for printing
1453	Constantinople captured by Ottoman Turks
1454	Peace of Lodi between Venice and Milan
1455	Palazzo Venezia, Rome, built
1456	First Bible printed. François Villon's *Le Petit Testament*
1460	Palazzo Pitti, Florence, begun
1462	Marsilio Ficino, translator of Plato from Greek to Latin, appointed head of Platonic Academy of Florence, among Europe's chief intellectual centers
1463–79	Great Venetian–Turkish War; Venice obliged to pay annual tribute for Black Sea trade
1472	Dante Alighieri's *Divine Comedy*

THE RENAISSANCE 1400–1600

1477	first printed
1478	Sandro Botticelli's *Primavera*
	Inquisition established in Spain
1478–92	Lorenzo de' Medici, "The Magnificent", rules in Florence
1482–84	Venice at war with Ferrara; Venetian territory at its greatest extent
	Birth of Venus by Botticelli.
1484	Albrecht Dürer's self-portrait
1486	Pico della Mirandola, *Oration on the Dignity of Man*
1489	Venice annexes Cyprus
1490	Beginnings of ballet at Italian court
1492	Expulsion of Jews from Spain. Leonardo da Vinci draws a flying machine. Lorenzo de' Medici dies. Piero de' Medici becomes ruler of Florence
1494	French invasion begins Italian Wars. In Florence, theocracy of Girolamao. Savonarola, a Dominican friar, denounces Renaissance paganism
1495	*Holy Family with St. Elizabeth and the young St. John* by Andrea Mantegna. *Last Supper* by Leonardo da Vinci
1497	Expulsion of Jews from Portugal

1498	Savonarola burnt at stake
1499	French invade Italy, seize Milan
1500	Milan regained from French by Ludovico Sforza
1501–4	*David* by Michelangelo
1502	Peter Henlein constructs the "Nuremberg Egg", the first watch
1503	*Mona Lisa* by Leonardo da Vinci
1504	Spain captures Naples
1506	St. Peter's, Rome, rebuilding begun to designs by Bramante
1508–11	Villa Farnesina, Rome, by Baldassare Peruzzi
1508–12	Michelangelo paints ceiling of Sistine Chapel
1508–15	King's College Chapel, Cambridge
1511	*Adoration of the Trinity* by Albrecht Dürer
1512	**Copernicus' *Commentariolus*, in which he states that the Earth and planets orbit the Sun**
1515–30	Tudor palace of Hampton Court built outside London
1515–16	Statue of Moses by Michelangelo
1516	Establishment of Jewish ghetto in Venice

Nicolaus Copernicus

9

Heliocentric theory of Copernicus

THE RENAISSANCE 1400–1600

Niccolo
Machiavelli

Illustration from
Gargantua

St. Peter's
Basilica

Year	Event
1516	*Orlando Furioso* by Ludovico Ariosto
1517	*Madonna of the Harpies* by Andrea del Sarto
1518	*Assunta* by Titian
1519	**Charles I of Spain elected Holy Roman Emperor Charles V.** Château of Chambord by Pierre Nepveu
1522	Beginning of Habsburg–Valois Wars in Italy
1527	**Sack of Rome by German and Spanish mercenaries.** Castiglione's *The Courtier*
1528	Founding of Capuchin Order. Palace of Fontainebleau begun by Diego de Siloe. Granada Cathedral begun
1529	Treaty of Cambrai between Emperor Charles V and Francis I of France
1532	Machiavelli's study of realpolitik, *Il Principe* (*The Prince*)
1533	*The Ambassadors* by Hans Holbein
1534	Statue of Hercules and Cacus, Florence, by Bacio Bandinelli. *Gargantua* by Rabelais
1534–41	*Last Judgement* by Michelangelo
1536–40	Dissolution of the monasteries in England
1537	Sansovino's façade of the Doge's Palace loggietta, Venice
1538	The *Urbino Venus* by Titian
1542	Inquisition established in Rome
1545	*Venus, Cupid, Time, and Folly* by Agnolo Bronzino
1545–54	*Perseus* by Benvenuto Cellini
1545–63	**Council of Trent begins the Counter-Reformation**
1546	Michelangelo designs the dome of St. Peter's
1547	Ivan the Terrible gains power in Russia. First predictions of the astrologer Nostradamus
c. 1548	Potatoes brought to Europe from South America
1550	*Lives of the Artists* by Georgio Vasari. *Odes* by Pierre Ronsard
1550–51	Villa Rotonda, Vicenza, by Andrea Palladio
1553	*Venus and Adonis* by Titian
1554–67	*Mars and Neptune* by Jacopo Sansovino
1555	Michelangelo's sculpture *Pietà*
1558	France regains Calais from England

THE RENAISSANCE 1400–1600

1559	**Treaty of Cateau-Cambresis ends Habsburg-Valois and Italian Wars.** *Battle of Carnival* by Pieter Brueghel the Elder
1560	Uffizi Palace begun by Giorgio Vasari
1561–65	Town Hall, Antwerp, begun by Cornelius Flock
1563	*Tower of Babel* by Brueghel the Elder
1563–86	Escorial Palace, Spain, by Juan de Toledo and Juan de Herrera
1564–87	*Life of Christ and Scenes of the Passion* series begun by Tintoretto
1565	*Alexander and the Family of Darius* by Paolo Veronese
1569–71	Revolt of the Moriscos in Spain
1570	Abraham Ortelius' first modern atlas. *Leda* by Tintoretto
1570–71	Turks capture Cyprus from Venice
1571	**Battle of Lepanto.** Holy League (Pope, Venice, and Spain) defeats Turks in last great galley battle
1572	*Lusiads* by Camoens
1573	*The Feast in the House of Levi* by Veronese
1575	El Greco arrives in Spain

1579	Union of Utrecht forms Dutch republic
1580	**Philip II annexes Portugal and its empire.** *Essais* by Michel de Montaigne
1581	*Gerusalemme Liberata* by Torquato Tasso
1581–85	*The Tortoise Fountain* by Landini
1582	Gregorian calendar introduced
1585	Quirinale Palace, Rome, by Domenico Fontana
1587	Drake destroys Spanish fleet at Cadiz
1587–91	Rialto Bridge, Venice, built
1588	Spanish Armada launched against England
1589	*Bacchus* by Caravaggio
1590	First microscope built by Janssen. William Shakespeare begins to write his plays
1594	Henri of Navarre crowned Henri IV of France. Tyrone Rebellion in Ireland begins
1596	Galileo develops heat measurement
1597	Bankruptcy of Spanish Crown
1600	Giordano Bruno burned for heresy by Inquisition

El Greco

9

Michel de Montaigne

Galileo Galilei

EUROPEAN EXPLORATION 1400–1600

Vasco da Gama

Slave ship

1402–6	Europeans conquer three Canary Islands
1418–19	Exploration of Madeira Island
1425	West Africa assigned to Portugal
c. 1427–32	Portuguese discover and settle the Azores
1446	Fernão Gomes discovers Cape Verde and Senegal
1447	Map of world drawn by Toscanelli
1448	Beginning of Portuguese empire in Africa. Portuguese build fort at Arguin in Mauritania
1452	**Pope allows Portuguese and Spanish to practise slavery**
1455–57	Alvise da Cadamosto explores Senegal and Gambia rivers
1470–71	João de Santavern reaches Gold Coast
1472	Lopo Goncalves crosses Equator
1482	Portuguese establish fort at Elmina, Gold Coast. Diego Cão reaches Congo River mouth
1487	Bartolomeu Diaz's voyage round Cape of Good Hope
1492–1504	**Columbus discovers New World** and makes further voyages of discovery to Central America
1493–1898	Spanish Caribbean–American empire
1494	**Treaty of Tordesillas between Spain and Portugal marking their halves of the world for exploration**
1497	John Cabot discovers Newfoundland while searching for the Northwest Passage
1498	**Vasco da Gama reaches India by sea.** John Cabot's second voyage
1499	**Amerigo Vespucci's first voyage to America**
1500–1	Pedro Cabral discovers Brazil and travels to India
1501–2	Vespucci's second voyage to America
1503	Portuguese trading post of Cochin, China, established. Portuguese set up first East Africa trading post at Zanzibar
1508–15	Spanish conquer Puerto Rico and Cuba
1510	Portuguese capture Goa in India
1510–11	**Importation of slaves to the Americas begins**

EUROPEAN EXPLORATION 1400–1600

1511 Portuguese capture Malacca (Malaya)

1513 Portuguese arrive in Moluccas (Spice Islands) and begin trading. Jorge Alvarez lands near Canton, Ponce de Léon claims Florida

1515 Portuguese capture Hormuz in the Persian Gulf

1518–1824 Spanish Latin American empire

1519 Spanish found Panama City

1519–21 **Hernán Cortés' conquest of Mexico**

1519–22 **Ferdinand Magellan's circumnavigation**

1520–22 First Portuguese mission to Beijing

1521 Magellan claims the Philippines for Spain

1521–55 Portuguese expand into inland Brazil

1521–61 Failed Spanish attempt to colonize Florida

1522 Spanish conquer Nicaragua and found New Spain. **Spanish discover Inca empire**

1524 Verrazano explores coast of North America and enters New York Bay.

1527–35 Spanish found Guatemala City

1528–36 Conquest of Yucatan, Mexico. Narvarez' Florida expedition

1530–1822 Portuguese empire in Brazil

1531 Spanish found Guadalajara, Mexico

1531–33 **Conquest of Peru by Pizarro**

1532 Spanish found Cartagena, Colombia. Henri Cartier discovers St. Lawrence River

1534–42

1536 Spanish found Buenos Aires; later destroyed by Indians

1537 Spanish found Asunción, Paraguay

1538 Spanish found Bogotá, Colombia

1540–61 Spanish conquest of Chile

1541 Hernando de Soto discovers Mississippi River. Coronado, explores New Mexico, Colorado, and Texas

1542 Antonio da Mota reaches Japan. Cabillo discovers California

1545 Opening of Spanish Potosi silver mines in Bolivia. Spaniard Retes finds northern New Guinea coast

1546 Mayan revolt against Spanish conquerors crushed

Hernán Cortés

9

Francisco Pizarro

EUROPEAN EXPLORATION 1400–1600

Francisco d'Almeida, first governor of Angola

African statue of a Portuguese soldier

1549–51 Francis Xavier introduces Christianity to Japan

1553 Willoughby and Chancellor round North Cape and reach Archangel

1557 Portuguese settlement at Macao, China

1565 Portuguese found Rio de Janeiro after destroying French colony. First permanent Spanish colony in Florida after French are ousted

1567 Mandana discovers Solomon, Marshall, and Ellice Islands.

1569 Spanish found Caracas, Venezuela

1570–71 Mercator's world map

1574 Spain begins colonization of the Philippines
Portuguese found Luanda, Angola

1578–80 Drake's circumnavigation

1578–84 Gilbert's attempts at colonization of North America

1580 Spain annexes Portugal. Spain refounds Buenos Aires

1584–90 Raleigh's missions to colonize Roanoke Island, North Carolina

1592 Portuguese settle at Mombasa on East African coast

1595 First Dutch posts on Guinea coast. Mendana discovers Marquesas and Santa Cruz Islands

1596 Dutch set up trading posts on Sumatra. Spanish found Monterey

1596–97 Barents discovers Bear Island and Spitzbergen

THE AMERICAS 2000 BC – AD 1550

c. 2000 BC	Maya culture in southern Mexico, Guatemala, and Belize
c. 1200	Olmec culture along Gulf of Mexico
c. 900	Chavin culture in northern Peru
c. 800	First Tiahuanaco culture in Bolivia
c. 400	Olmec culture wanes
c. 300	Teotihuacan culture in central Mexico
c. 200	Chavin culture wanes, replaced by Mochica culture
c. 100	Nazca culture in southern Peru
c. 30	Olmec "long count" dating inscriptions provide accurately calculated dates
AD c. 250	**Golden age of Maya culture begins**
c. 350	Teotihuacan empire at peak
c. 600	Mochica culture wanes. Teotihuacan empire declines
c. 750	Toltecs destroy Teotihuacan empire
c. 900	Golden age of Maya culture fades
c. 1000	Chimu culture in northwest Peru
c. 1100	Inca culture in Peru emerges
c. 1200	Toltecs conquered by Aztecs
c. 1370	Chimu culture under Nancan Pinco expands into Andes

1440	Montezuma I Aztec ruler
1471	Tupa Inca ruler. Incas conquer Chimu
1492	**Columbus discovers New World**
1493	Huayna Capac Inca ruler
c. 1500	Chibcha culture of Colombia destroyed. Nazca culture disappears. Aztec ruler Ahuizotl extends empire
1501	Coelho explores Brazilian coast
1502	**Montezuma II Aztec ruler**
1504	Hernán Cortés, Spanish conquistador, arrives in Cuba
1509	Aztecs defeat Spanish in Colombia
1511	Velázquez conquers Cuba
1519	Cortés begins invasion of Mexico
1520	Montezuma II killed while prisoner of Cortés
1521	Cortés takes Tenochtitlan; last Aztec ruler, Cuauhtemoc, surrenders
1525	Huayna-Capac dies; civil war
1527	Atahualpa defeats his brother Huascar in civil war. Pizarro in Panama
1532	Atahualpa defeated by Pizarro
1533	Atahualpa executed by Pizarro
1535	**Pizarro completes conquest of Inca empire**

Mayan stone calendar

9

Aztec sacrifice to the sun god

Cortés attending Christian conversions

THE REFORMATION 1500 – 1780

Luther's
annotated Bible

Luther
administers the
sacrament

1505 Martin Luther joins the Augustinian Order of monks

1510 Luther visits Rome

1517 **Luther's 95 theses against the sale of clerical indulgences are nailed to Wittenberg church door**

1518 Huldreich Zwingli called to be minister in Zürich

1519 **Luther questions infallibility of the Pope.** Zwingli begins Swiss Reformation

1520 Luther is declared a heretic by Pope Leo X and excommunicated but protected by Elector Frederick the Wise of Saxony. Beginnings of Anabaptist (radical Reformist) movement in Germany under Thomas Münzer

1521 **Diet of Worms bans Luther and all new doctrines.** Pope confers title "Defender of the Faith" on Henry VIII of England

1522 Luther returns to Wittenberg; condemns fanatics and iconoclasts. Finishes translating New Testament

1523 Zwingli's program of reform in 67 theses; Reformation adopted in Zürich

1524 **Zwingli abolishes Catholic mass in Zürich**

1525 Luther marries an ex-nun

1526 Luther's German Mass. Anabaptists settle as Moravian Brothers in Moravia

1527 Lutheranism established in Sweden. First Protestant university established in Marburg

1528 Austrian Anabaptist Balthasar Hubinair burned at the stake in Vienna. Reformation begins in Scotland

1529 Luther and Zwingli hold discussion on Eucharist at Marburg. Diet of Speyer; Lutheran-inclined states protest at Catholic domination of diet and are called "Protestant"

1530 Schmalkaldic League formed by Protestant princes and imperial cities

1531 Zwingli killed at Battle of Kappel with Swiss Catholic reformers.

1532 Inquisition in Portugal
Reformation in France

THE REFORMATION 1500 – 1780

1534 First complete translation of Luther's Bible. Act of Supremacy in England. **Jesuit Order founded by Ignatius Loyola**

1535 English clergy renounce authority of Pope. Thomas More executed for loyalty to Rome and refusal to accept Henry VIII as head of English Church. Anabaptist John of Leiden tortured to death. Study of canon law forbidden in Cambridge, England

1536 Act of Parliament declares authority of Pope void in England. Reformation in Denmark and Norway. Calvin's *Instructions in Christ*. Dissolution of the monasteries begins in England, followed by Pilgrimage of Grace, an uprising against it

1536–39 Lutheranism becomes the faith of Denmark, Norway, and Baltic states

1537 Pilgrimage of Grace and similar risings put down

1538 **Calvin expelled from Geneva;** settles in Strasbourg. Destruction of relics and shrines in southern

1540 England Order of Jesuits confirmed by Pope Paul III

1541 Calvin brings Reformation to Geneva. John Knox leads Calvinist Reformation in Scotland

1542 **Pope Paul III reintroduces Inquisition in Rome**

1543 First Protestant burned at the stake by Spanish Inquisition Transylvania becomes Lutheran

1545 First session of Council of Trent to discuss Catholic reform

1545–47 Death of Luther

1546 Schmalkaldic War; Charles V defeats Protestant League. *Chambre ardente* created in France for trial of heretics

1547

1549 Only new Book of Prayer can be used in England. Agreement between Calvin and followers of Zwingli on Holy Communion

1550 Jews persecuted in Bavaria

1551–52 Second session of Council of Trent

1553–58 Catholic Restoration in England under Mary I

1555 Knox returns to Scotland from exile

Destruction of Catholic relics

9

John Calvin

Huldreich Zwingli

THE REFORMATION 1500 – 1780

French Protestants tortured by Catholics

Catherine de Medici, a leading Catholic

Year	Event
1555	Peace of Augsburg; a compromise giving princes right to chose and enforce their subjects' faith. In Germany Lutheran states to enjoy equal rights with Catholics
1557	*Index of Forbidden Books* issued by Pope. First Presbyterian church founded in Scotland by Knox
1558	Lutherans at Seville and Valladolid
1559	First national synod of French Huguenot Calvinists
1560	Scottish National Church established. Beginnings of Puritanism in England
1561	First Calvinist refugees from Flanders settle in England. Edict of Orléans suspends persecution of Huguenots
1562	**Third session of Council of Trent reforms Catholic Church; Counter-Reformation begins.** 1200 French Huguenots massacred at Vassy leads to First War of Religion
1563	**Completion of Anglican Church's establishment.** Counter-Reformation begins in Bavaria
1564	Death of Calvin.
1566	Calvinist riots in the Netherlands. Regent Margaret of Palma abolishes Inquisition. Synod of Antwerp forms Calvinist Church of the Netherlands
1570	Peace of St. Germain-en-Laye ends third civil war in France. Huguenots gain amnesty
1571	Reconciliation between Charles IX of France and Huguenots
1572	**St Bartholomew's Day Massacre;** 2000 Huguenots are killed in Paris on Charles IX's orders
1573	Religious tolerance in Poland
1577	Henry of Navarre recognized as head of Huguenots
1579	Catholic Reform commission founded in Austria. Protestants expelled from Bavaria
1593	Henry of Navarre becomes Catholic
1594	Edict of St. Germain-en-Laye grants Huguenots freedom of worship
1598	**Edict of Nantes grants Huguenots equal political rights**
1600	Persecution of Catholics in Sweden

THE REFORMATION 1500 – 1780

1606	under Charles IX. Giordano Bruno burned as a heretic
	Penal laws against Papists in England
1609	Catholic League of German princes formed against Protestant Union. Emperor Rudolf II permits religious freedom in Bohemia
1609–14	Expulsion of Moriscos from Spain
1611	Cardinal Pierre de Bérulle founds French Congregation of the Oratory
1615	Galileo Galilei faces Inquisition for the first time
1616	Catholic oppression intensifies in Bohemia. Copernicus declared a heretic
1618	Thirty Years' War begins after closure of Czech protestant churches by Catholic authorities
1620	Battle of White Mountain. Habsburg Counter-Reformation defeats Czech Protestants
1622	Congregatio de Propaganda Fide unites Catholic missionaries
1625	Sisters of Mercy established in Paris
1628	Ignatius Loyola canonized by Pope Gregory XV

1629	Catholic Edict of Restoration of church property in Germany which had been secularized since 1555
1632	Galileo declared a heretic
1633	**Galileo forced by Inquisition to renounce theories of Copernicus**
1640	Cornelius Jansen's *Augustinus* published posthumously. Begins Jansenist disputes
1648	**A bull of Pope Innocent X condemns the Peace of Westphalia, which ends the Thirty Years' War**
1673	Test Act excludes Roman Catholics from both houses of English Parliament
1684	93 Jewish families expelled from Bordeaux
1685	Louis XIV revokes Edict of Nantes and exiles French Protestants
1686	Roman Catholics readmitted to English army
1759	Jesuits banned in Portugal
1764	Jesuits banned in France
1767	Spain bans Jesuits
1773	Pope Clement XIV bans all Jesuits

Protestants murdering Catholics in Prague

9

Pope selling indulgences

PROTESTANT EUROPE 1600–1700

Thirty Years' War

Gustav Adolphus

1600 Protestants expelled from Austria

1608 Protestant states of Rhineland form Protestant Union under Christian of Anhalt and Frederick IV of the Palatinate

1609 English Baptist Church founded by John Smyth and Thomas Hewys

1611 King James Bible in England

1618–19 General synod of Calvinists at Dodrecht, Holland

1618 **War in Bohemia starts Thirty Years' War.** Protestant nobles invade Czech royal palace.

1619 Richelieu recalled by Louis XIII.
Aug Diet of Bohemia elects Frederick

1620 End of Bohemian independence. Massacre of Protestants in Valtelline
Jul Princes of Protestant Union sign Treaty of Ulm with Catholic League to maintain German neutrality in Bohemian War

1621 Huguenots rebel against Louis XIII

1621–23 **Palatinate War**

1622 Richelieu created cardinal. Treaty of Montpellier ends Huguenot rebellion

1623 Holy Roman Emperor Ferdinand II grants Maximilian, Duke of Bavaria, the Upper Palatinate

1624–29 **Danish War**

1624–42 Richelieu administration in France

1625 Apr Ferdinand appoints Wallenstein commander in chief. Mansfeld defeated by Wallenstein at Dessau

1625–48 Netherlands joins anti-Spanish coalition

1626 Peace of La Rochelle between Huguenots and French Crown
Aug Catholic League defeats Christian IV of Denmark in Germany

1627 Wallenstein conquers Silesia. Tilly conquers Brunswick
May Renewed constitution for Bohemia by Ferdinand

1628 Gustav Adolphus of Sweden enters Thirty Years' War
Jul Ferdinand issues a renewed constitution for Moravia

1629 Mar Ferdinand orders the return of all lands taken over by Protestants since 1552

1630 Sep Treaty of Altmark extricates Gustav Adolphus from war against Poland. Gustav Adolphus invades Germany
Aug Wallenstein replaced by Tilly

PROTESTANT EUROPE 1600–1700

1630–35		**Swedish War**
1631	Jan	Sweden signs Treaty with France
	May	Tilly and Catholic League destroy Magdeburg. Tilly defeated by Swedish and Saxon troops
1632	Nov	Gustav killed in Battle of Lützen
	Apr	Wallenstein reinstated by Ferdinand
1633		First Baptist Church in England
1634		Wallenstein assassinated
1635	Apr	Sweden renews French alliance with Treaty of Compiègne. France declares war on Spain
	Sep	Sweden signs treaty with Poland
1635–48		Franco–Habsburg War
1639		**Dutch destroy Spanish fleet in English Channel**
1641		English and Scottish Protestant settlers massacred by Catholics in Ulster
1642–46		**English Civil War** between Royalist forces of Charles I and Parliamentarians under Cromwell
1642		Mazarin succeeds Richelieu
1643	May	Mazarin destroys Spanish army at Rocroi, Ardennes
	Sep	Solemn League and Covenant: Scots Covenanters (Presbyterians)

	make alliance with Parliamentarians
1644	Battle of Marston Moor; Royalists defeated. English parliament bans religious festivities at Christmas
1645	Peace talks begun between Holy Roman Empire and France
1646	Sweden takes Prague and invades Bavaria with the French
1648	**Peace of Westphalia and Münster ends Thirty Years' War.** George Fox founds Society of Friends (Quakers) in England
1649	Charles I executed
1653–58	Cromwell Lord Protector of the Commonwealth
1655	Cromwell prohibits Anglican services in England
1660	Charles II restored
1667	Calvinists acknowledged by Lutherans
1678	John Bunyan's *Pilgrim's Progress*
1685	Edict of Nantes revoked
1688	**Glorious Revolution:** William III and Mary II proclaimed joint monarchs after James II of England exiled for pro-Catholic sympathies
1689	Act of Toleration in England

Execution of
Charles I

9

John Bunyan

Mary II

AMERICAN COLONIZATION 1600–1700

Advertisement for land in Virginia

Year	Event
1599–1634	Champlain's voyages in Canada
1607–9	**English settlement of Jamestown, Virginia**
1608	Quebec founded by French
1608–11	Henry Hudson explores east coast
1612	Earliest colonization of Bermudas from Virginia. Dutch use Manhattan as fur trading centre. Tobacco planted in Virginia
1613	English colonists in Virginia destroy French settlement at Port Royal, Nova Scotia. Prevent French colonization of Maryland
1614	Dutch Fort Nassau built on Hudson River. Virginian colonists stop French from settling Maine and Nova Scotia
1617	Walter Raleigh reaches mouth of Orinoco River in South America
1619	First African slaves arrive in North America in Virginia. First representative colonial assembly in America held at Jamestown, Virginia
1620	**Pilgrim Fathers leave Plymouth in the Mayflower** and land at New Plymouth, Mass.
1623	First English settlement in New Hampshire
1624	**Dutch settle in New Amsterdam.** Virginia becomes a royal colony
1626	Salem, Mass. settled. Dutch East India Company buys Manhattan Island from the native Indian chiefs
1627	Barbados claimed for England
1630	Puritans found Massachusetts colony
1630–40	Great Migration to America of 16,000 settlers
1631	Dutch West India Company founds settlement on Delaware River
1632	English settlers in Antigua and Montserrat
1633	Dutch settle in Connecticut
1635	English colonize Connecticut
1635–36	Rhode Island settled
1636	Harvard College founded
1636–37	Pequot Indian War in New England
1638–43	New Hampshire settled
1638–55	Swedes settle on Delaware River
1640–54	Maine settled
1642	Montreal, Canada, founded
1643	New England Confederation to govern in war and Indian relations

AMERICAN COLONIZATION 1600–1700

1649 Puritan exiles from Virginia settle in Providence, Maryland

1650 Wars against North American Indians begin

1654 First Jewish settlers arrive in New Amsterdam

1660 Puritans settle in New Jersey

1661 English conquer New Netherlands

1661–62 Suspension of Quaker persecution

1661–63 Connecticut and Rhode Island charters

1663–65 Charters given for the Carolinas

1663–69 Massachusetts annexes Maine

1664 New Amsterdam renamed New York

1668–88 Anglo-French struggle for Hudson Bay

1670 Charleston settled by English. English Hudson Bay Company incorporated by royal charter to trade in regions of North America

1672–73 Father Marquette and Louis Joliet explore environs of Chicago and upper Mississippi

1674 Treaty of Westminster recognizes inhabitants of New York and New Sweden as British subjects

1675–76 King Philip's Indian War

1676 Nathaniel Bacon leads rebellion in Jamestown

1679–82 La Salle explores Great Lakes and reaches mouth of Mississippi. Hannepin discovers Niagara Falls

1680–86 Royal government in New Hampshire

1682 Pennsylvania founded by William Penn. La Salle claims Louisiana territory for France and takes possession of Mississippi Valley

1683 First German immigrants in North America. Penn's treaty with Indians

1684 Bermudas become Crown property

1685 First French settlers in Texas. French Huguenots emigrate to North America

1686 First French settlers in Arkansas

1689 Massacre of French settlers near Montreal by Iroquois

1692 Witchcraft trials and hangings at Salem, Mass.

1693 Kingston, Jamaica founded. Carolina divided into North and South Carolina

1698 French begin to settle in Louisiana and on upper Mississippi

The *Mayflower*

9

William Penn

MOGUL INDIA 1500–1858

Taj Mahal

1526   **Babur, a descendant of Timur the Great, founds Mogul dynasty**

1539   Afghan ruler Sher Shah defeats Moguls and founds Sur dynasty

1555   Mogul Humayun reconquers empire from Surs

1556   Akbar, Babur's grandson, consolidates empire

1564   Akbar abolishes tax on non-Muslims (jizya); heralds new era of conciliation

1573–94   Akbar conquers Gujarat, Bihar, Bengal, and Kandabar

1634–48   **Shah Jehan, Akbar's grandson, builds Taj Mahal**

1669   Aurangzeb, son of Shah Jehan, bans Hindu faith

1681   Akbar, son of Aurangzeb, rebels.

1689   Aurangzeb conquers Deccan

1707   Aurangzeb defeats Marathas

1708   Aurangzeb succeeded by Bahadur Bahadur defeats Sikhs who had threatened the empire

1737   Marathas defeat Moguls at Delhi

1738–39   Nadir Shah of Persia invades Afghanistan and sacks Delhi

1756   Over 100 British die while imprisoned in "black hole" of Calcutta after ruler of Bengal region captures the city

1757   Robert Clive secures Bengal for the British after Battle of Plassey

1768   Gurkhas conquer Nepal

1775–81   Anglo–Maratha War results from alliance between Bombay government and ruler of Maratha

1781   Coote conquers Mysore

1795   British take Ceylon from Dutch

1799   Hindu royal family in Mysore

1816   Treaty with Gurkhas; Nepal in British sphere of influence

1824–26   Anglo–Burmese War ends with British acquisition of Assam

1838–42   Anglo–Afghan War ends with16,000 British troops evacuating Kabul

1843   **Slavery in India abolished**

1844–49   Anglo–Sikh Wars

1849   Sikh state ends as Britain annexes Punjab

1857   **Indian "Mutiny".** Revolt against British rule in India

1858   **Government of India passes from East India Company to Crown; Lord Canning becomes first viceroy**

CHINA AND JAPAN 1500–1900

1736–39	Mongols at war with Chinese
1751	China invades Tibet
1775	Britain takes over India–China opium trade from Portugal
1825	Muslim rebellion in Turkestan
1830	Chinese emigration to Malaya
1838–42	**First Anglo-Chinese Opium War**
1842	China opens ports to foreign trade; cedes Hong Kong to Britain. Japan relaxes rules against foreign ships
1846	Japan refuses to allow US warships dock
1850–64	Taiping Rebellion in China
1857–58	Second Opium War
1868	Last Tokugawa shogun abdicates
1881	**Political parties formed in Japan**
1882	French capture Hanoi
1885	Kuroda Kiyotaka first Japanese prime minister
1894–95	China at war with Japan over Korea; Japan takes Taiwan; Korea independent
1900	Boxer Rebellion attempts to oust foreign powers from China. Military domination begins in Japan

Taiping rebellion in China

9

1516	Portuguese begin trade with China
1523	Europeans expelled from China
1549–51	Francis Xavier makes Christian converts in Japan
1571	Nobunaga deposes Ashikaga, shogun in Japan
1582	Nobunaga assassinated; replaced by Hideyoshi
1587	Hideyoshi bans Christian missionaries from Japan
1600	Tokugawa defeats rivals; Japanese capital moved to Edo
1603–1867	Tokugawa shogunate in Japan
1621	Manchu under Nurbaci establish Jurchen state
1623	Persecution of Christians in Japan; English trade stops after eight seized and killed
1644	Manchu enter Beijing; establish Qing dynasty
1683	Manchu conquer Taiwan
1685	China opens ports to foreign trade
1692	Christianity tolerated in China
1715	British trading post in Canton
1707–17	China mapped
1727	China's border with Russia fixed
1736	Christianity banned in China

Boxer Rebellion in China

INDUSTRIAL REVOLUTION 1700–1850

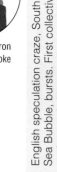

Smelting iron ore with coke

Mercury thermometer

South Sea Bubble bursts

Illustration from *Systema Naturae*

1702 Serfdom abolished in Denmark

1704 Earliest subscription library in Berlin

1709 First Copyright Act in Britain. 14,000 inhabitants of German Palatinate emigrate to North America; 100,000 Germans follow in the next hundred years. **Abraham Darby discovers method of smelting iron ore with coke**

1710 Porcelain factory at Meissen, Germany, founded

1712 Slave revolts in New York

1714 French surgeon Dominique Anel invents fine-pointed syringe for surgical purposes. D G Fahrenheit constructs mercury thermometer with temperature scale

1715 First Liverpool dock built

1716 *Diario di Roma*, first Italian newspaper, published

1717 School attendance in Prussia made compulsory

1718 First bank notes in England. Collegiate School of America transferred to new site in New Haven and renamed Yale University

1720 English speculation craze, South Sea Bubble, bursts. First collective settlement in Vermont

1721 Regular postal service between London and New England

1722 Workhouse Test Act introduced

1724 Gin drinking becomes popular in Britain. Paris Bourse opens

1726 Lloyd's List issued in London twice weekly

1727 Coffee first planted in Brazil. Quakers demand abolition of slavery

1730 Zinc smelting first practised in England

1731 English factory workers not allowed to emigrate to America

1733 John Kay patents shuttle loom

1735 Linnaeus' *Systema Naturae*, establishes principles of naming and classifying plants

1736 Manufacture of glass begins in Murano, Venice. Hard rubber, caoutchouc, comes to Britain

1742 **Cotton factories established in Birmingham and Northampton.** Anders Celsius

INDUSTRIAL REVOLUTION 1700–1850

Encyclopaedia Britannica appear

1769 James Watt patents steam engine. Richard Arkwright's waterframe, a spinning frame powered by water, is patented

1770 **James Hargreaves patents spinning jenny**

1771 Richard Arkwright opens first spinning mill in England

1773 Boston Tea Party; protest against tea duty in American colonies. **First cast-iron bridge built at Coalbrookdale, Shropshire**

1775 James Watt perfects his invention of the steam engine. Pierre-Simon Girard invents water turbine

1777 Co-operative workshop for tailors opens in Birmingham

1778 Act of Congress prohibits import of slaves into the United States

1779 Pope Pius VI begins draining Pontine Marshes. Samuel Crompton invents spinning mule

1781 Serfdom abolished in Austrian dominions

1782 Bank of America established in Philadelphia. Montgolfier brothers

James Watt's steam engine

9

invents centigrade thermometer

1743 East Indian yarns imported into Lancashire for manufacture of finer goods

1749 Giacobbo Rodriguez Pereire invents sign language

1754 First iron-rolling mill at Fareham, Hampshire

1756 First chocolate factory in Germany. Cotton velvets first made at Bolton, Lancashire

1758 Ribbing machine invented for making ribbed stockings

1760 Josiah Wedgwood founds pottery works in Staffordshire

1761 Society of Arts, London, opens first exhibition of agricultural machines. Bridgewater Canal is first canal in Britain

1762 Cast iron converted into malleable iron in Scotland

1763 First Chambers of Commerce in New York and New Jersey.

1765 Earliest use of ponies in mines. Spallanzani suggests preserving by hermetic sealing

1768 First weekly installments of the

James Hargreaves' spinning jenny

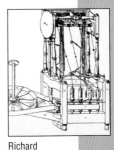

Richard Arkwright's weaving machine

INDUSTRIAL REVOLUTION 1700–1850

Montgolfier brothers' balloon

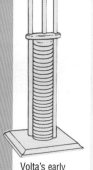

Volta's early battery

Fulton's steam boat

1783 construct air balloon. James Watt invents double-acting rotary steam engine

1784 A paddle-wheel steamboat is sailed on Saône River, France. **English ironmaster Henry Cort introduces puddling and rolling processes for manufacture of wrought iron.**

1785 Andrew Meikle, a Scottish millwright, invents threshing machine. Edmund Cartwright invents power loom. **Chemical bleaching invented. James Wall and Matthew Boulton install a steam engine with rotary motion in a cotton-spinning mill at Pupplewick, Nottinghamshire**

1786 Earliest attempts at internal gas lighting in Germany and England

1789 **First steam-driven cotton factory in Manchester**

1790 First steam-powered rolling mill built in England

1793 Eli Whitney introduces the cotton gin

1794 Abolition of slavery in French colonies

1795 Joseph Bramah invents hydraulic press

1796 **Edward Jenner introduces vaccination against smallpox**

1797 **England begins to export iron.** Merino sheep are introduced to Australia

1800 Alessandro Volta produces first electricity from a cell, the first form of battery

1802 Richard Trevithick constructs light-pressure steam engine. First practical steamship on the Clyde, Scotland. West India docks built in London

1803 American inventor, Robert Fulton, propels a boat by steam power

1806 Francis Beaufort designs a scale to indicate wind strength

1807 Abolition of slave trade by Britain. Street lighting by gas in London

1810 Techniques for canning food developed

1811 Luddites destroy industrial machines in northern England

1812 Philippe Girard invents machine for

INDUSTRIAL REVOLUTION 1700–1850

Rocket, steam locomotive 1829

9

1834 **Abolition of slavery in British colonies.** Cyrus Hall McCormick patents reaping machine in the US. Walter Hunt of New York constructs one of the first sewing machines. Poor Law Amendment Act: all poor to go to the workhouse. Louis Braille invents reading system for the blind

1835 Samuel Colt takes out English patent for single-barrelled pistol and rifle

1837 Electrical telegraph patented

1838–48 Chartist Movement in Britain

1839 Charles Goodyear makes commercial use of rubber possible by vulcanization

1844 Wood pulp paper invented

1845 Hydraulic crane patented by William G Armstrong. E B Bigelow constructs power looms for making carpets

1846 Britain repeals Corn Laws

1847–48 Great Irish Famine

1848 **Communist Manifesto published by Marx and Engels**

Samuel Colt's repeating hand gun

1814 spinning flax. George Stephenson constructs first practical steam locomotive

1815 Humphry Davy invents miner's safety lamp. First steam warship, USS *Fulton*, built

1815–16 **English economic crisis leads to large-scale emigration to North America**

1824 Erie Canal, US, finished

1825 Stockton–Darlington Railway opens: first in world to carry passengers. Expansion of trade union movement in Britain

1826 **Joseph Niepce produces photos on metal plates**

1828 Building of Baltimore–Ohio railroad begins: first in US to carry passengers and freight

1829 First co-operative stores in US. Shillibeer's omnibus becomes part of London's public transport

1830 French tailor Barthélemy Thimmonier devises a stitching machine

1833 First British Factory Act provides a system for factory inspection.

Early Goodyear tire

US WAR OF INDEPENDENCE 1765–83

Benjamin Franklin appeals for union

Anti-Stamp Act propaganda

George Washington

1765	Stamp Act; US colonies rebel against British taxes
1773	**Boston Tea Party; cargo of tea thrown overboard in Boston harbour to protest against British taxes**
1775 Apr	First skirmishes of war between Minutemen and British soldiers at Lexington
Jun	British victory at Battle of Bunker's Hill
Jul	**George Washington assumes control of Continental army**
Nov	Montreal taken from British
1776 Jan	Thomas Paine calls for full American independence in pamphlet *Common Sense*
Feb	British forces defeated near Wilmington, North Carolina
Mar	Continental fleet captures New Providence in the Bahamas. British evacuate Boston. Congress authorizes privateering
Jun	Declaration of American Independence drafted by Thomas Jefferson
Jul	**Declaration of Independence adopted**
Aug	British victory at Long Island
Sep	British occupy New York
Oct	Americans defeated at Lake Champlain and forced to retreat
Dec	American victory at Battle of Trenton. Washington captures 1,000 mercenaries
1777 Jan	American victory at Princeton
Jul	La Fayette joins Washington
Aug	American victories at Oriskany and Bennington
Sep	British win Battle of Brandywine; La Fayette wounded
Oct	Articles of Confederacy; first organizing document of the US
Dec	Washington winters at Valley Forge
1778 Feb	France signs treaty of alliance with Americans
Apr	British peace commission; American naval raid on Whitehaven, England
Jun	British evacuate Philadelphia; stalemate at Battle of Monmouth
Jul	French fleet arrives

US WAR OF INDEPENDENCE 1765–83

Mar **Articles of Confederation ratified.** Costly British victory in Battle of Guildford Courthouse

May–Aug British campaign in Virginia

Jun Congressional peace commission

Aug–Oct Yorktown campaign

Sep French naval victory in Battle of Chesapeake Bay

Oct **British capitulation at Yorktown**

1782 Mar British government defeated in vote on war and forced to resign

Apr Peace talks in Paris

Jul British evacuate Savannah

Sep Formal peace negotiations begin

Nov **Preliminary peace treaty signed**

Dec British evacuate Charleston

1783 Feb Cessation of hostilities

Apr Congress ratifies peace treaty; 7,000 loyalists sail home from New York

Jun American army disbanded

Sep **Treaty of Paris signed by Britain, France, Spain, and the United States**

Nov British leave New York

Declaration of Indepedence

9

Jul–Aug Franco-American attack on Newport repulsed; Americans evacuate Rhode Island

Dec British capture Savannah

1779 Feb American victory at Vincennes

Jun Spain declares war on Britain but refuses to acknowledge American independence, fearing for her possessions

Aug Congressional peace terms approved by Congress

Sep American naval victories in North Sea

Oct Franco-American attempt to recapture Savannah fails

1780 Mar Russia suggests a league of armed neutrality

May **Fall of Charleston to the British**

Jul French reinforcements land

Aug British victory at Battle of Camden

Sep West Point surrender plot by Benedict Arnold discovered

Oct American victory at Battle of King's Mountain

1781 Jan Mutiny in Pennsylvania crushed. American victory at Cowpens

Thomas Jefferson

FRENCH REVOLUTION 1789–99

French Revolution, Storming of the Bastille

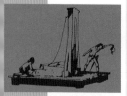

Execution by guillotine

French Revolutionary propaganda

1789 May **Estates General meet at Versailles**

- Jun Third Estate forms National Assembly and takes Tennis Court Oath

Jul **Storming of the Bastille**

- Aug Declaration of the Rights of Man
- Oct Royal Family brought from Versailles to Paris. National Assembly moves to Paris

1790 Jun Hereditary nobility and titles abolished; Louis XVI accepts constitution

1791 Jun Flight to Varennes; Louis XVI's escape thwarted
- Sep National Assembly dissolved
- Oct Legislative Assembly elected

1792 Apr France declares war on Austria and Prussia (First Coalition)
- Jun Mob attacks Tuileries Palace, Paris
- Sep Monarchy abolished

1793 Jan **Louis XVI executed**

- Feb War declared on Britain and Holland
- Mar War declared on Spain
- Apr Committee of Public Safety formed
- Jul Robespierre elected to Committee of Public Safety

Sep **Reign of Terror begins**

- Oct Republican calendar adopted. Execution of Marie Antoinette

1794 Apr Danton executed
- Jun Festival of the Supreme Being
- Jul Robespierre executed

1795 Feb Separation of Church and State

Apr **Bread riots in Paris**

- May Revolutionary Tribunal suppressed
- Oct Napoleon appointed major-general. The Directory of five members established to rule France

1796 Apr Italian campaigns begin

1797 Jul Italian campaigns end
- Oct Treaty of Campo Formio between France and Austria

1798 Feb French occupy Rome
- Apr French invade Switzerland
- Jul Battle of the Pyramids; France conquers Egypt
- Aug Battle of the Nile; French navy defeated by British
- Dec Second Coalition (Russia and Britain)

1799 Jan Formation of Republic of Naples
- Nov Napoleon overthrows Directory
- Dec Napoleon appointed First Consul

NAPOLEONIC WARS 1800–15

1800 Jun Battle of Marengo; France defeats Austria

1801 Mar Spain cedes Louisiana to French
Apr Nelson destroys Danish fleet at Copenhagen

1802 Mar Peace of Amiens between France and Britain
Aug New constitution. Napoleon Consul for life

1803 Apr USA purchases Louisiana from France
Oct France threatens to invade England

1804 May Napoleon proclaimed emperor

1805 Oct Battle of Trafalgar: Britain defeats Franco-Spanish fleet
Dec France defeats Austria and Russia at Battle of Austerlitz; signs Treaty of Pressburg

1806 Oct France occupies Berlin. Battle of Jena; France defeats Prussia
Nov Poland invaded

1807 Jun French defeat Russian and Prussian forces at Friedland
Nov France occupies Portugal

1808 Mar France invades Spain
Dec British troops land at Lisbon

1809 Jul Battle of Wagram; France defeats Austria
Dec Napoleon divorces Josephine

1810 Apr Napoleon marries Marie Louise of Austria

1812 Jun Russian campaigns begin
Jul Battle of Salamanca; Britain defeats France in Spain
Sept Battle of Borodino; Russians retreat. French advance to Moscow

Oct–Dec French retreat from Russia

1813 Jun Battle of Vittoria; Britain defeats France in Spain
Aug Battle of Dresden; Napoleon defeats allies
Oct Battle of Leipzig; allies defeat Napoleon

1814 Apr Napoleon abdicates; exiled to Elba
Nov Congress of Vienna opens to redefine Europe

1815 Mar Napoleon returns to Paris
Jun Congress of Vienna closes. **Battle of Waterloo; Napoleon defeated.** Napoleon abdicates again; exiled to St. Helena
Jul Louis XVIII returns to Paris

9

Napoleon Bonaparte

POST-NAPOLEONIC EUROPE 1810–50

Queen Victoria

Austrian coat of arms

Civil unrest in 1848

1811–20	Regency in Britain
1815	Congress of Vienna closes. Corn Laws passed in Britain
Sep	Holy Alliance formed between Prussia, Austria, and Russia
1816	Carl August of Saxe-Weimar grants first constitution in Germany
1818	**Allied army of occupation leaves France.** Prussia divided into 10 provinces
1819	Customs union in Germany (Zollverein) formed
1820	Revolutions in Italy, Portugal, and Spain. Spain cedes Florida to USA
1821	Greek uprising against Turkey
May	**Death of Napoleon on St Helena**
1822	Turkish invasion of Greece. Bottle riots in Dublin: Orangemen attack viceroy
Oct	Congress of Verona opens, to discuss European difficulties
1823	War between France and Spain
1824	Death of Byron in Turko-Greek war at Missolonghi
1825	**World's first railway opens between Stockton and**

1827	**Darlington.** Trade unions recognized as legal in England
	Battle of Navarino; destruction of Turkish fleet by Britain, France, and Russia
1828	Turko-Russian War. Duke of Wellington becomes British prime minister
1830	Revolutionary uprisings in Germany. Separation of Holland and Belgium. **Revolution in Paris**
1831	Electoral Reform Bill introduced into House of Commons
1834	Spanish Inquisition finally suppressed. Slavery ended in British possessions
1836	The Peoples' Charter launches first workers' movement in Britain
1837	**Accession of Queen Victoria in Britain.** Liberal constitution in Spain
1839	First British Opium War with China
1840	Louis Napoleon makes an attempt to lead Bonapartist uprising against July Monarchy
1847–48	Great Irish Famine

POST-NAPOLEONIC EUROPE 1810–50

1848

Communist Manifesto published by Marx and Engels. Unsuccessful revolt by Germans in Schleswig-Holstein

Feb Ferdinand II of Naples is forced to concede a constitution. In France July Monarchy overthrown. Louis-Philippe abdicates and Louis Napoleon elected president of France. Second Republic established

Feb-Mar Rulers of Tuscany and Piedmont and the Pope forced to grant constitutions

Mar Metternich, Austrian chancellor, dismissed and flees. Revolt in Vienna. Revolts in Venice, Berlin, and Parma. Street fighting in Milan against Austrians forces Austrian troops to withdraw. Piedmont declares war on Austria. Republic of St. Mark set up in Venice. Hungarian Diet adopts March Laws of autonomy

Jun Habsburg power restored. Emperor Ferdinand of Austria abdicates. Franz Joseph becomes emperor. Second uprising in Paris. Czech revolts suppressed by Austrian troops

Jul Piedmontese defeated at Custoza by Austrians

Sep Croats invade Hungary

Nov Pope Pius IX flees from Rome to Kingdom of Naples

1848-49 Revolution in the Austrian Empire

1849 Russians intervene to help crush Hungarian Revolution. Austria retakes Venice

Mar Piedmontese defeated by Austrians at Novara. Charles Albert of Sardinia abdicates in favour of his son, Victor Emmanuel II

Jun Danes secure constitution from Frederick VII

Aug End of Republic of St. Mark

1850 Apr Pope Pius IX returns to Rome with French military help

Karl Marx

9

Frederick
William IV
of Prussia

EUROPEAN NATIONALISM 1840–1914

British soldiers in the Crimea

Garibaldi

Otto von Bismarck

Paris Commune poster

Year	Event
1851	Great Exhibition in London
1852	Cavour becomes prime minister of Piedmont
1852–70	Second emperor of France, Napoleon II
1853–56	**Crimean War**
1859	Franco-Austrian war in northern Italy. Liberation of Lombardy from Austrians
1860	**Garibaldi sails from Genoa to Sicily with I Mille and takes Sicily and Naples**
1861	King of Naples surrenders at Gaeta. Kingdom of Italy announced; excludes Rome and Venetia. Victor Emmanuel is announced king of Italy
1862	**Alexander II of Russia frees the serfs** Garibaldi captured in bid for Rome. Bismarck becomes Prussian minister-president
1863–64	Second Polish Revolution
1864	German-Danish War over Schleswig-Holstein Red Cross formed in Geneva
1866	Austro-Prussian War (or Seven Weeks' War). Battle of Königgratz. Prussians defeat Austrians. Italy gains Venetia by allying with Prussia against Austria
1866–68	Cretan Revolt against Turks
1867	Dual Monarchy of Austria–Hungary organized. Garibaldi's second bid for Rome fails
1867–71	North German Confederation established
1870	**Unification of Italy complete.** Rome becomes Italian capital
1870–71	Franco–Prussian war. Siege of Paris
1870–1914	Third Republic in France
1871	Creation of German empire (Second Reich). **Paris Commune rising fails**
1872	League of Three Empires (Dreikaiserbund) between Germany, Austria–Hungary, and Russia
1873–74	First Spanish republic declared
1873–76	Second Carlist War in Spain
1874–80	Disraeli becomes British prime minister
1876	Bulgar Revolt against the Turks
1877–78	Russo-Turkish War
1878	Serbia, Montenegro, and Romania

EUROPEAN NATIONALISM 1840–1914

1879 become independent with Berlin Congress. Britain gains Cyprus

1881 Alliance of Germany and Austria Tsar Alexander II of Russia murdered

1882 Triple Alliance between Italy, Germany, and Austria

1885–86 Serbian–Bulgarian War

1886 First Irish Home Rule Bill

1886 Year of Three Empires in Germany

1890 Bismarck dismissed by Emperor Wilhelm II

1893–94 Franco-Russian Alliance

1894–

1906 Dreyfus Affair in France

1897 Greco-Turkish War over Crete

1899 First Hague Peace Conference

1901–5 Separation of Church and State in France

1904–5 Russo-Japanese War

1904 Anglo-French Entente signed: "Entente Cordiale"

1905 Kaiser's visit to Tangier precipitates First Moroccan Crisis. Norwegian–Swedish union dissolved

1905–6 Revolution in Russia

1906 Conference of Algeciras in Spain, between Germany, France, and Britain

1907 Second Hague Peace Conference Anglo-Russian Entente

1908 Austria annexes Bosnia and Herzegovina

1910 Portuguese Revolution

1911 Second Moroccan or Agadir Crisis

1911–12 Tripolitanian War between Turks and Italians

1912–13 First Balkan War between Balkan League and Turkey

1913 Second Balkan War; Bulgaria attacks former allies. Treaty of Bucharest

1914 **Archduke Francis Ferdinand murdered in Sarajevo**

Siege of Paris

Assassination of Alexander II

French meet Moroccan resistance

US CIVIL WAR 1861–66

CHARLESTON
MERCURY
EXTRA:

Passed unanimously at 1.15 o'clock, P. M., December 20th, 1860.

AN ORDINANCE

To Dissolve the Union between the State of South Carolina and other States united with her under the compact entitled "The Constitution of the United States of America."

We, the People of the State of South Carolina, in Convention assembled, do declare and ordain, and it is hereby declared and ordained.

That the Ordinance adopted by us in Convention, on the twenty-third day of May, in the year of our Lord one thousand seven hundred and eighty-eight, whereby the Constitution of the United States of America was ratified, and also, all Acts and parts of Acts of the General Assembly of this State, ratifying amendments of the said Constitution, are hereby repealed; and that the union now subsisting between South Carolina and other States, under the name of "The United States of America," is hereby dissolved.

THE

UNION
IS
DISSOLVED!

South Carolina leaves the Union

Abraham Lincoln

1861 Apr   Confederate batteries open fire on Fort Sumter. Lincoln calls for volunteers. Union naval forces begin blockade of Confederate ports and coastline

Jul   Confederate victory at first Battle of Bull Run

Aug   Missouri remains in Union after Battle of Wilson's Creek

Nov   Confederate commissioners seized from British ship by Union patrol

Dec   War between Union and Great Britain averted by their release

1862 Jan   Lincoln orders general offensive

Jan/Feb/Apr   Union victories in Tennessee and Kentucky culminating in Battle of Shiloh

Mar–Jun   Confederate forces pin down Union troops in Shenandoah Valley

Apr   Confederacy adopts conscription. New Orleans taken by Union.

May–Jun   Battle for Richmond at Seven Pines indecisive

Jun–Jul   Seven Days' Battle ends with Confederate withdrawal towards Richmond

Aug   Union forces defeated in second Battle of Bull Run

Sep   Confederacy invades Maryland. Drawn battle takes place near Sharpsburg. Lincoln issues preliminary proclamation on the emancipation of slaves

Dec   Confederate victory at Fredericksburg. Lincoln weathers cabinet crisis

1863   Jan   Emancipation proclamation

Feb   Congress establishes National Banking System. French attempt at mediation

May–Jul   Union forces besiege and take Vicksburg to split Confederacy geographically

Jun   West Virginia afforded statehood by the Union

Jul   Union victory at Battle of Gettysburg. Anti-conscription riots in New York

Sep   British and French governments deny shipbuilding facilities to Confederacy. Indecisive Battle of Chickamauga

Nov   Gettysburg war cemetery

US CIVIL WAR 1861–66

1864

Mar–May Union forces advance south and west

May Indecisive battles with heavy casualties in The Wilderness and at Spotsylvania

May–Sep Union advance through Georgia

Jun Battles at Chickahominy and Cold Harbor and siege of Petersburg cause heavy Confederate losses. Union Confederate naval losses. Union presidential election campaign begins

Jul Confederate advance toward Washington rebuffed

Jun–Oct Second Shenandoah Valley campaign

Sep Atlanta falls to Union forces

inaugurated with address by Lincoln. Union victory at Battle of Chattanooga reinforces geographical split of Confederacy

Nov Lincoln re-elected

Nov–Dec Union advance toward Savannah

Dec Union victory at Battle of Nashville. Savannah falls

1865

Jan–Mar Union advance through North and South Carolina

Feb Hampton Roads conference fails to agree terms. Union forces capture Charleston

Mar Confederacy agrees to arm slaves for military duties

Apr Confederate forces evacuate Petersburg and Richmond. Lincoln inaugurated for second term. Confederate forces surrender at Appomattox. Lincoln assassinated

May Confederate capitulation. Reconstruction proclamation

Dec Abolition of slavery

1866 Apr Civil Rights Act grants citizenship to African Americans

First naval battle between iron ships

Unionist general Ulysses S. Grant

Confederate leader Robert E. Lee

9

AFRICA 400–1914

The hand of Fatima. Symbol of the five pillars of Islam.

Xhosa warrior

Zulu warrior

c. 400 AD	Kingdom of Ghana founded
429–534	Vandal kingdom in North Africa
640–710	Islamic conquests in northern Africa
c. 690	Songhay empire founded in Niger
968–1171	Fatamid dynasty in Egypt
c. 1100–1440	Great Zimbabwe complex built in stone in Zimbabwe
c. 1200	Rise of Kilwa Sultanate
1235	**Foundation of Mali Kingdom**
1350	Songhay empires at their height
c. 1400	Shona civilization of Great Zimbabwe
1402	Ethiopian embassy to Venice
1433	**Tuaregs from the Sahara sack Timbuktu**
1448	Portuguese set up first fort at Arguin in Mauritania
1497	Vasco da Gama rounds the Cape of Good Hope
1505–1821	Funj empire in Sudan
1517	**Ottomans take Cairo**
1626	First French settle in Senegal and Madagascar
1628–29	War between Mozambique and Portugal
1629	Mozambique becomes a Portuguese protectorate
1632–55	Gondar Ethiopian empire
1650	Bambara kingdom of West Africa founded
1651	Swedes take Gold Coast from Dutch
1652	Dutch found Cape Colony
1658	French establish town of St Louis in Senegal
1659–60	War between Xhosa and Dutch settlers
1660	Rise of Bambara kingdoms in upper Niger
1662–84	English occupation of Tangier
1670	Bambara kingdoms defeat Mandingo empire
1697	French attempt to colonize West Africa under André de Brue
1729	Portuguese lose Mombasa to Arabs
1779–81	First Xhosa War between Boers and Xhosa people
1790–	Rise of the Fulani in northern Nigeria
1798–99	Napoleon's campaign in Egypt
1801	Egypt formally restored to sultan
1802	British reconquer the Cape Colony
1805	
1808	**Britain and US outlaw slave trade**
1816–28	**Zulu kingdom is created**

AFRICA 400–1914

1820	Egypt conquers Sudan. British settlers arrive in Cape Colony
1822	Liberia is established by freed African Americans
1824–31	First Anglo-Ashanti War
1830–47	**French conquest of Algeria**
1834–35	British defeat the Xhosa
1835–37	**Great Boer Trek from Cape Colony**
1843	Britain annexes Natal
1844	Treaty of Tangier ends French war in Morocco
1846–47	British defeat Xhosa again
1849	Livingstone's first journey in Africa
1850–78	Nine Xhosa Wars in South Africa
1852	Britain recognizes the Transvaal as an independent Boer republic
1854	Britain recognizes Orange Free State. Egypt grants French engineer de Lesseps concession to build Suez canal
1868	Britain annexes Lesotho
1869	**Suez Canal opens**
1879	Anglo-Zulu War
c. 1880	**"Scramble for Africa" begins**
1881	French seize Tunis
1882	British occupation of Egypt
1882	De Brazza negotiates with King Makoko to establish a French colony on the North bank of Congo river
1883	Mahdist state in Sudan. Kruger becomes president of South African Republic
1883–5	German colonization in East and West Africa
1885	Berlin Conference on Africa; Congo recognized as Leopold of Belgium's personal territory
1885–	Spanish African empire
1975	
1896	Battle of Adowa; Ethiopians defeat Italians
1899	British take Sudan
1899–	**Anglo-Boer Wars**
1902	
1904	France proclaims a constitution for Federation of West Africa
1912	Founding of African National Congress
1914–18	First World War; campaigns in German Togoland, Cameroon, Southwest Africa, and Tanganyika

King Makoko of the Teke

9

Stamp from British Central Africa

US WESTERN EXPANSION 1800–1900

Original flag of the United States

Gold discovered in California

Native American leader Chief Jospeh opposes US expansion

1800 Thomas Jefferson wins presidential election

1803 Ohio becomes 17th state of the US. US secures land in the gulf of Mexico to northwest, including Louisiana and New Orleans from France (Louisiana Purchase)

1811 Indians defeated at Tippecanoe, Indiana

1812 Louisiana becomes 18th state of the US

1814 Battle of Horseshoe Bend ends Creek Indian War begun in 1812

1816 Indiana becomes 19th state of the union

1817 Mississippi becomes 20th state of the union. Nov Beginning of Seminole Indian War, after Indians retaliate following attacks

1818 Illinois becomes 21st state

1819 Florida purchased from Spain. Alabama becomes 22nd state

1820 Maine becomes 23rd state

1821 Missouri becomes 24th state

1823 Monroe doctrine closes the American continent to further colonial settlements by European powers

1824 South Pass, Wyoming discovered, allowing passage through the Rockies

1825 Creek Indian Treaty signed, obliging Creeks to cede all territory in Georgia

1828 First railroad built for the transportation of passengers and freight

1830 **First covered wagon trek from Missouri River to Rockies**

1832 Black Hawk Indian War ends with massacre at Bad Axe River

1835 Texas declares its right to secede from Mexico

1836 American rebels massacred by Mexican forces at the Alamo. Texas wins independence and becomes a republic. Arkansas is 25th state

1837 Michigan is 26th state. First covered wagons reach California

1845 Florida becomes 27th state, Texas becomes 28th

1846 Westward migration of Mormons.

US WESTERN EXPANSION 1800–1900

1847 Beginning of Mexican War. Iowa becomes 29th state

1848 Discovery of gold in California leads to first gold rush
Mexican War ends: the US secures Texas, New Mexico, California, Utah, Nevada, Arizona, parts of Colorado, and Wyoming from Mexico in return for a large indemnity. Wisconsin becomes 30th state

1850 California becomes 31st state
1858 Minnesota becomes 32nd state
1859 Oregon becomes 33rd state
1860 Abraham Lincoln elected 16th president of the US; South Carolina secedes from the Union in protest

1861 Kansas becomes 34th state. Confederate states break away from the Union
Apr Civil War begins at Fort Sumter, South Carolina

1862 Union forces defeated at Bull Run and Fredericksburg

1863 **"Emancipation proclamation" effective from 1 Jan; all slaves in rebelling areas declared free**
Arizona and Idaho become US territories. West Virginia becomes 35th state. Lincoln delivers "Gettysburg Address," while dedicating a national cemetery

1864 General Sherman defeats Confederate army at Atlanta and occupies Savannah. Nevada becomes 36th state

1865 Apr Confederate states formally surrender at Appomattox
May Abraham Lincoln assassinated. **Civil War ends**

1867 Nebraska becomes 37th state. Alaska purchased from Russia. Gold discovered in Wyoming

1876 Colorado becomes 38th state
1880 Railroad mileage now in operation in the US: 141,000 km

1889 North Dakota, South Dakota, Montana, and Washington join the Union. Oklahoma opened to non-Indian settlement

1890 Idaho and Wyoming join the Union
1896 Utah becomes 45th state

Atlantic and Pacific coasts linked by rail

9

AM I NOT A MAN AND A BROTHER

Slaves gain freedom

Civil War advances millitary technology

AUSTRALASIA 1768–2000

James Cook

Maoris sign Treaty of Waitangi

1768–79 James Cook discovers Hawaii, New Caledonia, and other Pacific islands

1770 Cook claims east coast of Australia for Britain and calls it New South Wales

1787 **New South Wales is established as a convict colony. Britain ships convicts to Australia**

1793 **Arrival of first free settlers in New South Wales**

1798–99 George Bass and Matthew Flinders sail around Tasmania

1800s Settlers, traders, and slave traders settle on Pacific islands

1829 Western Australia is established as a colony

1840 Britain formally annexes New Zealand; Treaty of Waitangi signed with Maoris

1845–72 Settlers on North Island defeat Maoris in New Zealand Wars

1851 Australian colony of Victoria is established. Gold is discovered in New South Wales and Victoria

1852 Britain grants New Zealand self-government

1856 Britain grants self-government to all the colonies except Western Australia

1859 Queensland separates from New South Wales

1860 Maori uprising in New Zealand

1865 Wellington becomes capital of New Zealand

1868 Britain ends transportation of convicts

1893 **New Zealand becomes the first nation to grant women the vote**

1898 Germany and the US take over Spain's possessions in Micronesia

early 1900s Germany also holds parts of Nauru, New Guinea and part of Samoa, and US controls Hawaii and the rest of Samoa. France and Britain also hold islands

1901 **Australian colonies federate to become self-governing Commonwealth of Australia**

1907 New Zealand becomes a dominion within the British empire

1914–18 Australia and New Zealand join with Britain in World War I

AUSTRALASIA 1768–2000

1927 Australian capital transferred from Melbourne to Canberra

1936–38 New Zealand sets up a social security programme for all citizens

1939–45 **Australia and New Zealand fight with the Allies in World War II**

1946 Nuclear testing by US starts on Bikini and Enewetak atolls and on Johnston Island. Britain carries out nuclear tests on Christmas Island

1951 Australia and New Zealand sign ANZUS Treaty

1962 Western Samoa becomes independent

1965 France begins nuclear tests on Tuamotu Island

1967 **Australian constitution changed to allow programmes to aid Aborigines**

1968 Nauru becomes independent

1970 Britain grants independence to Fiji, Tonga, and the Solomon Islands

1975 Sep Papua New Guinea becomes independent from Australia

Nov Constitutional crisis in Australia when Prime Minister Whitlam is dismissed by Governor-General.

1978 Britain grants Tuvalu independence

1979 Britain's Gilbert Islands become independent as Kiribati

1980 New Hebrides become independent and are renamed Vanuatu

1985 New Zealand bans nuclear weapons and nuclear-powered ships in its harbours

1986 **Many American Trust Territories made self-governing except Guam and Caroline Islands**

1987 Fiji becomes a republic and leaves Commonwealth after coup

1994 Palau becomes independent from US

1995 France restarts underground nuclear tests on Mururoa Atoll

1996 Labour Party defeated in Australian general election

Apr 35 people shot dead by lone gunman in Port Arthur, Tasmania

1999 Nov Queen retained as head of state in Australia after Referendum

2000 Sydney hosts the Olympic Games

New Zealand and Australian troops fight in World War I

9

Australia enters World War II

LATIN AMERICA 1800–2004

Pedro I, Emperor of Brazil

Mexican Revolution 1911–1920

Cuban Revolution 1959

Year	Event
1810–26	**Spanish-American wars of independence**
1811	Paraguay independent
1816	Argentina independent
1818	Chile independent
1819	Colombia independent
1820–21	Peru independent. Costa Rica independent
1821	Guatemala independent. Mexico independent
1822	Brazil independent
1823 Dec	**US president Monroe issues Monroe Doctrine, banning European states from colonizing American republics**
1825	Bolivia independent. Uruguay independent
1826	Last Spanish garrisons in Peru and Chile surrender
1830	Venezuela independent. Ecuador independent
1838	Honduras independent. Nicaragua independent
1849	El Salvador independent
1865	Paraguay declares war on Argentina, Brazil, and Uruguay
1870	Paraguay ends war, having lost territory and over half its population
1903	Panama becomes independent, supported by the US
1914	Panama Canal opened
1966	Guyana independent
1975	Suriname independent
1981	Belize independent
1982	Argentina and UK at war over Falkland (Malvinas) Islands. UK retains control
1984	US-backed counter-revolutionary group launches offensive against Nicaraguan government.
1989	US invades Panama, leader General Noriega arrested
1991	Panama regains control of Canal
1992	12-year civil war ends in El Salvador. UN Earth Summit held in Rio. Noriega convicted in US court on drug charges; links with CIA revealed
1994	US intervention in Haiti reinstates elected president Aristide
2000	Socialist Ricardo Lagos elected Chilean president
2004	President Aristide of Haiti forced to resign and flee by rebels

WORLD WAR I 1900–19

Jun **Archduke Ferdinand murdered at Sarajevo by Serbian nationalist**

Jul Austria–Hungary with German support, declares war on Serbia. Russia mobilizes its forces in support of Serbia

Aug **Germany declares war on Russia and France. Britain enters war after Germany invades Belgium.** Russia declares war on Turkey. France and Britain declare war on Turkey. Russians invade east Prussia. Germans occupy Liège. Battles of Namur and Mons. Germans occupy Lille. Russians defeated at Tannenberg

Sep Battle of Marne; Germans retreat. Russians defeated in Battle of Masurian Lakes. Russians invade Hungary

Oct First Battle of Ypres; German offensive halted. Turkey attacks Russia

Nov Hindenburg appointed German commander in the east

FOR PRESIDENT

WOODROW WILSON

Woodrow Wilson elected US president

9

Battle of the Marne

1901 Queen Victoria dies
1902 Triple Alliance between Germany, Austria, and Italy renewed for further six years
1903 Jun King Alexander and Queen Draga of Serbia murdered
1904 Apr French–British "Entente Cordiale" established. Russo-Japanese war breaks out over Manchuria
1905 Mar Theodore Roosevelt wins US presidential election
1908 **Oct Austria annexes Bosnia and Herzegovina**
1910 Japan annexes Korea
1911 Sep Italo-Turkish Tripolitanian War begins
Oct Winston Churchill appointed First Lord of the Admiralty
1912 Oct Montenegro declares war on Turkey. Bulgaria and Serbia mobilize their armies
Dec Armistice is secured
1913 Feb Outbreak of second Balkan War
Mar Woodrow Wilson wins US presidential election
1914 Peace treaty signed by Serbia and Turkey

Heavy artillery

WORLD WAR I 1900–19

Women in Industry poster

US recruitment poster

1915

Dec Germans take Lodz in Poland

1915 German airships bomb British ports in East Anglia. Turkish army attacks Suez Canal

Feb German blockade of Britain begins

Mar Battle at Neuve-Chapelle

Apr Initial landings at Gallipoli

Apr–May Second Battle of Ypres. **Germans use poison gas for first time**

May Sinking of Cunard liner *Lusitania* by German U-boat

Jun First Battle of Isonzo

Sep Battle of Loos. First Zeppelin attack on London. Czar Nicholas II takes over command of the Russian army. Dardanelles campaign begins. Anglo-French landings at Gallipoli

Oct Edith Cavell executed in Brussels

Dec Douglas Haig becomes British commander-in-chief in France. Russians forced back on Eastern front

1916

Jan First Zeppelin raid on Paris. Australian and New Zealand forces withdraw from Gallipoli

Feb Battles of Verdun

May Battle of Jutland; German fleet retreats. Sinn Fein Easter Rebellion in Dublin

July Battles of Somme. British take possession of the whole Sinai peninsula. Anzacs arrive in France

Aug Italy declares war on Germany

Sept British use tanks on Western Front

Dec Lloyd George becomes British prime minister. Germany sends peace note to Allies. T E Lawrence (of Arabia) appointed British political and liaison officer to Faisal's army

1917

Feb Germans withdraw on Western front. Bread rationed in Britain. General Pershing arrives in Paris to head American forces. Russian Black Sea fleet mutinies at Sebastopol

Apr US and Cuba declare war on Germany.

Jun British royal family renounces German names and titles. German aircraft attack London

Aug China declares war on Austria and Germany

Jul Third Battle of Ypres begins

WORLD WAR I 1900–19

Oct–Nov Italian army defeated at Caporetto

Nov British and US forces take Passchendaele to end Third Battle of Ypres. First tank battles take place at Cambrai. Revolution breaks out in Russia; Lenin appointed chief commissar

Dec US declares war on Hungary and Austria. German–Russian armistice signed at Brest Litovsk

1918 Jan President Wilson issues 14 point peace plan. Meat and butter rationed in London

Mar Transfer of Soviet government to Moscow. Germans bomb Paris

Jul Second Battle of Marne. Ex-Tsar Nicholas of Russia and family are executed in Russia

Sep Allied offensive on the Western Front opens

Oct Fall of Damascus. Turkish resistance crumbles in Palestine. **Germany sues for peace.** Germany suspends submarine warfare

Nov German fleet mutinies at Kiel. Republic declared in Bavaria. German republic proclaimed. **Allies at Versailles agree on peace terms for Germany signed Nov 11.** Revolution in Berlin. Kaiser Wilhelm abdicates and flees to Holland. Austria proclaims union with Germany

Dec President Wilson arrives in Paris for Peace Conference at Versailles

1919 Jan Peace conference opens at Versailles. National Socialist party founded in Germany

Feb First League of Nations meeting in Paris. Mussolini founds Fasci del Combattimento

Apr Habsburg dynasty exiled from Austria

Jun German peace treaty signed at Versailles. German fleet scuttled at Scapa Flow

Jul Blockade of Germany ended

German propaganda poster

9

Mussolini founds Fascism

CIS AND THE BALTIC STATES 1900–2004

Lenin leads the Russian Revolution

Joseph Stalin

Year	Event
1901	Social Revolutionary Party founded
1903–21	Pogroms in Russia
1904–05	Russo–Japanese War; Russia loses
1905–6	Abortive Russian Revolution. General strike. Mutiny on battleship *Potemkin*
1917 Mar	Revolution in Russia; Tsar abdicates
1917 Nov	"October Revolution;" Lenin appointed chief commissar. Trotsky commissar for foreign affairs. Counter-revolution led by Kerensky fails
1917–22	**Civil War.** Communists defeat anti-communist opponents
1918	Murder of Russian royal family
1919	Third International founded
1919–21	Russo–Polish War
1922	Stalin becomes general secretary of Communist Party
1923	**The USSR formally established**
1924 Jan	Death of Lenin; power struggle between Stalin and Trotsky begins
1927	Trotsky is expelled from the Party
1928–32	First Five-Year Plan to expand the economy. Wealthy peasantry persecuted
1928	Grain shortage. Stalin orders immediate agricultural collectivism
1929	Trotsky is deported
1932–33	Famine and punishment of peasants farming smallholdings; approximately 15 million die
1933–37	Second Five-Year Plan to produce consumer goods
1933–38	**Stalin's Great Terror purge**
1938–42	Third Five-Year Plan to produce armaments
1939	Stalin–Hitler non-aggression pact. Russo–Japanese Mongolian border war. USSR invades Finland, and is expelled from the League of Nations
1939–40	Russo-Finnish War
1940	Trotsky assassinated in Mexico on Stalin's orders. Russia annexes Baltic states
1941	**Germany invades USSR, breaking 1939 pact**
1942–43	Battle of Stalingrad leads to Russian victory in 1943
1945	Yalta conference between Roosevelt, Stalin, and Churchill
1946–47	**Cold War begins**
1949	USSR tests atomic bomb

World War II

CIS AND THE BALTIC STATES 1900–2004

Year		Event
1950		Sino-Soviet Treaty of Alliance
1953		Death of Stalin. Khrushchev becomes Party first secretary
1954		Malenkov premier of the USSR
1955		Bulganin succeeds Malenkov
1956		Russia invades Hungary. Khrushchev denounces Stalin at Party Congress
1958		Khrushchev succeeds as leader
1961		Kennedy–Khrushchev summit
1964		Khrushchev falls from power and Brezhnev is elected as Party leader
1968		Red Army invades Czechoslovakia
1973		Brezhnev–Nixon summit
1982		Brezhnev dies, replaced by Andropov
1984		Andropov dies, replaced by Chernenko
1985		Gorbachev becomes Soviet leader
1986		Nuclear accident at Chernobyl. **Gorbachev begins policies of perestroika (reconstruction) and glasnost (openness)**
1987	Mar	US–USSR arms reduction treaty
1988	May	Troops impose curfew in Azerbaijan
		USSR withdraws from Afghanistan
	Oct	Latvia and Lithuania demand self-rule
1990	Nov	Estonia insists on sovereignty
	Jan	Azerbaijan erupts in violence
	Mar	Lithuania declares independence
	May	Yeltsin elected Russian president
	Jul	Yeltsin quits the Communist Party
1991	Jan	Soviet troops sent to Lithuania and Latvia
	Dec	**End of USSR. Eleven republics form Commonwealth of Independent States (CIS)**
1992		**Formal end of cold war.** Russia adopts drastic economic reforms
1993		Coup against Yeltsin defeated
1994		Chechenia declares independence. Russian troops sent; fighting starts
1996	Jul	Yeltsin re-elected. Chechenia peace agreement; troops pull out
1998	Mar	Yeltsin sacks his government
1999	Oct	Russian troops enter Chechenia
2000	Mar	Vladimir Putin becomes Russian president
2003	Nov	Eduard Shevardnadze resigns as Georgian president after protests
2004	May	Estonia, Latvia and Lithuania join European Union
	Dec	Protests in Ukraine result in election as president of Viktor Yushchenko

Hungarian resistance to Soviet forces

9

Gagarin first man to orbit Earth

Nuclear warning at Chernobyl

THE 1930s

Economic
depression

Japan invades
China

The Long March
in China

Italy occupies
Ethiopia

1929 Oct Wall Street Crash leads to world-wide economic depression

1930
Mar Gandhi begins campaign of civil disobedience in India

Apr Ras Tafari becomes Emperor Haile Selassie of Ethiopia. Amy Johnson first woman to fly solo UK–Australia

Jun Last French troops leave Rhineland

Aug First major Arab–Jewish conflict in Palestine

Sep German elections; National Socialists emerge as major political force

1931 Japan invades Manchuria

1932 Series of inconclusive elections in Germany

Jan Japanese occupy Shanghai

May French Prime Minister Doumer assassinated

1933 Jan Hitler appointed Chancellor of Germany

Feb Parliament building (Reichstag) burned

Mar Roosevelt becomes US president. Boycott of Jewish businesses in Germany begins

Jun Roosevelt launches "New Deal" to help US economy

Aug First Nazi concentration camps

Dec Prohibition laws repealed in USA

1934 Feb Civil war in Austria

May Mazaryk elected Czech president

Jun "Night of the Long Knives;" SS units used by Hitler to eliminate opposition. Hitler and Mussolini meet in Venice

Jul Nazi revolt in Austria

Aug Hitler assumes title of Führer (leader)

Sep USSR joins League of Nations

Oct Mao Zedong leads "Long March"

1935 Apr Dust storms hit US "breadbasket" states. Hitler announces German rearmament, in defiance of League of Nations

Oct Italy invades Ethiopia. Haile Selassie flees to French Somaliland

Dec Chiang Kai-shek elected president of Chinese Executive

1936 Mar Nazi troops enter Rhineland

Jul Spanish civil war begins between Franco's Fascists and Republican forces

THE 1930s

May Nazi revolt in Brazil is suppressed

Sep Chamberlain meets Hitler at Munich Conference. Germans and British sign agreement handing the Czech Sudetenland to Germany. Failed Nazi plot in Chile

Oct Hitler invades Czechoslovakia. Panic in USA as Orson Welles broadcasts *War of the Worlds*

Nov "Kristallnacht" pogroms throughout Germany. Japan withdraws from League of Nations

1939 Jan Atomic fission achieved

Mar Spanish Civil War ends. Franco takes control. Annihilation of Czechoslovakian state

Apr Italy annexes Albania

May Spain withdraws from League of Nations

Sep Germany invades Poland; World War II begins

Spanish Civil War

9

Adolf Hitler

Nov General Franco's Fascist government receives recognition from Hitler and Mussolini.

Aug Olympic Games held in Berlin as showcase for Aryan supremacy. Black American Jesse Owens dominates athletics events

Oct Franco appointed chief of Spanish nation

Nov Rome–Berlin axis formed

Dec Abdication of King Edward VIII

1937 Jan Show trials in USSR, as Stalin purges political opponents

Apr Franco's army destroys town of Guernica

May Giant airship, the *Hindenburg*, explodes as it tries to land in New Jersey. Egypt joins League of Nations

Aug Japanese take Beijing

Sep Armies of Chiang Kai-shek and Mao Zedong join to combat Japanese

Nov Japanese capture Shanghai

1938 Mar Germany annexes Austria. Mexico seizes US and British oil fields

Germany invades Poland

WORLD WAR II 1935–45

US Neutrality
Act

Nazi occupation
of Bosnia
Herzegovina

Britain prepares
for gas warfare

1935 Hitler announces German rearmament

1936 Germany occupies demilitarized Rhineland

1938 German troops enter Austria, which is declared part of Germany

Aug Germany mobilizes

Sep British premier Neville Chamberlain returns from Munich with a peace accord to avoid Czech crisis

Oct German troops enter Sudeten territory in Czechoslovakia

Nov Pogroms throughout Germany

1939 Mar Germany annihilates Czechoslovakian state and renounces naval agreement with Britain

Apr Italy annexes Albania. Japan occupies Hainan. US renounces Japanese trade agreement. Hitler denounces non-aggression pact with Poland.

Aug Hitler–Stalin non-aggression pact

Sep Germany invades Poland. Britain and France declare war on Germany. **World War II begins.** USSR invades Poland from the east; also invades Finland

Dec Battle of River Plate; German *Graf Spee* is scuttled. Roosevelt declares US neutral

1940 Mar Finland surrenders territory to USSR after 14-week war

Apr Germany invades Denmark and Norway. Italy declares war on France and Britain. Hitler names Hermann Goering reichs-marschall

May Germany invades Belgium, the Netherlands, and Luxembourg

May–Jun British forces evacuated from Dunkirk. Germany occupies the Channel Islands

Jun Germans enter Paris. Marshall Pétain concludes armistice with Germany

Aug Battle of Britain

Sep Daytime bombing of London and SE Britain begins. Italy advances into Egypt but is forced to retreat

Oct Night-time bombing of Britain. War spreads to North Africa. Roosevelt re-elected US president

Sep–Nov Blitz on London

1941 Feb Rommel arrives in North Africa

WORLD WAR II 1935–45

Apr British take control of Iraq
Apr–May British invade Ethiopia and Abyssinia
Jun Germany invades USSR. Blitz on Coventry, Britain. Rommel attacks Tobruk. Allies take Lebanon and Syria
Apr Greece falls to Germany
May Germans invade Crete
Aug Allies control Iran
Sep Siege of Leningrad begins
Dec **Japan bombs Pearl Harbor.** US and Britain declare war on Japan. Germany and Italy declare war on the USA. China enters war on the side of the Allies. Japan occupies Thailand, invades Philippines and Malaya, and takes Hong Kong
1942 Jan **Under Hitler, Germany embarks on the "Final Solution" – the systematic removal of Jews, gypsies, homosexuals, communists, and dissidents.** Japan takes Manila
Feb Japan invades Burma and

Singapore surrenders
Mar Japan invades Dutch East Indies. British bomb Lübeck and Cologne. US bombs Tokyo
May Americans win Battle of Coral Sea
Jun **Battle of Midway Island stops Japanese eastward expansion.** Rommel takes Tobruk. Battle of El Alamein; Rommel defeated by Montgomery
Aug Battle of Guadalcanal; US raid on Japanese-occupied Solomon Islands
Sep Battle of Stalingrad begins
Sep–Oct Germany launches V2 rocket
1943 Jan First daytime bombing of Berlin
Feb Russian victory at Stalingrad. Battle of the Atlantic; German U-boats defeated
Apr Massacre in Warsaw ghetto
Jul Allies land in Sicily. Mussolini overthrown and anti-fascist Badoglio takes over
Sep US troops invade Italian mainland. **Italian armistice signed** American landings in Bay of Salerno

Battle of Britain

9

Pearl Harbor

Anti-semitic propaganda

WORLD WAR II 1935–45

US bomber

Battle of
Iwo Jima, 1945

Formation of
the United
Nations

1943 Oct Italy declares war on Germany. US forces regain control of islands in Pacific. Russians cross Dnieper River and retake Smolensk

Nov Russians retake Kiev. Allied "round-the-clock" bombing of Germany begins

1944 Jun D-Day Normandy landings. Strategic bombing of Japan begins

Jul Assassination attempt on Hitler fails

Jul–Aug British and North American troops take northern France

Aug German armies driven from Soviet Union. Paris falls to Allies

Sep Soviet armistice with Romania and Finland. Battle of Arnhem. Bulgaria declares war on Germany. Germans evacuate Greece. German frontier crossed

Oct Battle of Leyte Gulf; Japanese fleet decisively defeated. Soviet troops invade Germany. Moscow conference between Churchill and Stalin

Dec Battle of the Bulge. **Yalta Conference between**

Churchill, Roosevelt, and Stalin. President Roosevelt dies; succeeded by Truman

1945 Jan Soviet troops invade Poland, Austria, and Hungary and enter Czechoslovakia

Jan–May Allies regain Burma

Feb Allies reconquer Manila

Apr Mussolini executed. Vienna liberated

Apr Hitler commits suicide

May Germany surrenders

May Berlin falls to Soviet troops

May–Jun Allies take possession of Borneo

June Allies regain Philippines. United Nations charter signed

Aug US drops atomic bombs on Hiroshima and Nagasaki. Japan formally surrenders. Nuremberg war criminal trials begin

1946 Oct First Nazi war criminals sentenced at Nuremburg trials. Goering and 10 others sentenced to death; Hess sentenced to life imprisonment. Goering commits suicide

AFRICA 1940–2004

Apartheid in
South Africa

9

Kenyan
independence
demonstrations

Togo gains
independence

Algerians fight for
independence

1941 British take Italian East Africa

1942 Battle of El Alamein

1950 **Population Registration Act
in South Africa classifies
people by race**

1951 Libyan independence

1952 Eritrea comes under Ethiopian rule

1952 Oct Mau Mau-instigated violence
begins. Kenyan government
declares state of emergency

1953 Mar Massacre at Lari in Rift Valley turns
opinion against Mau Mau

1953–55 Serious anti-French rioting in
Morocco

1954–62 **Algerian War.** A nationalist revolt
against French rule, ending in
Algerian independence

1956 Sudan, Morocco and Tunisia gain
independence

1956–7 **Suez Crisis.** Egypt nationalizes
Suez Canal, followed by invasion by
Israel and Anglo-French military
intervention. UN sends in peace-
keeping forces.

1957 Ghana becomes first black African
country to gain independence

1958 Guinea gains independence

1960 Kenyan state of emergency lifted.
Western Sahara made a province
of Spain. Benin, Cameroon, Central
African Republic, Chad, Congo,
Gabon, Ivory Coast, Madagascar,
Mali, Mauritania, Niger, Nigeria,
Senegal, Somalia, Togo, Upper
Volta, and Zaire gain independence

**Mar Sharpeville riots in South
Africa;** 67 people die; widespread
condemnation of South Africa

1961 UN general assembly condemns
apartheid. Sierra Leone, Tanganyika,
and Zanzibar gain independence.
South Africa leaves Commonwealth

1962 Algeria, Burundi, Rwanda, and
Uganda win independence

1963 Kenya gains independence.
Organization of African Unity
founded

1964 **Nelson Mandela and other
African National Congress and
Pan-African Congress leaders
given life sentences.**
Malawi and Zambia gain
independence. Tanganyika and
Zanzibar unite to form Tanzania

AFRICA 1940–2004

Nigerian
Civil War

Ethiopia suffers
drought and
civil war

1965	Gambia becomes independent
1966	Botswana and Lesotho gain independence
1967 May	Conflict in Nigeria leads to secession of Biafra and civil war
1968	Equatorial Guinea, Mauritius, and Swaziland gain independence
1969	Military officers led by Colonel Gaddafi overthrow king in Libya
1970 Jan	Nigerian civil war ends
1971 Jan	Major-General Idi Amin seizes power in Uganda
1974	Haile Selassie, emperor of Ethiopia, is deposed. Guinea Bissau gains independence
1975	Suez Canal reopens. Partition of Western Sahara between Morocco and Mauritania. Angola, Cape Verde, Comoros, Mozambique, and São Tomé and Principe gain independence
1976	Invasion of Uganda by dissident Ugandans and Tanzanians
1977	Djibouti gains independence
1977–78	Ogaden War between Somalia and Ethiopia
1979	Mauritania withdraws from Western Sahara which comes under Moroccan occupation
1980	White-minority rule ends in Rhodesia – renamed Zimbabwe
1981	President Sadat of Egypt is assassinated
early 1980s	**Severe drought in Africa; Ethiopia devastated**
1984	Western countries begin airlift to relieve famine
1986	South African government declares state of emergency. US air force bombs Libya
1987	Chad defeats Libya
1988 Apr	Sudanese refugees flee to Ethiopia, worsening situation
June	Two million black workers in South Africa strike in protest against apartheid
Aug	South African and Cuban troops withdraw from Angola
1990	UN cuts aid to refugees because of Ethiopia–Somalia War
Feb	**Nelson Mandela released after 26 years in prison**
	Mandela and de Klerk begin talks
1991 Mar	Severe famine in Sudan

AFRICA 1940–2004

May Violent clashes in South African townships between ANC and Zulu Inkatha supporters.

Jun South Africa repeals all apartheid laws

Jul US ends economic sanctions of South Africa

Nov Violent clashes break out in Somalia

1992
Jan Algeria's president forced to resign

Apr UN air embargo on Libya starts

Jun 39 die in Zulu Inkatha movement attack on ANC squatter camp

Oct Renewed violence in Angola

Dec US forces sent to Somalia to ensure food deliveries

1993 May Eritrea independent from Ethiopia

1994 Mar Peace agreement in Somalia. US troops withdraw

Apr Genocide in Rwanda. ANC wins first majority elections in South Africa; Nelson Mandela becomes president

Jun Agreement to end Djibouti civil war

Oct Peace agreement in Angola

1995 Feb UN troops withdrawn from Somalia

Apr Escalating violence in Burundi

Oct Nigerian military rule extended for three years. Comoros coup fails.

Nov Ken Saro-Wiwa and eight other Ogoni activists executed in Nigeria

Dec Eritrea and Yemen clash over Red Sea islands

1996 Jan Coups in Niger and Sierra Leone.

Mar-Apr Violence in Liberian capital, Monrovia

Apr Sanctions imposed on Nigeria

Oct Rebellion in Eastern Zaire sparks humanitarian crisis. Zaire and Rwanda brought to brink of war

1997 Algeria racked with violence by Islamic extremists. Thousands die

May Mobutu regime in Zaire collapses.

Nov 70 tourists and police massacred by Islamic militant group in Luxor, Egypt

1998 May Eritrea and Ethiopia go to war over disputed border region

1999 Jun Thabo Mbeki succeeds Nelson Mandela as South African president

2002 Mar Zimbabwe suspended from the Commonwealth following intimidation in presidential elections

2003 Aug Charles Taylor, president of Liberia, forced out in civil war

2004 May Peace deal between Sudan rebels and government after 21-year war

Assassination of President Sadat of Egypt

HOW LONG MUST WE KEEP ON DYING IN THIS WAY?

Appeals against apartheid

9

Civil war in Mozambique

Algerian civil conflict

THE COLD WAR 1945–92

MARSHALLPLAN

Marshall Plan aids Europe

Czechoslovakia invaded by Soviet troops

British Bloodhound missile

1945 USSR occupies eastern Germany

1946–47 Cold War begins

1946 USSR organizes Communist governments in Bulgaria and Romania

1947 Marshall Aid Plan (US funding for West European reconstruction). Communists take control in Hungary

1948 Communists take full control of Czechoslovakia. Communist coup in Poland. **Berlin Blockade and Airlift.** USSR helps set up North Korean "people's republic"

1949 **COMECON (Council for Mutual Aid and Assistance) set up.**
Apr North Atlantic Treaty Organization (NATO) formed

May Federal Republic of Germany formed

Aug USSR tests atomic bomb

Oct Communist Democratic Republic of Germany formed. People's Republic of China proclaimed

1950–53 Korean War

1950 North Korea invades South Korea. McCarran Act in the USA calls for severe restrictions against communists. Friendship Treaty signed between US and USSR. China enters Korean War in support of North Korea

1952 Aug 16,000 people escape from East to West Berlin

Nov US tests its first hydrogen bomb

1953 Khrushchev becomes Communist Party first secretary

Jan McCarthy becomes chairman of US Senate Subcommittee on Investigations

Aug USSR sets off its first hydrogen bomb

1954 Sep US and seven other nations sign Southeast Asia Collective Defense Treaty to prevent further communism spreading

1955 Warsaw Pact signed between East European communist countries

1956 Nov Russia invades Hungary

1957 Jun USSR launches Sputnik 1 satellite

1958 Jan US launches its first satellite

1960 U2 spy plane affair as a US plane is shot down in USSR. USSR withdraws aid to China. Fidel

THE COLD WAR 1945–92

1961
Castro's government in Cuba becomes openly communist

Jan US ends diplomatic relations with Cuba

Apr Bay of Pigs incident (US-sponsored invasion of Cuba fails)

Jun Kennedy–Khrushchev summit in Vienna to discuss disarmament

Aug Berlin Wall built

Sep US and USSR resume nuclear testing

1962
USSR, agrees to send arms to Cuba. **Cuban missile crisis** (USSR agrees not to base nuclear weapons in Cuba)

1963
Jul Nuclear testing ban is signed by US, USSR, and Great Britain

Aug US and USSR agree on "hot line" from White House to the Kremlin

1964–75
Vietnam War (US involved 1965–73)

1967
Jun China explodes its first hydrogen bomb. US and USSR discuss disarmament

1968
Warsaw Pact countries invade Czechoslovakia

1969
US and USSR begin SALT (Strategic Arms Limitation Talks)

1972
US president Nixon visits USSR for SALT I treaty. Nixon visits China

1973
Brezhnev–Nixon summit

1973–75
Helsinki Conference helps reduce East–West tension

1977
US reveals neutron bomb

1979
US–USSR SALT II treaty

1979–80
Soviet troops invade Afghanistan

1982
US and USSR START (Strategic Arms Reduction Talks) commence

1985
Gorbachev becomes Soviet leader

1986
Reagan–Gorbachev summit in Iceland

1987
INF (Intermediate Nuclear Forces) Treaty

1988
USSR withdraws from Afghanistan

1990
East and West Germany are reunited

1991
Jul Warsaw Pact dissolved

Dec Formation of Commonwealth of Independent States to replace USSR. Effective end of Cold War

1992
Yeltsin and Bush declare formal end of Cold War

American ICBM

9

Campaigns for nuclear disarmament

THE USA 1945–2004

Neil Armstrong is the first man on the Moon

Martin Luther King assassinated

John F. Kennedy assassinated

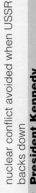

Racial conflict in Arkansas

1945 Apr Roosevelt dies; Vice-president Truman takes over

Aug World War II ends after atomic bombs dropped on Hiroshima and Nagasaki, Japan

1945 Sep US forces enter Korea

1947 Jun US launches Marshall Plan to pay for the reconstruction of Europe

1950 US intervention against communist North Korea.

1954 May Racial segregation in schools ruled unconstitutional by Supreme Court

1955 Black community leaders killed. Racial segregation in public life ruled unconstitutional

1957–58 Schools desegregation leads to civil unrest and use of National Guard

1959–60 US imposes trade embargo on Cuba after leader Batista ousted by Fidel Castro

1960 US spy plane shot down by USSR

1961 CIA-backed invasion of Cuba by exiles ends in Bay of Pigs defeat

1962 Oct US and USSR have massive stand-off over nuclear build-up in Cuba; nuclear conflict avoided when USSR backs down

1963 Nov President Kennedy assassinated. Alleged assassin, Lee Harvey Oswald, assassinated. Civil rights movement grows

1964 Race riots flare. US intervention in Vietnam War begins

1965–67 Escalation of US involvement in Vietnam includes bombing raids. Opposition to involvement grows Opposition to Vietnam War grows

1968 Apr Civil rights leader Martin Luther King assassinated. Widespread rioting follows

Jun Presidential candidate Robert Kennedy assassinated

1969 Jul Withdrawal from Vietnam begins Neil Armstrong becomes first man on moon

1972 Feb China visited by President Nixon. Bombing in Vietnam resumes

1973 Ceasefire in Vietnam and evacuation of troops. Oil crisis as Arabs ban sales to US

1974 Aug Nixon resigns as a result of Watergate scandal

THE USA 1945–2004

1979 US stops support for Nicaragua. American hostages taken in Iran

1980 Attempt to rescue hostages a fiasco; President Carter loses support

1981 Mar Assassination attempt on President Reagan. Hostages released

1983 Marines killed in Iran. Invasion of Grenada

1985 Trade ban imposed on Nicaragua. US and USSR begin arms reduction negotiations

1986 Libyan missile attack on US frigate *Stark*, killing 37. Military strikes launched in retaliation. US troops in Bolivia. Iran-Contra scandal

1987 Wall Street slump triggers international economic downturn. US–USSR arms limitation agreement

1988 Jul Iranian civil aircraft shot down, killing 290 people. Further arms treaties signed with USSR

1989 US invades Panama to overthrow president Manuel Noriega

1991 Jan US leads the UN's Desert Storm operation against Iraq, after the invasion of Kuwait

1992 Apr Riots in Los Angeles
Dec US intervenes in Somalia

1993 Jan Bill Clinton inaugurated as president
Jun US launches missiles on Baghdad

1994 Feb Trade embargo on Vietnam lifted
Mar US troops withdrawn from Somalia
Sep US intervention in Haiti to reinstate President Aristide

1995 Apr Oklahoma City bombing kills 168
Nov Bosnian peace agreement signed at Dayton, Ohio. Clinton visits Ireland to promote the peace process

1996 Nov Clinton re-elected for second term

1998 Jan Extra US troops sent to Gulf during Iraq weapons inspection crisis

2000 Dec George W. Bush elected president

2001 Sep Al-Qaeda terrorists crash airliners into World Trade Center and Pentagon. Another hijacked plane crashes near Pittsburgh
Oct US declares 'War on Terror' and leads invasion of Afghanistan

2003 Mar US leads invasion of Iraq
Dec Iraqi dictator Saddam Hussein captured by US troops

2004 Nov Bush re-elected president

Wall Street slump

US troops intervene in Somalia

Oklahoma City bombing

Destruction of the World Trade Center

THE MIDDLE EAST 1914–2005

State of Israel
formed

Suez crisis

Yasser Arafat

1916	Arab revolt against Turks
1917	Balfour Declaration promises
	Zionists a national home in Palestine
1919–23	**Ottoman Empire collapses**
1923	Turkey declares a republic
1926	Lebanese republic established
1932	Iraq becomes independent
1944	Syria becomes independent
1946	Jordan becomes independent
1948 May	**State of Israel created**
1948–49	First Arab–Israeli War
1956	Egypt seize the Suez Canal.Britain, France and Israel invade the canal region. Second Arab–Israeli War; Israel occupies the Gaza Strip
1961	Ben-Gurion forms a new coalition government
1962–70	Yemen Civil War; monarchy overthrown
1967	**Six-Day War.** Israel reoccupies the Gaza Strip and also the Golan Heights and West Bank. South Yemen becomes independent
1969	Yasser Arafat is elected the leader of the Palestinian Liberation Organization. Golda Meir becomes Israel's fourth prime minister
1971	Bahrain, Qatar, and the United Arab Emirates gain independence
1973	Fourth Arab–Israeli war. Arab oil embargo
1974	Turkey invades and partitions Cyprus
1977	President Sadat of Egypt visits Israel to offer peace
1978	Begin and Sadat share Nobel Peace Prize
1979	**Iranian revolution.** Ayatollah Khomeini gains power after shah flees the country. Israeli–Egyptian Peace Treaty signed. USSR invades Afghanistan
1979–81	US–Iranian crisis over US embassy siege
1980	US–Iranian hostage rescue fiasco. Iran–Iraq War begins. Iraq invades
1981	Sadat assassinated
1982	Israel invades Lebanon. Iran invades Iraq
1983	247 US marines and 58 French troops killed by a car bomb in Lebanon. Arafat expelled from Syria
1984	Multinational peace-keeping corps withdraws from Lebanon

THE MIDDLE EAST 1914–2005

US General Norman Schwartzkopf

9

Saddam Hussein

1985		Israelis leave Lebanon
1988		US bombs Iran oil base. Iraq attacks tankers at Iranian oil terminal. End of Iran–Iraq War after Iran accepts UN peace terms. USSR withdraws from Afghanistan
1990	May	North and South Yemen unite
	Aug	Iraqi forces attack Kuwait
1991		US–Iraq peace talks fail.
	Feb	**Operation Desert Storm commences Gulf War. Saddam sets Kuwait oil wells ablaze. Land war begins. Allies defeat Iraqi forces**
	Jul	Lebanese army attacks PLO
	Oct	Arab–Israeli peace talks in Madrid
	Dec	Many Kurd refugees die during winter, unable to return to Iraq after supporting Allies in Gulf War.
1992	Jun	Rabin elected Israeli prime minister
	Nov	Israeli tanks move into Lebanon after Hezbollah attacks on towns
1993	Jul	Iraq accepts UN weapons monitoring after US military attacks.
	Sep	Arafat and Rabin agree on self-government for Gaza Strip and West Bank. PLO ends armed struggle
1994	Feb	Hebron Mosque massacre
	Apr–Jul	North Yemen wins Yemeni civil war
	Oct	Israel and Jordan sign peace treaty
	Nov	Iraq recognizes Kuwait
1995	Nov	Yitzhak Rabin, Israeli prime minister, assassinated
1996	Sep	Taliban militia takes Afghan capital
1997	Jul/ Sep	Many killed by suicide bombs in centre of Jerusalem
1998	Aug	Iraq stops cooperating with UN weapons inspectors
	Dec	US air strikes on Iraq
2001	Feb	Sharon elected Israeli prime minister
	Oct	Taliban and Al-Qaeda forces in Afghanistan attacked by US and British forces
2003	**Mar**	**Iraq invaded by US and British forces but with no UN mandate**
	Dec	Iraqi leader Saddam Hussein captured by US forces
2004	Apr	Israel announces unilateral withdrawal from West Bank
2005	Aug	Israel begins withdrawal from Gaza strip

SOUTH AND EAST ASIA 1940–2004

Japanese occupy Burma

Formation of the People's Republic of China

Taiwan becomes an independent nation

Korean War

1941 Japan takes Hong Kong, Thailand, and Malaya

1942 Japan takes Singapore and Burma

1944 **Independent republic of Vietnam formed.** Ho Chi Minh is president

1945 **Atomic bombs dropped on Japanese cities of Hiroshima and Nagasaki; end of World War II, Japan surrenders.** Chinese Civil War begins

1946 The Philippines become independent

1947 Aug **India gains independence. State of Pakistan created**

1948 Communists capture Manchuria. USSR sets up communist rule in North Korea. Soviet troops withdraw

Jan Burma gains independence. Mahatma Gandhi assassinated in India

Aug South Korea gains independence

1948–60 Malayan emergency

1949 USA withdraws troops from South Korea. **Communists control China** Chiang Kai-shek resigns as president of China and Chinese nationalists flee to Taiwan

Oct Chinese People's Republic formally proclaimed

Dec Indonesia becomes independent Republic of Indonesia proclaimed. North Korean forces invade South Korea. China occupies Tibet

1950

1950–53 **Korean War**

1953 Vietnamese rebels attack Laos

1954 French defeat at Dien Bien Phu. Indochina split into North and South Vietnam, Cambodia, and Laos. Communists occupy Hanoi

1957 Aug Malaya given independence

1963 Malaya expanded to form Malaysia

1965–75 **Vietnam War between communist north and non-communist south**

1965 US ground troops enter Vietnam War. Singapore given independence

1966–77 **China's Cultural Revolution**

1968 North Vietnam launches Tet Offensive

1970 US troops enter Cambodia

1971 India and Pakistan go to war over East Pakistan (Bangladesh)

1972 Jan State of Bangladesh established

Feb US president Nixon visits China.

SOUTH AND EAST ASIA 1940–2004

1973 Jan Ferdinand Marcos declares martial law in the Philippines. Ceasefire and withdrawal of US forces from Vietnam agreed

1974 May India tests its first nuclear bomb

1975 **Khmer Rouge take Phnom Penh.** Cambodia becomes known as Kampuchea. Communist forces overrun South Vietnam. Immediate pulling out of all US troops

1976 Formal reunification of Vietnam. Death of Mao Zedong

1978 Vietnam invades Kampuchea, ending Pol Pot's regime

1979 China invades Vietnam

1980 Trial of Gang of Four in China

1983 Aug Benigno Aquino killed in Philippines

1984 Jun Indian troops storm the Golden Temple, holy to Sikhs, in Amritsar

Oct Indian Prime Minister, Indira Gandhi, assassinated

Dec Chemical plant leak in Bhopal, central India, kills thousands

1986 President Marcos exiled; Corazon Aquino succeeds in Philippines

1989 Jun Pro-democracy students killed in Tiananmen Square, Beijing, China

1990 May Aung San Suu Kyi wins elections in Burma but kept under house arrest

1991 Jan Thai army stages coup

Apr Peace talks begin in Cambodia

1992 May Clashes between army and pro-democracy movement in Thailand.

1993 May General elections in Cambodia and coalition government formed

1994 Jul North Korean leader, Kim Il Sung, dies. Khmer Rouge banned in Cambodia after peace talks fail

1996 Jan Massive Tamil bombing in Colombo

1997 Feb Deng Xiaoping, China's leader, dies

Jul Hong Kong handed back to China

1998 Apr Pol Pot, Khmer Rouge leader, dies.

May President Suharto of Indonesia resigns after mass protests

1999 Aug East Timor votes for independence from Indonesia.

2000 May Former Indonesian president Suharto arrested for corruption

2002 May East Timor established as a new nation

Oct Al-Qaeda terrorist bombs kill 202 on Indonesian island of Bali

2004 Dec Tsunami kills more than 250,000 in Indonesia, Thailand and across the Indian Ocean

Vietnam War

9

Pol Pot

Aung San
Suu Kyi

EUROPE 1970–2005

Civil unrest in
Northern Ireland

Margaret
Thatcher

Polish trade
union banner

Berlin Wall
dismantled

1972 Jan 'Bloody Sunday' shootings in Ulster
Aug–Sep The 18th Olympic games held in Munich; Israeli athletes murdered by terrorists
1973 Britain, Ireland, Denmark join EEC
1974 Revolution in Portugal led by military initiates democratic reforms
1975 Juan Carlos becomes first King of Spain for 44 years, after General Franco's death
1978 John Paul becomes first Polish Pope.
Nov In Spain, right-wing army officers attempt coup
1979 Margaret Thatcher becomes first woman prime minister in Europe
1980 **Polish trade union Solidarity founded**
May **President Tito of Yugoslavia dies.**
Aug Solidarity gains major concessions from Polish government
Major demonstrations calling for nuclear disarmament
1981 Feb Right-wing forces attempt coup in Spain; MPs held hostage
May Francois Mitterrand elected

president of France.
Dec Polish reforms reversed; martial law imposed
1982 Apr–Jun Britain goes to war with Argentina over the Falkland Islands
Oct A socialist government is voted into office in Spain
1985 Jul Live Aid concert takes place to raise money for African famine victims
1986 Spain and Portugal join the EEC
Feb Olof Palme, Swedish prime minister, murdered
1987 Mar 184 die in Zeebrugge ferry disaster
Mrs Thatcher wins third general election in Britain
Oct Stockmarket crashes in US and London trigger European recession
1988 Dec US airliner crashes onto Scottish town of Lockerbie after mid-air explosion
1989 Apr Polish Solidarity movement legalised
Sep Hungary opens borders to East German refugees
Oct Ruling Communist party in Hungary dissolves itself
Nov East German leader and Politburo resign. **Berlin Wall opened.** Czech leader and Politburo resign;

EUROPE 1970–2005

non-communist government formed

Dec Civil war in Romania; President Ceausescu executed

1990 Jan Yugoslavia allows new political parties. German unification treaty is ratified

Oct East and West Germany reunited

Dec Lech Walesa elected Polish president

1991 Mar Anti-communist protests in Yugoslavia

Jun Slovenia and Croatia declare independence

1992 May UN imposes sanctions on Serbia

Jul UN forces control Sarajevo airport

Aug–Nov Racist violence in eastern Germany

1993 Jan Czechoslovakia splits into Czech Republic and Slovakia

Mar Bosnians accept UN peace plan

Apr IRA bomb damages City of London

May Bosnian Serbs reject UN peace plan

1994 Mar Far-right-wing election win in Italy

Jul IRA announces ceasefire

1995 Sep NATO bombing of Bosnian Serbs transforms balance of power

Nov Dayton agreement on peace in Bosnia. US troops arrive in Bosnia

1996 Feb IRA abandons ceasefire, bombing London's Canary Wharf complex

Sep Elections held in Bosnia

1997 Feb Civil unrest sparked off in Albania

May Labour party wins general election in Britain by huge majority

Jul Large protests in Spain after ETA murders. IRA restores ceasefire in Northern Ireland

Aug Death of Diana, Princess of Wales

1998 Serious unrest in Kosovo

Apr Peace agreement reached in Northern Ireland talks

1999 Mar NATO launches air strikes on Serbia to force President Milosevic to cease hostilities in Kosovo

Jun Milosevic accepts Kosovo peace deal

Aug Massive earthquake in western Turkey

Oct Milosevic overthrown in Yugoslavia

2000 Jan Euro currency introduced in 12 European countries

2002 Feb Milosevic war crimes trial opens in The Hague

2003 Mar Zoran Djindjic, Serbian prime minister, assassinated

2004 Mar Al-Qaeda terrorists attack Madrid trains killing more than 200

May Ten countries join the EU, bringing the total to 25

2005 Jul Suicide bombers target London transport system. Over 50 killed

Princess Diana dies

Slobodan Milosevic

New European currency

The European Union in 2005

ORIGIN AND SIZE

How the Universe came about is a mystery. However, many scientists today accept the "Big Bang" theory which suggests that the Universe started with a huge explosion in which matter was created and scattered through space, which was also created. This produced atomic particles which turned into the hydrogen atoms that now make up 90 per cent of the Universe. The hydrogen cloud expanded and then broke up into separate clouds forming galaxies of stars like our own Milky Way galaxy.

Age and size

Research proves that the Universe is still expanding. It might do so forever or eventually collapse inward. Astronomers believe that the Universe is 13,000 million to 14,000 million years old.

Measuring space

No one knows how large the Universe is, but ways have been devised to measure distance and space. For example, based on the Earth's orbit: a light year (ly) is the distance light travels at a speed of 186,282 miles per second (mi/s) or 299,792.458 km/s through space every year. An astronomical unit (au) is the distance between the Earth and the Sun. A par sec (pc) is the distance at which a base line of 1 au in length subtends an angle of 1 second.

```
1 au = 93,000,000 mi = 149,600,000 km
1 ly = 5,878,000,000,000 mi = 9,460,500,000,000 km
1 pc = 19,174,000,000,000 mi = 30,857,200,000,000 km
1 ly = 63,240 au
1 pc = 206,265 au = 3.262 ly
```

The scale of the Universe is enormous. The diagram opposite illustrates this fact. Each of the cubes has sides 100 times longer than the previous cube.

Big Bang theory states that the Universe has expanded from a single point in space and time

1 Cube side 950 au (0.015 ly)
Contains the entire Solar System.

2 Cube side 1.5 ly
This is the whole Solar System surrounded by Oort clouds of comets believed to be the original source of comets which pass through the Solar System. It surrounds the Sun at about a distance of 40,000 au (2–3 ly).

3 Cube side 150 ly
The Solar System and the nearer stars.

4 Cube side 15,000 ly
This contains the nearer spiral arms of our galaxy.

10

5 Cube side 1.5 million ly
This comprises the whole of our galaxy, Large and Small Magellanic Clouds, and nearby galaxies in the Local Group.

6 Cube side 150 million ly
This contains the whole of the Local Group and the Pisces, Cancer, and Virgo clusters of galaxies.

7 Cube side 1.5 billion ly
This holds all the known clusters and super clusters of galaxies and all other known objects in space. This is the limit of our current knowledge of the Universe.

GALAXIES AND STARS
Galaxies

Galaxies are giant groups of stars, planets, gas, dust, and nebulae that form "islands" in space. Over 1 billion galaxies have been detected and some have measured from 1000 ly to 10 million ly across.
Galaxies are classified by their shape

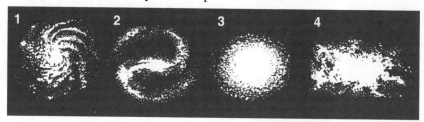

1 Spiral galaxies Our galaxy, the Milky Way, is a spiral galaxy with arms wrapped around its nucleus, or centre. It takes about 225 million years to spin round once.

2 Barred spiral A barred spiral has a short bar, into which most of its stars are concentrated, and arms emerging from opposite ends. Nearly 30 per cent of galaxies are spirals or barred spirals.

3 Elliptical galaxy These galaxies do not have spiral arms. They are shaped mainly like a huge ball, either spherical or very flattened like a rugby ball.

4 Irregular These galaxies have no particular shape and only make up 10 per cent of galaxies.

What are stars?

Stars are beaming spheres of gas. Deep inside them heat is created when hydrogen is turned into helium. Like the Sun, many stars shine continuously for thousands of millions of years before they fade.

Celestial poles

On Earth we have a North and a South Pole and in space there are equivalents called the North and South Celestial Poles. The Earth's axis joins the North and South Poles and if it was extended it would point to the North and South Celestial Poles.

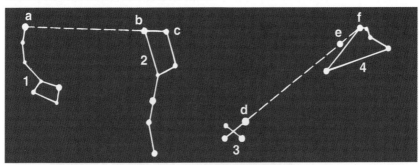

10

North Celestial Pole

In the diagram the North Celestial Pole is roughly marked by the star Polaris (**a**) in the constellation Ursa Minor (**1**). Polaris is only a short distance from the true pole. To find Polaris we find Ursa Major (**2**) and extend the imaginary line joining two stars known as the Pointers (**b**, **c**).

South Celestial Pole

No star marks the South Celestial Pole. Sigma Octantis (**e**) is the nearest visible star. To find the South Celestial Pole, find the constellation of the Southern Cross (**3**), then draw an imaginary line to meet the constellation Octans (**4**) at point **f**. Sigma Octantis is to be found between **d** and **f**.

Side view of our galaxy

1 Location of Earth and its sun

CONSTELLATIONS
Northern hemisphere

1 Virgo
2 Coma Berenices
3 Leo
4 Cancer
5 Canes Venatici
6 Boötes
7 Canis Minor
8 Gemini
9 Ursa Major
10 Corona Borealis
11 Serpens
12 Auriga
13 Ursa Minor
14 Draco
15 Hercules
16 Ophiuchus
17 Orion
18 Taurus
19 Perseus
20 Cassiopeia
21 Cepheus
22 Lyra
23 Cygnus
24 Aquila
25 Aries
26 Andromeda
27 Pisces
28 Pegasus

For over 2000 years stars have been divided into artificial groups called constellations. What we see today was originally suggested by the ancient Greeks who gave the stars names of characters from their mythology. No new constellations have been named since the middle of the 18th century. Astronomers recognize 88 constellations and call them by their Latin names.

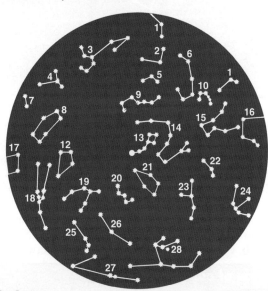

The five nearest stars

Name	Constellation	Apparent Magnitude	Distance (light years)
1 Proxima Centauri	Centaurus	+11.1	4.24
2 Alpha Centauri	Centaurus	−0.01	4.39
3 Barnard's Star	Ophiuchus	+9.5	6.0
4 Wolf 358	Leo	+13.6	7.8
5 Lalande 21185	Ursa Major	+7.7	8.2

Southern hemisphere

The first people to study the stars of the southern hemisphere were the explorers of the 17th and 18th centuries. The stars of the southern skies are never visible in the northern hemisphere but they are more spectacular because this part of the world faces the centre of our galaxy. The charts below show the major constellations.

1 Virgo
2 Corvus
3 Libra
4 Hydra
5 Centaurus
6 Ophiuchus
7 Scorpius
8 Crux
9 Vela
10 Monoceros
11 Triangulum Australe
12 Carina
13 Puppis
14 Canis Major
15 Sagittarius
16 Pavo
17 Octans
18 Dorado
19 Columba
20 Lepus
21 Orion
22 Tucana
23 Capricorn
24 Grus
25 Phoenix
26 Eridanus
27 Piscis Austrinus
28 Aquarius
29 Cetus

10

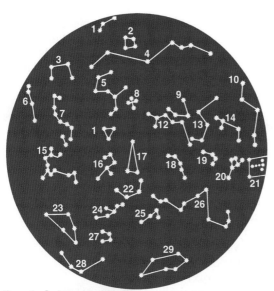

The five brightest stars

Name	Constellation	Apparent Magnitude	Absolute Magnitude	Distance (light years)
1 Sirius	Canis Major	−1.44	+1.5	8.6
2 Canopus	Carina	−0.62	−5.5	313
3 Alpha Centauri	Centaurus	−0.01	+4.1	4.39
4 Arcturus	Boötes	−0.05	−0.3	37
5 Vega	Lyra	+0.03	+0.6	25

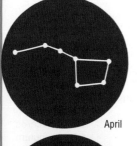

April

Northern constellations

The constellations of the northern hemisphere vary throughout the year. Watch the Big Dipper (Ursa Major) in April and in October.

October

Cygnus X-1

The star Cygnus X-1 has a black hole orbiting it which draws off matter

a Giant star Eta Cygni
b Drawn-off matter
c Black hole

April

Southern constellations

The positions of the southern constellations also vary throughout the year. Look out for the Southern Cross (Crux) in April and again in December.

December

PULSARS, BLACK HOLES, QUASARS

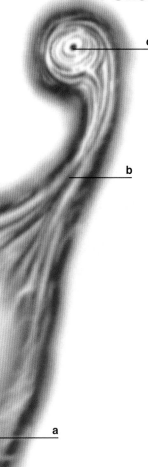

A star whose mass is more than 1.5 times that of the Sun will end its life as a small dense star called a pulsar. A very massive star – one with a mass more than three times that of the Sun – may collapse further to become a black hole.

Pulsars Neutron stars are called "pulsars" because they give out radio waves which are received on Earth as regular, rapid pulses. The pulse rate slows down as the neutron star ages. Pulsars are detected with radio telescopes. The average diameter of a neutron star is 6 mi, and so they are almost undetectable with optical telescopes.

Black holes are invisible and can only be detected by their effect on stars near them. Black holes warp space and time: time stops at their edges. The gravity in black holes is so great that not even light can escape from them. Anything coming close to a black hole is pulled into it and vanishes from our universe forever. No one has yet proved that black holes definitely exist.

Quasars "Quasar" is an abbreviation of "quasistellar object", i.e. an object that appears to be a star. When seen by optical telescopes, quasars look like ordinary faint stars. When seen by radio telescopes, they are clearly not stars but distant objects that give out massive amounts of energy. The diameter of our galaxy is 1 million ly. The diameter of a typical quasar is less than 11 ly.

10

SOLAR SYSTEM

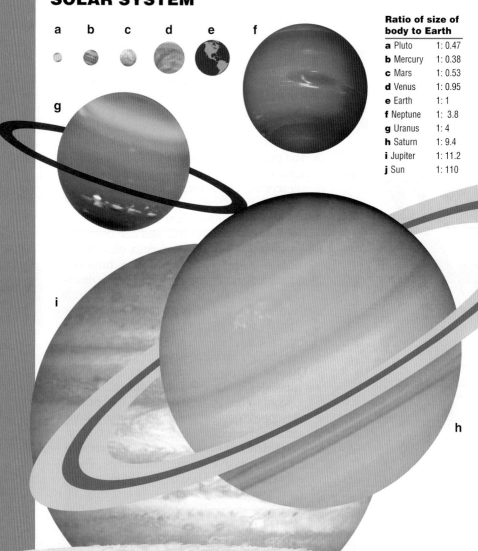

a b c d e f g i h j

Ratio of size of body to Earth

a Pluto	1: 0.47
b Mercury	1: 0.38
c Mars	1: 0.53
d Venus	1: 0.95
e Earth	1: 1
f Neptune	1: 3.8
g Uranus	1: 4
h Saturn	1: 9.4
i Jupiter	1: 11.2
j Sun	1: 110

Planetary distances

	Mean distance from the Sun (in millions)		Mean distance from Earth (in millions)	
	mi	km	mi	km
1 Mercury	36	58	50	80.8
2 Venus	67	108	25	40.4
3 Earth	93	150	–	–
4 Mars	141	227	35	56.8
5 Jupiter	484	778	367	591
6 Saturn	887	1427	744	1198
7 Uranus	1784	2869	1607	2585
8 Neptune	2796	4497	2678	4308
9 Pluto	3661	5888	2670	4297

10

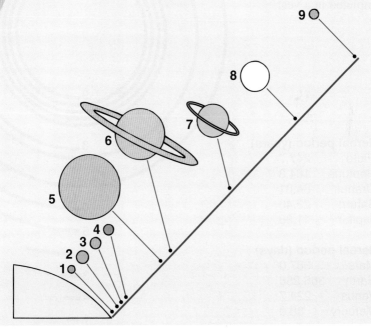

Orbits and rotation

All the planets in the
Solar System move
around the Sun. Each
planet also rotates on its
axis. The sidereal period
calculates the time taken
by a planet to orbit the
Sun once. For Earth it is
approximately 365 days.
The diagram compares
the planets' sidereal
periods. Black lines
show how much of a
planet's orbit has been
completed in a year.

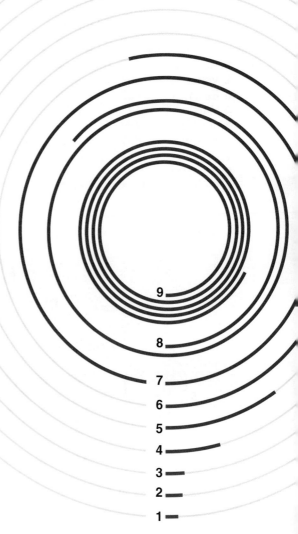

Sidereal period (years)
1 Pluto   247.7
2 Neptune   164.8
3 Uranus   84.01
4 Saturn   29.46
5 Jupiter   11.86

Sidereal period (days)
6 Mars   687.0
7 Earth   365.256
8 Venus   224.7
9 Mercury   88.0

Planetary data

	Mercury	Venus	Earth
Mean distance from Sun	0.39 au	0.72 au	1.00 au
Distance at perihelion	0.31 au	0.72 au	0.98 au
Distance at aphelion	0.47 au	0.73 au	1.02 au
Closest distance to Earth	0.54 au	0.27 au	
Average orbital speed	28.75 mi/s	21.7 mi/s	18.5 mi/s
Rotation period	58.6 days	243 days	23 hr 56 min
Sidereal period	88 days	225 days	365 days
Diameter at equator	3030 mi	7520 mi	7926 mi
Mass (Earth's mass = 1)	0.06	0.82	1
Surface temperature	662 °F (day) −274 °F (night)	896 °F	72 °F
Gravity (Earth's gravity = 1)	0.38	0.88	1
Density (density of water = 1)	5.5	5.25	5.517
No. of satellites	0	0	1
No. of known rings	0	0	0
Main gases in atmosphere	no atmosphere	carbon dioxide	nitrogen, oxygen

10

Planetary data (continued)

	Mars	Jupiter
Mean distance from Sun	1.52 au	5.20 au
Distance at perihelion	1.38 au	4.95 au
Distance at aphelion	1.67 au	5.46 au
Closest distance to Earth	0.38 au	3.95 au
Average orbital speed	14.97 mi/s	8.14 mi/s
Rotation period	24 hr 37 min	9 hr 50 min
Sidereal period	687 days	11.86 years
Diameter at equator	4,222 mi	88,734 mi
Mass (Earth's mass = 1)	0.11	317.9
Surface temperature	−9 °F	−238 °F
Gravity (Earth's gravity = 1)	0.38	2.64
Density (density of water = 1)	3.94	1.33
No. of satellites known	2	16
No. of rings known	0	1
Main gases in atmosphere	carbon dioxide	hydrogen, helium

Saturn	Uranus	Neptune	Pluto
9.54 au	19.18 au	30.06 au	39.36 au
9.01 au	18.28 au	29.8 au	29.58 au
10.07 au	20.09 au	30.32 au	49.14 au
8.01 au	17.28 au	28.8 au	28.72 au
5.97 mi/s	4.23 mi/s	3.36 mi/s	2.92 mi/s
10 hr 14 min	16 hr 10 min	18 hr 26 min	6 days 9 hr
29.46 years	84.01 years	164.8 years	247.7 years
74,566 mi	31,566 mi	30,137 mi	3725 mi
95.2	14.6	17.2	0.002–0.003
−292 °F	−346 °F	−364 °F	−382 °F
1.15	1.17	1.2	not known
0.71	1.7	1.77	not known
19	5	2	1
1000+	9	0	0
hydrogen, helium	hydrogen, helium, methane	hydrogen, helium, methane	methane

10

SUN, EARTH, MOON

The Earth and the Moon are about the same age, 4.6 billion years old, though they were formed separately. Earth has large oceans, a protective atmosphere, and a surface which is active and constantly changing. The Moon is dead, a barren airless world a quarter of the size of the Earth. The Sun, thought to be 5 billion years old, is a star. It generates light and heat and its enormous gravitational pull keeps all the planets in their orbits.

1 The Earth's orbit around the Sun
The Earth completes an orbit of the Sun every 365.25 days.

2 The Moon's orbit around the Earth
The Moon completes one orbit of the Earth every 28 days.

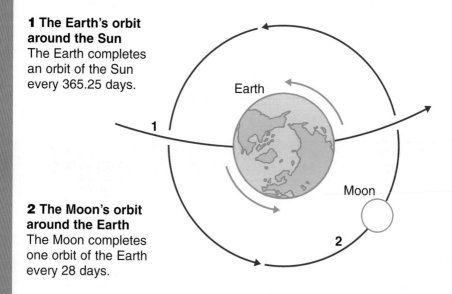

The Sun has a diameter of 865,000 miles. The Earth's diameter is 7930 miles and the Moon's diameter is 2170 miles

The Sun is a mass of glowing hydrogen gas which is so hot and compressed that hydrogen atoms fuse to make helium. This reaction generates huge amounts of energy which reach us in the forms of heat and light. The Sun's energy is shared out over the whole Earth. Its energy is more spread out in some areas and more concentrated in others.

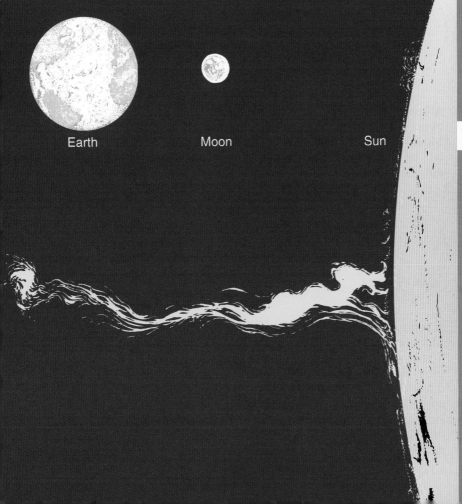

Earth   Moon   Sun

10

ECLIPSES

An eclipse occurs when the passage of all or part of an astronomical body moves into the shadow of another.

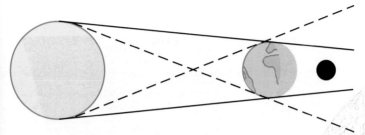

A lunar eclipse happens when the Earth is in a direct line between the Sun and the Moon. The Moon will then be in the Earth's shadow and it will be unable to receive direct sunlight. Normally only three eclipses of the Moon occur in one year.

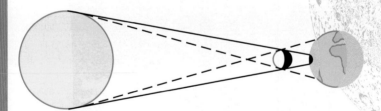

A solar eclipse is different. To our eye the Sun and the Moon seem to be the same size, though in reality the Sun is 400 times larger than the Moon. It is also 400 times further away from the Earth. If the Moon is in a direct line between the Sun and the Earth then the Moon appears to cover the Sun's photosphere (its visible surface). This would mean that any section of the Earth directly in the Moon's shadow would experience a total eclipse of the Sun and areas around it a partial eclipse.

In the time it takes the Moon to orbit Earth once it completes exactly one rotation on its axis – consequently only one side of the Moon is ever visible from Earth

Types of eclipse

Three types of eclipse are possible. A total eclipse (**1**) when the Sun's disk is completely but briefly obscured. This can last from a split second up to a maximum of 7 minutes 31 seconds. However, the corona - the luminous plasma "atmosphere" of the Sun extending millions of miles into space - can be seen. A partial eclipse (**2**) is when the Moon's disk only obscures part of the photosphere. An annular eclipse (**3**) occurs if the Moon is too far away to totally cover the Sun. A bright ring of light is visible around the eclipsed Sun.

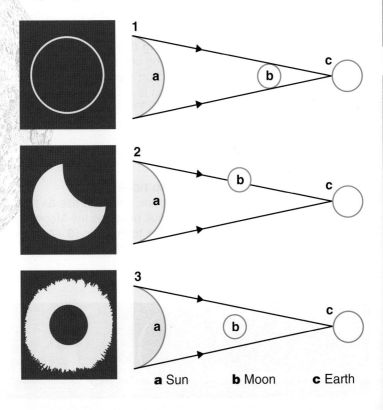

a Sun   **b** Moon   **c** Earth

10

TIDES

A tide is the rise and fall of water throughout the Earth's oceans. Occurring every 12 hours, 26 minutes, tides are created by the Moon's pull of gravity on the water and sometimes even the Sun's pull.

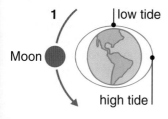

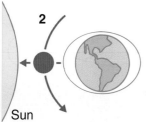

When the Earth is nearer to the Moon (**1**), water is pulled toward the Moon, producing a high tide. A high tide happens on the opposite side of the Earth at the same time. Tides occur about every 12 hours because of the Earth's rotation.

Spring tides

Spring tides occur when the Moon and the Sun are directly in line (**2**). The Moon is either in front of or behind the Earth. This produces a very high tide occurring twice a month.

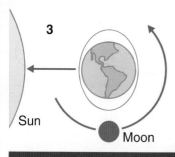

Neap tides

The tide does not rise as high as normal because the Moon is at right angles to the Sun (**3**). A neap tide occurs twice a month.

The phases of the moon
1 New moon
2, 3, 4 Shows more each day
5 Full moon
6, 7, 8 Shows less each day

PHASES OF THE MOON

The Moon only reflects sunlight; it produces no light of its own. From Earth we can see the amount of the lit half as it changes from day to day. These normal changes are known as phases of the Moon. The diagram shows how the Moon appears to us on selected nights within a month. It takes 29 days, 12 hours, 44 minutes and 3 seconds before a new moon occurs again. The phases have different names. For example, a waxing moon means one that is increasingly visible, a waning moon is less visible, and a gibbous moon is between half and full phase.

10

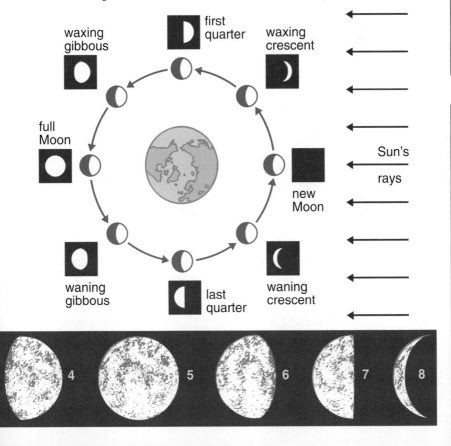

ASTRONOMICAL TIME
Units of time
Listed below are the ways of measuring time that are
artificially derived, as opposed to astronomical methods.
Years, months, weeks
Below are some widely used names for periods of time.

Name	Period	Name	Period
millennium	1000 years	leap year	366 days
half-millennium	500 years	year	365 days
century	100 years	year	12 months
half-century	50 years	year	52 weeks
decade	10 years	month	28–31 days
half-decade	5 years	week	7 days

Days, hours, minutes
Below are listed the basic subdivisions of a day and their
equivalents.

1 day = 24 hours = 1,440 minutes = 86,400 seconds
1 hour = 1/24 day = 60 minutes = 3600 seconds
1 minute = 1/440 day = 1/60 hour = 60 seconds
1 second = 1/86,400 day = 1/3600 hour = 1/60 minute

Seconds
Greater precision in measuring time has required seconds (s)
to be broken down into smaller units, using standard metric
prefixes.

1 tetrasecond (Ts)	10^{12} s	31,689 years
1 gigasecond (Gs)	10^{9} s	31.7 years
1 megasecond (Ms)	10^{6} s	11.6 days
1 kilosecond (ks)	10^{3} s	16.67 minutes

1 millisecond (ms)	10^{-3} s	0.001 seconds
1 microsecond (µs)	10^{-6} s	0.000 001
1 nanosecond (ns)	10^{-9} s	0.000 000 001
1 picosecond (ps)	10^{-12} s	0.000 000 000 001
1 femtosecond (fs)	10^{-15} s	0.000 000 000 000 001
1 attosecond (as)	10^{-18} s	0.000 000 000 000 000 001

Astronomical time

Time can be measured by motion; in fact, the motion of the Earth, Sun, Moon, and stars provided humans with the first means of measuring time.

Years, months, days

Sidereal times are calculated by the Earth's position according to fixed stars. The anomalistic year is measured according to the Earth's orbit in relation to the perihelion (Earth's minimum distance to the Sun). Tropical times refer to the apparent passage of the Sun and the actual passage of the Moon across the Earth's Equatorial plane. The synodic month is based on the phases of the Moon. Solar time (as in a mean solar day) refers to periods of darkness and light averaged over a year.

Time	Days	Hours	Minutes	Seconds
Sidereal year	365	6	9	10
Anomalistic year	365	6	13	53
Tropical year	365	5	48	45
Sidereal month	27	7	43	11
Tropical month	27	7	43	5
Synodic month	29	12	44	3
Mean solar day	0	24	0	0
Sidereal day	0	23	56	4

TIMELINE OF SPACE EXPLORATION

1957 First satellite, *Sputnik 1*, launched (Oct 4). Jodrell Bank radio telescope, England.

1958 NASA founded. First US satellite *Explorer 1* finds Van Allen radiation belts.

1959 Russian robotic probe *Luna 2* hits the Moon.

1960 First weather satellite: *Tiros 1*.

1961 First US-crewed space flight (Alan Shephard). First crewed space flight by Yuri Gagarin in *Vostok 1*: single orbit. Parkes radio telescope completed west of Sydney, Australia.

1962 John Glenn is first American to orbit the Earth. *Telstar 1* first TV-relay satellite.

1962 First dual mission (*Vostok 3* and *4*).

1963 Quasars first identified from Mt Palomar Observatory, California. First woman in space: Valentina Tereshkova in *Vostok 6*.

1965 Gemini missions practice two-person flight, spacewalks, and docking. First spacewalk: Alexei Leonov from *Voskhod 6*.

1966 *Surveyor* (uncrewed) lands on Moon. *Venera 3* (uncrewed) hits Venus.

1967 Death of *Apollo 1* crew in a fire on the ground (first US astronauts to be killed). First pulsar identified by Jocelyn Bell from Cambridge, England.

1968 *Apollo 8* makes first crewed orbit of Moon.

1969 Neil Armstrong, then Buzz Aldrin from *Apollo 11* (July 31), first to walk on Moon. Five more Apollo Moon landings. First space walk transfer between *Soyuz 5* and *4*.

1970 First space station launched, *Salyut 1*, but 3 cosmonauts die on return flight. First Chinese and Japanese satellites.

1973 First US space station: *Skylab* (4 missions).

1975 First international space docking: *Apollo 18* and *Soyuz 19*. First photos from Venus's surface by *Venera 9*. European Space Agency (ESA) founded.

1976 First Mars surface landing, by uncrewed *Viking 1*.

1978 Rings of Uranus recorded.

1979 First spacecraft, *Pioneer 11*, visits Saturn.

1981 First space shuttle flight.

1983 First US woman in space: Sally Ride aboard shuttle *Columbia*. *Pioneer 10* (launched 1972) first probe to leave Solar System.

1986 24th US space shuttle flight: *Challenger* explodes (Jan 28) killing crew of seven. *Voyager 2* (launched 1977) reaches Uranus; finds ten more moons. European space probe *Giotto* passes through tail of Halley's comet.

1988 *Discovery* resumes space shuttle flights more than two years after loss of *Challenger*. First permanently crewed space station *Mir* sets 366-day crew duration record in orbit.

1989 Space shuttle launches *Galileo* probe.

1990 *Magellan* space probe arrives at Venus. *Hubble Space Telescope* launched but flaws discovered.

1993 *Hubble* repaired. *Mars Observer* (launched 1992) reaches Mars. *Pioneer 10* reaches 3.3 billion miles from Earth, making it the most distant human-made object.

1995 *Galileo* probe reaches Jupiter.

1997 Successful docking of space shuttle *Atlantis* and Russian *Mir* space station. *Pathfinder* probe lands on Mars after eight-month journey. *Cassini* probe launched on seven-year trip to Saturn.

2001 *NEAR-Shoemaker* probe becomes first spacecraft to touch down on an asteroid.

2003 Space Shuttle *Columbia* breaks up during atmospheric re-entry at the end of a mission. All seven crew members killed.

2004 Twin Mars Exploration Rovers *Spirit* and *Opportunity* arrive on Mars and begin 18-month exploration. *Cassini* probe becomes first spacecraft to enter orbit around Saturn. Intended to complete 74 orbits by 2008.

2005 *Huygens* probe lands on surface of Saturn's moon Titan. *Discovery* resumes space shuttle flights more than two years after loss of *Columbia*. *Mars Reconnaissance Orbiter* launched to arrive at Mars in 2006. *Deep Impact* probe releases solid metal impactor which strikes comet Tempel 1 emitting large amounts of material for study.

10

DELIVERY ROCKETS

1 Saturn V Built originally to send astronauts to the Moon. A three-stage launch vehicle. It stood 111 meters high and with fuel weighed 3207 tons. The USA made six landings on the Moon using the Saturn rocket.

2 Soyuz The first Soviet Soyuz mission was launched in 1967. It was designed for a crew of three men with three sections: the orbital module, the descent module, and the service module.

3 Ariane Ariane's main purpose is to put a satellite or space probe into space for the European Space Agency.

4 Gemini Titan The first manned Gemini flight took off in March 1965. It carried two astronauts.

5 Vostok In April 1961 this Soviet spacecraft carried the first man into space and completed one orbit of the Earth.

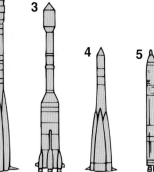
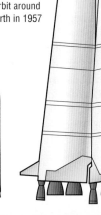

Russian R-7 rocket – launched the first artificial Satellite into orbit around the Earth in 1957

CREWED SPACEFLIGHT

The space shuttle is a reusable launcher. At lift-off the shuttle is thrust into space by two solid-fuel booster rockets (**1**). The used rockets then parachute away into the ocean (**2**) from where they are recovered and then reused. The large fuel tank is abandoned (**3**) 8 minutes into the flight. The spacecraft goes into orbit (**4**) and delivers its load. After the mission the shuttle begins descent (**5**) protected by hundreds of heat-resistant tiles. It coasts back to Earth (**6**) like a glider and lands on a runway (**7**).

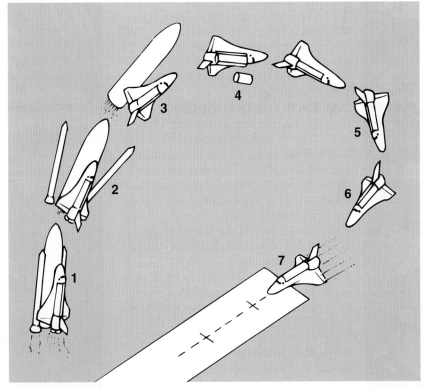

See page 503 to find out more about the space shuttle's rockets

SATELLITES

A satellite is a spacecraft placed into orbit with equipment for sending pictures and radio signals back to Earth.

1 Spy satellites generally operate in polar orbit to cover the whole Earth as it turns. They survey military movements and pick up communications between countries. The USA has a missile-warning satellite.

2 The IUE (International Ultraviolet Explorer) is a science research satellite. It has made thousands of discoveries and has enabled astronomers to weigh a black hole and to discover more about the Sun, stars, and comets.

3 An Earth resources satellite is roughly the size of a family car. These satellites can cross over the whole Earth as it rotates. Images from the Landsat satellite have helped to survey areas of minerals, forest growth, and disasters.

4 Communication satellites, of which the US Comstar is one, can relay 18,000 telephone calls over the whole of the USA. It can also send dozens of television channels.

5 Telescopic satellites have a clear view of the Universe and can transmit images of space far beyond what was previously known. They normally lie above the Earth's atmosphere.

6 Weather satellites can see how the clouds move and how temperatures are changing. They are used by weather forecasters to predict weather days ahead.

SPACECRAFT

1 The Mercury capsule carried one space pilot. The capsule was bell-shaped to reduce the enormous heat encountered on re-entry into the atmosphere. The heat shields were made from layers of glass fibre and plastic and the astronaut's cabin was double-skinned for protection.

2 Apollo command and service module was used for Moon-landing. It carried life-support systems, communication and navigation equipment, re-entry and landing equipment. It was manned by three astronauts and built in three sections: the lunar module (used to go to and from the surface of the Moon), the command module, and the service module and engine.

3 The Soviet Soyuz spacecraft was built to shuttle crews backward and forward from established space stations. It was designed for three men. It consisted of three sections: an orbiting module, a descent module, and a service module.

4 The Shuttle transport system was first launched in 1981 with the assistance of two solid propellant boosters. The space shuttle is piloted to its destination, discharges its crew and cargo, and returns to earth. It is used to supply staff to the ISS and deliver additional contents and units for construction.

International Space Station (ISS) began assembly in 1998 – it is a co-venture of many nations

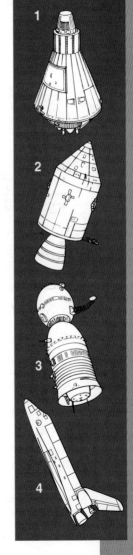

HISTORIC NUMBER SYSTEMS

Different civilizations have developed their own systems for writing numbers. Here we show numerals from eight such systems.

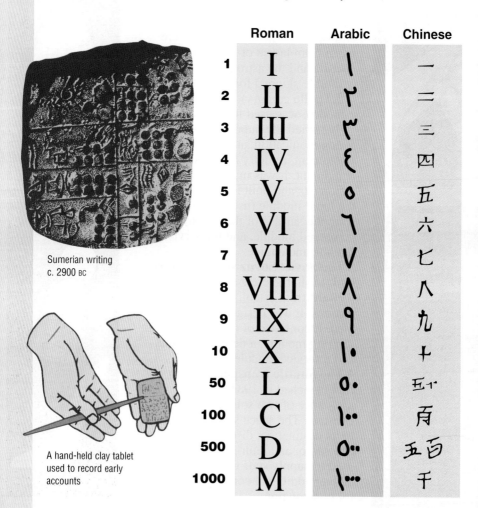

Sumerian writing
c. 2900 BC

A hand-held clay tablet
used to record early
accounts

	Roman	Arabic	Chinese
1	I	١	一
2	II	٢	二
3	III	٣	三
4	IV	٤	四
5	V	٥	五
6	VI	٦	六
7	VII	٧	七
8	VIII	٨	八
9	IX	٩	九
10	X	١٠	十
50	L	٥٠	五十
100	C	١٠٠	百
500	D	٥٠٠	五百
1000	M	١٠٠٠	千

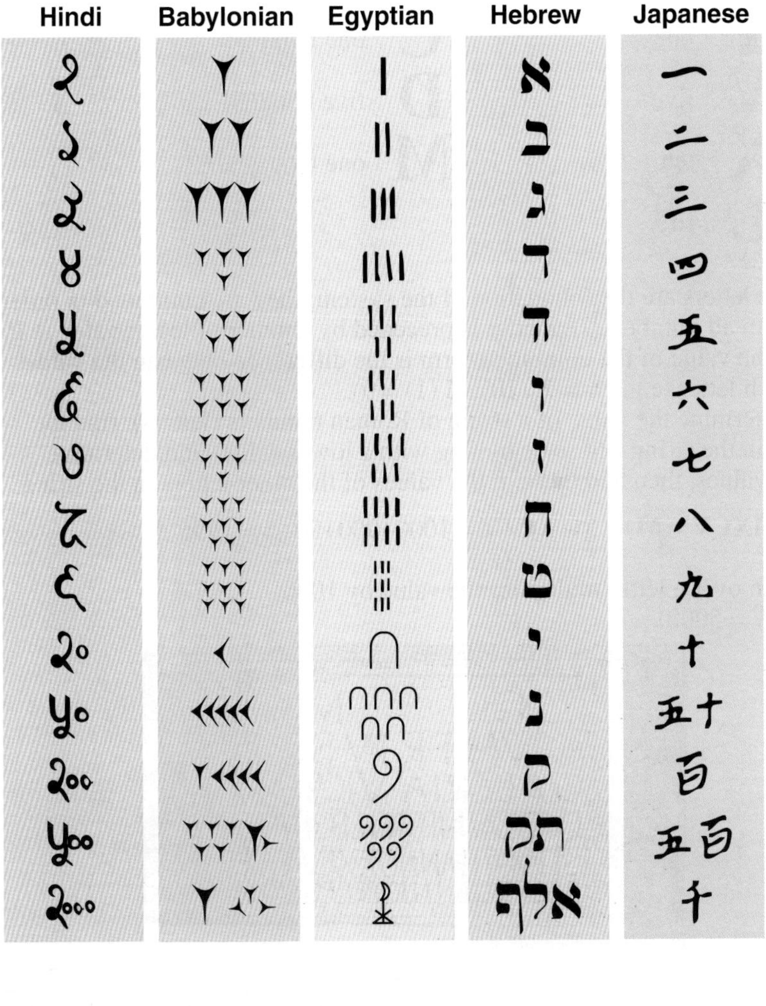

Hindi	Babylonian	Egyptian	Hebrew	Japanese

Roman number system

The Roman system is a method of notation in which the capitals are modelled on ancient Roman inscriptions. The numerals are represented by seven capital letters of the alphabet:

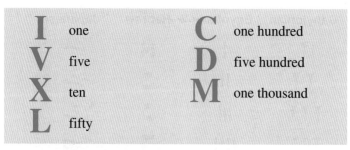

I	one	**C**	one hundred
V	five	**D**	five hundred
X	ten	**M**	one thousand
L	fifty		

These letters are the foundation of the system; they are combined in order to form all numbers. If a letter is preceded by another of lesser value (e.g. IX), the value of the combined form is the difference between the values of each letter (e.g. IX = X (10) – I (1) = 9).

To determine the value of a string of Roman numbers (letters), find the pairs in the string (those beginning with a lower value) and determine their values, then add these to the values of the other letters in the string:

MCMXCV = M+CM+XC+V = 1000+900+90+5 = 1995

A dash over a letter multiplies the value by 1000 (e.g. $\bar{V}$ = 5000).

Roman tombstone with numerals

1 I	12 XII	35 XXXV	100 C
2 II	13 XIII	40 XL	200 CC
3 III	14 XIV	45 XLV	300 CCC
4 IV or IIII	15 XV	50 L	400 CD
5 V	16 XVI	55 LV	500 D
6 VI	17 XVII	60 LX	600 DC
7 VII	18 XVIII	65 LXV	700 DCC
8 VIII	19 XIX	70 LXX	800 DCCC
9 IX	20 XX	75 LXXV	900 CM
10 X	25 XXV	80 LXXX	1000 M
11 XI	30 XXX	90 XC	2000 MM

11

NAMES FOR NUMBERS

Many numbers have names. Some of these names are in everyday use, while others apply in more specialized areas such as music and multiple births, and for sums of money. Some names for specialized numbers have the same first part (prefix). These prefixes indicate the number to which the name refers.

Everyday use

$^1/_{10}$	Tithe	20	Score
2	Pair, couple, brace	50	Half-century
6	Half a dozen	100	Century
12	Dozen	144	Gross
13	Baker's dozen		

Twins

Musicians

1	Soloist	5	Quintet
2	Duet	6	Sextet
3	Trio	7	Septet
4	Quartet	8	Octet

Triplets

Slang for money

1¢	Penny	25¢	Quarter, two bits
5¢	Nickel	1$	Buck
10¢	Dime		

Quadruplets

Multiple births

2	Twins	5	Quintuplets (quins)
3	Triplets	6	Sextuplets
4	Quadruplets (quads)		

Quintuplets

Sextuplets

Numerical prefixes

Prefixes in numerical order

$^1/_{10}$ Deci-

$^1/_2$ Semi-, hemi-, demi-

1 Uni-

2 Bi-, di-

3 Tri-, ter-

4 Tetra-, tetr-, tessera-, quadri-, quadr-

5 Pent-, penta-, quinqu-, quinque-, quint-

6 Sex-, sexi-, hex-, hexa-

7 Hept-, hepta-, sept-, septi-, septem-

8 Oct-, octa-, octo-

9 Non-, nona-, ennea-

10 Dec-, deca-

11 Hendeca-, undec-, undeca-

12 Dodeca-

15 Quindeca-

20 Icos-, icosa-, icosi-

Biped

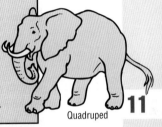

Quadruped **11**

Prefixes in alphabetical order

Bi-,	**2**	Pent-, penta-	**5**	
Dec-, deca-	**10**	Quadr-, quadri-	**4**	
Deci-	$^1/_{10}$	Quindeca-	**15**	
Demi-	$^1/_2$	Quinqu-, quinque-	**5**	
Di-	**2**	Quint-	**5**	
Dodeca-	**12**	Semi-	$^1/_2$	
Ennea-	**9**	Sept-, septem-, septi-	**7**	
Hemi-	$^1/_2$	Sex-, sexi-	**6**	
Hendeca-	**11**	Ter-	**3**	
Hept-, Hepta-	**7**	Tessera-	**4**	
Hex-, hexa-	**6**	Tetr-, tetra-	**4**	
Icos-, icosa-, icosi-	**20**	Tri-	**3**	
Non-, nona-	**9**	Undec-, undeca-	**11**	
Oct-, octa-, octo-	**8**	Uni-	**1**	

Hexaped

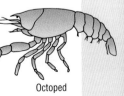

Octoped

Prefixes in order of value	Value
*Atto-	0.000,000,000,000,000,001
*Femto-	0.000,000,000,000,001
*Pico-	0.000,000,000,001
*Nano-	0.000,000,001
*Micro-	0.000,001
*Milli-	0.001
*Centi-	0.01
*Deci-	0.1
Semi-, hemi-, demi-	0.5
Uni-	1
Bi-, di-	2
Tri-, ter-	3
Tetra-, tetr-, tessera-, quadri-, quadr-	4
Pent-, penta-, quinqu-, quinque-, quint-	5
Sex-, sexi-, hex-, hexa-	6
Hept-, hepta-, sept-, septi-, septem-	7
Oct-, octa-, octo-	8
Non-, nona-, ennea-	9
Dec-, deca-	10
Hendeca-, undec-, undeca-	11
Dodeca-	12
Quindeca-	15
Icos-, icosa-, icosi-	20
Hect-, hecto-	100
*Kilo-	1000
Myria-	10,000
*Mega-	1,000,000
*Giga-	1,000,000,000
*Tera-	1,000,000,000,000

Egyptian measurements
a Digit, one finger width
b Palm (= four digits)
c Hand (= five digits)
d Cubit, elbow to finger tips (= 28 digits, 20.6 in)

*These prefixes can be used in the SI system of units

MULTIPLICATION GRID

Below is a grid of numbers which gives you quick reference to multiplication tables and answers to division calculations.

Multiplication

In order to multiply 6 by 7, for example, look down the column with 6 at the top. Continue down the column until you reach row 7. The number in the square where column 6 and row 7 meet gives the answer of 42.

Division

To divide 63 by 9, for example, look down the column with 9 at the top until you find 63. Look along the row to find the row number. The answer is 7.

Inca grain abacus and knotted-string record keeper

11

Row	Column											
	1	2	3	4	5	6	7	8	9	10	11	12
1	1	2	3	4	5	6	7	8	9	10	11	12
2	2	4	6	8	10	12	14	16	18	20	22	24
3	3	6	9	12	15	18	21	24	27	30	33	36
4	4	8	12	16	20	24	28	32	36	40	44	48
5	5	10	15	20	25	30	35	40	45	50	55	60
6	6	12	18	24	30	36	42	48	54	60	66	72
7	7	14	21	28	35	42	49	56	63	70	77	84
8	8	16	24	32	40	48	56	64	72	80	88	96
9	9	18	27	36	45	54	63	72	81	90	99	108
10	10	20	30	40	50	60	70	80	90	100	110	120
11	11	22	33	44	55	66	77	88	99	110	121	132
12	12	24	36	48	60	72	84	96	108	120	132	144

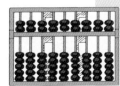

European abacus

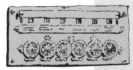

Mechanical calculating machine

MATHEMATICAL SYMBOLS

$+$	plus or positive	$\geqq$	greater than or equal to
$-$	minus or negative	$\leqq$	less than or equal to
$\pm$	plus or minus, positive or negative	$\gg$	much greater than
$\times$	multiplied by	$\ll$	much less than
$\div$	divided by	$\sqrt{\ }$	square root
$=$	equal to	∞	infinity
$\equiv$	identically equal to	$\propto$	proportional to
$\neq$	not equal to	Σ	sum of
$\not\equiv$	not identically equal to	Π	product of
$\approx$	approximately equal to	Δ	difference
$\sim$	of the order of or similar to	$\therefore$	therefore
$>$	greater than	$\angle$	angle
$<$	less than	$\parallel$	parallel to
$\not>$	not greater than	$\perp$	perpendicular to
$\not<$	not less than	$:$	is to (ratio)

ARITHMETIC OPERATIONS

The four basic arithmetic operations are addition, subtraction, multiplication, and division. Each part of an arithmetic operation has a specific name.

16th century abacus inscribed on a table

11

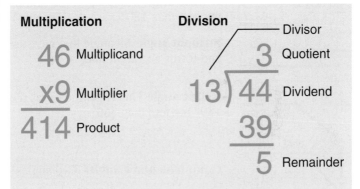

Addition		Subtraction	
29	Addend	74	Minuend
+6	Addend	-16	Subtrahend
35	Sum	58	Difference

Multiplication		Division	
46	Multiplicand		Divisor
x9	Multiplier	3	Quotient
414	Product	13)44	Dividend
		39	
		5	Remainder

Fraction		Simple (or vulgar) fraction	
5/8	5	Numerator	9/7	9	Numerator
	8	Denominator		7	Denominator

16th century mathematics student using blackboard and chalk

GEOMETRY
Angles
Angles can be measured using two different units. Both of these are divisions of a circle. Degrees are the more widely used unit of measurement but radians are also used for some types of mathematics (see page 293).

Acute angle This is an angle that measures more than 0° but less than 90°.

Right angle An angle that measures exactly 90°. The lines at right angles are perpendicular to one another.

Obtuse angle This is an angle of more than 90° but less than 180°.

Straight angle An angle that measures 180° and forms a straight line.

Reflex angle This angle measures more than 180° but less than 360°.

Complementary angles Two angles whose sum is 90°.

Supplementary angles Two angles whose sum is 180°.

Conjugate angles Two angles whose sum is 360°.

Angles in circles

Degrees (A) A circle is divided into 360 equal parts called degrees (°). One degree is the angle at the center of a circle which cuts off an arc that is 1/360 of the circumference. Below is a quarter of a circle divided into 90 degrees (°).

Radians (B) One radian is the angle between 2 radii of a circle which cuts off on the circumference an arc equal in length to the radius. 1 radian (rad) equals 57.296°. There are 2π (approximately 6.28) radians in a circle. Below is an angle of 1 radian.

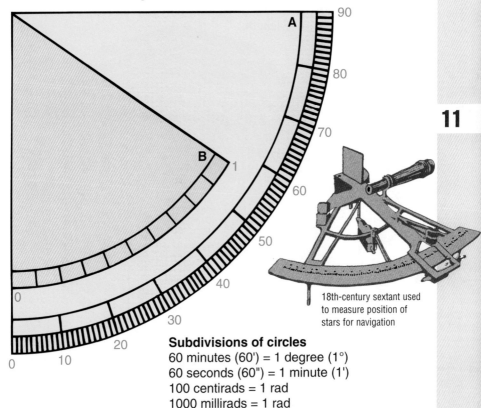

18th-century sextant used to measure position of stars for navigation

11

Subdivisions of circles

60 minutes (60') = 1 degree (1°)
60 seconds (60") = 1 minute (1')
100 centirads = 1 rad
1000 millirads = 1 rad

Traditional Chinese division of a square known as a Tangram – used to form shapes such as the figures shown below

Polygons

A polygon is a plane figure, or a shape with three or more straight sides. *Poly* is the Greek word for many and *gonia* means angle. There are irregular and regular polygons. Regular polygons have sides which are all the same length and angles which are all the same size. Irregular polygons have sides which are different lengths and angles of different sizes. The table opposite lists the names and number of sides of the first 10 regular polygons. The diagram below shows the 10 polygons all drawn with sides of the same length.

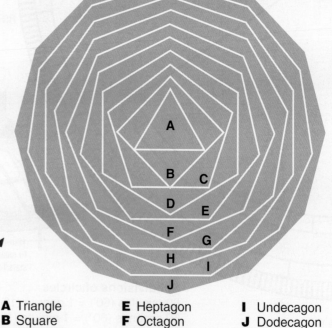

A Triangle   **E** Heptagon   **I** Undecagon
B Square   **F** Octagon   **J** Dodecagon
C Pentagon   **G** Nonagon
D Hexagon   **H** Decagon

	Name of polygon	Number of sides	Each internal angle	Sum of internal angles
	Triangle	3	60°	180°
	Square	4	90°	360°
	Pentagon	5	108°	540°
	Hexagon	6	120°	720°
	Heptagon	7	128.6°	900°
	Octagon	8	135°	1080°
	Nonagon	9	140°	1260°
	Decagon	10	144°	1440°
	Undecagon	11	147.3°	1620°
	Dodecagon	12	150°	1800°

11

Quadrilaterals

A quadrilateral is a four-sided polygon or a four-sided plane figure.

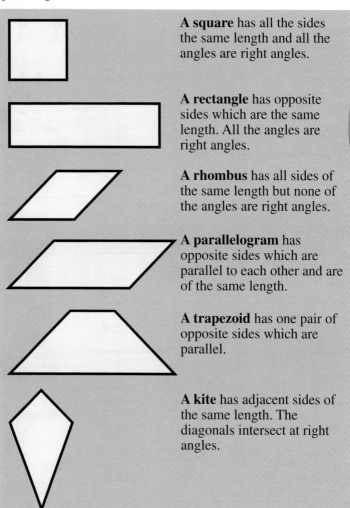

A square has all the sides the same length and all the angles are right angles.

A rectangle has opposite sides which are the same length. All the angles are right angles.

A rhombus has all sides of the same length but none of the angles are right angles.

A parallelogram has opposite sides which are parallel to each other and are of the same length.

A trapezoid has one pair of opposite sides which are parallel.

A kite has adjacent sides of the same length. The diagonals intersect at right angles.

Triangles

Shown below are six types of triangle. The sum of the internal angles of any flat triangle is always 180°.

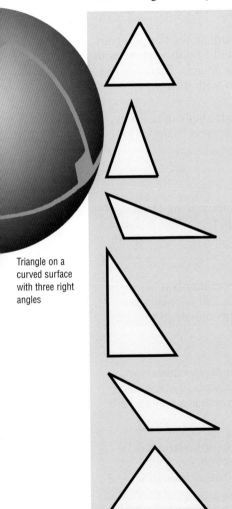

Triangle on a curved surface with three right angles

An equilateral triangle has all the sides of the same length. All the internal angles are equal.

An isosceles triangle has two sides which are of the same length and two angles which are of equal size.

A scalene triangle has all the sides of different lengths and has all the angles of different sizes.

11

A right-angle triangle is a triangle which contains one right angle of 90°.

An obtuse-angle triangle is a triangle which contains one obtuse angle – an angle over 90°.

An acute-angle triangle is a triangle which contains three acute angles. These are each less than 90°.

Solids

Solid shapes are three-dimensional. This means they have length, width, and depth. A polyhedron is a solid shape with polygons for faces, or sides. Opening out a polyhedron gives a shape called a net.

All the faces of a regular solid are identical regular polygons of equal size. A regular polyhedron will fit into a sphere with all the vertices, or edges, touching the sphere. There are five regular solids which are shown below with their nets.

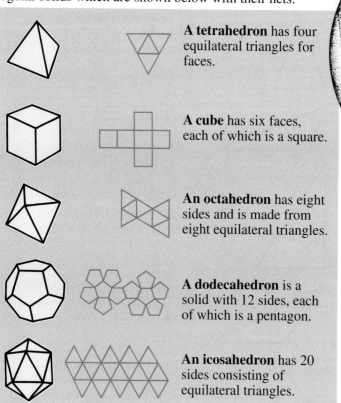

A tetrahedron has four equilateral triangles for faces.

A cube has six faces, each of which is a square.

An octahedron has eight sides and is made from eight equilateral triangles.

A dodecahedron is a solid with 12 sides, each of which is a pentagon.

An icosahedron has 20 sides consisting of equilateral triangles.

Semi-regular figures have two or more types of polygon as their faces. Like regular solids they fit into a sphere with all the vertices touching the sphere. Below are six semi-regular solids.

Any regular solid can be placed in a sphere so that all its corners touch the sphere

 A truncated octahedron has 14 faces made of squares and hexagons.

 A cuboctahedron also has 14 faces. These consist of triangles and squares.

 A truncated cuboctahedron has 26 faces which are made of squares, hexagons, and octagons.

11

 A truncated icosahedron has 32 faces which consist of pentagons and hexagons.

 An icosidodecahedron has 32 faces made up of triangles and pentagons.

 A truncated icosidodecahedron has 62 faces consisting of squares, hexagons, and decagons.

Geometry of area
Abbreviations
a = length of top
b = length of base
h = perpendicular height
r = length of <u>radius</u>

$$\pi = 3.1416$$

The working formula

Circle

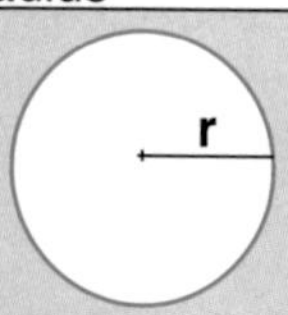

$$\pi \times r^2$$

Rectangle

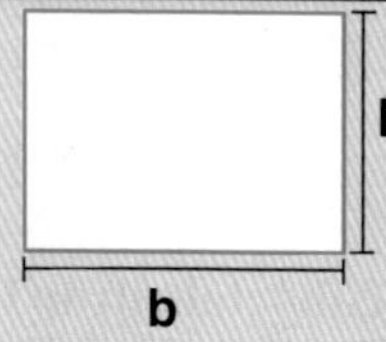

$$b \times h$$

Parallelogram

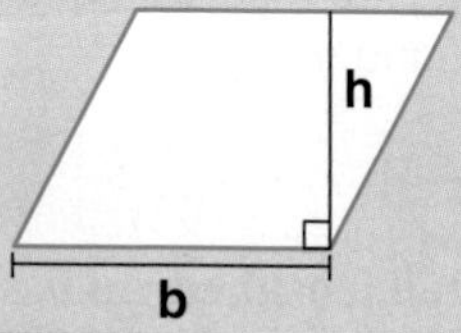

$$b \times h$$

The mathematical constant π is the ratio of a circle's circumference to its diameter. It is commonly used in mathematics, physics, and engineering. Pi has been calculated to more than 16 million decimal places

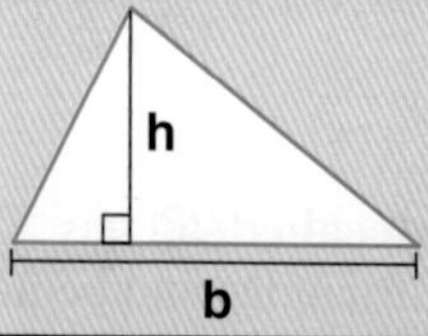

Triangle

$$^1/_2 \times b \times h$$

Trapezoid

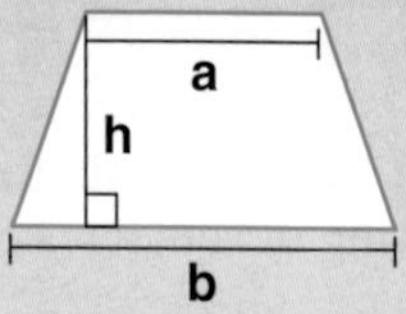

$$\frac{(a + b) \times h}{2}$$

$$\pi = 3.14159265358979323846$$

Geometry of volume
Abbreviations

b=breadth of base **l** =length of base
h=perpendicular height **r** =length of radius

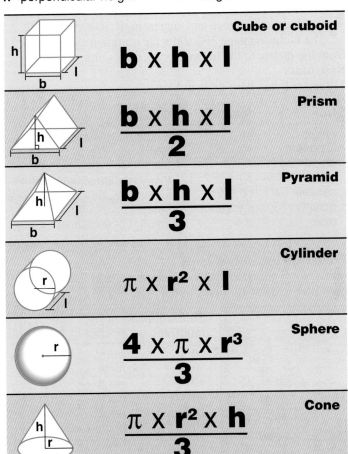

Cube or cuboid

$$b \times h \times l$$

Prism

$$\frac{b \times h \times l}{2}$$

Pyramid

$$\frac{b \times h \times l}{3}$$

Cylinder

$$\pi \times r^2 \times l$$

Sphere

$$\frac{4 \times \pi \times r^3}{3}$$

Cone

$$\frac{\pi \times r^2 \times h}{3}$$

11

26433832795028841971693993751

UNIT SYSTEMS
International System of Units
The International System of Units (or Système International d'Unités – SI) is the current form of the metric system that has been in use since 1960. In the US, the SI system is used in education, science and, increasingly, in everyday life.

The tables on page 303 show the common conversions from the metric to the imperial system of units.

Base units
There are seven base units in SI:

One meter is the average height of a 4-year-old

Unit	Symbol	Quantity
meter	m	length/distance
kilogram	kg	mass
ampere	A	electric current
kelvin	K	thermodynamic temperature
candela	cd	luminosity
second	s (or sec)	time
mole	mol	amount of substance

Prefixes to use with SI units
Prefixes are added to each of the base units to indicate multiples and submultiples of ten:

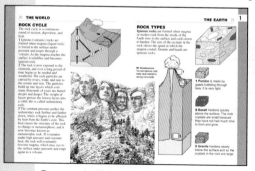

Two pages in this book cover 250 square centimeters

Submultiple/multiple	Prefix	Symbol
10^{-6}	micro-	r, μ
10^{-3}	milli-	m
10^{-2}	centi-	c
10^{-1}	deci-	d
10	deca-	da
10^{2}	hecto-	h
10^{3}	kilo-	k
10^{6}	mega-	M

Derived units

In addition, the SI system uses derived units. For example, velocity is given in meters per second (m/s, ms⁻¹). Other derived units in SI are referred to by special names: the watt (W) is a unit of power; the joule (J) is a unit of energy.

Common conversions

	Metric	Imperial
Length		
	1 millimeter (mm)	0.039 in
	1 centimeter (cm)	0.394 in
	1 meter (m)	3.281 ft = 1.094 yd
	1 kilometer (km)	1094 yd = 0.621 mi

One liter is just over two pints

	Metric	Imperial
Area		
	1 square millimeter (mm²)	0.015 in²
	1 square centimeter (cm²)	0.155 in²
	1 square meter (m²)	10.764 ft² = 1.196 yd²
	1 hectare (ha)	2.471 acres = 0.00386 mi²
	1 square kilometer (km²)	0.386 mi²

11

	Metric	Imperial
Volume		
	1 cubic centimeter (cm³)	0.061 in³
	1 cubic meter (m³)	35.315 ft³ = 1.308 yd³ = 220 gallons
	1 milliliter (ml)	0.034 fl oz
	1 centiliter (cl)	0.338 fl oz
	1 liter (l)	1.76 pts = 0.88 quarts = 0.22 gallons

One kilogram is just over two pounds

	Metric	Imperial
Weight		
	1 gram (g)	0.035 oz
	1 kilogram (kg)	2.205 lb = 35.28 oz
	1 tonne (t)	1.102 tons = 2204.623 lb

CONVERSION FORMULAE

Below are listed the multiplication/division factors for converting units of length from imperial to metric, and vice versa. For conversion formulae for area see pp. 306–7; for volume see pp. 307–10; for weight see pp. 310–11; for energy see p. 312; for speed see pp. 313–14; and for temperature see pp. 314–315. Note that two kinds of factors are given: quick, for an approximate conversion that can be made without a calculator; and accurate, for an exact conversion. The diagram drawn with each conversion shows an approximate visual comparison of the two units.

Length

Milli-inches (mils) Micrometers (μm)	**Quick**	**Accurate**
mils → μm	× 25	× 25.4
μm → mils	÷ 25	× 0.0394

Inches (in) Millimeters (mm)		
in → mm	× 25	× 25.4
mm → in	÷ 25	× 0.0394

Inches (in) Centimeters (cm)		
in → cm	× 2.5	× 2.54
cm → in	÷ 2.5	× 0.394

Feet (ft) Meters (m)		
ft → m	÷ 3.3	× 0.305
m → ft	× 3.3	× 3.281

Yards (yd) Meters (m)		
yd → m	÷ 1	× 0.914
m → yd	× 1	× 1.094

Fathoms (fm) Meters (m)		**Quick**	**Accurate**
fm → m		× 2	× 1.83
m → fm		÷ 2	× 0.547

Chains (ch) Meters (m)			
ch → m		× 20	× 20.108
m → ch		÷ 20	× 0.0497

Furlongs (fur) Meters (m)			
fur → m		× 200	× 201.17
m → fur		÷ 200	× 0.005

Kilometers (km) Yards (yd)			
yd → km		÷ 1000	× 0.00091
km → yd		× 1000	× 1093.6

Miles (mi) Kilometers (km)			
mi → km		× 1.5	× 1.609
km → mi		÷ 1.5	× 0.621

Nautical miles (n mi) Miles (mi)			
n mi → mi		× 1.2	× 1.151
mi → n mi		÷ 1.2	× 0.869

Nautical miles (n mi) Kilometers (km)			
n mi → km		× 2	× 1.852
km → n mi		÷ 2	× 0.54

11

Area

		Quick	Accurate
Circular mils (cmil) Square micrometers (μm²)			
cmil ⟶ μm²		× 500	× 506.7
▪ μm² ⟶ cmil		÷ 500	× 0.002
Square inches (in²) Square millimeters (mm²)			
in² ⟶ mm²		× 650	× 645.2
▪ mm² ⟶ in²		÷ 650	× 0.0015
Square inches (in²) Square centimeters (cm²)			
in² ⟶ cm²		× 6.5	× 6.452
cm² ⟶ in²		÷ 6.5	× 0.15
Square chains (ch²) Square meters (m²)			
ch² ⟶ m²		× 400	× 404.686
▪ m² ⟶ ch²		÷ 400	× 0.0025
Square miles (mi²) Square kilometers (km²)			
mi² ⟶ km²		× 2.5	× 2.590
km² ⟶ mi²		÷ 2.5	× 0.386

	Square miles (mi^2) Hectares (ha)	**Quick**	**Accurate**
	mi^2 ⟶ ha	× 250	× 258.999
	ha ⟶ mi^2	÷ 250	× 0.0039
	Hectares (ha) Acres		
	ha ⟶ acre	× 2.5	× 2.471
	acre ⟶ ha	÷ 2.5	× 0.405
	Square meters (m^2) Square yards (yd^2)		
	m^2 ⟶ yd^2	× 1	× 1.196
	yd^2 ⟶ m^2	÷ 1	× 0.836
	Square meters (m^2) Square feet (ft^2)		
	m^2 ⟶ ft^2	× 11	× 10.764
	ft^2 ⟶ m^2	÷ 11	× 0.093

11

Volume

	UK gallons (gal) US fluid gallons (fl gal)	**Quick**	**Accurate**
	UK gal ⟶ US fl gal	× 1	× 1.201
	US fl gal ⟶ UK gal	÷ 1	× 0.833

			Quick	Accurate
1 **1**	UK quarts (qt) US fluid quarts (fl qt)			
	UK qt ⟶ US fl qt		× 1	× 1.201
	US fl qt ⟶ UK qt		÷ 1	× 0.833
1 **1**	UK pints (pt) US fluid pints (fl pt)			
	UK pt ⟶ US fl pt		× 1	× 1.201
	US fl pt ⟶ UK pt		÷ 1	× 0.833
1 **1**	UK fluid ounces (fl oz) US fluid ounces (fl oz)			
	UK fl oz ⟶ US fl oz		× 1	× 0.961
	US fl oz ⟶ UK fl oz		÷ 1	× 1.041
1 **2**	UK fluid ounces (fl oz) Cubic inches (in³)			
	UK fl oz ⟶ in³		× 2	× 1.734
	in³ ⟶ UK fl oz		÷ 2	× 0.577
1 **16**	Cubic inches (in³) Cubic centimeters (cm³)			
	in³ ⟶ cm³		× 16	× 16.387
	cm³ ⟶ in³		÷ 16	× 00.061
1 **30**	UK fluid ounces (fl oz) Milliliters (ml)			
	UK fl oz ⟶ ml		× 30	× 29.574
	ml ⟶ UK fl oz		÷ 30	× 0.034
1 **1**	UK quarts (qt) Liters (l)			
	UK qt ⟶ l		× 1	× 1.137
	l ⟶ UK qt		÷ 1	× 0.880

1	UK gallons (gal)	**Quick**	**Accurate**
4.5	Liters (l)		
	UK gal ⟶ l	× 4.5	× 4.546
	l ⟶ UK gal	÷ 4.5	× 0.220

1	Liters (l)		
2	UK pints (pt)		
	l ⟶ UK pt	× 2	× 1.760
	UK pt ⟶ l	÷ 2	× 0.568

1	Cubic meters (m³)		
35	Cubic feet (ft³)		
	m³ ⟶ ft³	× 35	× 35.315
	ft³ ⟶ m³	÷ 35	× 00.028

1	Cubic meters (m³)		
1	Cubic yards (yd³)		
	m³ ⟶ yd³	× 1	× 1.308
	yd³ ⟶ m³	÷ 1	× 0.765

1	Cubic meters (m³)		
220	UK gallons (gal)		
	m³ ⟶ UK gal	× 220	× 219.970
	UK gal ⟶ m³	÷ 220	× 010.005

1	US fluid ounces (fl oz)		
30	Milliliters (ml)		
	US fl oz ⟶ ml	× 30	× 29.572
	ml ⟶ US fl oz	÷ 30	× 00.034

1	US fluid gallons (fl gal)		
4	Liters (l)		
	US fl gal ⟶ l	× 4	× 3.785
	l ⟶ US fl gal	÷ 4	× 0.264

11

			Quick	Accurate
1 **2**	Liters (l) US fluid pints (fl pt)			
	l ⟶ US fl pt		× 2	× 2.113
	US fl pt ⟶ l		÷ 2	× 0.473
1 **1**	Liters (l) US fluid quarts (fl qt)			
	l ⟶ US fl qt		× 1	× 1.056
	US fl qt ⟶ l		÷ 1	× 0.947
1 **264**	Cubic meters (m³) US fluid gallons (fl gal)			
	m³ ⟶ US fl gal		× 264	× 264.173
	US fl gal ⟶ m³		÷ 264	× 0.004
1 **227**	Cubic meters (m³) US dry gallons (dry gal)			
	m³ ⟶ dry gal		× 227	× 227.020
	dry gal ⟶ m³		÷ 227	× 0.004

Weight

The term "weight" differs in everyday use from its scientific use. In everyday terms, we use weight to describe how much substance an object has. In science, the term "mass" is used to describe this quantity of matter. Weight is used to describe the gravitational force on an object and is equal to its mass multiplied by the gravitational field strength. In scientific terms, mass remains constant but weight varies according to the strength of gravity. All units that follow are strictly units of mass rather than weight, apart from the pressure units kg/cm² and PSI.

		Quick	**Accurate**
Grains (gr) Grams (g)			
g ⟶ gr		× 15	× 15.432
gr ⟶ g		÷ 15	× 0.065
Ounces (oz) Grams (g)			
oz ⟶ g		× 28	× 28.349
g ⟶ oz		÷ 28	× 0.035
Ounces troy (oz tr) Grams (g)			
oz tr ⟶ g		× 31	× 31.103
g ⟶ oz tr		÷ 31	× 0.032
Stones (st) Kilograms (kg)			
st ⟶ kg		× 6	× 6.350
kg ⟶ st		÷ 6	× 0.157
Long (UK) tons (l t) Tonnes (t)			
l t ⟶ t		× 1	× 1.016
t ⟶ l t		÷ 1	× 0.984
Kilograms (kg) Pounds (lb)			
kg ⟶ lb		× 2	× 2.205
lb ⟶ kg		÷ 2	× 0.454

11

	Kilograms per square centimeter (kg/cm²) Pounds per square inch (PSI)		
	kg/cm² ⟶ PSI	× 14	× 14.223
	PSI ⟶ kg/cm²	÷ 14	× 0.070
	Tonnes (t) Short (US) tons (sh t)		
	t ⟶ sh t	× 1	× 1.102
	sh t ⟶ t	÷ 1	× 0.907
	Ounces troy (oz tr) Ounces (oz)		
	oz tr ⟶ oz	× 1	× 1.097
	oz ⟶ oz tr	÷ 1	× 0.911

Energy

	Kilowatts (kW) Horsepower (hp)	**Quick**	**Accurate**
	kW ⟶ hp	× 1.5	× 1.341
	hp ⟶ kW	÷ 1.5	× 0.746
	Calories (cal) Joules (J)		
	cal ⟶ J	× 4	× 4.187
	J ⟶ cal	÷ 4	× 0.239
	Kilocalories (kcal) Kilojoules (kJ)		
	kcal ⟶ kJ	× 4	× 4.187
	kJ ⟶ kcal	÷ 4	× 0.239

Speed

		Quick	Accurate
Miles per hour (mph)			
Kilometers per hour (km/h)			
mph ⟶ km/h		× 1.5	× 1.609
km/h ⟶ mph		÷ 1.5	× 0.621
Yards per minute (ypm)			
Meters per minute (m/min)			
ypm ⟶ m/min		× 1	× 1.094
m/min ⟶ ypm		÷ 1	× 0.914
Feet per minute (ft/min)			
Meters per minute (m/min)			
ft/min ⟶ m/min		÷ 3	× 0.305
m/min ⟶ ft/min		× 3	× 3.281
Inches per second (in/s)			
Centimeters per second (cm/s)			
in/s ⟶ cm/s		× 2.5	× 2.54
cm/s ⟶ in/s		÷ 2.5	× 0.394
International knots (kn)			
Miles per hour (mph)			
kn ⟶ mph		× 1	× 1.151
mph ⟶ kn		÷ 1	× 0.869
British knots (UK kn)			
International knots (kn)			
UK kn ⟶ kn		× 1	× 1.001
kn ⟶ UK kn		÷ 1	× 0.999

11

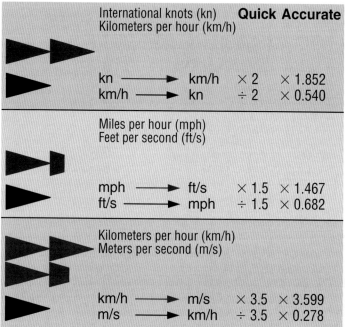

International knots (kn)   **Quick Accurate**
Kilometers per hour (km/h)

kn ———→ km/h   × 2   × 1.852
km/h ———→ kn   ÷ 2   × 0.540

Miles per hour (mph)
Feet per second (ft/s)

mph ———→ ft/s   × 1.5   × 1.467
ft/s ———→ mph   ÷ 1.5   × 0.682

Kilometers per hour (km/h)
Meters per second (m/s)

km/h ———→ m/s   × 3.5   × 3.599
m/s ———→ km/h   ÷ 3.5   × 0.278

°C   °F
100 — 210
90 — 200
    — 190
80 — 180
    — 170
70 — 160
    — 150
60 — 140
    — 130
50 — 120
    — 110
40 — 100
30 — 90
    — 80
20 — 70
    — 60
10 — 50
    — 40
0 — 32
    — 20
-10 — 10
    — 0
-20 — -10
-30 — -20

Temperature comparisons
a water boils   100 °C (212 °F)
b hot tea   38 °C (100 °F)
c blood heat   37 °C (98 °F)
d warm room   21 °C (70 °F)
e cold day   5 °C (41 °F)
f water freezes   0 °C (32 °F)
g in the freezer   –29 °C (–20 °F)

Temperature units

Below, the different systems of temperature measurement are compared: Fahrenheit (°F), Celsius (°C), Réaumur (°r), Kelvin (K) and Rankine (°R). Also listed are the formulae for converting temperature measurements from one system to another. The Kelvin is the base unit of temperature in the SI system.

Formulae

°F ➡ °C   (°F−32)÷1.8   °r ➡ K   (°r×1.25)+273.16
°C ➡ °F   (°C×1.8)+32   °R ➡ K   °R÷1.8
°F ➡ K   (°F+459.67)÷1.8   K ➡ °F   (K×1.8)−459.67
°C ➡ K   °C+273.16   K ➡ °C   K−273.16

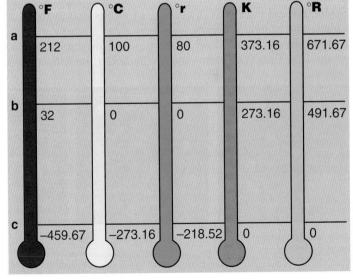

	°F	°C	°r	K	°R
a	212	100	80	373.16	671.67
b	32	0	0	273.16	491.67
c	−459.67	−273.16	−218.52	0	0

a boiling point of water   **c** absolute zero
b freezing point of water

11

ENERGY

Energy is the capacity for doing work. Energy and work have particular meanings in science. A man climbing some stairs or a car moving along are examples of actions that involve energy and work. Work is done whenever a force causes movement.

There are different forms of energy. Any form of energy can be changed into any other form of energy. Below are some of the important energy forms and the ways in which energy changes can be made.

1 Electrical energy is provided by an electrical current which is produced by the movement of electrons from one atom to another.

2 Chemical energy is stored in an atom or a molecule. It is produced by chemical reactions. It is stored in fuels and in food.

3 Radiant energy consists of rays, waves, or particles, especially electromagnetic radiation. This includes infra-red radiation, ultraviolet radiation, X-rays, gamma rays, and cosmic rays.

4 Nuclear energy uses the energy stored in an atom's nucleus.

5 Mechanical energy is the energy of things that move. It includes both kinetic and potential energy.

6 Heat energy is produced by the random movement of a substance's atoms. The faster the atoms move, the hotter the substance becomes.

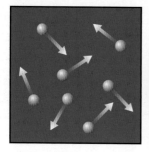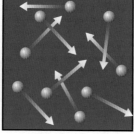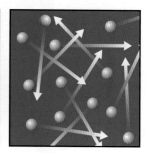

The faster atoms move
the greater the heat

Examples of energy changes

The diagram shows the energy changes in each situation, for example, in a dynamo, mechanical energy is converted to electrical energy.

a Dynamo
b Friction
c Electric motor
d Electric heater
e Light bulb
f Nuclear power station
g Atomic bomb

h Hot-air balloon
i Anything red- or white-hot
j Solar heating panels
k Solar cells
l Photosynthesis
m Batteries
n Oil furnace

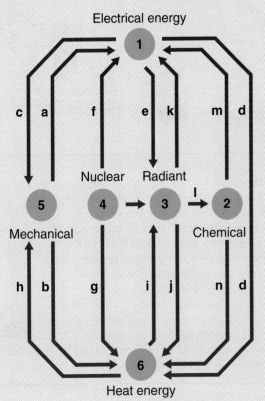

12

Kinetic and potential energy

In scientific terms a tile (**1**) falling off a roof (**2**) and breaking a pane of glass (**3**) below is doing work. The tile has energy. When the tile is falling it has kinetic energy. All moving objects have kinetic energy. Potential energy is the energy a stationary object has because of its state or position. The tile had potential energy because of its position above the ground and the force of gravity could act on it and make it move. Potential energy becomes kinetic energy when the object moves.

A skier has potential energy at the top of a mountain which becomes kinetic energy as he skies down the slope

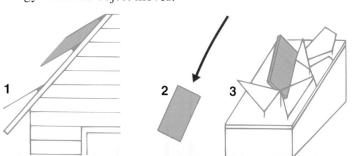

1 2 3

Einstein

Early last century a German scientist, Albert Einstein, suggested that matter was a form of energy. This theory was shown in his equation $E = mc^2$. E is the amount of energy produced, m is the mass and c (which is a constant) is the speed of light in a vacuum (300,000 km/s). Einstein's theory was proved by the development of nuclear energy. Nuclear power stations convert matter in an atom directly into heat energy.
Even in efficient power stations only a tiny amount of fuel is converted into energy. The rest remains as matter. Einstein's theory makes it possible to calculate the huge amount of energy that could be released if the whole of the available mass could be converted into pure energy.

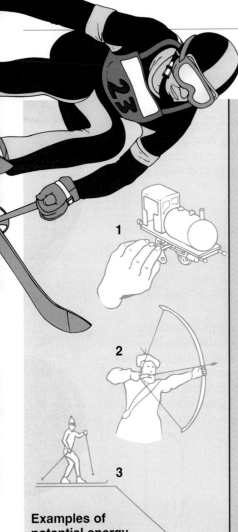

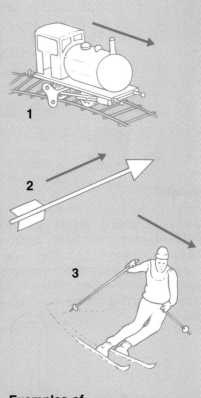

Examples of potential energy
1 stored in a spring
2 stored in a stretched bow
3 on top of a hill

Examples of kinetic energy
1 moving clockwork train
2 arrow in flight
3 downhill skier

12

VOLUME, WEIGHT, MASS, DENSITY

Volume

Volume is the amount of space occupied by an object. The volume of a hollow object can be measured by the amount of water needed to fill it. The volume of solid objects (such as cubes) can be found by suspending them in water in a measuring cylinder and observing how much the water level rises. The greater the volume of the object, the greater the change in water level. Displaced water equals the volume of the object.

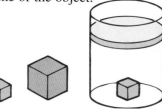

A soccer ball is 9 inches in diameter and weighs 16 oz

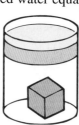

Weight

Weight is the force with which gravity pulls an object toward the ground. Weight varies with the force of gravity. Gravitational forces decrease with distance from the Earth's centre. The further away an object moves from the Earth's centre the lighter it becomes. Weight is measured using a spring balance. A lighter object will extend the spring balance less than a heavier one.

A bowling ball is 8½ inches in diameter and weighs 16 lb

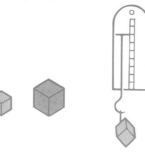

Mass

Mass is the amount of matter an object contains. The greater an object's mass the more difficult it becomes to move. The mass of an object remains the same wherever it is. An object's mass can be measured on a beam balance to compare it with objects whose mass is known already.

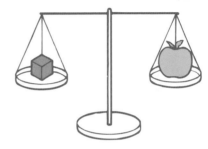

Density

Density is mass per unit volume. This means that if an object with a small volume has the same mass as an object with a large volume, the smaller object is said to have a greater density. Density is calculated by dividing the mass of an object by its volume.

The four cubes below represent 4 g each of platinum (**1**), granite (**2**), lead (**3**), and milk (**4**). The denser the material the smaller the volume for a fixed mass.

12

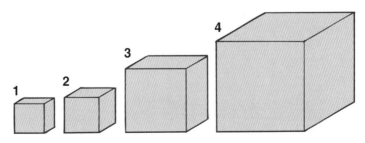

FORCES

Forces can change an object's shape, size, or the speed or direction in which it is travelling. Force is measured in newtons (N). 1 N is the amount of force needed to give a 1 kg mass an acceleration of 1 metre per second per second (1 m/s^2). This means with each second that passes the mass travels 1 m/s faster than it did the previous second.

Gravity

Gravity is the natural force pulling one object towards another. Its strength depends on the mass of the objects involved. Because the Earth is so large, objects on it are pulled towards it more than they are pulled towards each other. Earth's gravity exerts a pull of 9.8 N on a mass of 1 kg, so its weight on Earth is 9.8 N.

An apple is pulled towards the centre of the Earth. The Earth's mass is greater than the apple's mass, so its gravitational pull is stronger. An apple's mass is 0.1 kg. The pull of gravity gives the apple its weight. The weight of the apple = mass x gravity (= 0.1 x 9.8). The apple weighs 0.98 N.

An athlete able to jump 3 ft on Earth would be able to jump 18 ft on the Moon with the same effort because the gravitational pull of the Moon is weaker

Pressure

A force acting over a small area has a greater effect than a force acting over a large area. Pressure is "force per unit area." It is calculated by dividing the force by the area over which it is acting. The Earth's atmosphere has weight, and therefore exerts pressure (1 m³ of air weighs about 12 N). Atmospheric pressure can be measured using a barometer. In the diagrams below 1 kg exerts $^1/_{100}$ kg over each of the squares in diagram (**1**). In diagram (**2**) the weight is distributed over one square only. Therefore the full 1 kg of pressure is exerted on the small square.

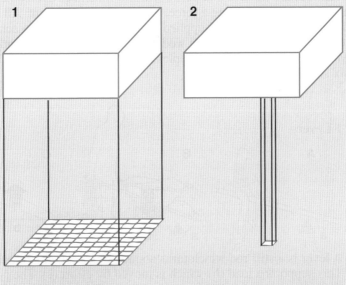

1 1 kg over 1 m² has a pressure of $^1/_{100}$ kg per cm²

2 1 kg over 1 cm² has a pressure of 1 kg per cm²

12

A plough is a form of wedge

MACHINES

Machines are devices that perform work. Machines overcome resistance at one point by applying a force, usually at another point. All machines depend on energy being supplied. There are six types of machine: the lever, the inclined plane, the wedge, the screw, the wheel, and the pulley. Most machines, however complex, are all based in some way on these six simple machines.

1 Levers

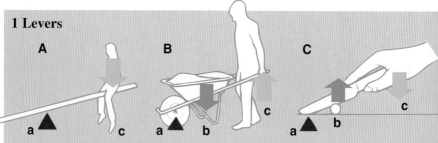

A lever is a stiff rod which turns about a point called a fulcrum (**a**). This supports a load (**b**) which is moved by effort (**c**). The positions of these elements create three types of lever. The nearer the fulcrum is to the load, the less effort is needed and the machine's mechanical advantage is greater.

A counterbalance is a form of lever

2 Inclined plane

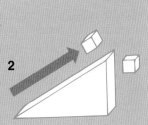

An inclined plane is a flat sloping surface. Much less effort is needed to move an object up an inclined plane than a vertical face.

3 Wedge

A wedge is a machine made of two inclined planes (**3a**). The smaller the angle formed by the wedge, the smaller the force needed for moving the load. Both the chisel (**3b**) and axe (**3c**) shown are examples of wedges.

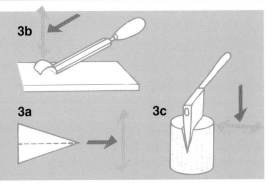

12

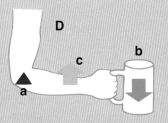

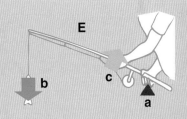

A seesaw (**A**) has a fulcrum in the centre. This is where the lever pivots. A wheelbarrow (**B**) and a knife (**C**) have the fulcrum at one end with the load in the centre. The effort is exerted at the opposite end to the fulcrum. Raising your arm to lift an object (**D**, **E**) has the load furthest away from the fulcrum. The effort is exerted in the centre.

4 Screw

A screw is an inclined plane which spirals around a pole (**4a**). A screw is much easier to get into a piece of wood than a nail. An Archimedean screw is a cylinder with a screw inside (**4b**). It lifts river water to irrigate fields in the Middle East.

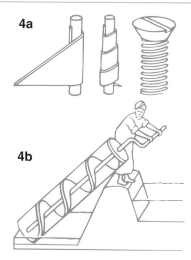

5 Wheel and axle

A wheel and axle is a form of lever but it is capable of moving a load further than a lever, helping to move loads overland.

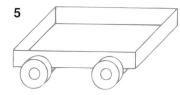

6 Pulley

The pulley is a wheel over which a rope or belt passes (**6a**). It is a form of wheel and axle which helps to change the direction of the force. A rope is pulled while the other end raises a load. A block and tackle has two pulleys (**6b**), one attached to a fixed support while the other moves with the load.

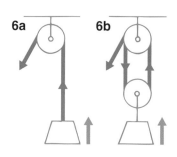

Medieval builders made extensive use of pulleys

MOTION

Everything in the Universe is in motion. The Earth moves around the Sun, and the Solar System is moving in its galaxy. People and animals move around by using their limbs, moved by muscles. Some animals, such as earthworms, move by contracting and squeezing muscles.

Speed
The rate of motion is called speed. It is measured by calculating the distance moved in a certain time.

Acceleration
Objects that are accelerating are increasing their speed. The faster the speed of an object increases, the greater its acceleration.

Velocity
Velocity is the rate at which an object changes position. An object's velocity describes its speed and the direction in which it is moving. An object travelling at a constant speed but moving in more than one direction has a changing velocity.

12

Laws of motion
The study of how objects move is called mechanics. Isaac Newton (1643–1727) discovered the laws that govern this. His three laws of motion are:
1 An object remains at rest or moves in a straight line until a force acts upon it.
2 When a force acts on a moving object its rate of acceleration is proportional to the force and in the direction of the force.
3 Action and reaction are equal and opposite. This means that the action of a force always produces a reaction in the object.

ELECTRICITY

Electricity involves the flow of electric charges which are either positive or negative. Electricity is about the way atoms behave. Atoms are made of subatomic particles. These are electrons which are negatively charged, protons which are positively charged, and neutrons which are neutral.

Properties of charged particles

Charged particles react to each other in specific ways.

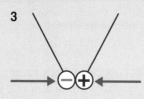

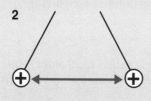

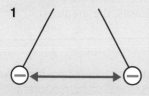

1 Two negatively charged particles repel or push against each other.

2 Two positively charged particles repel each other.

3 Two oppositely charged particles attract each other.

Electrons

Electrons move around the nucleus of an atom at high speeds. When negatively charged electrons move from atom to atom, the energy released is electricity.

Michael Faraday demonstrating the principles of electricity

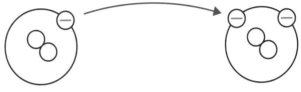

Ions

Ions are atoms or groups of atoms that are electrically charged because they have lost or gained one or more electrons. An atom is usually neutral because the number of positively charged protons in the nucleus equals the number of negatively charged electrons.

An electrically neutral atom (**1**) has an equal number of electrons and protons.

When an atom has an electron removed (**2**), it becomes a positive ion because it has one more proton than electrons. When an atom gains an electron, it becomes a negative ion. It has one more electron than protons.

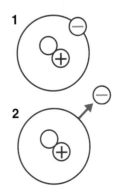

12

ELECTRIC CURRENT

An electric current is a continual flow of electrons through a conductive material, such as copper wire. This illustration represents static electricity.

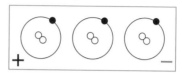

Direct current

Direct current (DC) will flow in one direction only, from the negative to the positive terminal within the electric circuit, as the electrons move between the atoms in one direction only. A good example of this is the electric current produced by a battery.

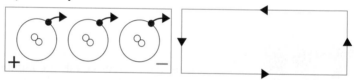

Alternating current

Alternating current (AC) will change its direction of flow at regular intervals. The electrons move between each other in one direction and then in another very quickly. They generate energy as they move. A domestic electricity supply can convert alternating current to direct current.

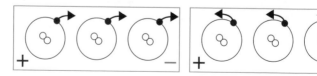

MAGNETISM

Magnetism is the name given to the invisible force which attracts some materials to each other and which acts between electric currents. Magnetism is produced by "ferromagnetic" metals. They have tiny molecules which act like miniature magnets and are called dipoles. If a bar is unmagnetized (**1**), the dipoles form closed chains, their opposite ends (poles) attract and there are no free poles. In a magnetized bar (**2**), the chains are broken and the dipoles are aligned, producing free poles at each end of the bar.

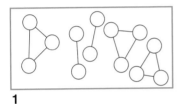

1

2

Opposite ends of a magnet have opposite polarity

12

Magnetic fields

A magnet is surrounded by a magnetic field which is invisible. The magnetic field is strongest at its north and south poles. Two different poles of two magnets attract each other.

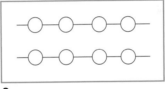

N   S   N   S

Two like poles repel each other.

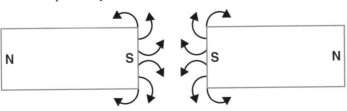

N   S   S   N

Some magnets are stronger than others

ELECTROMAGNETISM

An electromagnet is a magnet which only produces magnetism because of an electric current flowing through a wire. Electromagnets are usually made from a piece of wire coiled around many times to increase the magnetic effect. The magnetic field created by the coil can be increased further by putting a magnetic material, such as an iron rod, inside the coil. The current flowing through the coil causes the iron to become temporarily magnetic.

Creating an electromagnetic field

When an electric current is passed along a wire, a magnetic field is created around it (**1**).

When the wire is wrapped around a piece of metal, leaving the north and south poles free, the metal becomes magnetized (**2**). This is now an electromagnet. Scrap metal merchants often use large electromagnets to pick up old cars. When the electric current is turned off the magnet loses its power and a car can be dropped in another spot.

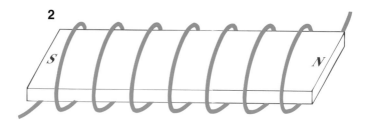

Electromagnetic waves

Light, radio waves, X-rays, and other forms of radiant energy are transmitted through space as energy waves called electromagnetic waves. These waves have crests (**1**) and troughs (**2**), just like waves formed when a stone is thrown into still water. The distance between the waves' crests is called the wavelength (**3**). It is measured in metres. The number of waves per second is called the frequency and it is measured in hertz (Hz). All electromagnetic waves travel at the speed of light. This is the frequency of an electromagnetic wave multiplied by its wavelength.

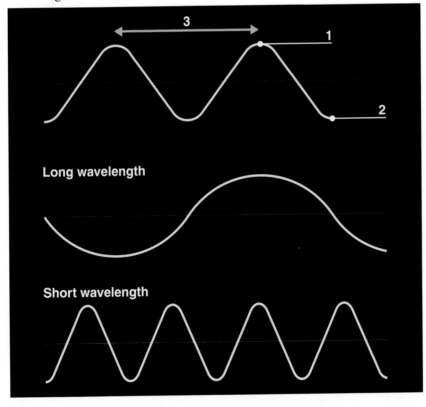

Long wavelength

Short wavelength

12

ELECTROMAGNETIC SPECTRUM

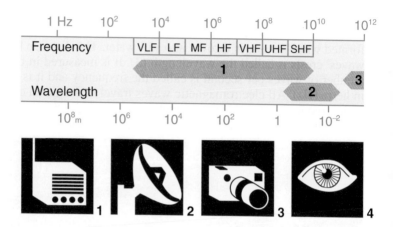

Above is a diagram of the electromagnetic spectrum, showing the different forms of energy in order of frequency and wavelength. The top part of the diagram shows the frequency in hertz (Hz); the lower part measures the wavelength in metres.

1 Radio waves

These waves transmit television and radio signals. This section of the spectrum is divided into bands, from VLF (very low frequency) – used for time signals – to SHF (super-high frequency) – used for space and satellite communication.

2 Radar and microwaves

Radar bounces off objects, allowing unseen objects to be located; microwaves can cook food quickly.

3 Infra-red waves

These invisible waves are emitted by all objects that radiate heat.

4 Visible light

The spectrum of colors which we can see, from violet at the highest

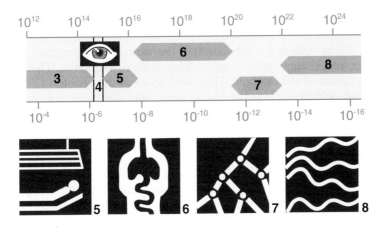

frequency, through indigo, blue, green, yellow, and orange to red at the lowest frequency end. The visible spectrum can be seen in a rainbow or with a prism. It was the first part of the spectrum to be discovered.

5 Ultraviolet light

In small amounts, these waves produce vitamin D and cause skin to tan; in larger amounts they can damage living cells.

6 X-rays

X-rays are capable of passing through many materials that are opaque to light. Their most familiar use is the photographing of internal structures of the body for medical purposes.

7 Gamma rays

Emitted during the decay of some radioisotopes, these waves can be very damaging to the body.

8 Cosmic rays

Caused by nuclear explosions and reactions in space, nearly all of these waves are absorbed by the Earth's atmosphere.

12

LIGHT

Light is produced by electromagnetic waves which have a particular range of frequencies and wavelengths. Each color we see has a different wavelength, ranging from violet which is 3.9×10^{-7} m to red which is 7.8×10^{-7} m. White light is a combination of the various wavelengths which produce red, orange, yellow, green, blue, indigo, and violet. These are the seven colors of the rainbow. They are known as the visible spectrum. Most objects, such as the Moon, rocks, and plants, do not produce light. They are seen by the light that they reflect. The Sun, stars, and electric lights give off their own light.

How light travels

Light travels in a straight line. This can be seen in a simple test using a light bulb. Three cards, each with a pinhole in the same place, are set up in front of the light bulb. The light can only be seen through the holes when all three cards are in a straight line.

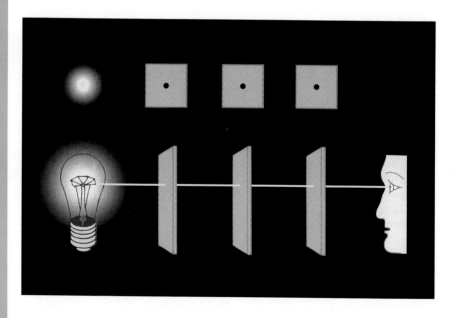

Visible spectrum

A glass prism (**1**) splits a beam of white light (**a**) into seven colors in the visible spectrum (**b**). The second prism (**2**) combines the colors to give white light again (**c**). When it rains and the Sun is shining, the raindrops act as a giant prism splitting the sunlight into the colors of the rainbow.

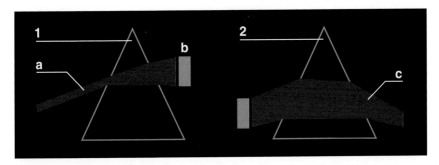

Colored substances

When white light falls on colored objects or surfaces, most objects absorb some wavelengths in the spectrum and reflect others. The wavelengths an object reflects give it its color. For example, a white object reflects all the colors of the spectrum (**1**). A black surface absorbs all the colors (**2**). A red surface (**3**) appears red because it reflects the red wavelengths but absorbs all the others.

12

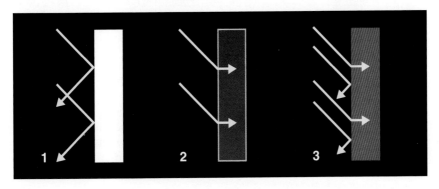

LIGHT INTENSITY

Light intensity diminishes as the square of the distance between the light source and the lit surface increases. For example, the amount of light falling on a 1 cm square (**1**) from a light source will spread over four squares that are placed twice as far from the light (**2**). And the light will fall on nine squares which are placed three times as far from the light source (**3**).

Mirrors

Mirrors and other shiny surfaces change the direction in which light rays travel by reflecting the light.

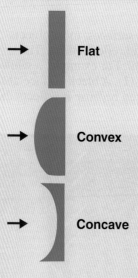

Flat

Convex

Concave

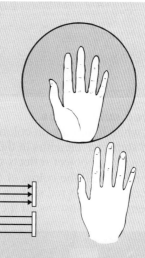

Flat mirror

A flat mirror produces an image which appears to be the same distance behind the mirror as the original object is in front of it. The image is the same way up and the same size as the object, but it is reversed.

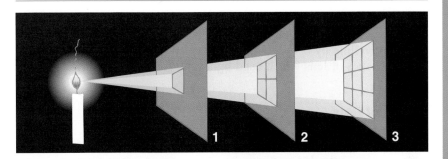

12

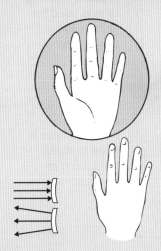

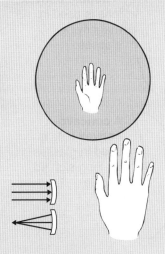

Convex mirror
A convex mirror gives a larger field of vision than a flat mirror of equal size. The image seen in a convex mirror is upright but reversed and larger than the original object.

Concave mirror
A concave mirror produces an image which is smaller than the original.

LENSES

Lenses and other transparent materials change the direction in which light is travelling by bending it. This is called refraction. There are various shapes of lens which bend light in different directions.

Types of lens

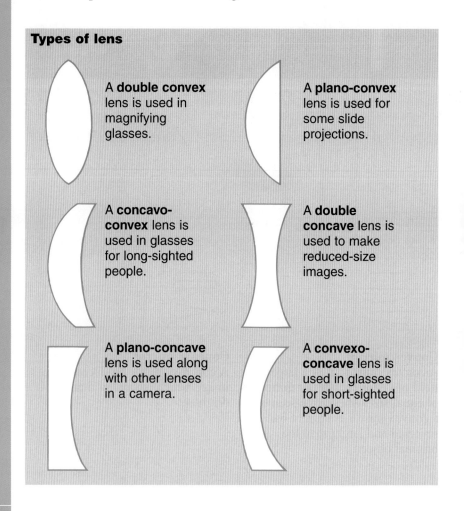

A **double convex** lens is used in magnifying glasses.

A **plano-convex** lens is used for some slide projections.

A **concavo-convex** lens is used in glasses for long-sighted people.

A **double concave** lens is used to make reduced-size images.

A **plano-concave** lens is used along with other lenses in a camera.

A **convexo-concave** lens is used in glasses for short-sighted people.

Concave lens

A concave lens is thinner at the centre than at the edges. It bends parallel light rays outward as they pass through the lens. A concave lens produces a reduced image which is the right way up and appears on the same side as the original object. This is a virtual image and it cannot be focused onto a screen.

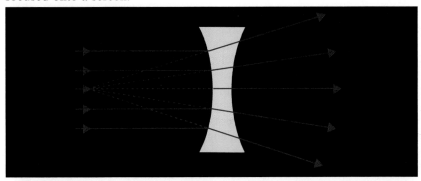

Convex lens

12

A convex lens is thicker in the centre than at the edges. It bends light rays inward to meet at a focal point behind the lens, producing a real image. The distance from the centre of the lens to the focal point is the focal length. An object which is less than one focal length from the lens becomes an enlarged image, the correct way up on the same side of the lens. If the object is moved further away a reduced, inverted image is seen on the opposite side of the lens.

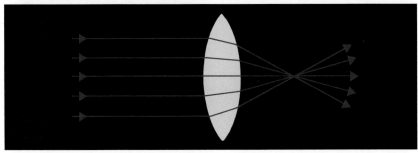

SOUND

Sound travels in the form of waves in air. Sound waves can also travel through water, metal, or any other material but they cannot travel through a vacuum. Sound travels at different speeds in different mediums, for example, it travels faster through water than air.

How sound is produced

The illustration shows how sound is produced when a metal tuning fork (**1**) vibrates backwards and forwards. The bar's vibrations send pressure waves through the air. Our ears detect waves of certain frequencies which we hear as sound.

The prongs of a tuning fork vibrate outwards, compressing air molecules nearby (**2**) and creating high pressure. As the fork vibrates inwards (**3**), the air expands, leaving an area of low pressure. Sound waves have many different frequencies, wavelengths (**4**), and amplitudes (**5**).

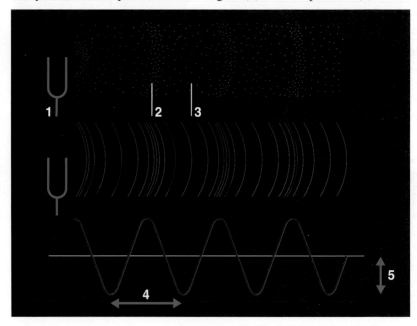

Pitch and quality

A sound's pitch and quality, whether it is high or low,
depends on its frequency or its wavelength.

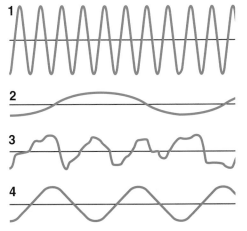

1 Short-wavelength or
high-frequency waves give
high-pitched sound.

2 Long-wavelength or low
frequency waves give
low-pitched sound.

3 Irregular waves give noise.

4 Regular waves give music.

12

How sound travels

Sound travels much faster through some mediums than others. The
chart below shows the effectiveness of some mediums in
transmitting sound.

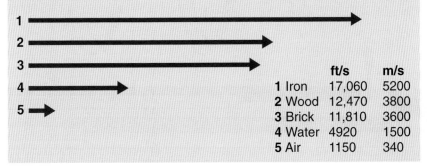

	ft/s	m/s
1 Iron	17,060	5200
2 Wood	12,470	3800
3 Brick	11,810	3600
4 Water	4920	1500
5 Air	1150	340

DECIBELS

The decibel (dB) is the unit used for the loudness of a sound, or its sound pressure.

Decibel scale

The decibel scale is relative and increases in stages, beginning with the tiniest sound change that can be heard by a human being (0–1 dB). A 20 dB sound is ten times louder than a 10 dB sound and 30 dB is 100 times louder than 10 dB. A noise around the level of 120 dB or higher is likely to be damaging to human hearing. Even higher levels can cause permanent ear damage.

Wave amplitude

One of the main properties of a sound wave is its amplitude. This is the distance between a wave crest or trough and an in-between line of balance (**1**). The greater the amount of energy transmitted in a sound wave, the greater is the wave's amplitude and the louder the sound.

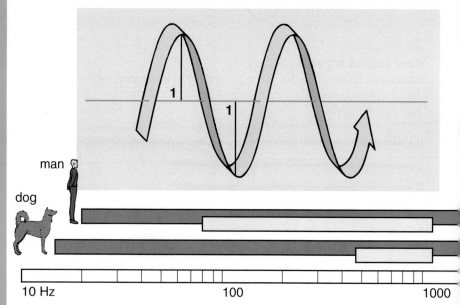

man

dog

10 Hz   100   1000

The chart shows the decibels of various sounds at certain distances and the effects on the human ear.

1 Human minimum 0 dB
2 Soft whisper at 15 ft 30 dB
3 Inside an urban home 50 dB
4 Light traffic at 50 ft 55 dB
5 Conversation at 3 ft 60 dB
6 Pneumatic drill at 50 ft 85 dB
7 Heavy traffic at 50 ft 90 dB
8 Loud shout at 50 ft 100 dB
9 Aeroplane taking off at 2000 ft 105 dB
10 Inside full-volume disco 117 dB
11 Aeroplane taking off at 200 ft 120 dB
12 Pain threshold for humans 130 dB
13 Aeroplane taking off at 100 ft 140 dB

Different animals are able to hear and produce sounds across different ranges.

☐ Range of sounds emitted

☐ Range of sounds heard

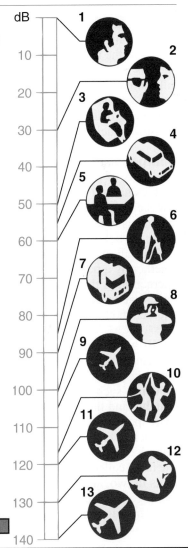

dB
10
20
30
40
50
60
70
80
90
100
110
120
130
140

10,000   100,000 Hz

12

NUCLEAR PHYSICS

Nuclear physics is essentially the study of what occurs in the nucleus, or heart of an atom. A nucleus is approximately a thousand million millionth of a meter across. The human eye cannot see the nucleus but information about it and the particles inside it is obtained by smashing nuclei and observing the results.

Composition of an atomic nucleus

The study of the properties of the atomic nucleus has led to many important advances in science, medicine, and technology. An atomic nucleus is made up of protons and neutrons. These particles make up 99.9 per cent of the mass of all matter. The nucleus is mainly held together by a powerful force called the strong interaction or the strong nuclear force. It is this force that causes protons and neutrons to interact and bind together.

Radioactive emissions

Most nuclei are stable and they do not break down easily. However, the nuclei of some elements, such as radium and uranium, are unstable and they are radioactive. They break apart spontaneously and release energy as radioactive emissions called alpha, beta, and gamma rays. An understanding of nuclear reactions called fission, when a heavy nucleus splits in two, and fusion, when two light nuclei join together, has enabled scientists to release the tremendous energy of the nucleus for practical use.

Atomic particles colliding in a cloud chamber

Nuclear fission

Nuclear fission is the production of energy from the splitting of an atom's nucleus.

1 When the nucleus of an atom of uranium is struck by a neutron it causes fission.

2 The combined reactions produce an unstable atom.

3 Energy in the form of heat is released by the splitting atom.

4 Two or three additional neutrons are also produced. These new neutrons can cause further uranium nuclei to split, resulting in a continuous chain reaction.

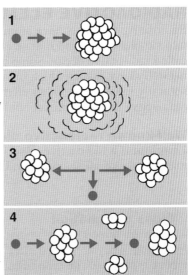

12

Nuclear fusion

Nuclear fusion is the production of energy from the joining together of atoms to form larger atoms.

1 When two isotopes of hydrogen, deuterium (hydrogen 2), and tritium (hydrogen 3) collide, fusion takes place.

2 The combination produces energy by the release of a neutron.

3 It also produces a larger atom of helium.

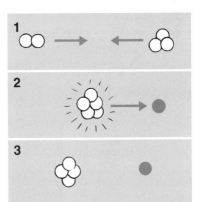

RADIOACTIVE ELEMENTS

Radioactive elements have atoms which tend to break down into simpler atoms and radiate energy. This process is called radioactive decay. Some elements which occur naturally have nuclei which break down, making them naturally radioactive. Other elements can be made radioactive under certain conditions in nuclear reactors.

Well-known radioactive elements

Uranium is a radioactive silver-white metal and it is the main source of nuclear energy. Uranium is plentiful but it is

Types of radiation

There are three kinds of radiation which are given out by a radioactive element. They are called after letters in the Greek alphabet: α alpha, ß beta, γ gamma. The type of radiation given out depends on the radioactive element. Some radioactive elements give off more than one type of radiation.

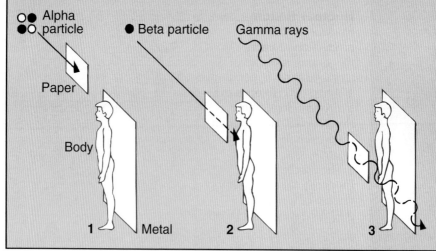

Alpha particle

Paper

Body

1 Metal

Beta particle

2

Gamma rays

3

only found in tiny amounts in most rocks where it occurs. It is highly reactive. Uranium is used chiefly as fuel for nuclear reactors and also for making atomic bombs.
Plutonium is a radioactive metallic element. Almost all plutonium is produced artificially and only a very small amount occurs naturally. Plutonium is highly poisonous because it rapidly gives off radiation in the form of alpha rays. Plutonium is also extremely explosive.
Thorium is a naturally-occurring radioactive metal which is more abundant than uranium. It has one of the highest known melting points at 6026 °F.

1 Alpha radiation
The emission of alpha particles. When a nucleus emits a fragment called an alpha particle it loses two protons and two neutrons. This gives it a positive electrical charge. Alpha particles are emitted with high energy but they lose it rapidly passing through matter and can be stopped by two sheets of paper.

2 Beta radiation
The emission of negative beta particles, which are electrons. Some nuclei emit positive electrons, or positrons. Beta particles travel almost at the speed of light. Beta radiation is about 100 times more penetrating than alpha radiation.

3 Gamma radiation
Gamma rays are similar to X-rays but with shorter wavelengths. Gamma rays have no electrical charge. They move at the speed of light and can travel long distances. Gamma radiation does not change the nucleus which is left behind. It is also much more penetrating than alpha or beta radiation.

12

MATTER

Matter on Earth is made up of atoms forming solids, liquids, and gases. **An element** is a single substance which cannot be broken down chemically into simpler substances. Zinc, oxygen, and gold are elements. There are about 90 elements which occur naturally and about another 20 elements have been produced artificially but not all of these have been recognized.

A compound is made of two or more elements chemically joined to form a new substance which has different qualities from the elements which produced it. Water is a compound. It is a liquid made from two elements, hydrogen and oxygen. In a compound the proportions of the elements are always the same.

A mixture is made from two or more substances which have not been chemically joined. Each element can be separated without a chemical change. A mixture can have ingredients in any proportion.

Examples of mixtures

A solution is a mixture of two or more substances which cannot be separated by using mechanical methods such as filtering. A solution can be a solid, a liquid, or a gas but the most common are liquids. The dissolved substance spreads evenly in the substance in which it dissolves.

A suspension is a mixture where one substance spreads evenly through another without dissolving. It includes solids in liquids or gases, gases in liquids, and liquids in gases. Suspensions containing very small particles are called colloids.

An emulsion is a liquid which is evenly spread through another liquid. Droplets of one liquid are evenly spread in the other but in time the two separate. This can be delayed by adding emulsifying agents. Paints and cosmetic lotions are examples of emulsions.

Changes

Matter can change its form

Solids like butter can be heated to turn to liquid

SOLIDS, LIQUIDS, AND GASES

Solid
A solid takes up a specific amount of space. Its molecules cannot move around freely, although they are not completely still. A solid will not alter its shape unless it is forced to do so.

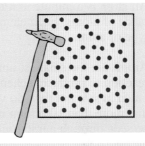

Liquid
A liquid also occupies a specific amount of space but, unlike a solid, it can alter its shape easily. A liquid will take the shape of any container into which it is poured. The molecules in a liquid can move around, but only in a limited way.

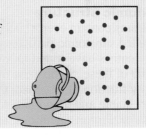

Gas
A gas does not have a specific shape or size. Its molecules can move around completely freely so a gas will spread out to fill a container. If the gas is not restricted it will continue to expand.

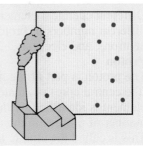

13

Liquids from melted butter form oil

Gases from heated oils form vapor

ATOMS AND MOLECULES

An atom is a minute unit of matter. Everything around us is made of atoms. Each element is made up of one particular type of atom.

Atoms are the smallest units that can take part in a chemical reaction to produce a chemical change. They do not vary much in size but they do vary in weight. Atoms are so small that more than 10 billion make up the tiniest object that can be seen through a microscope.

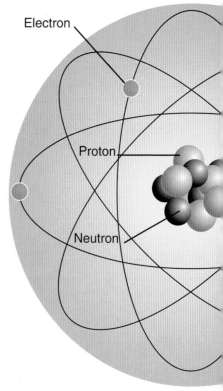

Atomic structure

Atoms contain even smaller units called subatomic particles. Scientists have found more than 200 of these. Some exist for only a tiny fraction of a second. Others are stable and do not break down easily. Protons, neutrons, and electrons are stable particles. Different chemical elements have different numbers of protons, neutrons, and electrons.

Proton

The proton is part of the nucleus (the central core) of an atom. An element is identified by the number of protons in the atom. This is called the atomic number. If an atom gains or loses a proton, it becomes an atom of a different element. A proton has a positive electrical charge of 1 unit. It has a mass of 1.6726×10^{-27} kg.

Neutron

A neutron is also part of the nucleus. The number of neutrons in an atom can vary without the element changing identity. Forms of an element with different numbers of neutrons in the nucleus are called an element's isotopes. A neutron is electrically neutral as it carries no charge. It has a mass of 1.6748×10^{-27} kg.

Electron

Electrons move around the nucleus of an atom at high speed. The arrangement of electrons in an atom determines the element's chemical behavior. An electron has a negative charge of 1 unit. Atoms are electrically neutral as they have the same number of electrons as protons. An electron has a mass of 9.1096×10^{-31} kg.

Molecules

Two or more atoms joined together form a molecule. The atoms may come from the same element or from different elements. Molecules that contain atoms from two or more elements make up a compound. When a molecule is broken down it splits into the atoms of the elements from which it was made. Molecules can be made of two atoms or thousands of atoms. For example, an oxygen molecule only has two atoms but a rubber molecule has between 13,000 and 65,000 atoms.

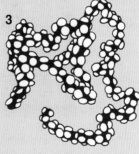

1 Oxygen molecule: 2 atoms. **2** Water molecule: 3 atoms
3 Rubber molecule: 13,000–65,000 atoms

13

PERIODIC TABLE

Calcium, gold, and hydrogen are chemical elements which are examples of basic chemical substances. They cannot be broken down into simpler forms. This gives each element distinctive properties. The Periodic Table gives information about all the 115 known elements. (Elements 113, 115 and 117 are not known, but are included in the table to show their expected positions. Elements 110–118 have not yet been officially named.)

1 H								
3 Li	4 Be							
1 Na	12 Mg							
19 K	20 Ca	21 Sc	22 T	23 V	24 Cr	25 Mn	26 Fe	27 Co
37 Rb	38 Sr	39 Y	40 Zr	41 Nb	42 Mo	43 Tc	44 Ru	45 Rh
55 Cs	56 Ba	57-71 -	72 Hf	73 Ta	74 W	75 Re	76 Os	77 Ir
87 Fr	88 Ra	89-103 -	104 Rf	105 Db	106 Sg	107 Bh	108 Hs	109 Mt

57 La	58 Ce	59 Pr	60 Nd	61 Pm	62 Sm	63 Eu
89 Ac	90 Th	91 Pa	92 U	93 Np	94 Pu	95 Am

The Periodic table was devised in 1869 by the Russian chemist Dmitri Mendeleyev. The table groups elements into seven lines or periods. As we read from left to right the elements become less metallic. The elements in each vertical group have similar chemical properties. Further information about the elements is given on pages 356–61.

Dmitri Mendeleyev devised the Periodic Table

																	2 He
			5 B	6 C	7 N	8 O	9 F	10 Ne
			13 Al	14 Si	15 P	16 S	17 Cl	18 Ar
28 Ni	29 Cu	30 Zn	31 Ga	32 Ge	33 As	34 Se	35 Br	36 Kr
46 Pd	47 Ag	48 Cd	49 In	50 Sn	51 Sb	52 Te	53 I	54 Xe
78 Pt	79 Au	80 Hg	81 Tl	82 Pb	83 Bi	84 Po	85 At	86 Rn
110 Ds	111 Rg	112 Uub	113 Uut	114 Uuq	115 Uup	116 Uuh		

64 Gd	65 Tb	66 Dy	67 Ho	68 Er	69 Tm	70 Yb	71 Lu
96 Cm	97 Bk	98 Cf	99 Es	100 Fm	101 Md	102 No	103 Lr

13

CHEMICAL ELEMENTS

Chemical element; symbol; atomic number (relative atomic mass); origin of name; date of discovery.

Actinium; Ac; 89 (227.027 8); from the Greek *aktis*, ray; 1899

Aluminum; Al; 13 (26.98); from the Latin *alum*, an ore; 1827

Americium; Am; 95 (243); after America; 1944

Antimony; Sb; 51 (121.75); origin unknown; Latin *stibium*, antimony; before 1500

Argon; Ar; 18 (39.948); from Greek *argos*, inactive; 1894

Arsenic; As; 33 (74.9216); from Greek *arsenikon*, yellow ore containing arsenic; 1250

Astatine; At; 85 (210); from Greek *astatos*, unstable; 1940

Barium; Ba; 56 (137.33); from Greek *barys*, heavy; 1808

Berkelium; Bk; 97 (247); after Berkeley, California; 1950

Beryllium; Be; 4 (9.012 18); from Greek *beryllos*, beryl; 1798

Bismuth; Bi; 83 (208.980); from the German *wismut;* 1753

Bohrium; Bh; 107 (262); after Danish physicist Niels Bohr*;* 1981

Boron; B; 5 (10.81); from Arabic *burak*, borax; 1808

Bromine; Br; 35 (79.904); Greek *bromos,* unpleasant smell; 1826

Cadmium; Cd; 48 (112.41); after Cadmus, founder of Thebes; 1817

Caesium; Cs; 55 (132.905); from Latin *caesius*, bluish-gray; 1860

Calcium; Ca; 20 (40.08); from Latin *calx*, lime; 1808

Californium; Cf; 98 (251); after California; 1950

Carbon; C; 6 (12.011); from Latin *carbo*, charcoal; prehistoric

Cerium; Ce; 58 (140.12); after the asteroid Ceres; 1803

Chlorine; Cl; 17 (35.453); from Greek *khloros*, green; 1797

Chromium; Cr; 24 (51.996); from Greek *khroma*, color; 1797

Cobalt; Co; 27 (58.933 2); from German *kobold*, goblin; 1735

Glen Seaborg discovered americium

Sir Humphrey Davy discovered barium

Copper; Cu; 29 (63.546); from Latin *cuprum*, Cyprus metal; prehistoric

Curium; Cm; 96 (247); after Marie and Pierre Curie; 1944

Darmstadtium; DS; 110(271); after Darmstadt, Germany, 1994

Dubnium; Db; 105 (262); after the Dubna Institute, Moscow; 1967

Dysprosium; Dy; 66 (162.50); from Greek *dysprositos*, hard to get at; 1896

Einsteinium; Es; 99 (254); after Albert Einstein; 1952

Erbium; Er; 68 (167.26); after Ytterby, a Swedish town; 1843

Europium; Eu; 63 (151.96); after Europe; 1896

Fermium; Fm; 100 (257); after physicist Enrico Fermi; 1952

Fluorine; F; 9 (18.998 4); from the mineral fluorspar; 1771

Francium; Fr; 87 (223); after France; 1939

Gadolinium; Gd; 64 (157.25); after chemist, Gadolin; 1880

Gallium; Ga; 31 (69.72); from Latin *Gallia,* France; 1875

Germanium; Ge; 32 (72.59); from Latin *Germania,* Germany; 1886

Gold; Au; 79 (196.967); Old English *gold*; Latin, *aurum;* prehistoric

Hafnium; Hf; 72 (178.49); from Latin *Hafnia*, Copenhagen; 1923

Hassium; Hs; 108 (265); from Latin *Hassias*, Hess (the German state); 1984

Helium; He; 2 (4.002 60); from Greek *helios*, Sun; 1895

Holmium; Ho; 67 (164.930); from Latin *Holmia*, Stockholm; 1878

Hydrogen; H; 1 (1.007 9); from Greek *hydor*, water; *genes*, producing; 1766

Indium; In; 49 (114.82); from indigo line in its spectrum; 1863

Iodine; I; 53 (126.905); from Greek *iodes*, violet; 1811

Iridium; Ir; 77 (192.22); from Latin and Greek *iris*, rainbow; 1803

Iron; Fe; 26 (55.847); Old English *iren*; Latin *ferrum;* prehistoric

Krypton; Kr; 36 (83.8); from Greek *kryptos*, hidden; 1898

Marguerite Perey discovered francium

13

Henry Cavendish discovered hydrogen

Joseph Black
discovered
magnesium

Joseph
Priestley
discovered
nitrogen

Lanthanum; La; 57 (138.906); Greek *lanthanein*, to lie unseen; 1839

Lawrencium; Lr; 103 (260); after physicist Ernest Lawrence; 1961

Lead; Pb; 82 (207.2); Old English *lead*; Latin *plumbum*; prehistoric

Lithium; Li; 3 (6.941); from Greek *lithos*, stone; 1817

Lutetium; Lu; 71 (174.97); after *Lutetia*, old name for Paris; 1907

Magnesium; Mg; 12 (24.305); after Magnesia, in Thessaly; 1808

Manganese; Mn; 25 (54.938); alteration of Latin *magnesia;* 1774

Meitnerium; Mt; 109 (266); after Austrian physicist Lise Meitner*;* 1982

Mendelevium; Md; 101 (258); after chemist Mendeleyev; 1955

Mercury; Hg; 80 (200.59); after planet; Latin *hydrargynum;* prehistoric

Molybdenum; Mo; 42 (95.94); from Greek *molybdos*, lead; 1778

Neodymium; Nd; 60 (144.24); Greek *neo*, new; *didymos*, twin; 1885

Neon; Ne; 10 (20.179); from Greek *neo*, new; 1898

Neptunium; Np; 93 (237.048); after planet Neptune; 1940

Nickel; Ni; 28 (58.69); from German *kupfernickel*, devil's copper; 1751

Niobium; Nb; 41 (92.9064); after Niobe in Greek myth; 1801

Nitrogen; N; 7 (14.006 7); from nitre, saltpetre; Greek *genes*, producing; 1772

Nobelium; No; 102 (259); after Alfred Nobel; 1958

Osmium; Os; 76 (190.2); from Greek *osme*, smell; 1903

Oxygen; O; 8 (15.999 4); from Greek *oxys*, acid; *genes*, producing; 1774

Palladium; Pd; 46 (106.42); after asteroid Pallas; 1803

Phosphorus; P; 15 (30.973 8); from Greek *phosphorus*, light-bearing; 1669

Platinum; Pt; 78 (195.08); from Spanish *plata*, silver; 1735

Plutonium; Pu; 94 (244); after planet Pluto; 1940

Polonium; Po; 84 (209); from Latin *Polonia*, Poland; 1898

Potassium; K; 19 (39.098 3); after potash; Latin *kalium*, alkali; 1807

Praseodymium; Pr; 59 (140.908); Greek *prasios*, green; *didymos*, twin; 1885

Promethium; Pm; 61 (145); after Prometheus in Greek myth; 1945

Protactinium; Pa; 91 (231.036); from Greek *protos*, first; *actinium;* 1917

Radium; Ra; 88 (226.025); from Latin *radius*, ray; 1898

Radon; Rn; 86 (222); from radium; 1900

Rhenium; Re; 75 (186.207); from Latin *Rhenus*, Rhine; 1925

Rhodium; Rh; 45 (102.906); from Greek *rhodon*, rose; 1803–4

Roentgenium; Rg; 111 (272); after Wilhelm Roentgen; 1994

Rubidium; Rb; 37 (85.467 8); from Latin *rubidus*, ruby; 1861

Ruthenium; Ru; 44 (101.07); from Latin *Ruthenia*, Russia; 1844

Rutherfordium; Rf; 104 (261); after New Zealand physicist Lord Rutherford; 1964

Samarium; Sm; 62 (150.36); after mineral samerskite; 1879

Scandium; Sc; 21 (44.955 9); from Latin *Scandia*, Scandinavia; 1879

Seaborgium; Sg; 106 (263); after American nuclear chemist Glenn T. Seaborg; 1974

Selenium; Se; 34 (78.96); from Greek *selene*, moon; 1817

Silicon; Si; 14 (28.085 5); from Latin *silex*, flint; 1823

Silver; Ag; 47 (107.868); Old English *siolfor*, Latin *argentum;* prehistoric

Sodium; Na; 11 (22.989 8); from soda; Latin *natrium;* 1807

Strontium; Sr; 38 (87.62); after Strontian, a Scottish village; 1808

Sulfur; S; 16 (32.06); from Latin *sulfur;* prehistoric

Tantalum; Ta; 73 (180.948); after Tantalos in Greek myth; 1802

Technetium; Tc; 43 (97); from Greek *tekhnetos*, artificial; 1937

Tellurium; Te; 52 (127.60); from Latin *tellus*, earth; 1782

Lisa Meitner discovered protactinium

13

Marie Curie discovered radium

Jons Jacob
Berzelius
discovered
vanadium

Terbium; Tb; 65 (158.925); after Ytterby, town in Sweden; 1843

Thallium; Tl; 81 (204.383); from Greek *thallos*, green shoot; 1861

Thorium; Th; 90 (232.038); after Thor, Norse god of thunder; 1828

Thulium; Tm; 69 (168.934); from Latin *Thule*, Northland; 1879

Tin; Sn; 50 (118.71): Old English *tin*; Latin *stannum*; prehistoric

Titanium; Ti; 22 (47.88); after Titans in Greek myth; 1791

Tungsten; W; 74 (183.85); Swedish *tung sten*, heavy stone; 1781

Ununbium; Uub; 112 (277); (temporary name); 1996

Ununhexium; Uuh; 116 (289); (temporary name); 1999

Ununpentium; Uup; 115(288); (temporary name); 2004

Chemical elements by symbol

Ac	Actinium	**Cl**	Chlorine	**He**	Helium
Ag	Silver	**Cm**	Curium	**Hf**	Hafnium
Al	Aluminum	**Co**	Cobalt	**Hg**	Mercury
Am	Americium	**Cr**	Chromium	**Ho**	Holmium
Ar	Argon	**Cs**	Caesium	**Hs**	Hassium
As	Arsenic	**Cu**	Copper	**I**	Iodine
At	Astatine	**Db**	Dubnium	**In**	Indium
Au	Gold	**Ds**	Darmstadtium	**Ir**	Iridium
B	Boron	**Dy**	Dysprosium	**K**	Potassium
Ba	Barium	**Er**	Erbium	**Kr**	Krypton
Be	Beryllium	**Es**	Einsteinium	**La**	Lanthanum
Bh	Bohrium	**Eu**	Europium	**Li**	Lithium
Bi	Bismuth	**F**	Fluorine	**Lr**	Lawrencium
Bk	Berkelium	**Fe**	Iron	**Lu**	Lutetium
Br	Bromine	**Fm**	Fermium	**Md**	Mendelevium
C	Carbon	**Fr**	Francium	**Mg**	Magnesium
Ca	Calcium	**Ga**	Gallium	**Mn**	Manganese
Cd	Cadmium	**Gd**	Gadolinium	**Mo**	Molybdenum
Ce	Cerium	**Ge**	Germanium	**Mt**	Meitnerium
Cf	Californium	**H**	Hydrogen	**N**	Nitrogen

Ununquadium; Uuq; 114 (285); (temporary name); 1998

Ununtrium; Uut; 113 (288); (temporary name) 2004

Uranium; U; 92 (238.029); after planet Uranus; 1789

Vanadium; V; 23 (50.9415); after Vanadis, Norse goddess; 1801

Xenon; Xe; 54 (131.29); from Greek *xenos*, strange; 1898

Ytterbium; Yb; 70 (173.04); after Ytterby, town in Sweden; 1907

Yttrium; Y; 39 (88.905 9); after Ytterby, town in Sweden; 1828

Zinc; Zn; 30 (65.39); from German *zink*; 1800

Zirconium; Zr; 40 (91.224); from German *zirkon* and originally Persian *zargun*, golden; 1789

Sir William Ramsay discovered xenon

Na	Sodium	**Rb**	Rubidium	**Te**	Tellurium
Nb	Niobium	**Re**	Rhenium	**Th**	Thorium
Nd	Neodymium	**Rf**	Rutherfordium	**Ti**	Titanium
Ne	Neon	**Rg**	Roentgenium	**Tl**	Thallium
Ni	Nickel	**Rh**	Rhodium	**Tm**	Thulium
No	Nobelium	**Rn**	Radon	**U**	Uranium
Np	Neptunium	**Ru**	Ruthenium	**Uub**	Ununbium
O	Oxygen	**S**	Sulfur	**Uuh**	Ununhexium
Os	Osmium	**Sb**	Antimony	**Uuq**	Ununquadium
P	Phosphorus	**Sc**	Scandium	**Uup**	Ununpentium
Pa	Protactinium	**Se**	Selenium	**Uut**	Ununtrium
Pb	Lead	**Sg**	Seaborgium	**V**	Vanadium
Pd	Palladium	**Si**	Silicon	**W**	Tungsten
Pm	Promethium	**Sm**	Samarium	**Xe**	Xenon
Po	Polonium	**Sn**	Tin	**Y**	Yttrium
Pr	Praseodymium	**Sr**	Strontium	**Yb**	Ytterbium
Pt	Platinum	**Ta**	Tantalum	**Zn**	Zinc
Pu	Plutonium	**Tb**	Terbium	**Zr**	Zirconium
Ra	Radium	**Tc**	Technetium		

13

GROUPING THE ELEMENTS

The Periodic Table (see pages 354–55) is a way of ordering and comparing chemical elements. It gives information about all known chemical elements.

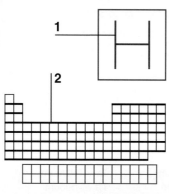

Periods

Each element is shown by its symbol (**1**) in the table. The elements are arranged in seven rows called periods (**2**). They are read from left to right and show a progression from metals to non-metals. Hydrogen does not clearly belong to any of the classes.

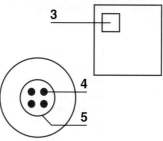

Elements are arranged in the periods according to their atomic number, from 1 to 118. This appears in the top left corner of each box (**3**). The number states how many protons (**4**) are in the element's nucleus (**5**). Protons are positively charged particles in an atom's centre.

Groups

Each column in the table is a group, read vertically. It contains elements with similar properties. There are eight major groups of elements, arranged according to how many electrons (**6**), negatively charged particles, are in the outer shell of the atom (**7**). Elements have between 1 and 8 electrons in the outer shell. Elements in each group behave similarly.

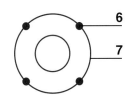

Alkali metals (1)

Lithium, sodium, potassium, rubidium, caesium, and francium are the elements in Group 1 of the Periodic Table. Alkali metals are so reactive that they are stored in oil to protect them from oxygen and water vapor in the air. Their melting and boiling points are low for metals, they float in water, and they can be cut with a knife. They react with water to form alkaline solutions.

Alkaline-earth metals (2)

The elements in Group 2 are beryllium, magnesium, calcium, strontium, barium, and radium. These elements are greyish-white in color. They are all malleable although

13

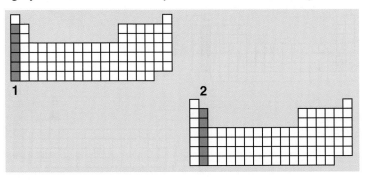

varying in hardness. The alkaline-earth metals have a pair of electrons on the outermost shell which can be removed from their atoms relatively easily to form positive ions. This gives them their particular chemical quality. They are not as reactive as the alkali metals.

Halogens (3)

Halogens are the elements in Group 7. They are fluorine, chlorine, bromine, iodine, and astatine. They are so reactive they never occur free in nature. Instead, they are found combined with metals in salts such as sodium chloride. This has led to them being called halogens, or salt-formers. Halogens occur in compounds with negative ions. Astatine is the only element in the group that does not occur in nature.

Noble gases (4)

Group 8 contains very unreactive elements. This group includes helium, neon, argon, krypton, xenon, and radon. They are all colorless gases at room temperature, with low melting and boiling points. They all exist as separate single atoms. Until 1962 no compounds of the noble gases were known and chemists thought they were completely unreactive, calling them inert gases.

Carbon (5)

Carbon is an important element. It is a nonmetallic element and forms only 0.2 per cent of the Earth's crust. Carbon is

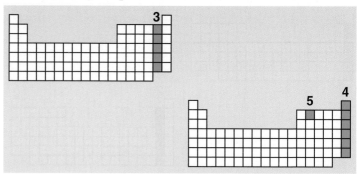

found naturally both in pure forms and in combination with other elements. Carbon occurs naturally in three forms: diamond, graphite, and charcoal. In diamond the carbon atoms are arranged regularly in a framework. Each atom is surrounded by four others producing a strong crystal structure and making diamond the hardest substance known. In graphite each atom is surrounded by three others. This produces a layer pattern, and makes graphite soft. Charcoal has a non-regular structure.

Carbon is a unique element because of the huge number and variety of its compounds. Carbon is the basis of organic chemistry and all living systems. The extensive and varied chemistry of carbon results from its ability to form single, double, and triple bonds with itself and other elements.

Transition elements (6)
The elements (highlighted) in this part of the table are called transition metals. Each element differs from its neighbor in another numbered period by the number of electrons (**a**) in its next to outer electron shell (**b**).

Lanthanide and actinide series (7)
The two bottom rows of the table are lanthanides and actinides. They are shown separately because their properties are so similar that they only cover two elements on the main table. Lanthanides are rare metallic elements. Actinides are chemically similar to them. Uranium is an actinide.

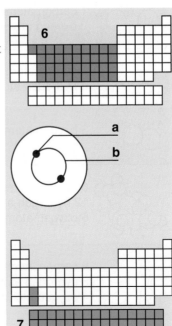

13

CHEMICAL SYMBOLS

A chemical symbol is a letter or a pair of letters which stands for a chemical element. The symbols are used in chemical equations and formulae. A chemical formula is a group of symbols used to describe different molecules.

Atoms joined together	Formula	Name
2 oxygen atoms	O_2	oxygen
2 hydrogen atoms + 1 oxygen atom	H_2O	water
1 carbon atom + 2 oxygen atoms	CO_2	carbon dioxide
1 carbon atom + 4 hydrogen atoms	CH_4	methane
3 oxygen atoms	O_3	ozone
6 carbon atoms + 12 hydrogen atoms + 6 oxygen atoms	$C_6H_{12}O_6$	glucose
9 carbon atoms + 8 hydrogen atoms + 4 oxygen atoms	$C_9H_8O_4$	aspirin

CHEMICAL REACTIONS

In a chemical reaction molecules in a substance gain or lose atoms or they are rearranged. Four main types of chemical reaction occur:

A combination reaction (1) This occurs when two or more substances combine to form a compound.

Decomposition (2) This occurs when a chemical compound breaks up, forming simpler substances.

Replacement (3) This occurs when a compound loses one or more elements but gains other elements to replace them.

Double decomposition (4) This is when two decomposing compounds exchange atoms to form two new compounds.

Common chemical reactions

13

Combustion is a rapid burning that occurs when oxygen combines quickly with another substance. **Corrosion** happens on metal surfaces when they react with air, chemicals, or moisture. **Destructive distillation** is the decomposition of substances in a closed container. **Digestion**, in animals, involves the breakdown of food by protein catalysts called enzymes. **Dissociation** is the break-up of a compound's molecules into simpler ingredients which may be recombined. **Electrolysis** occurs when an electric current passed through a liquid breaks up its parts. **Fermentation** is a change to organic substances caused by enzymes. **Oxidation** occurs when a substance loses electrons. These are gained by another substance, which undergoes **reduction**. The two reactions occur together (**redox** reaction).

BIOCHEMICAL CYCLES

The Earth's resources are constantly being used and reused. Biochemical changes recycle some of the key elements required by living things.

The oxygen cycle

The oxygen cycle is a vital part of life on Earth. All living things need oxygen to live and breathe.

1 Oxygen is in the air.

2 The oxygen is breathed in by animals.

3 It is breathed out as carbon dioxide which is a carbon–oxygen compound.

4 The carbon dioxide is absorbed by plants which combine it with water to make food.

5 Plants release the surplus oxygen into the air.

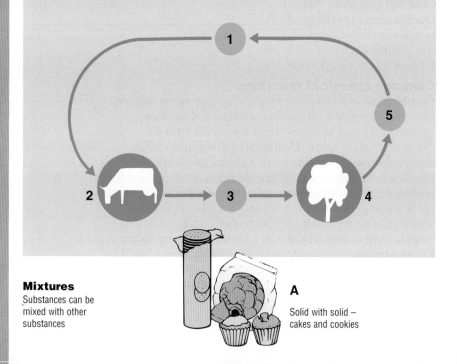

Mixtures

Substances can be mixed with other substances

A

Solid with solid – cakes and cookies

The carbon cycle

Carbon compounds make up the living tissues of all plants and animals. The carbon cycle is the circulation of carbon between living organisms and their surroundings. It describes the processes which increase and decrease the amount of carbon dioxide in the environment.

1 Carbon dioxide is in the air.

2 It is breathed in, or absorbed by plants.

3 Animals eat the plants.

4 Carbon dioxide is breathed out as waste by plants and animals.

5 Dead plants and animals are broken down by bacteria.

6 Bacteria convert the carbon compounds to carbon dioxide and the cycle starts again.

7 The remains of living organisms which have been dead a long time and microscopic organisms form fossil fuels.When burnt, carbon dioxide enters the atmosphere.

8 Volcanoes release carbon dioxide into the air.

13

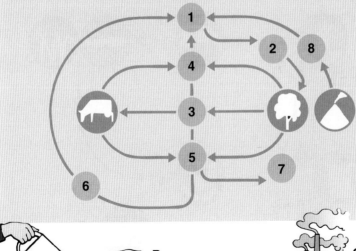

B
Solid with liquid –
jello or disolvable tablets

C
Solid with gas –
industrial smoke

The nitrogen cycle

All plants and animals need nitrogen, present in proteins and nucleic acids. Most living things, however, cannot use nitrogen directly from the atmosphere.

1 Nitrogen in the air.

2 Nitrogen in the atmosphere is trapped by some plant roots.

3 Plants use nitrogen for making proteins.

4 Animals eat plant proteins.

5 The proteins in dead organisms and in body wastes are converted to ammonia by bacteria and fungi.

6 Other bacteria convert the ammonia to nitrates.

7 Artificial nitrates added to soil as fertilizer. When too much is added, water supplies become polluted with nitrates.

8 Plants absorb the nitrates.

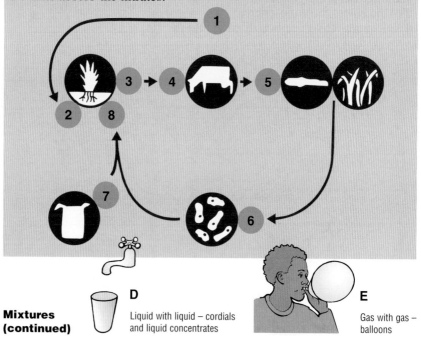

Mixtures (continued)

D
Liquid with liquid – cordials and liquid concentrates

E
Gas with gas – balloons

The sulfur cycle

Sulfur is an important part of almost every protein.

1 Sulfates, or sulfur–oxygen compounds, are absorbed by plant roots.

2 The oxygen in the sulfates is replaced by hydrogen in a plant process making amino acids.

3 Animals eat the plants.

4 In dead animals and plants the amino acids which contain sulfur are broken down by decomposer microorganisms to obtain hydrogen sulfide.

5 Bacteria extract sulfur from sulfides.

6 Other bacteria combine sulfur with oxygen to produce sulfates.

13

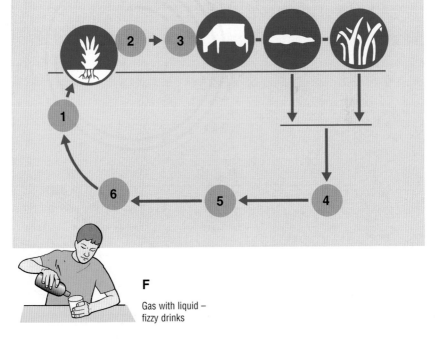

F

Gas with liquid –
fizzy drinks

EVOLUTION

The clock below marks key events in the Earth's history. They appear as if on a 12-hour clock which represents millions of years. The Earth (**1**) formed 4.6 billion years ago which is 12 hours ago. The first life on Earth (**2**) began 3.5 billion years ago in the form of single-cell organisms. Plants and animals (**3, 4**) appeared 1 billion years ago. Most fossils (**5**) were formed from 590 million years ago. On the next page are first appearances of animal and plant life on Earth in millions of years, which occurred in the last two hours.

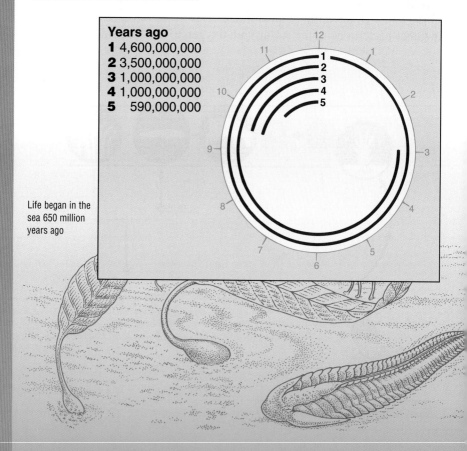

Years ago
1 4,600,000,000
2 3,500,000,000
3 1,000,000,000
4 1,000,000,000
5   590,000,000

Life began in the sea 650 million years ago

First appearance of life forms

The creatures today evolved from earlier species and some appeared in their present forms earlier than others. Crustaceans were among the first animals. They appeared nearly 650 million years before humans. Midway between their first appearance and that of humans, the insects developed their characteristics 380 million years ago.

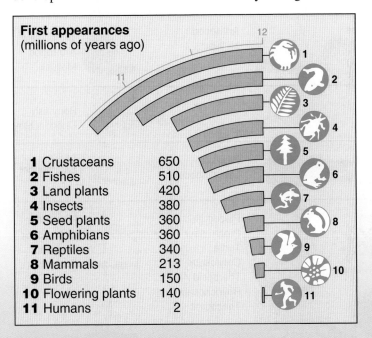

First appearances
(millions of years ago)

1	Crustaceans	650
2	Fishes	510
3	Land plants	420
4	Insects	380
5	Seed plants	360
6	Amphibians	360
7	Reptiles	340
8	Mammals	213
9	Birds	150
10	Flowering plants	140
11	Humans	2

14

AGE OF DINOSAURS 245–65 million years ago

TRIASSIC (245–208)   JURASSIC (208–144)

Plants 	Fern Cycad Conifer	 Conifer Cycad Ginkgo
Invertebrates 	Arthropod Mollusc	Tentaculate Arthropod Mollusk
Fishes		Bony fish Chondrichthyan
Amphibians	Frog Labyrinthodont	Salamander
Reptiles 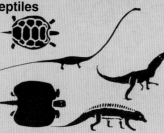	Placodont Protorosaur Turtle Cotylosaur Therapsid Rhynchosaur Thecodont	Plesiosaur Ichthyosaur Pterosaur Crocodilian
Birds		*Archaeopteryx*
Mammals	Prototherian	Prototherian

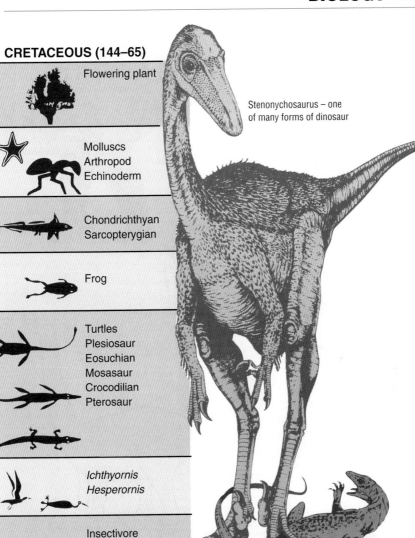

CRETACEOUS (144–65)

Flowering plant

Molluscs
Arthropod
Echinoderm

Chondrichthyan
Sarcopterygian

Frog

Turtles
Plesiosaur
Eosuchian
Mosasaur
Crocodilian
Pterosaur

Ichthyornis
Hesperornis

Insectivore

Stenonychosaurus – one
of many forms of dinosaur

14

DINOSAURS

Brachiosaurus

There were two main groups of dinosaurs. The Ornithischians had a hip joint similar to that of a bird. The Saurischian dinosaurs had hips similar to those of a lizard.

Saurischian dinosaurs
Two main groups developed.
1 Theropods were flesh-eating, two-legged creatures.
The *Tyrannosaurus* was typical of these creatures.
2 Sanropods had four legs and were mainly plant-eaters. The *Diplodocus* is the most familiar of this group.

Ornithischian dinosaurs
There are four suborders.
1 Stegosaurs were giant lizards with spiky tails and large bony plates on their backs.
2 Ceratopsians were horned dinosaurs. The *Triceratops* had three horns, as its name suggests.
3 Ornithopods were fast-moving, ostrich-like creatures. The *Dromicelomimus* was possibly the fastest of all the dinosaurs.
4 Ankylosaurs were large, heavy creatures with protective plates covering their bodies.

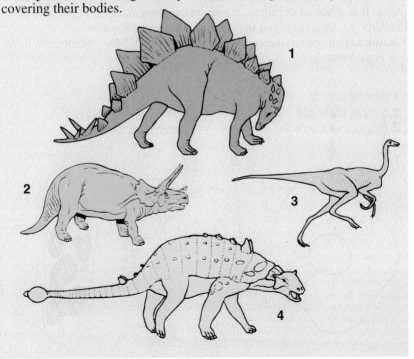

14

CELLS

Living things are made of cells. Animal cells (**1**) and plant cells (**2**) share some characteristics of cells, although, in any plant or animal, the cells are specially developed to do certain jobs. All cells contain the following elements:

Cytoplasm (**a**) a transparent jelly-like substance, in which the chemical reactions of life occur.

Cell membrane (**b**) a skin around a cell which allows the entry and exit of materials.

Nucleus (**c**) the cell's control centre, containing hereditary material (chromosomes).

Plant cells have additional features. These are:

Cell wall (**d**) outside the membrane, which gives the cell rigidity and shape. It is made of cellulose, a non-living substance.

Plastids (**e**) units involved in making and storing food.

Vacuoles (**f**) large cavities containing air or fluid. Many plant cells have one large vacuole.

1 Simple animal cell
2 Simple plant cell
3 Single cell *Euglena*

4 Bacteria cell
5 Specialized animal cell
  (nerve cell)

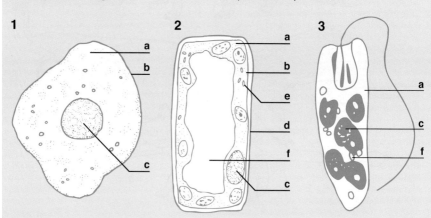

Structure of an
animal cell

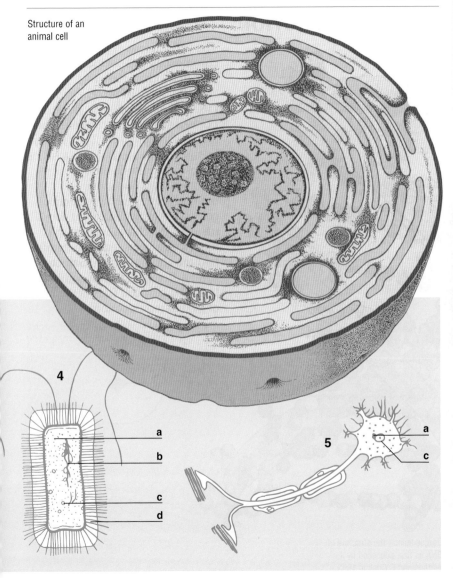

4

a
b
c
d

5

a
c

14

CELL REPRODUCTION

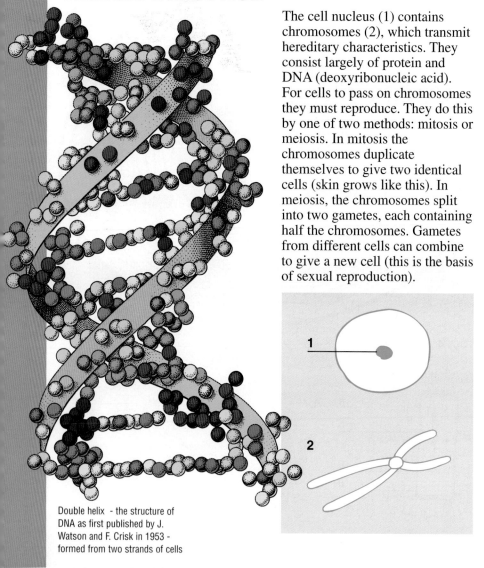

The cell nucleus (1) contains chromosomes (2), which transmit hereditary characteristics. They consist largely of protein and DNA (deoxyribonucleic acid). For cells to pass on chromosomes they must reproduce. They do this by one of two methods: mitosis or meiosis. In mitosis the chromosomes duplicate themselves to give two identical cells (skin grows like this). In meiosis, the chromosomes split into two gametes, each containing half the chromosomes. Gametes from different cells can combine to give a new cell (this is the basis of sexual reproduction).

Double helix - the structure of DNA as first published by J. Watson and F. Crisk in 1953 - formed from two strands of cells

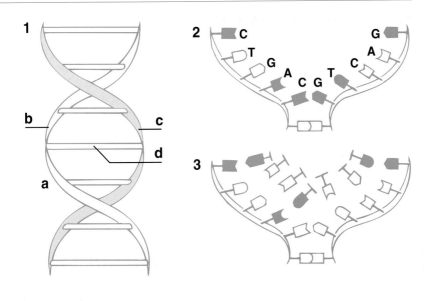

DNA

1 DNA groups are assembled in spiral form (**a**). Each strand (**b**, **c**) of the spiral ribbon is linked to its partner with cross-strands (**d**) by 'bases' called cytosine (**C**), thymine (**T**), guanine (**G**), and adenine (**A**). The order of these bases gives the genetic code.

2 When chromosomes begin to duplicate, the DNA ladder unzips.

3 Each side gains a new matching side made from chemicals within the cell.

4 Two independent DNA spirals are now formed.

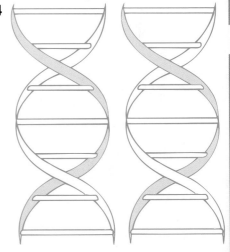

14

GENES AND GENETICS
Sex determination

A baby's sex depends on the chromosomes it receives from each parent. Each of its mother's cells includes a pair of X-shaped sex chromosomes. Each of the father's cells includes a pair made of an X and a Y-shaped sex chromosome. The baby inherits one sex chromosome from each parent. If it inherits two Xs it will be a girl. If it inherits an X and a Y it will be a boy. Here are various ways in which (**a**) the mother and (**b**) the father can pass on sex cells to create (**c**) a female or (**d**) a male.

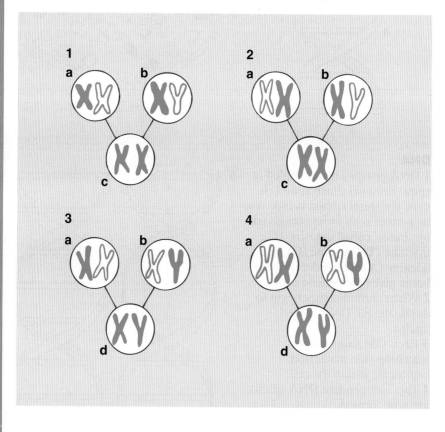

Inherited traits

A child inherits certain character traits from its parents as well as similarities in physical appearance, such as the same colour eyes or hair. These are coded in genes, which are units carried on chromosomes. Each type of gene occurs in a pair and we inherit one gene from each parent in each pair. In the inherited pair of genes, the dominant gene will overpower the weaker, or recessive, gene. The diagram below shows the gene for brown eyes dominating the gene for blue eyes in four out of five cases.

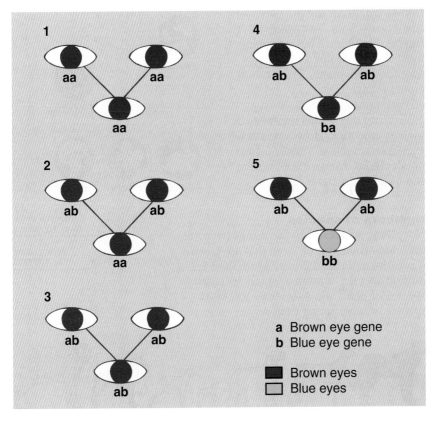

1

aa   aa
aa

4

ab   ab
ba

2

ab   ab
aa

5

ab   ab
bb

3

ab   ab
ab

a Brown eye gene
b Blue eye gene

Brown eyes
Blue eyes

14

LIFE FORMS

The five kingdoms

All living things are divided, or classified, into five major groups called kingdoms. The plant and the animal kingdoms are the two best-known ones. Fungi are another kingdom. They are plant-like but they do not make their own food like plants. Protists and monera make up two more kingdoms. Most protists are one-celled organisms such as amoebae. However, a few exceptions, such as seaweeds, are multicellular. Monera are bacteria and blue-green algae.

Living organisms

Protists

Monera

Animals Plants Fungi

Numbers of species

Not all the species of living things have yet been identified, but of those that are known it is estimated that there are more than 1.2 million species of animal, about 300,000 species of plant and more than 100,000 species of other living things.

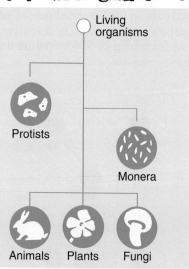

Animals more than 1.2 million

Others more than 100,000

Plants about 300,000

Classification systems

All living organisms are classified, or divided into groups of organisms. The system is based on a series of levels with the five kingdoms at the top and more than a million species at the bottom. Each kingdom is divided and subdivided so that organisms with similar features are classified together at each level. The dogrose *Rosa canina,* for example, is a species in the *Rosa* genus. It is part of the Rosaceae family, which belongs to the Rosales order. This order is in the Dicotyledon class, which is in turn a member of the division known as Angiospermophyta, one of the 10 main divisions in the plant kingdom (see over).

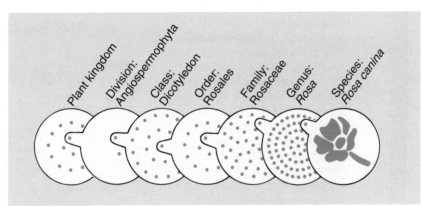

14

The dog family has many subgroups of species

PLANT KINGDOM

Plant life on Earth 420 million years ago

Apart from the traditional groupings (shown opposite), botanists also divide plants into groups determined by plant structure. The simplest group in this system consists of the algae and one-celled organisms (**1**). This is now recognized as the monera kingdom. These plants do not have any phloem or xylem which, in other plants, provide a network to carry water or food from one part of the plant to another.

The other major group (**2**), the plant kingdom, includes plants that have phloem and xylem to carry water, mineral salts, and food between the roots, stem, and leaves. This group is called the tracheophytes. Tracheophytes are further divided into two groups: plants such as clubmosses, ferns, and horsetails (**3**) which do not flower and do not form seeds, and plants that bear seeds (**4**). There are two sorts of seed-bearing plants. Conifers and cycads are one. They belong to the gymnosperm family (**5**) which have seeds and cones. The others are angiosperms (**6**), flowering plants and trees that bear seeds protected in an ovary.

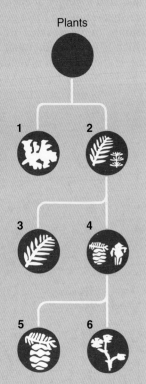

Plants

PLANT CLASSIFICATION

The largest and most long-lived organisms on Earth are plants

Traditional groupings of the plant kingdom

Plant kingdom

- Bryophytes
  - Liverworts
  - Mosses
  - Hornworts
- Psilophyta
- Clubmosses
- Horsetails
- Ferns
- Cycads
- Ginkgoes
- Ephedra
- Conifers
- Angiosperms
  Flowering plants
  - Dicots
  - Monocots

- Plant kingdom
- Division
- Class

PLANT CHARACTERISTICS

Common name	Division	Class	Vascular tissue
Mosses Liverworts Hornworts	Bryophyta	Musci Hepaticae Anthocerotae	Absent
Whiskferns Clubmosses Horsetail ferns	Psilophyta Lycopodophyta Spenophyt Filicinophyta		Present
Conifers Girgkoes Gnetophytes Cycads	Coniferales Girgkophyta Gnetophyta Cycadophyta		Present
Flowering plants	Angiospermophyta	Monocotyledoneae Dicotyledoneae	Present

Structure	Habitat
Multicellular; no true roots, stems, or leaves	Moist areas on land
Multicellular; true roots, stems, and leaves	Moist areas on land
Multicellular; true roots, stems, and leaves	Land
Multicellular; true roots, stems, and leaves	Land

Non-flowering plants

Flowering plants

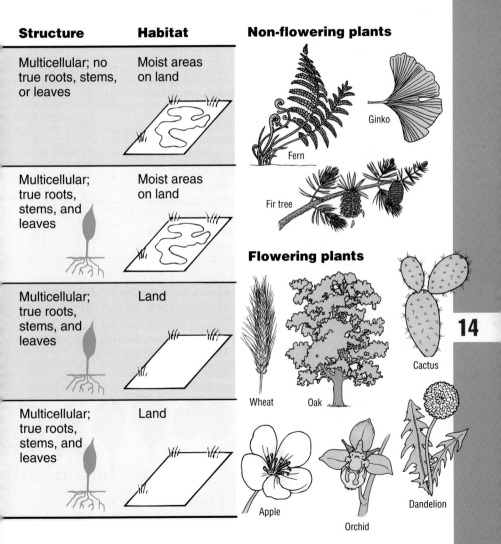

Ginko

Fern

Fir tree

Wheat

Oak

Cactus

Apple

Orchid

Dandelion

14

PLANT STRUCTURE AND FUNCTION

Breathing and feeding

Plants as well as animals breathe. The plant takes in carbon dioxide from the air (**1**) which combined with water makes sugar and waste oxygen. The sugar is stored and waste oxygen is given out (**2**). Plants use the stored sugar together with sunlight to make food, by a process that is known as photosynthesis.

A flowering plant

1 The roots keep the plant firmly in the soil.
2 The root hairs absorb water and minerals from the soil which the plant needs for growth and to stay healthy.
3 The stem carries the water and minerals to the leaves. Food made in the leaves is carried to the rest of the plant. The stem supports the leaves and flowers. It holds them in the air and light.
4 The leaves use sunlight to convert water and carbon dioxide into food.
5 The flowers are the plant's reproductive structure.

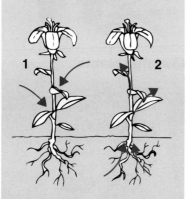

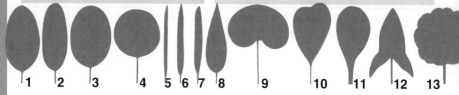

Leaf shapes
1 Elliptical
2 Oblong
3 Oval
4 Orbiculate
5 Acerose
6 Awl-shaped
7 Linear
8 Lanceolate
9 Reniform
10 Cuneate
11 Sagittate

Parts of a leaf
1 Dicotyledon leaf
2 Petiole, or leaf stalk
3 Midrib
4 Vein
5 Leaf blade margin

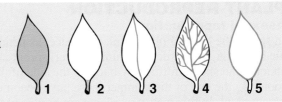

Inside a leaf
A cross section of a leaf magnified many times would show the following parts:
1 The epidermis.
2 A leaf cell.
3 A chloroplast, containing chlorophyll, a green pigment that helps plants use light energy to make food from water, minerals, and carbon dioxide and giving out oxygen as waste.
4 A stoma is a pore in the leaf. Stomata let out water vapor and waste oxygen. They let in carbon dioxide and oxygen.
5 A vein carrying water and minerals in and food out of the leaf.

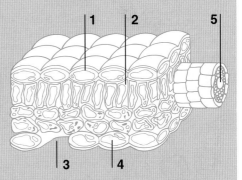

14

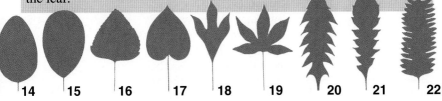

12 Spatulate	15 Obovate	18 Pedate	21 Lyrate
13 Peltate	16 Deltoid	19 Palmate	22 Pectinate
14 Ovate	17 Cordate	20 Runcinate	

PLANT REPRODUCTION
Asexual reproduction

In spring the buds of plants called herbaceous perennials (which do not die in winter, but lie dormant until spring) sprout and produce new shoots. The shoots formed by buds on the side of the plant often grow roots. By the end of the summer these have become independent of the parent plant. In this way, new plants are produced from buds without pollination or fertilization being necessary. This is a form of asexual reproduction. Flowering plants can reproduce themselves in a number of ways, including runners and rhizomes.

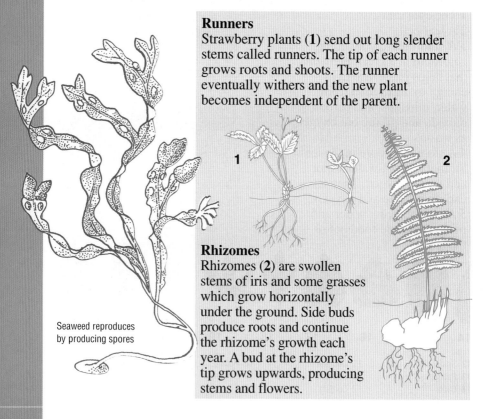

Seaweed reproduces by producing spores

Runners
Strawberry plants (**1**) send out long slender stems called runners. The tip of each runner grows roots and shoots. The runner eventually withers and the new plant becomes independent of the parent.

1

2

Rhizomes
Rhizomes (**2**) are swollen stems of iris and some grasses which grow horizontally under the ground. Side buds produce roots and continue the rhizome's growth each year. A bud at the rhizome's tip grows upwards, producing stems and flowers.

Sexual reproduction

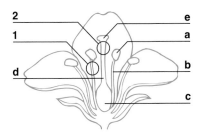

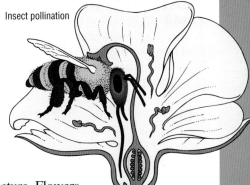

Insect pollination

A flower is a plant's reproductive structure. Flowers have stamens (**1**), or male reproductive organs. These have (**a**) anthers and (**b**) filaments, which produce pollen grains containing male sex cells. The pistil (**2**) is the female reproductive organ consisting of the ovary (**c**), the style (**d**), and the stigma (**e**). Here, pollen from another flower is received and pollination takes place. The male sex cells join the female one and the flower begins to produce seeds. Some flowers are self-pollinating.

Seed dispersal

14

1　　**2**　　**3**　　**4**　　**5**　　**6**

When flowering is over and the seeds are mature, the ovary or the individual seeds fall from the plant and scatter. The wind spreads poppy seeds (**1**) by shaking the dry ovary which has slits. It also spreads clematis seeds (**2**) which have feathers, dandelion seeds with parachutes (**3**), and winged sycamore seeds (**4**). Some seeds are carried by birds as they drop berries (**5**) in flight or eat and excrete the seeds. Animals also do this and sometimes seeds are carried in their fur, attached by the seeds' hooks or barbs (**6**).

FEATURES OF FRUITS AND FLOWERS
Fruits

A fruit is a flowering plant's ovary, holding seeds. The wall of a mature fruit has three layers collectively called the pericarp. There is an outer layer called the exocarp, a mesocarp, the middle layer, and an inner layer, or endocarp.

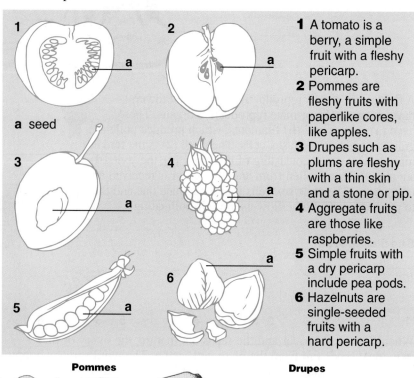

a seed

1 A tomato is a berry, a simple fruit with a fleshy pericarp.
2 Pommes are fleshy fruits with paperlike cores, like apples.
3 Drupes such as plums are fleshy with a thin skin and a stone or pip.
4 Aggregate fruits are those like raspberries.
5 Simple fruits with a dry pericarp include pea pods.
6 Hazelnuts are single-seeded fruits with a hard pericarp.

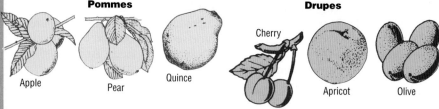

Pommes

Apple

Pear

Quince

Drupes

Cherry

Apricot

Olive

Flower forms

Flowers can be grouped together on stems in a variety of ways:

1 Spike (racemose spike)
2 Raceme (simple raceme) flower head)
3 Panicle
4 Cyme
5 Spadix (fleshy spike)
6 Umbel (simple umbel)
7 Capitulum
8 Composite head (discoid flower head)
9 Hollow flower head
10 Bostryx (helicoid cyme)
11 Cincinnus (scorploid cyme, curled cyme)

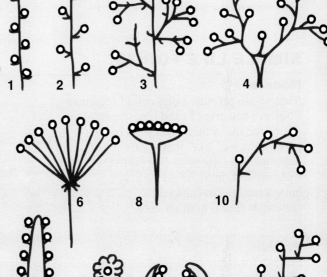

Nuts

Walnut

Coconut

Peanut

Berries

Grape

Blackcurrant

Strawberry

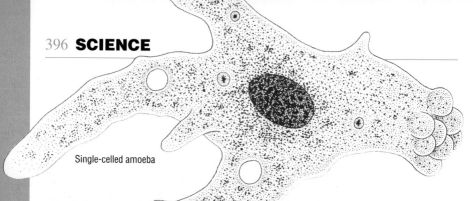

Single-celled amoeba

SIMPLE LIFE FORMS

Monera

Monera are primitive one-celled organisms.
They are bacteria (**1**) and blue-green algae
(**2**). Some make their own food by
photosynthesis, like plants, in
chloroplasts. Others take in particles
from around them. Monera do not
have a nucleus or organelles,
structures found in other cells.

Protists

Protists form another kingdom of one-celled organisms such as amoeba
(**3**), euglena (**4**), paramecium (**5**), and diatoms (**6**).They have a
well-defined nucleus and organelles. Paramecium have hair-like threads
which enable them to move. Euglenas make food using sunlight and they
move by beating a long whip-like part backward and forward. Amoebae
eat by wrapping themselves around food and then absorbing it through
the outer cell membrane.

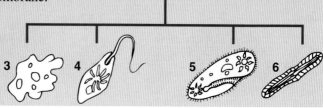

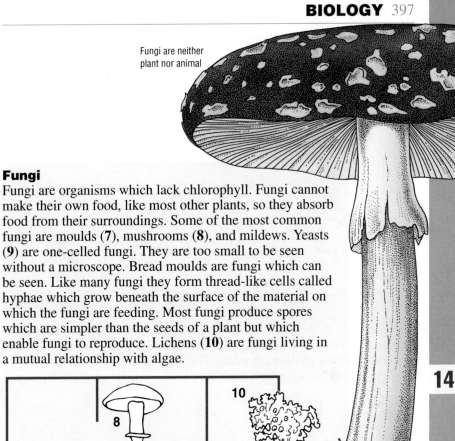

Fungi are neither
plant nor animal

Fungi

Fungi are organisms which lack chlorophyll. Fungi cannot
make their own food, like most other plants, so they absorb
food from their surroundings. Some of the most common
fungi are moulds (**7**), mushrooms (**8**), and mildews. Yeasts
(**9**) are one-celled fungi. They are too small to be seen
without a microscope. Bread moulds are fungi which can
be seen. Like many fungi they form thread-like cells called
hyphae which grow beneath the surface of the material on
which the fungi are feeding. Most fungi produce spores
which are simpler than the seeds of a plant but which
enable fungi to reproduce. Lichens (**10**) are fungi living in
a mutual relationship with algae.

14

ANIMAL KINGDOM

There are more than one million different kinds of animal in the animal kingdom. The animal kingdom is divided into smaller groups of animals with similar features, just as plants are classified (see page 385). If we look at the lion, *Panthera leo*, it is one of several species in the genus *Panthera*. This genus is one of several in the family Felidae.

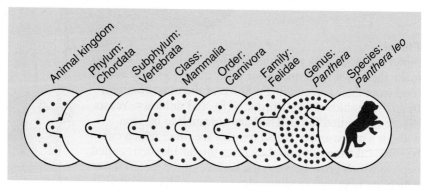

This family is in the order Carnivora, and carnivores belong to the class Mammalia. This class belongs with several others in the subphylum Vertebrata, of the phylum Chordata. This phylum is one of the many phyla in the animal kingdom. A phylum is equivalent to a plant division.

Animals include mammals, insects, fishes, reptiles and worms

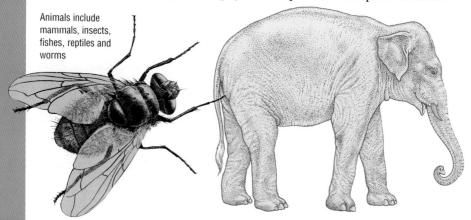

ANIMAL CLASSIFICATION

1 Porifera (sponges)
2 Coelenterata (coelenterates)
3 Platyhelminthes (flatworms)
4 Nematoda (roundworms)
5 Annelida (true worms)
6 Mollusca (molluscs)
7 Arthropoda (arthropods)
7a Chilopods (centipedes)
7b Diplopods (millipedes)
7c Crustacea (crustaceans)
7d Insecta (insects)
7e Arachnida (spiders)
8 Echinodermata (echinoderms)
9 Chordata (chordates)
9a Cephalochordate (amphioxus)
9b Vertebra (vertebrates)
9c Urochordata (sea squirts)
9bi Agnatha (jawless fish)
9bii Chondrichthyes (cartilaginous fish)
9biii Osteichthyes (bony fish)
9biv Amphibia (amphibians)
9bv Reptilia (reptiles)
9bvi Aves (birds)
9bvii Mammalia (mammals)

14

INVERTEBRATE CHARACTERISTICS

Phylum Common name	Locomotion	Number of body openings
Porifera Sponges	None	One
Coelenterata Coelenterates	Mostly sessile free floating	One
Platyhelminthes Flatworms	Muscles; cilia	One
Nematoda Roundworms	Muscles	Two
Annelida Segmented worms	Muscles	Two
Mollusca Molluscs	Muscles	Two

Invertebrates are animals with no backbones.

Tape worms can grow up to 50 feet long

Nervous system	Digestive system	Circulatory system
None	None	None
Present	Present	None
Present	Present	None
Present	Present	None
Present	Present	Present
Present	Present	Present

14

ARTHROPOD CHARACTERISTICS

Class and common names	External appearance	Body sections	Antennae
1 Chilopods Centipedes		Head and body segments	1 pair
2 Diplopods Millipedes		Head and body segments	1 pair
3 Crustacea Crabs, lobsters, water fleas		Cephalothorax and abdomen	2 pairs
4 Insecta Grasshoppers, butterflies, fleas		Head, thorax, and abdomen	1 pair
5 Arachnida Scorpions, ticks, spiders		Cephalothorax and abdomen	None

Mouth parts	Number of walking legs	Gas exchange
Mandibles	1 pair per 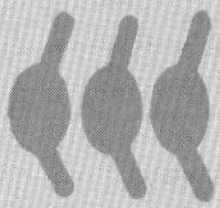	Tracheae segment
Mandibles	2 pairs per 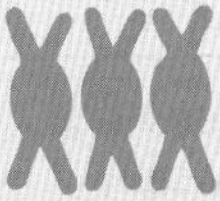	Tracheae segment
Mandibles	5 pairs in 	Gills most forms
Mandibles	3 pairs 	Tracheae
First pair of legs adapted to hold prey	4 pairs 	Tracheae, lungs

Some millipedes have 700 legs

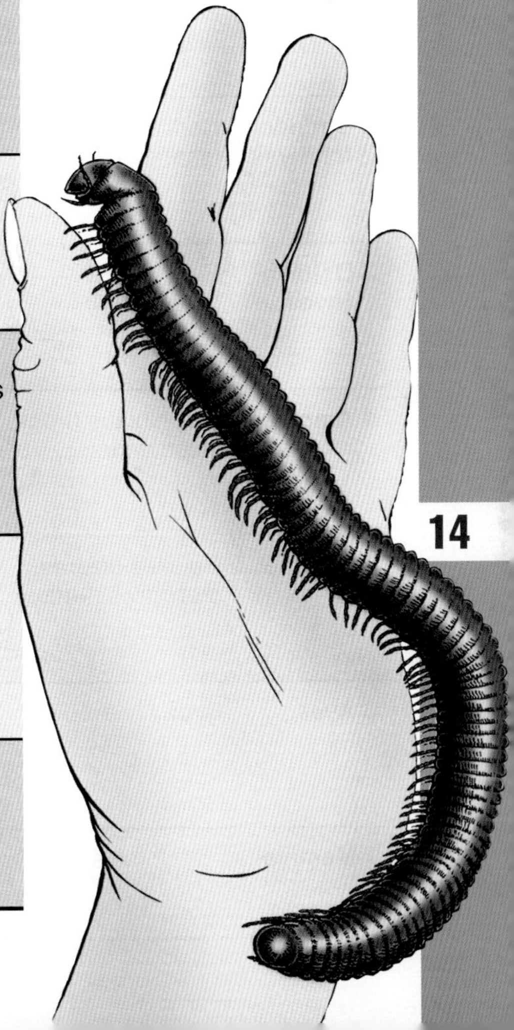

14

VERTEBRATE CHARACTERISTICS

Class	Examples	External	Integument appearance	Body temperature
1 Agnatha	Jawless fish (lampreys, hagfish)		Slimy skin	Cold-blooded
2 Chondr-ichthyes	Cartilaginous fish (sharks, rays)		Scales	Cold-blooded
3 Osteich-thyes	Bony fish (cod, perch)		Scales and slimy skin	Cold-blooded
4 Amphibia	Amphibians (frogs, salamanders)		Slimy skin most forms	Cold-blooded
5 Reptilia	Reptiles (lizards, crocodiles, turtles)		Dry, scaly	Cold-blooded
6 Aves	Birds		Feathers, scales on claws	Warm-blooded
7 Mammalia	Mammals		Hair	Warm-blooded

Body temperature	Limb structure	Gas exchange	Fertilization
No paired limbs	Gills	External	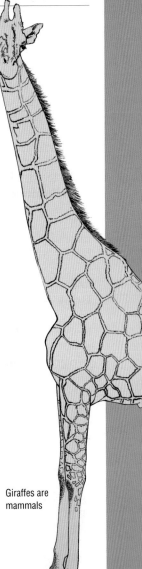
2 pairs of fins	Gills	Internal	
2 pairs of fins	Gills	External	
2 pairs of legs, no claws	Gills; lungs	External	
2 pairs of legs, claws	Lungs	Internal	
1 pair of wings, 1 pair of legs, claws	Lungs	Internal	
2 pairs of legs, claws in most forms	Lungs	Internal	

Giraffes are mammals

FISH

Fish are divided into two main groups – jawless and jawed fish. The jawed fish are divided into bony or cartilaginous fish according to the skeleton.

Jawless fish

Jawless fish belong to the class Agnatha. They include lamprey and hagfish and they are the most primitive fish and vertebrates. They lack jaws, paired fins, swim bladder, and scales. Lampreys have a sucker-like mouth and a toothed tongue. Hagfish have a slit mouth with sharp teeth. They both have a skeleton of cartilage.

Cartilaginous fish

This is the class Chondrichthyes, which consists of fish with a skeleton of tough gristly cartilage instead of bone. Sharks, rays, and chimeras belong to this class. All the fish have jaws and have tiny tooth-like scales and paired fins, but no swim bladder. They live mainly in saltwater.

Bony fish

The class Osteichthyes includes all fish with bony skeletons. The fish all have scales or bony plates and swim bladders. Bony fish divide into two groups. Modern bony fish (ray-finned) such as tuna, cod, catfish, and herring have skeletons mainly of bone. They form the larger group. Primitive bony fish include coelacanth and lungfish which have skeletons of bone and cartilage. They are related to fish that lived millions of years ago.

Classification of fish			
A	Jawless	**B2a**	Primitive fish
B	With jaws	**B2b**	Ray-finned
B1	Cartilaginous	**1**	Coelacanths
B2	Bony	**2**	Lungfish
B1a	Sharks	**3**	Sturgeon
B1b	Chimera	**4**	Perch

CLASSIFICATION OF FISH

Like the first fish,
lampreys do not
have jaws

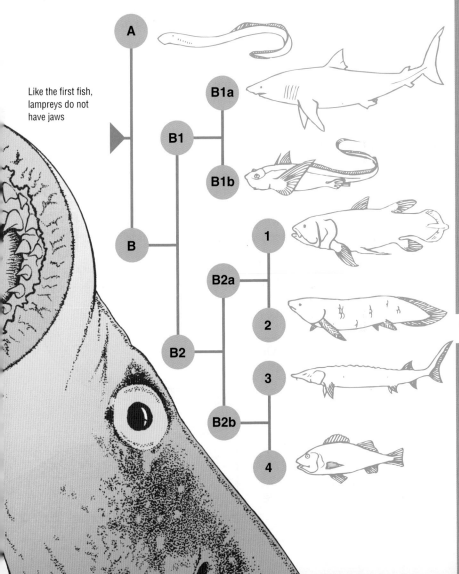

14

AMPHIBIANS

Amphibians include frogs, newts, and toads. They are cold-blooded vertebrates which are mainly scaleless and spend most of their time on land. Most lay eggs in water.

Caecilians

Caecilians are limbless, worm-like amphibians. They have rings around their bodies and some have scales. Caecilians burrow into the forest floor and river beds of tropical countries. The largest Caecilians are 5 ft long.

Tailed amphibians

Tailed amphibians are also called Caudata. They include salamanders and newts. They have four legs and a long body and tail. Most tailed amphibians start life as swimming larvae with feathery gills. As they grow older, they lose their gills and leave the water, with the exception of the axolotl and the olm, which keep their gills and remain in water.

Frogs and toads

Frogs and toads are tailless amphibians and form the order Anura. They have long hind legs and the majority are strong swimmers. Most frogs and toads start as swimming limbless tadpoles with feathery gills. As they grow they develop limbs and lose their gills.

Amphibian characteristics
- Metamorphosis from larvae to adult in most amphibians
- Skeleton mostly bone
- Heart has three chambers
- Mouth connects with two nostrils
- Four limbs
- Lungs, gills, or skin used for breathing
- Skin moist and scaleless
- Fertilization inside or outside the body

Some frogs can climb trees

Frogs

1 Eardrum usually visible
2 Skin smooth and damp – shed regularly. Absorbs oxygen from both air and water
3 Pulls eyes into head to close
4 Some secrete poison through skin to deter some predators
5 Tailless
6 Hind legs usually long – leaps rather than walks or hops
7 Slim-waisted body
8 Hind feet usually webbed

Toads

1 Skin may cover the eardrum
2 Skin dryish, warty, and shed regularly. Absorbs water and oxygen
3 Pulls eyes into head to close
4 Parotid glands secrete poison as defence against predators
5 Tailless
6 Hind legs short – hops, walks, or runs
7 Body short and squat
8 Hind feet usually webbed

14

Salamanders and newts

1 No ears
2 Skin smooth and warty – shed regularly. Absorbs water and oxygen
3 Eyelids do not move
4 Skin secretes poison
5 Long, often flattened tail
6 Limbs short; lost limbs regrow. Females have no rear limbs
7 Long, often thin body
8 Has toes without claws

Vipers can detect body heat

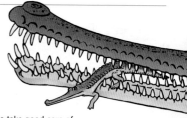

Crocodilia take good care of their young, here is a mother carrying her baby in her mouth

REPTILES

Reptiles are a class of land animals with dry-skinned, scaly bodies. They are cold-blooded vertebrates and include lizards, crocodiles, and tortoises.

Turtles and tortoises

This order is called Chelonia. Turtles and tortoises are four-legged toothless reptiles which have a protective shell. Tortoises are land-dwelling and turtles live either in salt or fresh water. Most tortoises eat plants but some turtles are carnivores. The leatherback turtle is the largest animal in this group. It is about 8 ft long.

Lizards and snakes

This order is called Squamata. The lizards usually have four legs but snakes have none. They have jaws which allow them to swallow large prey whole. The largest snake is the python, which can be 33 ft long. The Komodo dragon is the largest lizard (10 ft long and weighing 310 lb).

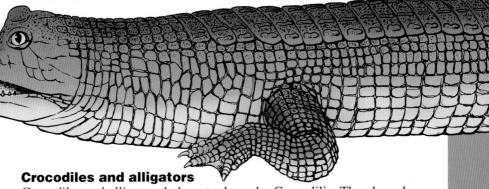

Crocodiles and alligators

Crocodiles and alligators belong to the order Crocodilia. They have long tails, short legs, and long jaws with sharp teeth giving them an elongated head. The largest reptile and the largest of the Crocodilians is the estuarine crocodile which may be more than 23 ft long.

Tuatara

Tuatara are lizard-like creatures with a beaked upper jaw and a scaly crest along the back. They are the sole survivors of the Sphenodontida order of reptiles. They only live on islands off New Zealand. Tuatara are about 23 in long, although the females are smaller.

14

Reptile characteristics
- Skin dry and leathery
- Skeleton mostly bone
  - Heart has four chambers
  - Lungs for breathing
  - Eggs are fertilized inside the body
- Eggs covered with waterproof shell
- Embryo protected by four membranes
- No metamorphosis

BIRDS

Birds make up the Aves class, one of the eight classes of vertebrates. Birds are the only animals with feathers. All birds hatch from eggs and have wings. Most birds can fly.

Birds have hollow bones which reduce body weight

Parts of a bird
1 Bill
2 Throat
3 Ear coverts
4 Claws
5 Tarsus
6 Secondary feathers
7 Primary feathers
8 Tail coverts
9 Tail feathers
10 Rump
11 Scapular feathers
12 Alula
13 Nape
14 Crown

Feather types
a Coverts – roost feathers
b Primary or flight feathers
c Down feathers
d Filoplumes

Bird orders

1 Struthioniformes (ostriches)
2 Rheiformes (rheas)
3 Casuariiformes (cassowaries)
4 Apterygiformes (kiwis)
5 Gaviiformes (divers)
6 Podicipediformes (grebes)
7 Sphenisciformes (penguins)
8 Proceillariiformes (albatross, petrels)
9 Pelecaniformes (cormorants, pelicans, gannets)

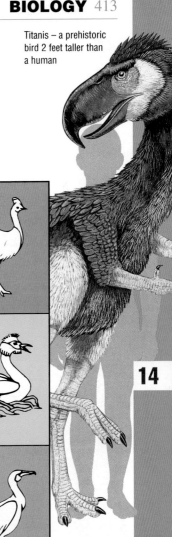

Titanis – a prehistoric bird 2 feet taller than a human

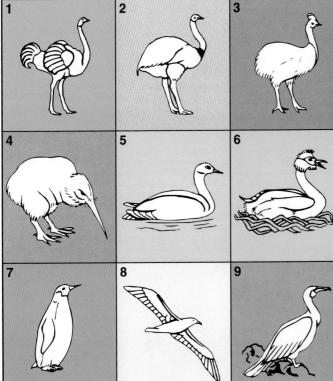

14

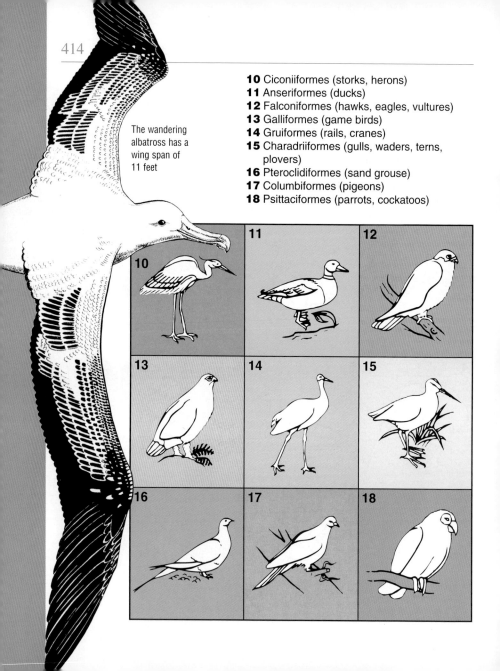

The wandering albatross has a wing span of 11 feet

10 Ciconiiformes (storks, herons)
11 Anseriformes (ducks)
12 Falconiformes (hawks, eagles, vultures)
13 Galliformes (game birds)
14 Gruiformes (rails, cranes)
15 Charadriiformes (gulls, waders, terns, plovers)
16 Pteroclidiformes (sand grouse)
17 Columbiformes (pigeons)
18 Psittaciformes (parrots, cockatoos)

19 Cuculiformes (cuckoos)
20 Strigiformes (owls)
21 Caprimulgiformes (nightjars)
22 Apodiformes (swifts, hummingbirds)
23 Coliiformes (mousebirds)
24 Trogoniformes (trogons)
25 Coraciiformes (kingfishers, hornbills, hoopoes, toucans)
26 Piciformes (woodpeckers)
27 Passeriformes (thrushes, sparrows, perching birds; 60% of all birds are in this order)

The humming bird beats its wings 480 times a minute

14

MAMMALS

The class Mammalia is one of the eight classes of vertebrates. All mammals are warm-blooded, they have hair, and the mothers suckle the young.

Monotremes

Monotremes are primitive animals. They lay eggs and have a horny beak. Only the young have teeth. This order consists of the duck-billed platypus from Australia and echnidas from Australia and New Guinea.

Marsupials

Marsupials give birth to poorly developed young which continue to grow attached to the mother's nipples in a pouch. The order includes the Australian bandicoots, koalas, kangaroos, and wombats, and the American opossums.

Placental mammals

Placental mammals, or Eutheria, are mammals whose young develop in the mother's body nourished by an organ called the placenta. The order includes primates, rodents, and grazing animals. The largest mammal is the blue whale.

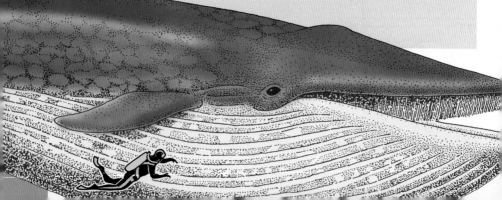

Mammal groups

Most mammals eat plants but some eat meat or insects.

Herbivores
Herbivores are the largest group of mammals. Their teeth and stomachs are adapted to eat only plants.

Carnivores
Carnivores are mammals that eat the flesh of other animals. Many are fast-moving animals which catch and hold their prey. They have claws and large canine teeth which rip flesh, eating chunks whole.

Omnivores
Omnivores eat both plants and meat.

Insectivores
Insectivores are small mammals that eat insects. Their teeth are adapted to crush the hard outer coating of insects to extract the soft body and juices. Insectivores mainly have pointed snouts.

14

Frugivores
Frugivores only eat fruit from trees and their bodies are adapted to life in the treetops.

The blue whale is the largest animal that has ever lived

MAMMAL CLASSIFICATION

Subclass
1 Prototheria (monotremes)
2 Theria

Infraclass
3 Metatheria (marsupials)
4 Eutheria (placentals)

Eutherian orders
a Chiroptera (bats)
b Edentata (sloths, armadillos, anteaters)
c Insectivora (moles, shrews)
d Pholidota (pangolins)

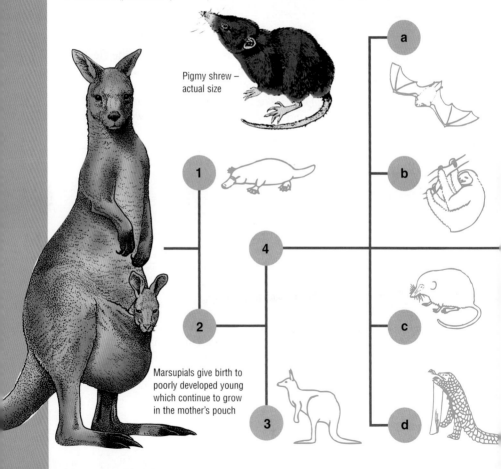

Pigmy shrew – actual size

Marsupials give birth to poorly developed young which continue to grow in the mother's pouch

e Primates (monkeys, apes)
f Rodentia (rats, mice)
g Lagomorpha (rabbits, hares)
h Cetacea (dolphins, whales)
i Carnivora (cats, wolves)
j Tubulidentata (aardvarks)
k Hyracoidea (hyrax)

l Proboscidea (elephants)
m Sirenia (sea cows)
n Perissodactyla (tapirs, horses, rhinoceroses)
o Artiodactyla (pigs, cattle, camels)
p Dermoptera (flying lemurs)

14

ANIMAL LIFE SPANS

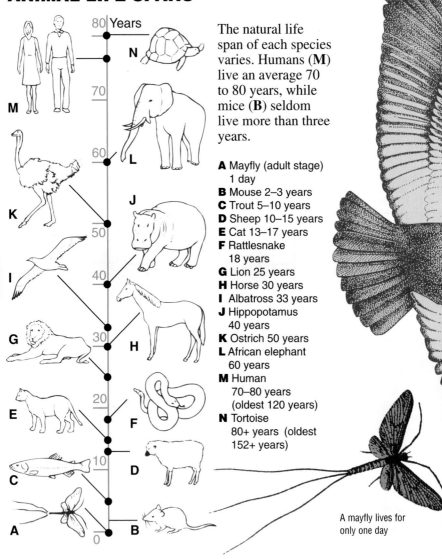

The natural life span of each species varies. Humans (**M**) live an average 70 to 80 years, while mice (**B**) seldom live more than three years.

A Mayfly (adult stage) 1 day
B Mouse 2–3 years
C Trout 5–10 years
D Sheep 10–15 years
E Cat 13–17 years
F Rattlesnake 18 years
G Lion 25 years
H Horse 30 years
I Albatross 33 years
J Hippopotamus 40 years
K Ostrich 50 years
L African elephant 60 years
M Human 70–80 years (oldest 120 years)
N Tortoise 80+ years (oldest 152+ years)

A mayfly lives for only one day

ANIMAL HEIGHTS AND DEPTHS

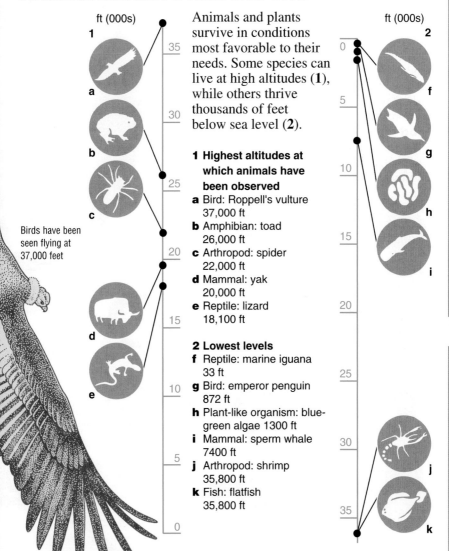

ft (000s)
1

Animals and plants survive in conditions most favorable to their needs. Some species can live at high altitudes (**1**), while others thrive thousands of feet below sea level (**2**).

Birds have been seen flying at 37,000 feet

ft (000s)
2

1 Highest altitudes at which animals have been observed
a Bird: Roppell's vulture 37,000 ft
b Amphibian: toad 26,000 ft
c Arthropod: spider 22,000 ft
d Mammal: yak 20,000 ft
e Reptile: lizard 18,100 ft

2 Lowest levels
f Reptile: marine iguana 33 ft
g Bird: emperor penguin 872 ft
h Plant-like organism: blue-green algae 1300 ft
i Mammal: sperm whale 7400 ft
j Arthropod: shrimp 35,800 ft
k Fish: flatfish 35,800 ft

14

ECOLOGY

The environment in which a particular animal or plant exists is called its habitat. In an untouched habitat, each organism is adapted to cope with the characteristics of the environment and its neighbors (either predators or prey). Within each habitat, organisms are linked to each other in various ways. Ecology is the study of these relationships.

Food web

A food web consists of interlinking food chains in a single habitat, in this case a wood. Arrows show the flow of food energy.

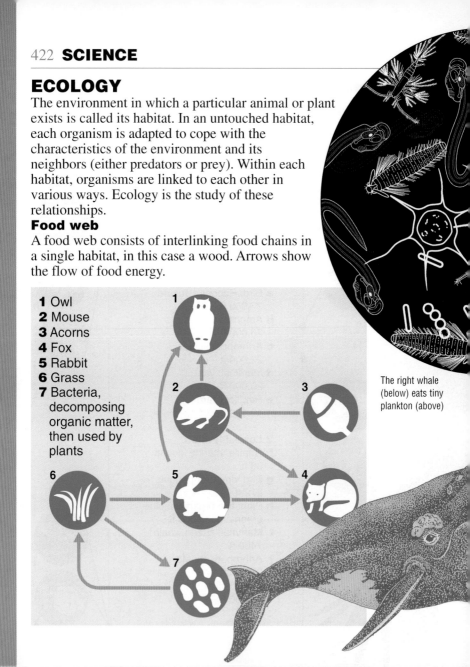

1 Owl
2 Mouse
3 Acorns
4 Fox
5 Rabbit
6 Grass
7 Bacteria, decomposing organic matter, then used by plants

The right whale (below) eats tiny plankton (above)

Food chain

A food chain consists of consumers and consumed. In this food chain, arrows show the flow of food energy along a chain consisting mainly of marine plants and animals.

1 Algae (food producers)
2 Animal plankton (primary consumers)
3 Herring (secondary consumers)
4 Cod (tertiary consumers)
5 People (quaternary consumers)

Food pyramid

A food pyramid consists of a broad base of food-producing plants supporting successively higher stages of consumers. Each stage provides food for a smaller weight of animals than from the stage below. The pyramid's apex consists of the top predator. The following example is of a food pyramid in 1 sq mi of East African grassland, but does not take into account small mammals.

1 14.6 million lb of plants
2 121,300 lb of large consumers (e.g. wildebeest, antelope)
3 410 lb of secondary consumers (e.g. lions, hyena, wild dog)

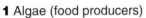

14

THE MAJOR BIOMES

Most animals live in specific areas of the world because they have precise ecological requirements. The Earth can be divided into regions, or biomes, which are determined by the main types of vegetation growing there.

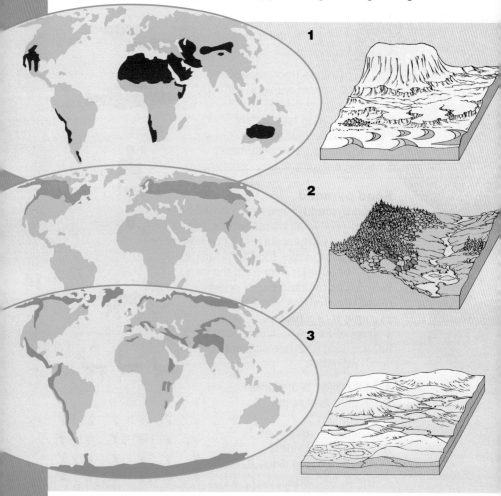

1 Deserts Deserts are dry areas of the world which receive very little rainfall and where dry winds blow across the land. Deserts can be hot or cold. They are found in North and South America, Africa, Asia, and Australia. Some deserts have vast areas of sand while others are covered in bare rocks. Plants may grow there. Animals that live in deserts include lizards, scorpions, rattlesnakes, roadrunner birds, and camels.

2 Coniferous forest Cold, snowy forests cover vast tracts of land in northern areas near the Arctic. Here summers are cool and short and the winters are severe. Evergreen conifers such as spruces, pines, firs, and larches grow here. Ermine, beavers, grizzly bears, and wolves live in the coniferous forests. In Russia, Siberian tigers and brown bears also live in the forests.

14

3 Arctic, tundra, and mountain The tundra lies between the coniferous forests and the Arctic. It is a flat and featureless plain where virtually the only vegetation is mosses and lichen. The polar regions are covered with snow and ice. Few animals and plants live here. Polar-type climates are also found at high altitudes. The Andes and the Himalayan mountains have a polar climate above a certain level. Animals living in these cold areas are musk oxen, penguins, polar bears, whales, seals, and yaks and llamas in the mountains.

MAJOR BIOMES (continued)

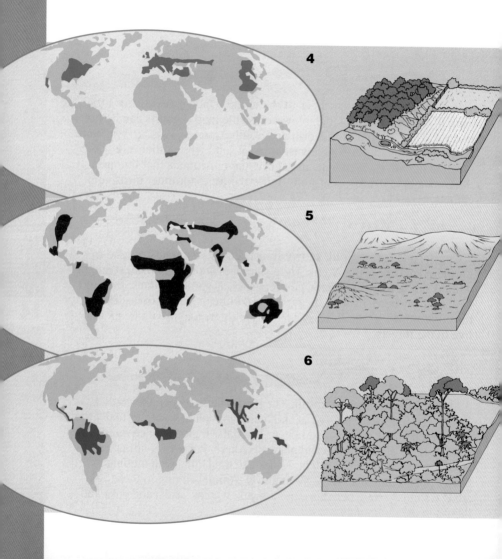

4 Deciduous forest Deciduous forests are found in the temperate parts of the world where the temperatures are cool to warm, such as Europe, eastern North America and eastern Asia. These areas all receive adequate rainfall. Vegetation includes evergreen trees, fruit trees, hardwoods, eucalyptus, poplar, oak, and birch. Animals of the deciduous forests are deer, bears, owls, and bats.

5 Grasslands There are grasslands throughout the world, in North and South America, Africa, and Australia. These areas are mainly flat, with trees and bushes providing food and shelter for the animals. The animals include a wide variety of herbivores. Some grasslands have many predators and carrion-eating animals. Giraffes, lions, antelopes, bison, coyote, and rabbits are animals of the grasslands.

14

6 Tropical rainforest Tropical rainforests are found around the tropics. They are the richest biomes with the greatest variety of plants and animals. The rainforests are hot, humid places which receive plenty of sunshine. Plants grow quickly and densely. Few large animals live in the rainforests, but there are many smaller ones such as jaguars, tapirs, monkeys, birds, and insects.

BODY SYSTEMS

An organ is a group of tissues working together to carry out a major
activity in the body, for example the heart or the liver. Groups of organs
form organ systems. Some organs play a part in more than one system.
Here we show 10 major systems. Later pages describe their parts
in detail.

1 Skeletal system Bones and joints, the scaffolding or framework of
the body.

2 Muscular system Muscles, elastic fibres that move limbs and drive
blood around the body.

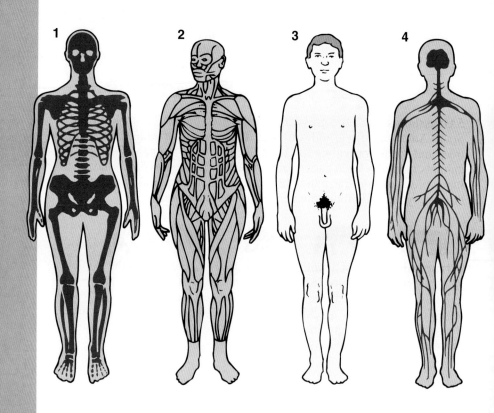

3 Skin, nails, and hair The skin, a barrier that protects the body and helps control its temperature.

4 Nervous system Brain, spinal cord, and nerves, the body's control centre and communication system, including the five senses.

5 Respiratory system The breathing organs, nose, windpipe, lungs, etc., which take in oxygen and remove carbon dioxide waste.

6 Circulatory system Blood vessels, heart, and lymphatic system, supplying cells, removing waste, and helping fight disease.

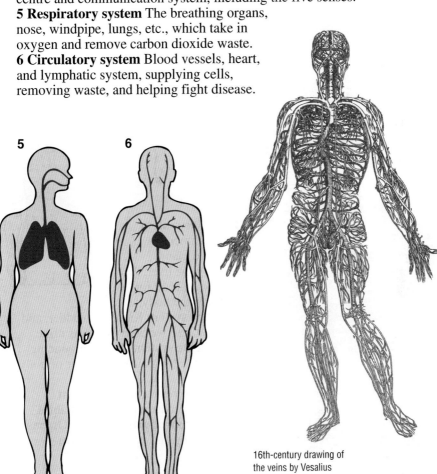

16th-century drawing of the veins by Vesalius

15

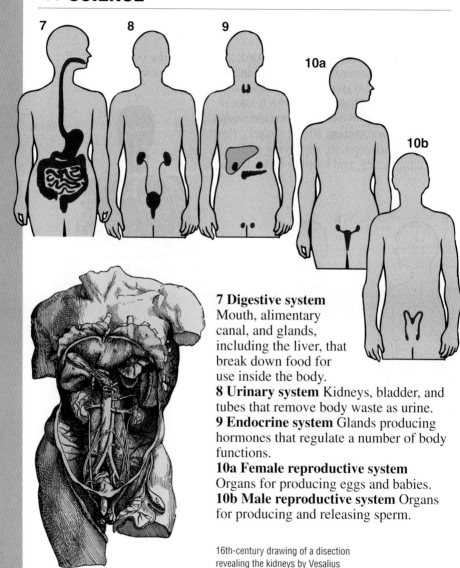

7 Digestive system
Mouth, alimentary
canal, and glands,
including the liver, that
break down food for
use inside the body.
8 Urinary system Kidneys, bladder, and
tubes that remove body waste as urine.
9 Endocrine system Glands producing
hormones that regulate a number of body
functions.
10a Female reproductive system
Organs for producing eggs and babies.
10b Male reproductive system Organs
for producing and releasing sperm.

16th-century drawing of a disection
revealing the kidneys by Vesalius

SKELETAL SYSTEM
Bone and cartilage
Bone is the hard, strong substance that forms the skeleton. Bones develop from soft connective tissue which is replaced by cartilage, the white springy substance also known as gristle, which becomes bone.

Bone structure
Bone is mainly calcium and phosphorus but one-third is living matter. This is chiefly the fibrous protein collagen. Bone has two types of tissue. In a long bone, hard dense compact tissue (**1**) forms the outside. A light, spongy honeycomb, or cancellous tissue (**2**) is in each bulging end. Marrow (**3**) is soft tissue contained in a cavity inside bones. Red marrow is involved with the manufacture of blood cells. Yellow marrow fills adult bones and contains fat cells.

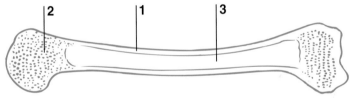

How bone is made
Bones are not dry, dead material; one-third of bone is living tissue with a constant turnover of cells carrying out the jobs of maintenance and repair. Bones are serviced by blood vessels, nerves, and lymph vessels (transporting body fluids) which run through a labyrinth of tiny canals. Special cells (osteoblasts) carry out repair work on bones, while others (osteoclasts) dissolve and break down damaged bones so that they can be repaired.

What bone does
Bone forms an inner framework for the body. It stores calcium, phosphorus, fat, and other substances. Bone also manufactures blood cells, and helps remove some harmful substances from blood.

15

Cartilage structure

Cartilage is formed of the hard protein collagen and the elastic protein elastin.

What cartilage does

Cartilage forms the skeleton in unborn babies. In an adult, cartilage gives shape to the nose and outer ears, keeps large airways open, links ribs, and buffers joints.

Joints

Joints are where two or more bones meet. A joint can be fixed or movable. Fixed joints help to protect abutting bones from damage caused by blows. Movable joints let bones move smoothly against one another. Many joints are held in place by bands of flexible tissue called ligaments, and buffered by smooth cartilage and fluid.

Types of joint

Joints vary greatly in complexity and range of movement, from a simple junction between two bones, as between skull bones, to the intricacy of, for example, the elbow.

The five principal types are:

1 Hinge joint (e.g. elbow)
2 Slicing joint (e.g. wrist)
3 Saddle joint (e.g. finger)
4 Ball and socket joint (e.g. hip)
5 Pivot joint (e.g.neck and skull)

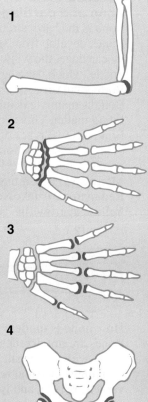

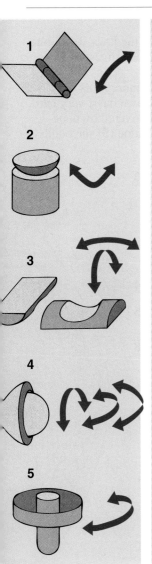

Principal bones

Identified are the most important human bones. Common names are also given.

1. Cranium (skull)
2. Mandible (jawbone)
3. Clavicle (collarbone)
4. Scapula (shoulder blade)
5. Sternum (breastbone)
6. Ribs
7. Humerus
8. Vertebrae (spine or backbone)
9. Radius
10. Ulna
11. Carpals (wrist bones)
12. Metacarpals
13. Phalanges (finger and toe bones)
14. Pelvis or pelvic girdle
15. Femur (thighbone)
16. Patella (kneecap)
17. Tibia (shinbone)
18. Fibula
19. Tarsals
20. Metatarsals

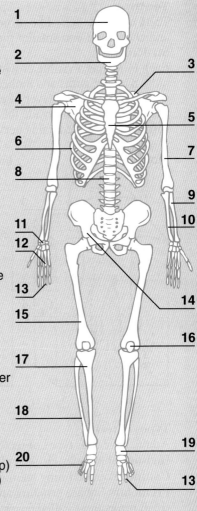

Teeth

Teeth are hard, bone-like projections set in sockets in the jaws. Teeth bite and chew food into smaller pieces as a first stage in food digestion.

Structure

Each tooth has a visible crown (**1**) rising from one or more roots (**2**) hidden by the gums and embedded in the jaw. The crown has a very hard, smooth, shiny, outer layer of enamel (**3**). The root is covered by bone-hard cementum (**4**). Inside the tooth, hard, yellow dentine (**5**) surrounds soft pulp (**6**) that contains nerves and blood vessels.

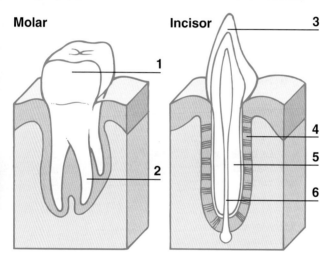

Molar   **Incisor**   3

1

2

4

5

6

Inside of the mouth

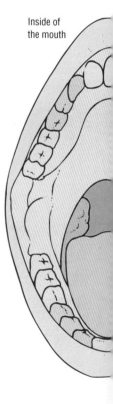

Types of teeth

Adults have four types of teeth.

Incisors Sharp, chisel-like cutting teeth, with one root.
Canines Pointed biting teeth, with one root.
Premolars Square grinding and crushing teeth, with two small projections called cusps, and one or two roots.
Molars Like premolars but larger, with up to five cusps and three roots.

Primary teeth

These teeth are also called deciduous or milk teeth. By about the age of two most children have gained 20 teeth (10 upper, 10 lower): 8 incisors, 4 canines, and 8 molars. Appearing in stages, usually between the age of 6 and 30 months, these teeth are usually lost from age 7–12 years to be replaced by permanent teeth.

Permanent teeth

An adult has 32 permanent or adult teeth (16 upper, 16 lower): 8 incisors, 4 canines, 8 premolars, and 12 molars.

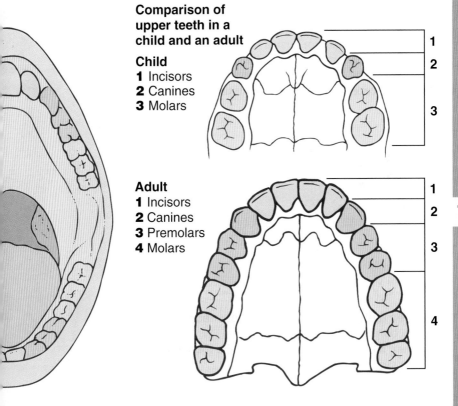

Comparison of upper teeth in a child and an adult

Child
1 Incisors
2 Canines
3 Molars

1
2
3

Adult
1 Incisors
2 Canines
3 Premolars
4 Molars

1
2
3
4

15

MUSCLES

Muscles are tough elastic tissues made of cells called muscle fibres. The body's more than 600 muscles account for 40 per cent of its weight. Muscles work limbs, lungs, and other parts of the body, and largely give it bulk and shape. They come in three main types. Skeletal muscles hold the bones of the skeleton together, they give the body shape, and make it move. They make up a large part of the arms, legs, abdomen, chest, and face. Smooth muscles are found in various organs. They control body processes such as digestion and are found in the stomach wall, intestines, blood vessels, and the bladder. Cardiac muscle is found in the heart.

How muscles work

Muscles pull but cannot push. This means to and fro movements need muscles that work in pairs with opposite effects. Bending and straightening the arm involves biceps (**a**) and triceps (**b**) muscles.

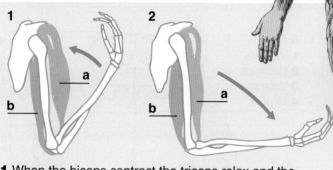

1 When the biceps contract the triceps relax and the arm bends.
2 When the triceps contract the biceps relax and the arm straightens.

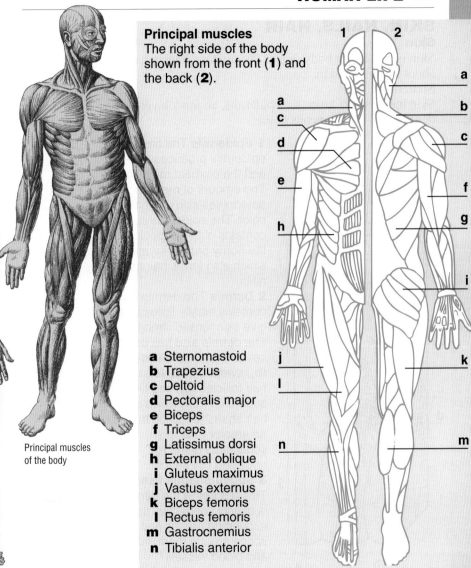

Principal muscles

The right side of the body shown from the front (**1**) and the back (**2**).

1   2

a
b
c
d
e
h
f
g
i
j
l
k
n
m

a Sternomastoid
b Trapezius
c Deltoid
d Pectoralis major
e Biceps
f Triceps
g Latissimus dorsi
h External oblique
i Gluteus maximus
j Vastus externus
k Biceps femoris
l Rectus femoris
m Gastrocnemius
n Tibialis anterior

Principal muscles
of the body

SKIN, NAILS, HAIR

Skin

Skin is the largest body organ. The average human has about 20 sq ft of skin.

Structure

Skin has an outer layer, the epidermis, an inner layer, the dermis, and subcutaneous tissue.

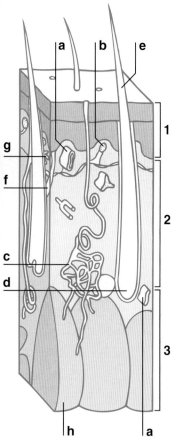

1 Epidermis The base of the epidermis produces new cells and the pigment melanin. The amount of melanin determines skin and hair color. The epidermis surface contains old, dying cells of the horny protein keratin, which also forms hair and nails.

2 Dermis The dermis contains elastic fibres that give skin tensile strength. The dermis also has blood vessels (**a**), nerve endings (**b**), sweat glands (**c**), and hair follicles (**d**), bag-like structures from which grow hair shafts (**e**). Each hair has an erector muscle (**f**), and a sebaceous gland (**g**) releasing oily sebum.

3 Subcutaneous tissue This lies below the dermis. It is mainly connective tissue supporting organs and filling space around them, fat (**h**), and blood vessels.

An adult human has about 20 sq ft of skin

What skin does

Skin provides a flexible, waterproof barrier that keeps in body fluids and keeps out bacteria and harmful rays from the Sun. Nerve endings in the skin sense heat, cold, pain, and pressure. Sweat glands and tiny blood vessels in skin help to control body temperature. Subcutaneous tissue buffers the body's internal structures against blows.

Nails

Nails form before birth. Certain epidermal cells in toes and fingers divide (**1**) and the upper cells accumulate hard keratin to produce a nail plate (**2**). This plate grows out of the nail groove (**3**) and over the skin, forming a fingernail or toenail.

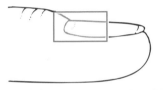
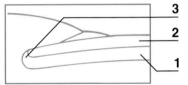

Hair

Hair forms before birth. First, part of the epidermis grows thicker (**a**). Then it invades the dermis (**b**) and forms a projection called a papilla (**c**). Its multiplying cells produce a hair (**d**) which accumulates the hard protein keratin as it grows up and away from its supply of nourishment. Other cells in the papilla form a keratinized root sheath (**e**) which produces a sebaceous gland (**f**).

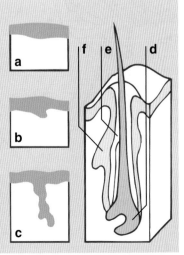

15

NERVOUS SYSTEM

The brain

The brain is the main part of the central nervous system, which also includes the spinal cord. It controls all of the body's processes. Most of the signals from the brain reach the body via the spinal cord.

The forebrain

The forebrain, where memory, the mind, and intelligence are based. This is also involved in body-part movements, receiving sensations, speech, hearing, and sight.

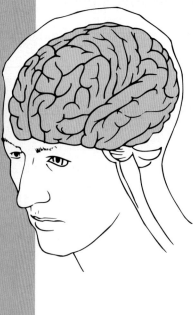

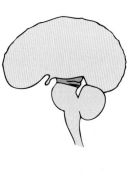

The midbrain

The midbrain, which works mainly as a relay station for messages to and from the brain. Eye movements are controlled here.

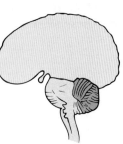

The hindbrain

The hindbrain, which coordinates complex body movements, especially of the arms and legs.

Structure

The cross-section (right) shows the five layers that guard the brain and help to shape it. Scalp (**1**), with hair, fat, and other tissue. Cranium (**2**), the part of the skull housing the brain. Its inner network of bony struts and dome-like shape give this structure its strength. Dura mater (**3**), the tough membrane embracing the brain. Arachnoid (**4**), the elastic "skin" enclosing the so-called subarachnoid space. Pia mater (**5**), a thin "skin" that clings closely to the brain's irregular surface.

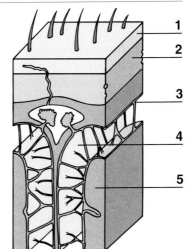

Functions

In this illustration of the left side of a human brain, the numbered areas are involved with the following functions:

1 Movement of body parts,
2 Speech,
3 Receiving body sensations,
4 Hearing,
5 Sight.

15

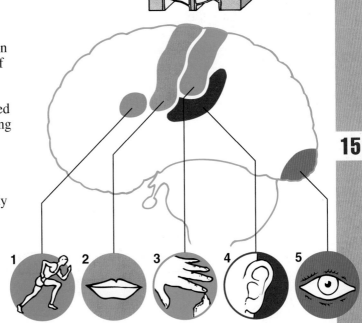

The senses
Ears

Ears contain structures that enable us to hear and keep our balance. The human ear is sensitive to sounds ranging in loudness from 10 to 140 decibels (10 million million times as loud as 10), and ranging in pitch from 20 to 20,000 hertz (cycles per second). The distance between both ears helps the brain to locate the source of sound.

How we hear

Sound waves that have been gathered by the ear pass through the auditory canal (**1**). The sound waves cause the eardrum (**2**) to vibrate. Vibrations from the eardrum are passed on and strengthened by the three ossicles: the malleus (hammer, **3a**), the incus (anvil, **3b**), and the stapes (stirrup, **3c**). The oval window (**4**) now vibrates. Vibrations pass into the fluid in the cochlea (**5**) where they are detected by special cells. Information is sent via the auditory nerve (**6**) to the brain.

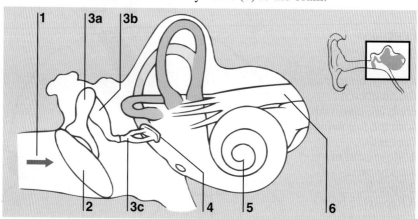

There are three semicircular canals in the ear which control balance.

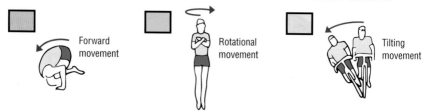

Forward movement

Rotational movement

Tilting movement

Sense of smell

Our sense of smell is less keen than a dog's, yet some people can identify 10,000 odors, all based on combinations of just seven. We smell substances whose molecules are breathed into the roof of each nasal cavity (**1**) and dissolved on a patch of olfactory membrane (**2**) armed with 100 million smell receptor cells equipped with tiny sensitive "hairs". Scent molecules react with these to stimulate nerve impulses in the receptor cells. Olfactory nerves transmit these signals to olfactory bulbs (**3**) then via olfactory tracts (**4**) to the front part of the cerebrum (**5**) of the brain.

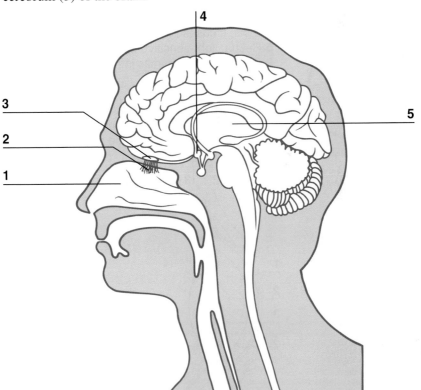

15

Eyes

Our eyes work by sensing the light that objects give off or reflect. Eyes look like two balls of jelly, each about 1 in across, set in sockets in the skull on each side of the nose. Nerves inside the eyes send signals to the brain, providing information on shape, size, color, and distance. The overlapping areas of vision of each eye help us to assess distance. Eyelids and eyelashes protect eyes from dust and injury.

Correcting hyper-metropia (long sightedness)

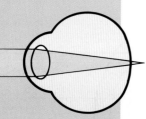

In long sightedness the eyeball is too small for the focusing power of the lens — light rays are not focused when they reach the retina

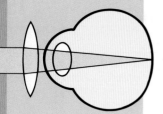

A convex lens causes light rays to converge slightly before they reach the lens of the eye — the eye is then able to focus them on the retina

Parts of an eye

1 Cornea: transparent tissue at front of eye
2 Iris: colored disc, controls size of pupil
3 Pupil: hole through which light enters eye
4 Lens: focuses light onto retina
5 Retina: light-sensitive nerve cells
6 Optic nerve: transmits information to brain

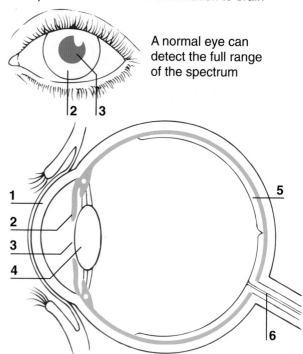

A normal eye can detect the full range of the spectrum

How we see Inside the eye, light rays from an object are bent by the cornea (**a**), lens (**b**), aqueous humor (**c**), which is fluid-like, and vitreous humour (**d**), which is jelly-like. These liquids help to bend the light so that the rays come to a focus on the retina (**e**) and produce an image. (The focused image is upside down, but the brain "sees" it the right way up.)

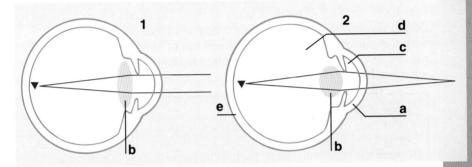

1 Light rays from a distant object are bent relatively slightly inside the eye. Its lens (**b**) has gently curved sides.
2 Light rays from a nearby object must be bent more sharply to bring them into focus. The lens (**b**) grows shorter and fatter, with strongly curved sides.

Correcting myopia (short sightedness)

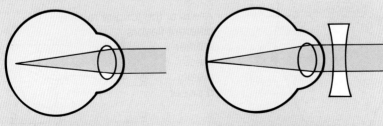

In short sightedness the eyeball is too large for the focusing power of the lens – light rays are focused before they reach the retina

A concave lens causes light rays to diverge slightly before they reach the lens of the eye – the eye is then able to focus them on the retina

15

Sense of touch

Touch is the sense that allows us to know we have made contact with an object. We learn shape, texture, and hardness from the sense of touch. Through touch, feelings of warmth, cold, pain, and pressure are experienced. Free nerve endings in the tissue give the sense of pain. There are several types of touch organs in the skin. One kind is found near hairs, another in hairless areas of skin. Yet another type is found in deeper tissues. We feel something when an object comes in contact with the sense organs and presses them out of shape or touches a nearby hair. Nerves then carry impulses to the brain which let us know what has happened.

Sense of taste

The organs of taste (the taste buds) are found on the tongue. Food is chewed and moistened with saliva, which carries tiny particles of the food to the taste buds. Taste buds in different areas of the tongue register the different flavors of food. At the same time, the olfactory system is stimulated, and the information from both tongue and nose combines to give the sensation the brain perceives as taste.

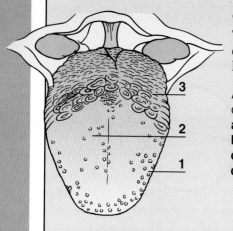

The tongue's surface

The tongue has three forms of senses called papillae. Fungiform (**1**) Filiform (**2**) Vallate (**3**)

Areas of the tongue register different flavors.
a bitter
b sour
c salty
d sweet

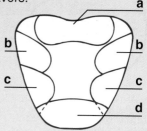

Skin sensitivity Some parts of the body are more sensitive to touch than others. This is because the end organs for touch are not scattered evenly over the body. Instead they are arranged in clusters. Feeling is greatest where there is a large number of end organs. The tip of the tongue, the lips, and fingertips are the areas most sensitive to touch. The area where sensitivity to touch is poorest is the back of the shoulders.

Skin structure
Specialized nerve endings in the skin send signals that the brain identifies as touch, pain, pressure, heat, and cold.

1. Free nerve endings (pain)
2. Merkel's disks (touch)
3. Meissner's corpuscles (touch)
4. Beaded nerve net (pain)
5. Krause's end bulbs (cold)
6. Ruffini corpuscles (heat)
7. Pacinian corpuscles (pressure, stretching, and vibration)
8. Hair organs (touch)
9. Hair
10. Epidermis
11. Dermis
12. Subcutaneous fat (fatty layer)
13. Nerve fibre

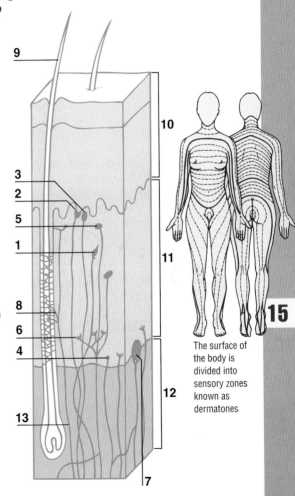

The surface of the body is divided into sensory zones known as dermatones

15

RESPIRATORY SYSTEM

The system consists of
the nose and mouth (**a**),
the throat (**b**),
the voice box (**c**),
the windpipe (**d**),
the lungs (**e**),
and the bronchus (**f**).

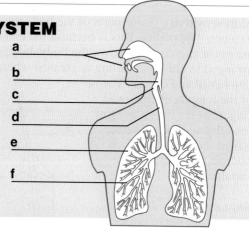

a
b
c
d
e
f

How we breathe

Lungs are operated by
the diaphragm (a
muscular sheet below
the lungs) and by
muscles that move
ribs up and out.
Breathing in Ribs
move up and out (**1**)
and the diaphragm
moves down (**2**). This
expands the chest
cavity and draws air
into the lungs.
Breathing out Ribs
move down and in (**3**)
and the diaphragm
moves up (**4**). This
contracts the chest
cavity and forces air
out of the lungs.

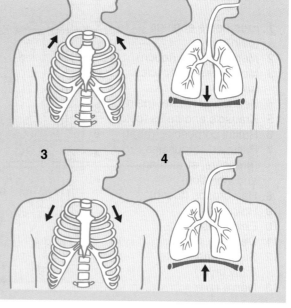

CIRCULATORY SYSTEM
Blood

Blood is a complex fluid that brings body tissues the food and oxygen they need to grow and live. It also helps remove waste products. Some substances in blood help fight disease.

Substances in blood

The four main ingredients of blood are plasma (**a**), red blood cells (**b**), white blood cells (**c**), and platelets (**d**).

What they do

Plasma is a straw-colored fluid that contains the other three constituents, along with foods, proteins, and waste. White blood cells or leucocytes (**1**), are big, rounded blood cells with variously shaped nuclei; special kinds of leucocytes attack harmful bacteria, viruses, and other foreign bodies. Red blood cells or erythrocytes (**2**), are the next largest cells in blood. They contain haemoglobin, the red substance that gives fresh blood its color. Red blood cells take oxygen from the lungs to body tissues. They also play a part in absorbing carbon dioxide waste from body tissues and taking it to the lungs. Platelets (**3**) are tiny disks that seal tears or cuts in damaged blood vessels. They also produce substances that make blood clot. Clotting stops an injured person bleeding to death.

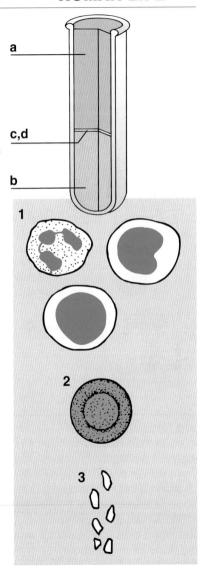

15

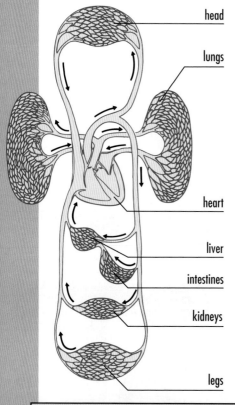

head

lungs

heart

liver

intestines

kidneys

legs

Arteries and veins

These are the largest blood vessels. Arteries (**1**) are large tubes carrying high-pressure blood away from the heart. They have thick, muscular walls. Arteries branch into countless tiny tubes called arterioles. Veins (**2**) are large tubes that return low-pressure blood to the heart. Veins have thinner walls than arteries. Veins are supplied by tiny blood vessels called venules. The tiniest blood vessels are capillaries. Capillaries (**3**) link arterioles and venules.

The heart's pumping action forces blood out through arteries into arterioles and capillaries. Foods in the blood pass out through capillaries' walls to nourish surrounding tissues. Wastes pass in through the walls, and oxygen enters capillaries next to the lungs. From capillaries, blood flows back to the heart through the venules and veins. Muscles near veins keep this blood on the move, and valves in big veins stop blood sinking back down in the legs and feet.

Blood facts and figures

- An adult man is likely to have 1 gallon of blood.
- About 55 per cent of blood is plasma.
- About 90 per cent of plasma is water.
- A healthy adult has about 20,000 billion red blood cells.
- Blood contains over 500 times more red cells and 25 times more platelets than white cells.
- Red blood cells live about 17 weeks.
- The body destroys about 120 million old red blood cells every minute.

1

2

3

1 Artery
2 Vein
3 Capillary

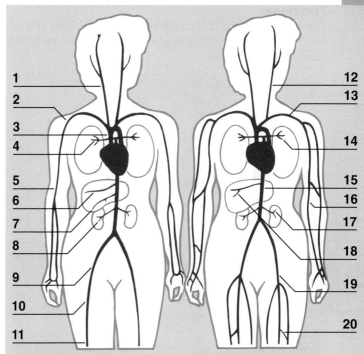

Important arteries
1 Carotid to head
2 Subclavian to arm
3 Aorta supplying all but lungs
4 Pulmonary to lungs
5 Brachial in arm
6 Hepatic to liver
7 Gastric to stomach
8 Renal to kidney
9 Iliac to thigh
10 Femoral in thigh
11 Tibial in leg

Important veins
12 Jugular from head
13 Subclavian from arm
14 Pulmonary from lung
15 Superior and inferior vena cava from all but lungs
16 Brachial in arm
17 Renal from kidney
18 Hepatic from liver
19 Iliac from thigh
20 Femoral in thigh

The heart

The heart is a muscular pump which drives blood around the body. Its nonstop action supplies oxygen and nutrients to body cells, and removes their waste products.

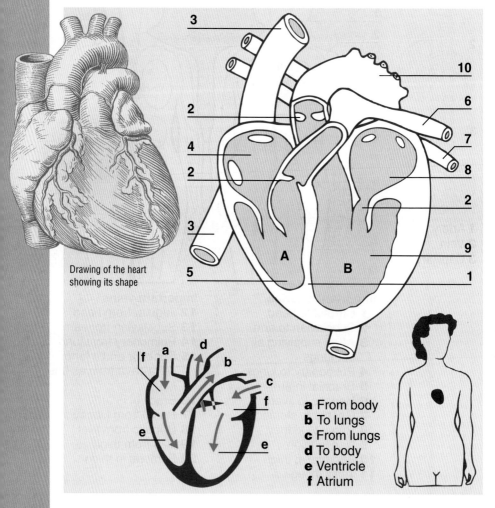

Drawing of the heart showing its shape

a From body
b To lungs
c From lungs
d To body
e Ventricle
f Atrium

Structure
The heart is a fist-sized hollow muscle with a broad top and pointed base. It lies roughly in the middle of the chest. A wall called a septum (**1**) divides the right side (**A**) from the left side (**B**). Each side has an inlet, outlet, and two chambers; atrium and ventricle. Valves (**2**) control the blood flow in and out.

How it works
The heart works as two pumps. As the heart relaxes, blood flows into both atria. As the atria contract, blood flows through valves into the ventricles. Lastly, the ventricles contract, forcing blood out of the heart.

Deoxygenated blood from the body flows via the superior vena cava and inferior vena cava (**3**) into the right atrium (**4**) and right ventricle (**5**) then out through the pulmonary artery (**6**) to the lungs.

Oxygenated blood from the lungs flows via the pulmonary vein (**7**) into the left atrium (**8**) and left ventricle (**9**) then out through the aorta (**10**) to the body. Each complete contraction produces one heartbeat.

Nerve signals to the heart keep heartbeats regular. But heartbeats speed up during exercise as the heart pumps faster and harder to satisfy the body's extra needs for blood and oxygen.

Lymphatic system
A body-wide network of vessels that traps fluid escaped from blood vessels, and returns it to the blood supply. This stops tissues swelling. The system also absorbs harmful bacteria and other dangerous substances.

Spleen
This organ plays a part in circulation and combating infection. It manufactures some of the blood formed in the body before birth, and contains cells that kill old or injured blood cells and destroy bacteria and parasites. It also produces antibodies – proteins that attack viruses and other agents of infection.

15

Drawing of the lymphatic system

DIGESTIVE SYSTEM
Structures and processes

Digestion happens in the alimentary canal, a tube 30 feet long with different parts. Waves of movement in its walls force food along. Food entering the mouth (**a**) is swallowed by the pharynx (**b**), then passes through the gullet or esophagus (**c**) to the stomach (**d**). This muscular bag churns food and dissolves some by releasing gastric juices. The gall bladder (**e**) and pancreas (**f**) release digestive juices in the duodenum (**g**), the first part of the small intestine (**h**). Most digested food enters the blood through tiny finger-like projections in the small intestine's walls. The large intestine (**i**) absorbs water and forms faeces, solid wastes expelled from the anus (**j**).

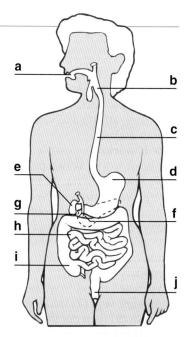

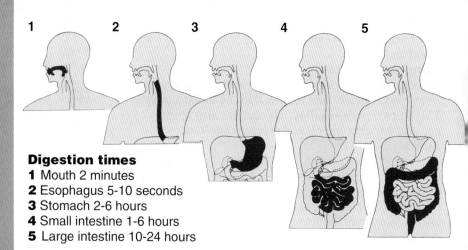

Digestion times
1 Mouth 2 minutes
2 Esophagus 5-10 seconds
3 Stomach 2-6 hours
4 Small intestine 1-6 hours
5 Large intestine 10-24 hours

Where digestion happens

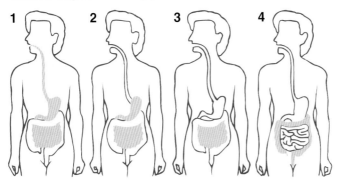

Different foods chiefly undergo digestion in specific parts of the digestive system.

1 Carbohydrates Mouth, esophagus, stomach, small intestine.
2 Proteins Stomach and small intestine.
3 Fats Small intestine.
4 Water (not a food) Absorbed in the large intestine.

The mouth

The mouth takes in food and starts the process of digestion. Lips (**a**) help us drink and bring food inside the mouth. Teeth (**b**) break food into smaller pieces. Salivary glands (**c**) produce saliva that moistens and softens food and begins digesting starches. The bony hard palate (**d**) and the soft palate (**e**) stop food entering and blocking the airway through the nose and upper throat or pharynx. The tongue (**f**) helps to form each mouthful into a ball or bolus, then moves it back into the throat for swallowing.

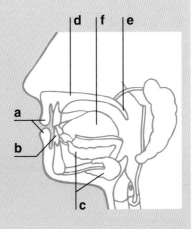

15

Position of the kidneys and bladder

URINARY SYSTEM
Kidneys

Kidneys are a pair of organs for filtering impurities from blood, and prevent poisons fatally accumulating in the body.

Structure

Kidneys are two bean-shaped objects behind the stomach, one on each side of the spine. Together, kidneys add up to the same size as the heart. Each kidney has three layers. From the outside in, these layers are the cortex (**1**), medulla (**2**), and pelvis (**3**). The cortex and medulla contain tiny blood filtration units called nephrons (**4**). (A single kidney has more than a million nephrons.) Urine, the waste product of filtration, collects in the kidney's pelvis.

The two kidneys

How they work

Blood for processing enters the medulla from the renal artery (**5**). Inside the medulla and cortex, the artery splits into tiny coiled blood vessels. Each coiled vessel is called a glomerulus (**8**). Almost completely surrounding this lies a pinhead-sized sac called Bowman's capsule (**9**). Pressure forces water and dissolved chemicals from the blood in the glomerulus into the Bowman's capsule. The filtered liquid then continues through a tubule (**10**) surrounded by capillaries (**11**). These tiny blood vessels reabsorb into the blood most of the water and such useful chemicals as amino acids. The treated blood then leaves the kidney via the renal vein (**6**). Meanwhile, wastes remaining in the convoluted tubule flow on via a collecting tubule to the kidney's pelvis. These wastes now form urine, an amber liquid largely made of water, uric acid, urea, and inorganic salts. From the kidney's pelvis, urine leaves the kidney through a tube known as the ureter (**7**). From there it passes into the bladder where it is stored until it is released.

One pair of kidneys can process 42 gallons of blood a day. Their urine output drops in sleep or during perspiration, and rises after someone has been drinking more liquid than usual.

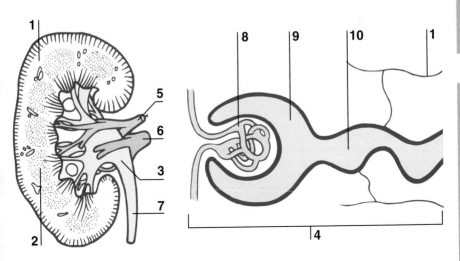

15

ENDOCRINE SYSTEM

Endocrine glands release into the blood hormones ("chemical messengers") that reach target glands and organs to control growth, reproduction, and the daily processes of living.

1 Hypothalamus releases hormones especially from the pituitary gland

2 Pituitary releases several hormones; one controls water reabsorbed into blood by kidneys, another is a growth hormone

3 Thyroid controls rates of growth in young and in adults controls rate of chemical activity

4 Parathyroid releases calcium from bones to blood

5 Adrenal glands produce several hormones including cortisone to accelerate conversion of proteins to glucose and adrenaline

6 Pancreas (contains some endocrine cells) secretes digestive juices and insulin

7 Ovaries in females produce several hormones called estrogens

8 Testicles in males produce testosterone

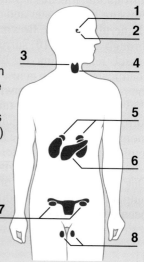

The sex glands

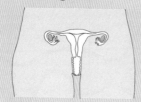

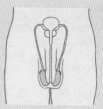

The ovaries The female glands produce estrogens containing female genetic material and the nutrients for the beginning of a new life.

The testes The male glands produce the sperm cells, testosterone, containing genetic material.

EXOCRINE SYSTEM

Exocrine glands produce substances released via ducts to other organs or the surface of the skin. Here are some major types and their products.

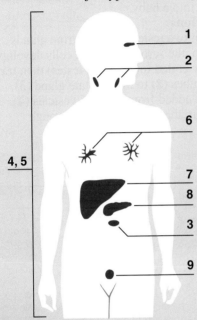

Exocrine system and digestion

1 Liver The body's largest organ, it stores vitamins, minerals, and glycogen. It also turns dangerous chemicals into harmless substances.

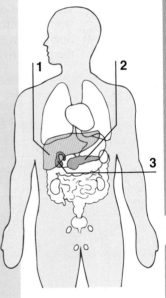

1 Lacrimal glands (tears)
2 Salivary glands (saliva)
3 Mucus glands (mucus)
4 Sweat glands of skin (sweat)
5 Sebaceous glands of skin

(sebum, oily substances which keep skin supple)
6 Mammary glands in women (milk)
7 Liver (bile)
8 Pancreas (digestive juices)
9 Prostate in men (seminal fluid)

2 Pancreas Stores enzymes that break down fats, proteins and carbohydrates.
3 Gallbladder Stores bile to use in the digestion of fats.

15

REPRODUCTIVE SYSTEM

Male

A man's sex organs produce the minute tadpole-shaped sex cells called sperm. A sperm that fertilizes an egg produces an embryo that develops into a baby.

Structures and functions

Sperm are produced in two testes (**1**), endocrine glands which hang in a pouch, the scrotum. Sperm cells develop in the epididymis (highly coiled tubes in the testes) then travel via two vas deferens tubes (**2**) to the prostate gland (**3**), where seminal fluid is added from seminal vesicles (**4**). Sperm then enter the urethra (**5**) and escape through the penis (**6**).

Male

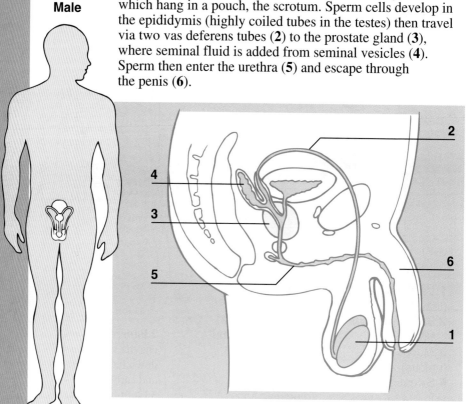

Female

A woman's reproductive system produces eggs and babies and provides these with nourishment.

Structures

The vagina (**1**) is a muscular tube opening between the rectum and urethra. A narrow neck, the cervix (**2**), leads to the womb or uterus (**3**), a hollow, muscular organ as big as a pear. Fallopian tubes (**4**) connect the uterus to the ovaries (**5**), where the eggs are produced. Breasts (**6**) are milk-producing glands.

Female

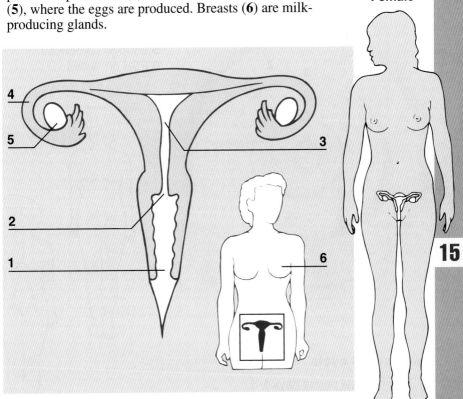

15

MENSTRUATION

Menstruation is a woman's monthly "period," when the vagina
discharges blood and mucus. This happens as part of the 28-day
menstrual cycle of egg production controlled by a hormone feedback
system run by the hypothalamus (**1**) and pituitary (**2**) in the brain.

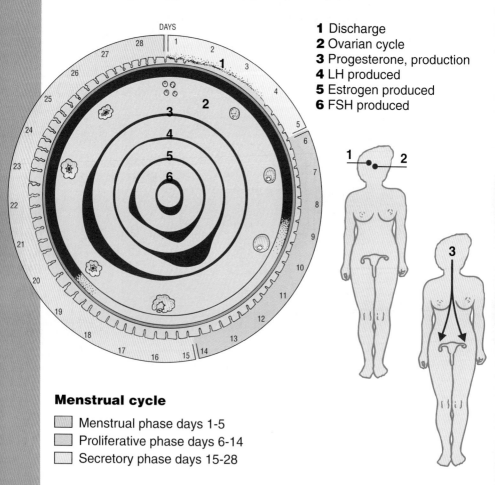

1 Discharge
2 Ovarian cycle
3 Progesterone, production
4 LH produced
5 Estrogen produced
6 FSH produced

Menstrual cycle

Menstrual phase days 1-5
Proliferative phase days 6-14
Secretory phase days 15-28

From day 1 Follicle-stimulating hormone or FSH (**3**) helps a new egg form in an egg follicle (**4**), which is a fluid-filled cavity in the ovary.
From day 4 The follicle produces the hormone estrogen (**5**), promoting growth of the uterus (**6**) and breasts (**7**), releasing luteinizing hormone or LH (**8**), which stimulates ovulation (and conversion of the ruptured follicle), and blocking FSH output.
From day 12 LH bursts the follicle, releasing an egg or ovum (**9**) and transforming the follicle into a solid body, the corpus luteum (**10**), yielding estrogen and the hormone progesterone (**11**).
From day 14 Progesterone stimulates thickening of the uterus wall and increased blood supply in preparation for the uterus receiving a fertilized egg. If fertilization fails to occur, the corpus luteum shrinks, LH, estrogen, and progesterone output fall, the uterus lining breaks up, and its bloody fragments escape in the monthly discharge.

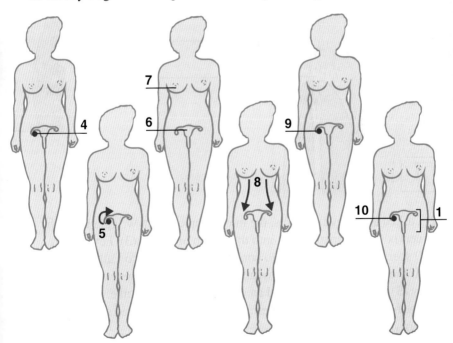

15

CONCEPTION

A new life starts when a sperm fertilizes an egg. During sexual intercourse, a man's penis releases millions of sperm into a woman's vagina.

The sperms' journey

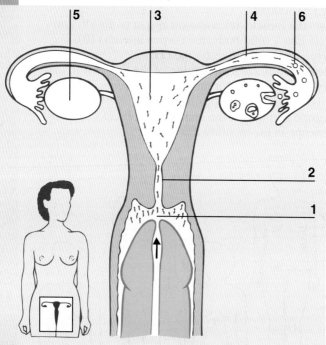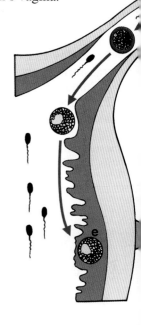

(**1**) Lashed along by their tails, the microscopic sperm wriggle through the cervix (**2**), a narrow neck, into the womb or uterus (**3**). Fewer than 3000 sperm probably survive to continue on into the two Fallopian tubes (**4**). If the woman has recently ovulated (released an egg or ovum from an ovary (**5**) some sperm may find an egg (**6**) already in a tube. If egg release has not occurred, the sperm can survive up to three days until an egg arrives.

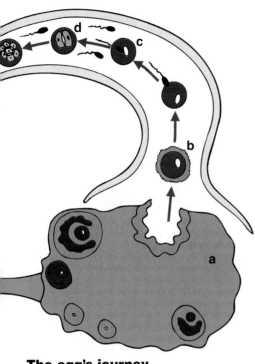

Fertilization

Fertilization occurs when sperm meet an egg as it passes down the oviduct. Hugely magnified, a tadpole-like sperm (**1**) fertilizes an egg or ovum (**2**) much larger than itself. The sperm's head, or nucleus, will stick to the ovum and fuse with the ovum nucleus. The ovum then gains a hardened wall to keep out other sperm.

An ovum can live for between 12 and 24 hours once it has been released, but sperm can live inside a female for 3–4 days. Each month there are therefore 3–4 days when fertilization can occur.

From puberty to old age, men's testes produce 10–30 billion sperm a month. Women are born with perhaps 350,000 immature eggs. Between puberty and menopause, at least one egg matures in an ovary each month and is released for possible fertilization. Only some 375 eggs mature throughout a lifetime.

The egg's journey
a ovary
b egg's journey
c fertilization
d division
e embedded in uterus wall

1

2

15

DEVELOPMENT OF A BABY

These line drawings show how an embryo becomes a fetus within the mother's uterus (womb), and they also show how the mother's body adapts and changes both for gestation and for the events of birth and nursing.

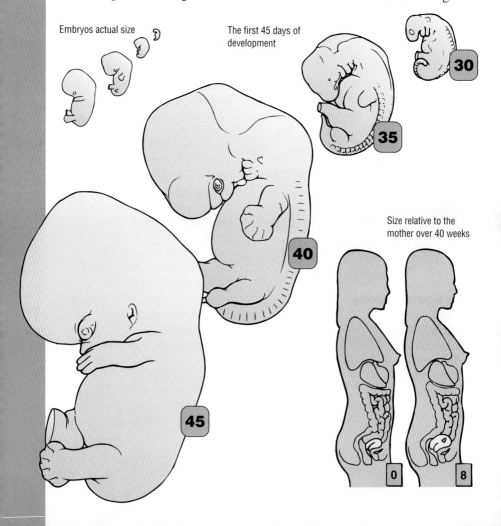

Embryos actual size

The first 45 days of development

Size relative to the mother over 40 weeks

The embryo

At conception, the fertilized egg comprises one single cell, known as a zygote. Following cell division, the zygote becomes a small bundle of cells that then implants in the lining of the uterus (womb), creating a placenta (a union of cells between mother and child) at the junction. From that time until week 8 of pregnancy, the developing child is technically described as an embryo.

The fetus

Well before week 8 of gestation, the developing child is protected from damage and pressure by a surrounding membranous sac filled with amniotic fluid. Its nutrition is supplied through the placenta via an umbilical cord. By week 8, the human embryo is less than 1 inch in length and has arms, legs, eyes, and eyelids. From week 8 to the time of birth is a period of sustained growth for the fetus; the length of the fetus increases some 20 times during that period, and the weight increases by around 1700 times. The embryo cells divide rapidly and have special functions, becoming muscles, bones, and organs. The later stages of an embryo when all the organs are present is called the fetus. A few weeks before the birth the embryo lies head down in the uterus with the head just above the cervix.

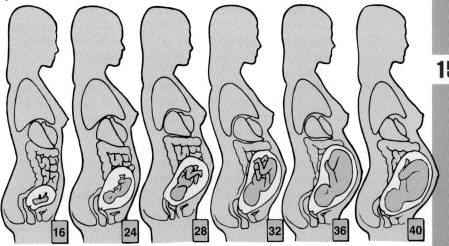

15

METHODS OF CONTRACEPTION

The following list gives types of contraceptive most commonly used by both male and female.

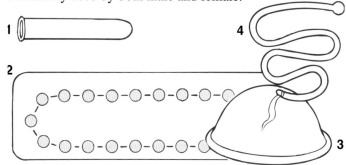

Condom (1) Also known as a sheath, rubber, or French letter, this is worn by the man over his erect penis and prevents sperm from entering the vagina. It also protects against sexually transmitted diseases. The female condom fits inside the woman's vagina.

Contraceptive pill (2) Taken by the woman, this contains the hormones estrogen and progesterone, or just progesterone, and acts by preventing ovulation (ripening and release of an egg by an ovary). There are often side effects, so the pill should be taken under medical supervision. A male pill is currently being developed.

Diaphragm (3) A rubber cap that is inserted by the woman to fit across her cervix, acting as a barrier to sperm. It should be used in conjunction with a spermicide cream or gel. Similar, but not as widely used in the US, is the cervical cap.

IUD (4) (intrauterine device) Also known as the coil or loop. This small plastic device is inserted in the uterus by a physician and left in place for several years. It helps to prevent conception by interfering with the implantation of fertilized eggs.

Female sterilization This involves cutting, tying, or removing all or part of the Fallopian tubes so that eggs cannot pass from the ovaries to the uterus and sperm cannot reach the egg. A hysterectomy (removal of the uterus) is not generally recommended for birth control.

Implants These are based on similar hormonal principles to those of the pill but are inserted under the skin to release progestogen into the bloodstream. They remain effective for 5 years. There can be side effects.

Mucus method This requires recognition of natural changes in the nature of cervical mucus during a woman's menstrual cycle, in order to recognize "safe" days. It is not one of the more reliable methods.

Postcoital methods These include a "morning after" pill, consisting of large doses of synthetic estrogen to be taken within 72 hours of intercourse; insertion of an IUD up to 5 days after intercourse; and menstrual extraction.

Rhythm method The calendar method requires that a couple avoid intercourse during those days of the menstrual cycle when a woman is most likely to conceive. The temperature method requires checking the small rise in temperature that a woman has when ovulation occurs. Both methods are unreliable on the whole, particularly if menstruation is not regular.

Spermicides These chemical products are inserted into the woman's vagina before intercourse and either kill sperm or create a barrier. They come as creams, jellies, foaming tablets, or pessaries, and should be used in conjunction with a diaphragm or condom.

Sponge The spermicide-impregnated sponge is inserted in the vagina prior to intercourse and left in place for 6 hours.

Vasectomy This simple surgical procedure involves the cutting and tying of both the tubes that connect the testes and the urethra so that semen ejected no longer contains sperm. It is reversible in only 50% of men.

Withdrawal This is the oldest method of birth control, by which the male takes his penis out of the vagina just prior to ejaculation. It is not considered a reliable method.

15

NUTRITION AND HEALTH
Health

Health is a state of physical, mental, and social well-being. Good health is the absence of disease, a balanced outlook on life and all the parts of the body working properly together. Knowledge of the human body is necessary to achieve good health. Good nutrition, exercise, rest, sleep, cleanliness, and medical and dental care help to maintain health.

Health guidelines

Cleanliness
Keeping clean helps to control the growth of bacteria and other germs which can cause diseases. Daily washing keeps the body free from dirt and also prevents skin infections. Hair should also be washed regularly. Daily dental care is also necessary to prevent tooth decay and disease.

Exercise
Exercise keeps the body fit and healthy. Vigorous exercise strengthens muscles and improves the circulatory and respiratory systems. Physical fitness benefits physical and mental health.

Rest and sleep
Rest helps to overcome tiredness and restores energy. Everyone needs rest and sleep but the amount required varies from person to person.

Calorie requirements

Children of both sexes below the age of ten have high calorie needs for their size. From there to the age of twenty the male has a greater requirement than the female. Later years show a marked reduction in calorie needs but still a gap between male and female needs.

Nutrition

Good food is essential for health and survival. A poor intake of food, poor absorption or use of nutrients by the body results in malnutrition. Overeating leads to obesity. Good nutrition is the proper amount of food each day.

Food provides certain chemical substances needed for good health. These are nutrients. They perform one or more of three functions:

1 provide materials for building, repairing, or maintaining body tissues;
2 help to regulate body processes;
3 serve as fuel to provide energy.

Medical care

Regular check-ups by a doctor and a dentist are important for safeguarding health. Doctors recommend that people call them at the first sign of illness. It is equally important to prevent disease, which can be by immunization.

Balanced diet

A balanced diet helps to provide all the substances needed by the body for healthy growth and development. These substances are called nutrients and they are classified into five main groups: proteins, vitamins, minerals, carbohydrates, and fats. Water is also essential for life. A balanced diet consists of a wide variety of foods such as fresh fruit and vegetables, meat, fish, cereals, dairy products, and eggs.

15

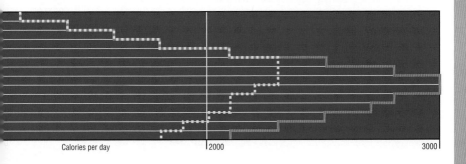

Calories per day   2000   3000

Nutrients in food

Foods give us proteins, carbohydrates, fats, vitamins, and minerals.

1 Proteins build and repair body cells. Meat, fish, eggs, milk, beans, grains, and nuts are rich in proteins.

2 Carbohydrates provide energy for rapid use. They include sugars in fruits, sugar cane, and sugar beet; starches in potatoes, bread, cereals such as wheat, rice, maize, oats, and barley, and vegetables.

3 Fats are concentrated stores of energy, found in butter, margarine, edible oils, meat, eggs, etc.

4 Vitamins in tiny quantities help regulate chemical processes inside the body. Different vitamins occur in fats and oils, fresh fruits and vegetables, liver, kidney, cereals, eggs, and yeast.

5 Minerals are necessary for the chemical activities of the body and for the construction of tissues. Minerals of certain kinds abound in milk, cheese, fish, and some green vegetables.

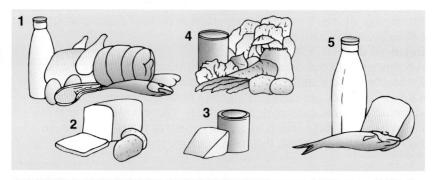

Calories
Calorie intake increases weight. Selecting foods with low calories assists in weight reduction.

High calories
Cakes, cookies, chocolate, nuts, cream, salami, puddings, jelly, honey

Food intake

The diagrams compare average daily calorie consumption of different foods per person in two regions. In the Western world people eat more food of more kinds than they do in the non-Western world.

American–European food consumption

Breakfast 1000 calories	cereals, milk, sugar, juice, coffee, fried foods, toast, marmalade	
Snacks 400 calories	tea, coffee, milk, sugar, cookies	
Lunch 1000 calories	soup, main dish, salad, bread, butter, dessert, coffee, milk, sugar, wine, or beer,	
Dinner 1100 calories	main dish, salad, bread, butter, dessert, coffee, sugar, milk, wine, or, beer	

3500 calories average daily intake

Asian–African food consumption

Breakfast, lunch, and dinner 2000 calories	rice, milk, pulses, vegetables, very little meat or fish	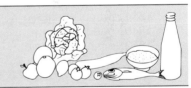

15

Medium calories
Mackerel, herring, anchovies, bananas, crackers, rice, pasta, eggs, cheese

Low calories
Onions, peppers, tomatoes, mushrooms, fruits, unsweetened tea, and coffee

TRANSPORT

Date	Invention	Inventor
c. 3480 BC	wheel	Sumerian civilization
AD 1712	piston steam engine	Thomas Newcomen
1769	steam engine (condenser model)	James Watt
1770	steam tricycle	Nicolas Cugnot
1783	full-size hot-air balloon	Jacques & Joseph Montgolfier
1797	parachute	Jacques Garnerin
1804	steam railway locomotive	Richard Trevithick
1826	car (gas-powered)	Samuel Brown
1839	bicycle	Kirkpatrick MacMillan
1843	railway (underground)	Charles Pearson
1844	propeller ship	Isambard Kingdom Brunel
1845	pneumatic tyre	Robert Thomson
1852	airship (nonrigid)	Henri Giffard
1852	lift	Elisha Otis
1853	glider	Sir George Cayley
1866	cable car	W. Ritter
1876	carburettor	Gottlieb Daimler
1879	electric railway	Ernst von Siemens
1884	steam turbine	Charles Parsons
1885	motorcycle	Gottlieb Daimler
1885	internal-combustion engine	Gottlieb Daimler
1885	gasoline engine	Karl Benz
1886	airplane (steam-powered)	Clement Adler

Columbia – first space shuttle

1892	diesel engine	Rudolf Diesel
1892	escalator	Jesse Reno
1897	turbine-propelled ship	Charles Parsons
1900	airship (rigid)	Ferdinand von Zeppelin
1902	disk brakes	Frederick Lanchester
1903	aeroplane	Orville & Wilbur Wright
1907	helicopter	Louis & Jacques Breguet
1926	rocket	Robert H. Goddard
1937	jet engine	Frank Whittle
1940	first serviceable helicopter	Igor Sikorsky
1954	swing-wing airplane	Grumman Co.
1959	hovercraft	Sir Christopher Cockerell
1959	rotary engine	Felix Wankel
1981	space shuttle	NASA
1990	joined-wings aircraft	Julian Wolkovitch
2005	Segway, one-person scooter	Dean Kamen

MEDICAL

Date	Invention	Inventor
c. 1280	spectacles	not known
1540	artificial limb	Ambroise Paré
1630	obstetric forceps	Peter Chemberlen
1714	mercury thermometer	Gabriel Fahrenheit
1775	bifocal lenses	Benjamin Franklin
1796	vaccination	Edward Jenner
1816	stethoscope	Théophile Laënnec
1817	dental plate	Anthony Plantson

1827	endoscope	Pierre Segalas
1846	anaesthetics	William Morton
1853	hypodermic syringe	Alexander Wood
1863	barbiturates	Adolf von Bayer
1865	antiseptics	Joseph Lister
1885	rabies vaccination	Louis Pasteur
1887	contact lenses	Adolf Frick
1895	X-ray	Wilhelm Röntgen
1903	electrocardiograph	Willem Einthoven
1928	antibiotics (penicillin)	Alexander Fleming
1955	contraceptive pill	Gregor Pincus
1957	pacemaker	Clarence W. Lillehie & Earl Bakk
1966	artificial blood	Clark & Gollan
1967	heart transplant	Christiaan Barnard
1973	CAT scan	Godfrey Hounsfield & Allan Cormack
1979	ultrasound scan	Ian Donald
1982	artificial heart	Robert Jarvik
1989	LipoScan	Home Diagnostic Inc.
1994	portable kidney dialysis	Dean Kamen
1999	Robotic heart surgery	Intuitive Surgery Inc.

COMMUNICATIONS

Joseph Lister's
antiseptic machine

Date	Invention	Inventor
c. 3500 BC	writing	Sumerian civilization
c. 1300 BC	parchment	Egyptian civilization
AD 105	paper	China
c. 1455	printing press	Johannes Gutenberg
1565	pencil	Konrad Gessner

Samuel Morse
and his telegraph

1774	electrical telegraphy	Georges Lesage
1787	mechanical telegraphy	M. Lammond
1826	photography (metal)	Joseph Niepce
1834	braille	Louis Braille
1835	photography (paper)	William Fox Talbot
1837	telegraph code	Samuel Morse
1868	typewriter	Christopher Sholes
1876	telephone	Alexander Graham Bell
1876	microphone	Alexander Graham Bell
1877	gramophone	Thomas Edison
1884	fountain pen	Lewis Waterman
1895	cinema	Auguste & Louis Lumière
1896	radio	Guglielmo Marconi
1898	tape recorder	Valdemar Poulsen
1900	loudspeaker	Horace Short
1902	facsimile machine	Arthur Korn
1925	television	John Logie Baird
1938	ballpoint pen	Laszlo & Georg Biro
1948	long-play record	Peter Goldmark
1956	video recorder	Ampex Co.
1957	Liquid Paper®	Bette Nesmith Graham
1978	compact disc (CD)	Philips (Netherlands)
2002	braille glove	Ryan Patterson

MILITARY

Alexander
Fleming

Date	Invention	Inventor
c. 200 BC	cannon	Archimedes
AD 950	gun powder	Chinese
1232	missile rocket	Mongolians
c. 1300	gun	not known
1718	machine gun	James Puckle
1776	submarine	David Bushnell

1835	revolver	Samuel Colt
1862	rapid-fire gun	R. Gatling
1916	tank	Ernest Swinton
1922	radar	A. Taylor & L. Young
1943	air-to-air missile	Herbert Wagner
1945	atomic bomb	O. Frisch, N. Bohr, & R. Peierls
1988	B2 stealth bomber	Northrop

DOMESTIC

Niels Bohr

Date	Invention	Inventor
c. 2500 BC	soap	Sumerian civilization
AD 1589	flush toilet	Sir John Harington
1679	pressure cooker	Denis Papin
1784	gas lighting	Jean-Pierre Minkhales
1810	food canning	Nicolas Appert
1816	fire extinguisher	George Manby
1826	safety match	John Walker
1830	lawnmower	Edward Budding
1849	safety pin	Walter Hunt
1851	sewing machine	Isaac Singer
1858	burglar alarm	Edwin Holmes
1860	linoleum	Frederick Walton
1862	refrigerator	James Harrison
1876	carpet sweeper	Melville Bissell
1879	electric light	Thomas Edison
1882	electric iron	Henry Seeley
1889	dishwasher	Mrs W. Cochran
1889	electric oven	Bernina Hotel, Switzerland
1893	zip fastener	Whitcombe Judson
1901	safety razor	King Camp Gillette

Allessandro Volta

1901	vacuum cleaner	Hubert Booth
1907	washing machine	Hurley Machine Co.
1926	aerosols	E. Rotheim
1927	toaster	Charles Strite
1929	frozen foods	Clarence Birdseye
1938	fluorescent light	General Electric Co.
1947	microwave oven	P. Spencer
1948	Velcro	George de Mestral
1955	nonstick pan	Mark Grégoir
1971	food processor	Pierre Verdon
1991	clockwork radio	Trevor Baylis
2004	Thinking Shoes	Adidas

Samuel Colt's revolver

SCIENCE

Date	Invention	Inventor
c. 1590	microscope	Zacharias Janssen
1644	barometer	Evangelista Torricelli
1650	air pump	Otto von Guericke
1654	slide rule	Robert Bissaker
1657	pendulum clock	Christiaan Huygens
1698	steam pump	Thomas Savery
1762	chronometer	John Harrison
1800	electric battery	Alessandro Volta
1814	spectroscope	Joseph von Frauenhofer
1824	electromagnet	William Sturgeon
1831	electric generator	Michael Faraday
1834	galvanometer	André Ampere
1839	vulcanized rubber	Charles Goodyear
1851	heat pump	Lord Kelvin
1855	bunsen burner	Peter Desdega

1870	plastics (celluloid)	John Wesley Hyatt
1870	electric motor (DC)	Zenobe Gramme
1888	electric motor (AC)	Nikola Tesla
1908	gyrocompass	Elmer Sperry
1911	superconductivity	Heika Onnes
1933	electron microscope	M. Knoll & E. Ruska
1935	radar	Robert Watson-Watt
1942	nuclear reactor	Enrico Fermi
1960	laser	Theodore Maiman
1981	scanning tunnelling microscope (STM)	IBM
1987	positron microscope	Michigan University

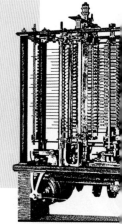

Charles Babbage's "analytical engine"

ELECTRONICS AND COMPUTING

Date	Invention	Inventor
1623	adding machine	Wilhelm Schickard
1822	"analytical engine"	Charles Babbage
1890	punched card machine	Herman Hollerith
1948	electronic computer	Frederick Williams
1948	transistor	W. Shockley, J. Bardeen & W. Brattain
1958	integrated circuit	Jack Kilby
1960	mini computer	Digital Corporation
1965	word processor	IBM
1965	mouse	Douglas Engelbart
1970	floppy disk	IBM
1972	microprocessor	Intel Corporation
1973	microcomputer	Trong Truong
1981	superchip	Hewlett-Packard
1985	transputer	Inmos Ltd.

James Hargreaves' spinning jenny

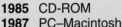

1985	CD-ROM	Sony/Philips
1987	PC–Macintosh interface	Micro Solutions
1989	interactive compact disc (CD-I)	Sony/Philips
1991	World Wide Web	Tim Berners Lee

ENGINEERING AND CONSTRUCTION

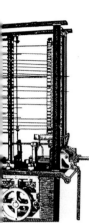

Date	Invention	Inventor
c. 6000 BC	bricks	Jericho
c. 4000 BC	saw	Egyptian civilization
c. 3700 BC	bronze	Sumerian civilization
c. 1500 BC	lathe	Greek civilization
c. AD 100	concrete	Roman civilization
c. 900	windmill	Persia
983	canal lock	Chiao Wei-Yo
1738	iron rails	Whitehaven Colliery, UK
1752	lightning conductor	Benjamin Franklin
1764	spinning jenny	James Hargreaves
1769	spinning frame	Richard Arkwright
1779	spinning mule	Samuel Crompton
1824	Portland cement	Joseph Aspdin
1860	steel production	Henry Bessemer
1861	pneumatic drill	Germain Sommelier
1867	dynamite	Alfred Nobel
1883	skyscraper	William Jenney
1892	reinforced concrete	François Hennebique
1895	electric drill	Wilhelm Fein
1912	stainless steel	Harold Brearley
1954	geodesic dome	R. Buckminster Fuller
1986	biometal	Dai Homma

Richard Buckminster Fuller's geodesic dome

MOVING: ON WATER
Floating

The arrows indicate relative values of weight and upthrust.

1 A raft floats because, overall, it is less dense than water. It settles at a point where its weight equals the upthrust produced by displaced water.

2 A raft sinks when its laden weight exceeds upthrust.

3 The boat's weight equals upthrust. It rides high in the water because overall it is much less dense than water.

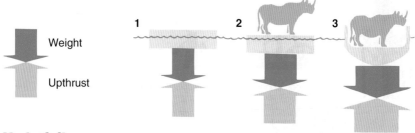

Weight

Upthrust

Hydrofoil

A hydrofoil boat uses an aerofoil-shaped device, the hydrofoil (**1**), to provide lift. At low speeds (**2**) lift from the hydrofoil is small. At higher speeds (**3**) increased lift raises the hull out of the water. With reduced friction between the hull and the water, higher speeds can now be attained.

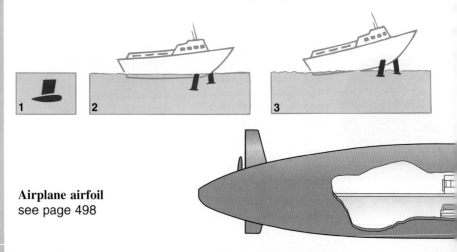

Airplane airfoil
see page 498

Submarine

Diving (1) Water is pumped into ballast tanks, and (**2**) air is expelled. The submarine's density is greater than that of the surrounding water and it sinks.

Neutral buoyancy (3) The submarine levels off when its overall density is the same as that of the surrounding water.

Rising (4) Compressed air is pumped into the ballast tanks, expelling the water. The submarine's density becomes less than that of the seawater and it rises to the surface.

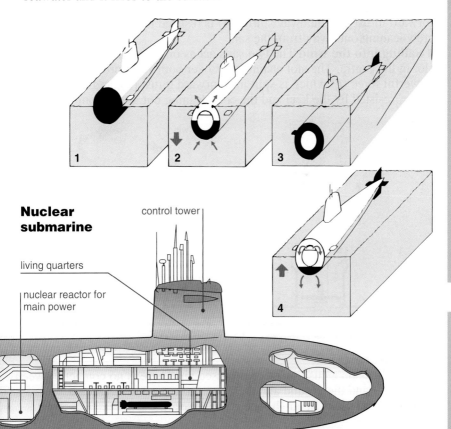

Nuclear submarine

control tower

living quarters

nuclear reactor for main power

17

Sailing boat

A simple yacht has two triangular sails – the jib (**a**) and the mainsail (**b**). A rudder (**c**) steers the boat in the required direction. A boat can make progress into the wind by tacking (following a zigzag course).

1 Sailing before the wind Forward thrust (**d**) is in the same direction as the wind.

2 Sailing with the wind on the quarter Forward thrust (**d**) is provided by the wind acting on the sail (**e**). A sideways thrust (**f**) is resisted by the boat's keel, which stops the boat shifting sideways.

3 Sailing across the wind The wind acting on the sail (**e**) provides the forward thrust (**d**). Sideways thrust (**f**) is resisted by the keel and the crew leaning out away from the sail.

4 Sailing into the wind The two sails act as one large aerofoil with a slot in the centre. The slot channels air over both sails, producing a powerful force (**g**) which is split into forward thrust (**d**), and a sideways thrust, resisted by the keel and the crew leaning out away from the sail.

Tacking
a to starboard
b to port

a

b

wind

route

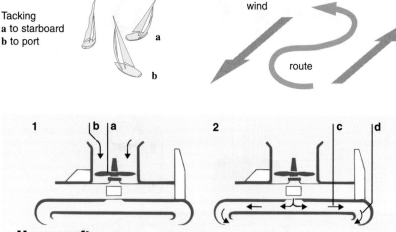

1 b a   2   c d

Hovercraft

This floats on a cushion of compressed air. There is no contact between the craft and the ground and therefore no friction to overcome.

1 A fan (**a**) sucks in air (**b**) and compresses it.

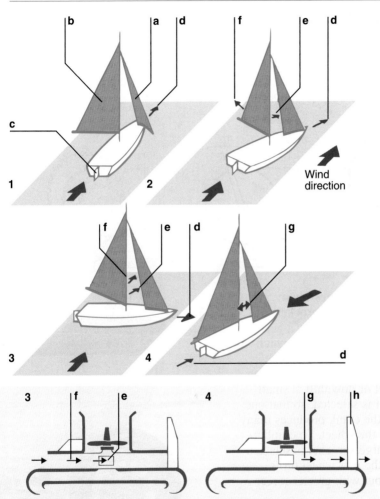

Wind direction

17

2 The air is forced down and along (**c**) and a flexible rubberized skirt
(**d**) keeps the cushion of air trapped.
3 Propellers (**e**) draw in air (**f**) for forward propulsion.
4 Air flow (**g**) is directed by a rudder (**h**) for steering.

MOVING: ON LAND
Bicycle

1 Propulsive force This is transmitted from the cyclist's legs via pedals (**a**) and a crank (**b**) through a chain (**c**) to a rear wheel sprocket (**d**). The crank rotates at low speed with high force, while the sprocket and rear wheel rotate at a higher speed with lower force.

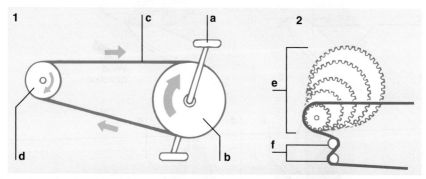

2 Derailleur gears These comprise several sprockets of different sizes (**e**) plus a gear change mechanism (**f**), which transfers the chain from one sprocket to the next. To ride on the level or downhill, a small sprocket is selected, so that one turn of the crank produces many turns of the wheel. To climb a hill, a large sprocket is selected so that the rear wheel turns slowly but with greater force.

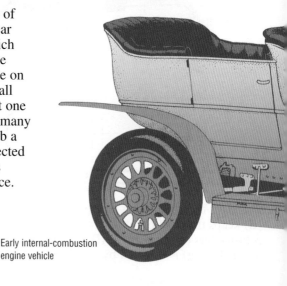

Early internal-combustion engine vehicle

Internal-combustion engines

Engines are machines that convert heat energy into mechanical energy to produce force or motion. As their name implies, internal-combustion engines burn fuel within the engine.

Piston engines

These are usually fuelled by gasoline or by diesel oil.

The gasoline engine A mixture of gasoline vapor and air is drawn into a cylinder (**1**), compressed (**2**), and then ignited by a spark (**3**). As the gasoline vapor/air mixture ignites, the burnt gases expand and move a piston within the cylinder. The piston is attached to a crankshaft, which provides rotational power.

The three main types of gasoline engine are the four-stroke, the two-stroke, and the Wankel rotary engine.

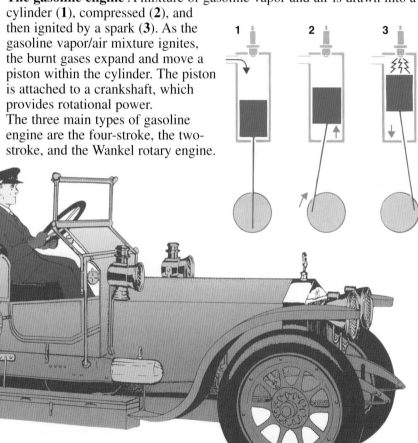

The four-stroke engine The piston (**a**) is connected to the crankshaft (**b**) via a big end (**c**). There are four piston strokes per cycle:

1 Induction stroke The inlet valve (**d**) opens and the piston moves down inside the cylinder, drawing in the gasoline/air mixture (**e**).

2 Compression stroke The piston rises, compressing the gasoline/air mixture. The inlet and exhaust valves are closed.

3 Power stroke A spark plug ignites the fuel (**f**) and the burning gases expand, forcing the piston down.

4 Exhaust stroke As the piston rises, burnt gases escape through an exhaust valve (**g**).

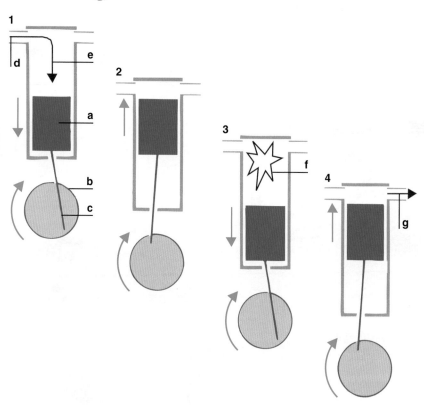

The two-stroke engine Less efficient than the four-stroke engine but cheaper and lighter. Valves are replaced by ports which are opened and closed by the piston as it moves. Two-stroke engines deliver a power stroke for every turn of the crankshaft. A four-stroke engine only does so for every other turn.

1 The piston (**a**) is at the top of the cylinder and the gasoline/air mixture is compressed. The exhaust port (**b**) and inlet port (**c**) are closed. When the spark ignites the compressed mixture (**d**), the piston is driven down on its power stroke.

2 The piston (**a**) is near the bottom of the power stroke, burnt gases have escaped through the outlet port (**b**) and gasoline/air is admitted through the inlet port (**c**).

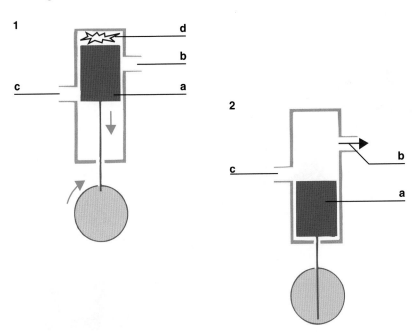

17

Wankel rotary engine Developed by the German engineer Felix Wankel in 1956, it has a triangular piston which rotates inside an oval combustion chamber. The power output is directly rotational, rather than via a crankshaft. It has a four-stage cycle similar to a four-stroke engine:

1 Induction stage of cycle Inlet (**a**) admits a gasoline/air mixture into chamber (**b**).

2 Compression The revolving piston (**c**) compresses the gasoline/air mixture.

3 Power A spark plug ignites (**d**) the compressed gasoline/air mixture and the gases expand, keeping the piston turning.

4 Exhaust Burnt gases escape through the exhaust port (**e**).

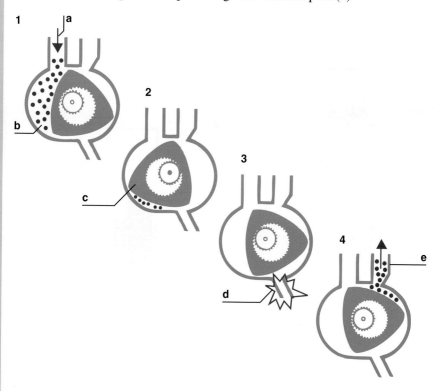

The diesel engine

This uses diesel oil as a fuel, which is sprayed into the cylinder as a liquid. It does not require an electrical ignition system as the oil/air mixture is ignited by pressure alone.

In a diesel engine the air is drawn into the cylinder first (**1**) and is compressed (**2**) to a much greater degree than in the gasoline engine. Because of this, the air in the diesel engine heats up and when a small amount of diesel oil is injected, it ignites spontaneously (**3**).

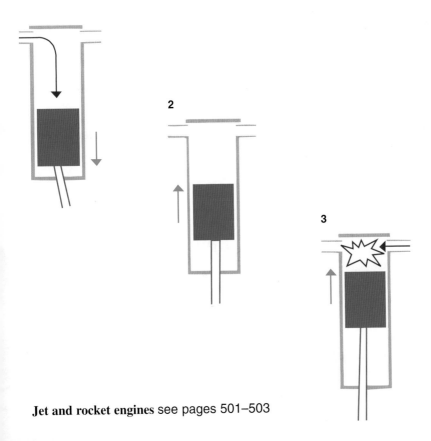

17

Jet and rocket engines see pages 501–503

Steam engines

A steam engine converts heat energy stored in steam into usable power. In the first engines, water was heated in a furnace and converted to steam. The steam expanded into a cylinder, forcing the piston up. A spray of water was then injected. This changed the steam back to water. The steam no longer held up the piston and it dropped down ready for the cycle to start again.

Double-acting steam engine

Many improvements were made. This engine was developed by James Watt and was used widely during the Industrial Revolution in the UK.

1 Steam (**a**) enters the steam chest (**b**) through an inlet.

2 Steam enters the upper piston cylinder (**c**) through an open valve (**d**). The piston is forced down. Steam in the lower cylinder (**e**) is pushed out of the valve into the exhaust (**f**).

3 As the axle (**g**) revolves, the piston starts to be forced up. More steam enters the steam chest.

4 As the piston rises, the lower valve (**h**) opens. Steam enters the lower piston cylinder, continuing to push up the piston. Steam from the upper cylinder enters the exhaust.

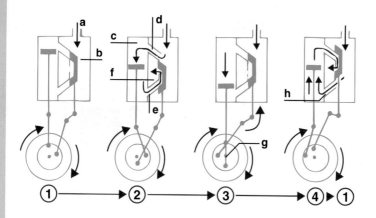

George Stephenson's
steam engine *Rocket*

Types of train

Steam locomotive

Largely superseded by diesel and electric trains, steam locomotives burn fuel, usually coal, in a firebox (**1**). Hot gases (**2**) are drawn through tubes in a boiler (**3**), turning water to steam. A regulator (**4**) controls the delivery of steam to a cylinder (**5**). Expanding and condensing steam pushes a piston (**6**) back and forth. This drives the wheels (**7**) via a connecting rod (**8**) and a coupling rod (**9**). Exhaust steam and boiler smoke escape through the chimney (**10**).

17

Diesel locomotive

The most common type, a diesel-electric locomotive is an electric locomotive that carries diesel engines as its power source. The power of the diesel engine (**1**) is transmitted to an electric generator (**2**). This drives traction motors (**3**) mounted on axles which drive the wheels (**4**).

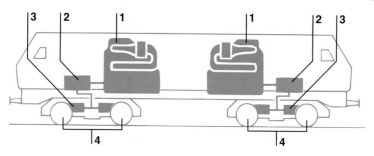

Electric locomotive

Electric trains take their power from an external supply. On electrified main-line railways this is usually from overhead wires (**1**) via a spring-loaded arm (**2**). The high-voltage overhead current is reduced by a transformer (**3**) and fed to a motor (**4**) which, through a system of connecting rods (**5**), drives a number of wheels (**6**). On suburban and underground trains (not shown) electricity is usually obtained from an electrified third rail.

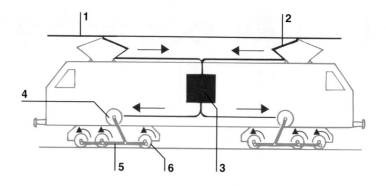

Motor car
1 Steering
The steering wheel (**a**) and steering column (**b**) rotate gears in a pinion (**c**) which moves a rack (**d**) to the left or right. This in turn connects to a steering arm (**e**) that turns the axle (**f**) of each front wheel.

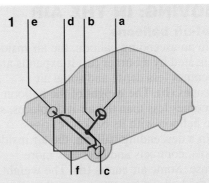

2 Transmission
The gearbox (**a**) and differential (**b**) convert engine revs to useful wheel revs. The clutch (**c**) disengages the gearbox from the engine (**d**), enabling gear changing. This shows a rear-wheel drive car. In front-wheel drive, the engine powers the front wheels.

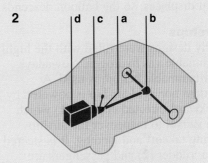

3 Suspension
This cushions vertical movement of the wheels, enabling a smooth ride. The front suspension consists of a shock absorber (**a**) and coil spring (**b**) attached to the chassis via a wishbone support (**c**). Rear suspension comprises leaf springs (**d**) and shock absorbers (**e**).

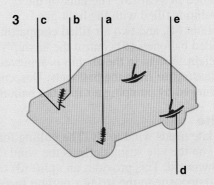

17

MOVING: IN THE AIR

Hot-air balloons

1 In an ascending balloon, the air inside is heated by a burner (**a**). It expands and becomes less dense and some air escapes (**b**). The weight of the balloon becomes less than the air it displaces, so the balloon with its basket (**c**) rises.
2 In a descending balloon, the air inside cools, contracts and becomes more dense. Some air enters (**d**). The weight of the balloon becomes more than the air it displaces, so the balloon descends.

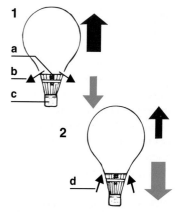

Arrow sizes show relative sizes of forces

↑ Upthrust   ↓ Weight

Airships

Early designs were filled with the highly flammable gas hydrogen. Nowadays, nonflammable helium is used. A modern nonrigid airship is powered by backward-directed engines (**1**) which can swivel to maneuver the airship during takeoff and landing. It is steered by a rudder (**2**) and passengers are carried in a car (**3**). The bulk of the airship is filled with the light gas helium (**4**), and two air-filled compartments called ballonets (**5**) control the airship's weight. Ascent in the airship is achieved by releasing air from the ballonets. Descent is achieved by pumping air into the ballonets.

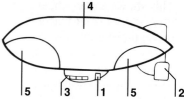

Kite

A kite needs wind to fly. The pulling force (**1**) on the kite string deflects the wind (**2**) downward. This provides an uplift (**3**) equal and opposite to the string's pulling force.

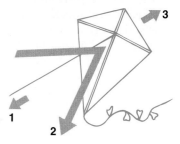

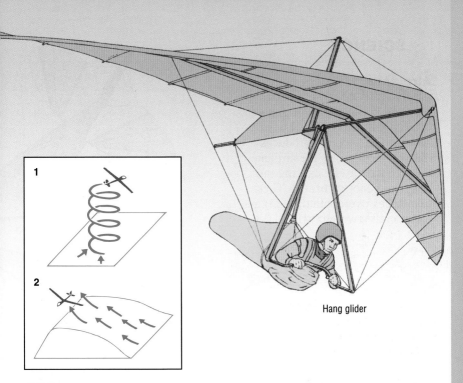

Hang glider

Gliders

A glider is a fixed-wing airplane which is unpowered while in flight. Gliders soar upward on air that is rising faster than the glider's rate of descent. Features such as thermals (**1**), rising currents of hot air, and upcurrents (**2**) found on the windward side of ridges, enable a glider to stay aloft for long periods.

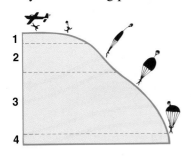

Parachute

When a parachutist jumps from the airplane he free falls (**1**) until the canopy opens (**2**). Upward forces called lift, and air resistance called drag, counteract the weight of the parachutist, slowing the rate of descent (**3**). Deceleration continues to a low constant speed of descent (**4**).

17

Airplanes

Airplanes fly because they are powered and their wings generate lift to hold them in the sky. An airplane's engine produces thrust which moves the airplane through the air (**1**), causing the wings to generate lift (**2**). These two forces overcome drag (**3**) and the aircraft's weight (**4**).

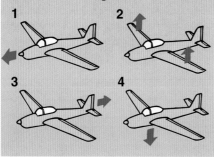

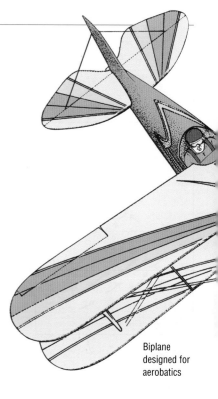

Biplane designed for aerobatics

Lift

An airplane's wing in cross-section is called an airfoil (**1**). Airflow (**2**) is faster over the wing than underneath it. The resulting low-pressure zone above (**3**) and high pressure zone below (**4**) generate lift (**5**).

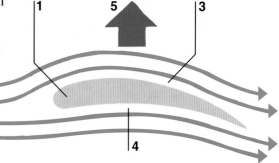

To manoeuvre an airplane it is necessary to control three types of movement: pitch (**1**), yaw (**2**), and roll (**3**).

Types of movement

Pitch is controlled by elevators (**a**) on the rear of the horizontal tail. Yaw is controlled by the rudder (**b**), a flap on the vertical tail fin. Roll is controlled by ailerons (**c**) on the outer trailing edges of the wings. When banking (turning) the rudder and ailerons are used together.

Controlling movement

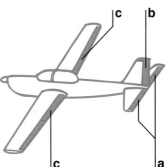

1 When diving, elevators are down.
2 When climbing, elevators are up.
3 When banking left, the left aileron is up, the right aileron down, and the rudder turned left.
4 When banking right, the right aileron is up, the left aileron down, and the rudder turned right.

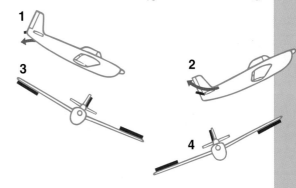

Helicopters

Revolving rotor blades (**a**) have an aerofoil cross section (**b**) and act like a plane's wings to create lift (**c**). The tail rotor helps maintain stability in flight (**d**).

1 At rest the blades sag down.
2 On takeoff the blades are raised.
3 To move forward the blades are tilted forward.
4 To move sideways the blades are tilted sideways.
5 To stop or go backward the blades are tilted back.

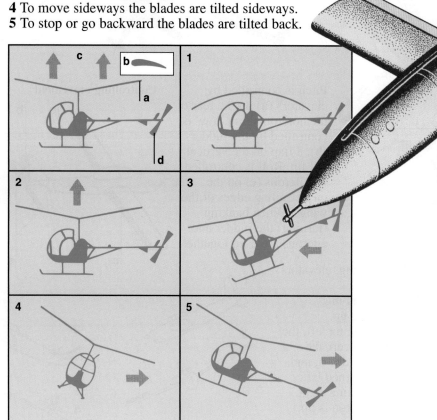

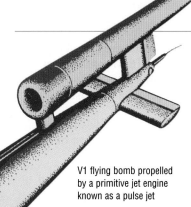

V1 flying bomb propelled by a primitive jet engine known as a pulse jet

Jet and rocket engines

Jet and rocket engines depend on Newton's Third Law of Motion: every action has an equal and opposite reaction. A rocket or jet aircraft is thrust forward by the force of hot gases spurting from the back of the engine. Jet engines get oxygen for combustion from the air around them. Rockets carry their own compressed air or oxygen supply and so can go outside the Earth's atmosphere.

Jet engines

Thrust is generated by a jet of exhaust gas discharged from a nozzle at the rear of the engine.

Four types of jet engine are shown here. All rely on air being sucked in (**a**), compressed (**b**), and ignited with fuel (**c**), then burnt gases being blown out of the back (**d**) to provide the forward thrust.

1 In the ramjet, used by high-speed military aircraft, flight speed is sufficient to suck in and compress air.

2 In turbojet engines, air is compressed by a compressor (**e**) which is rotated by a turbine (**f**) powered by the jet of exhaust gases.

1

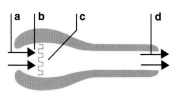

2

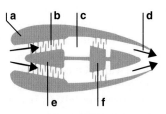

17

3 Modern turbofan engines, such as those used in subsonic jumbo jets, also have a compressor (**e**) and turbine (**f**). They differ from turbojet engines in that they have fans (**g**) at the front, and some compressed air travels through a bypass (**h**) and joins directly with the exhaust gases. This increases thrust and fuel economy.

4 In more traditional turboprop engines, the turbine (**f**) drives not only the compressor (**e**) but also a propeller (**i**) which provides most of the forward thrust.

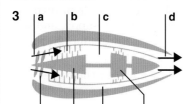

Key

a Air sucked in

b Air compressed

c Air/fuel mixture
   ignited

d Gases expelled

e Compressor

f Turbine

g Fans

h Bypass

i Propeller

Rocket engines

There are two types of rocket engine: those which burn solid fuel and those which burn liquid fuel.

1 Solid-fuel rocket engines burn fuel in a combustion chamber (**a**) that has an open end. The igniting fuel provides its own oxygen. As the fuel burns it produces gas which forces its way out of the open end of the rocket (**b**) as it expands, propelling the rocket forward. Once ignited, solid-fuel rocket engines cannot be shut off. They are used mainly as boosters which can be jettisoned from the space vehicle when spent.

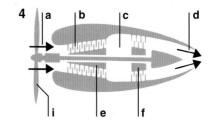

Solid-fuel rocket

2

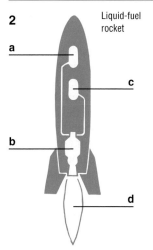

Liquid-fuel rocket

a

c

b

d

2 Liquid-fuel rocket engines. Rockets which burn liquid fuel carry a separate oxygen supply. Liquid hydrogen (**a**) is often used as fuel, and is fed into a combustion chamber (**b**) where it is ignited with liquid oxygen (**c**). The gas produced thrusts the rocket along (**d**). Speed of ignition is controllable, and liquid-fuel engines are used as space rocket main engines.

Space shuttle

The space shuttle has five major rocket engines. There are two large solid-fuel boosters (**1**) either side of the orbiter (**2**) and three liquid-fuel main engines (**3**) attached at the rear of the orbiter. The huge external tank (**4**) contains liquid nitrogen and liquid oxygen for the main engines. These five engines only take the shuttle into space. Smaller liquid-fuel engines are used to maneuver it in space.

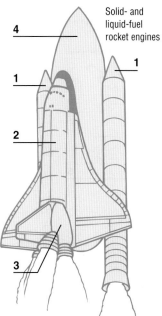

Solid- and liquid-fuel rocket engines

4

1

1

2

3

4 Third stage

5 Second stage

6 First stage

Saturn V – the largest liquid-fuel rocket ever built

ELECTRICAL DEVICES
Electric generators

These are used for large-scale production of electrical energy. They work by electromagnetic induction. Coils of wire (**1**) are mounted so they can be spun around in a magnetic field (**2**) between magnets (**3**, **4**). This means the magnetic field points one way through the coils, then the other way. The changing magnetic field produces a current around the coil. This type of generator is called an alternator because the increase and decrease of the magnetic field produces an alternating current (AC). A direct current (DC), where the current always flows in the same direction, has the coil connected to a commutator (**5**) which makes the current flow continuously in one direction as illustrated below.

In power stations, the energy from burning coal, oil, gas, or from a nuclear reaction is used to make steam. The steam drives a turbine to produce mechanical energy to turn the generator coils.

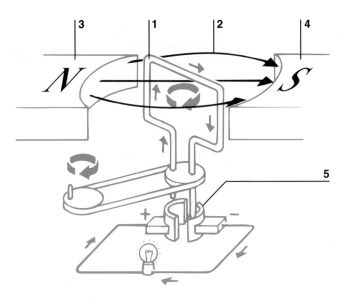

Turbines see page 507

Conventional power station

Coal (**1**) is delivered by conveyor belt to a boiler (**2**) where it is ground to a powder and ignited. Some power stations use gas or oil as an alternative fuel. Water inside pipes is heated to produce steam (**3**) which, under pressure, drives a steam turbine (**4**). This in turn powers an alternator (**5**) which delivers electricity to powerlines (**6**).

Used steam from the turbine (**4**) passes to a condenser (**7**). The condensed steam is recycled back to the boiler (**2**). Water used to cool the steam is sent to a cooling tower (**8**) and then recycled back to the condenser.

The flue gases (**9**) from the boiler (**2**) are passed through a dust extractor before release through tall chimneys (**10**).

A typical power station generates 60,000 kilowatts at 11,000 volts, enough to power a town of about 200,000 inhabitants.

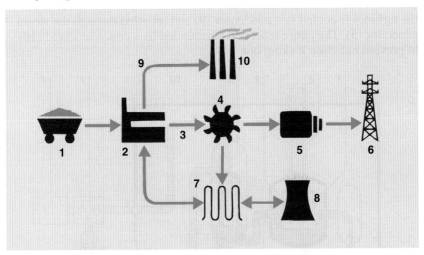

17

Coal is a dirty fuel which releases large amounts of sulfur and other pollutants into the air when it is burnt, leading to acid rain. Most power plants which burn fossil fuels use pollution control equipment to limit the release of pollution into the air. Cleaner ways of making electricity are provided by hydroelectric or geothermal power plants.

Nuclear power

This is generated by a nuclear reactor which converts nuclear (atomic) energy into thermal energy. A pressurized water reactor (PWR) is shown. In the reactor core (**1**) are fuel rods (**2**) containing uranium. When bombarded with neutrons (particles in an atom's nucleus), uranium atoms split, or undergo fission, and in so doing emit more neutrons, so starting a chain reaction which must be controlled. The breakdown products of uranium collide with water molecules in the reactor, and give off heat. This is the power source.

Control rods (**3**), when lowered over the fuel rods, slow down or stop the fission process. Water (**4**), superheated by the fission process and under pressure, passes to the steam generator (**5**) where it boils unpressurized water to steam. This superheated steam is then recycled via a pump (**6**) back to the reactor core. Steam from the steam generator powers a steam turbine (**7**) which in turn drives an electrical generator (**8**). Water from the turbines is cooled in a condenser (**9**) and recycled through the steam generator (**5**). The entire reactor is surrounded by a concrete shield (**10**) to prevent radiation leaking out.

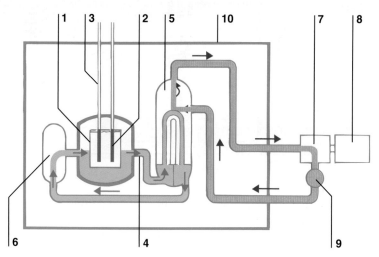

Neutrons see nuclear fission page 347

Hydroelectric power

Hydroelectric stations generate power using water turbines. Water in a reservoir (**1**) is held back by a dam (**2**) and enters an inlet (**3**) where it is directed to a turbine (**4**). The water strikes the turbine blades (**5**), rotating a drive shaft (**6**) which powers an electric generator (**7**). The water, having lost much of its energy, flows into the turbine's centre and leaves through an outlet pipe (**8**).

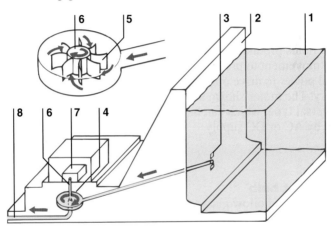

Wind power

The wind turbine has large aerofoil rotor blades (**1**) up to 160 ft (50 m) long to catch the wind. As the blades turn, a gearbox (**2**) ensures the drive shaft (**3**) rotates at high speed for efficient operation of the electric generator (**4**). Wind sensors (**5**) detect speed and direction of air movement and control the pitch, speed, and direction of the rotor blades so that power output is optimized.

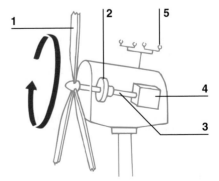

17

Electric motor

A very versatile power source. Electric current is fed to the stator coil (**1**), an electromagnet. Current is also fed to the brushes (**2**) in close contact with a commutator (**3**). This in turn is connected to a coil (**4**) in the rotor (**5**). The interaction between the rotor and stator magnetic fields produces a spinning movement to provide rotational power to drive other machinery. The motor shown is of a universal type, which can be powered by AC or DC supply.

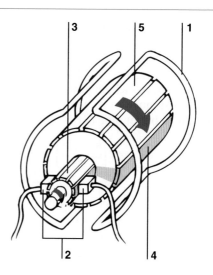

Electric light bulb

This consists of a hollow glass bulb (**1**) with a coil of tungsten wire inside called the filament (**2**). The filament is very thin and long, so resistance to the current is great and heat and light output is high. The bulb is filled with inert gas (**3**). The base of the bulb has screw thread or bayonet fittings (**4**) to keep it in place and a foot contact (**5**) which allows electric current to flow through the filament.

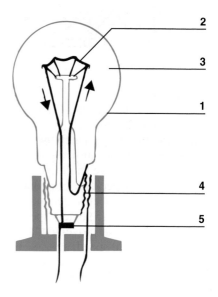

Electric circuit symbols

Name			Symbol
Battery			− ╎├ +
Bulb			
Connecting wire			
Off switch		Circuit broken	
On switch		Circuit made	
Ammeter		Measures amount of current in amps flowing in a circuit	Ⓐ
Voltmeter		Measures potential difference in volts	Ⓥ

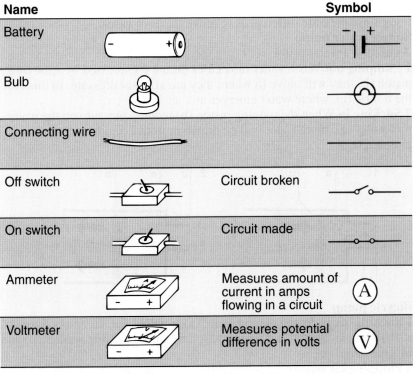

Diagram of an electrical circuit

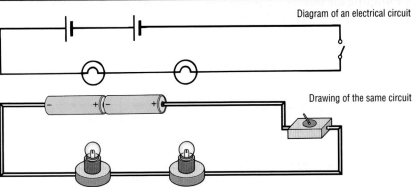

Drawing of the same circuit

MECHANICAL DEVICES
Pumps
Pumps use pressure differences to move fluids or gases.
Simple water pump
As used in a water pistol.
1 Pumping out When water molecules (**a**) are compressed by a moving piston (**b**) they will move to where they are at lower pressure; in this case the nozzle (**c**), where water emerges as a jet.
2 Sucking in When the moving piston (**b**) reduces pressure on the water molecules (**a**), more water will be drawn in from a region of higher pressure (**c**).

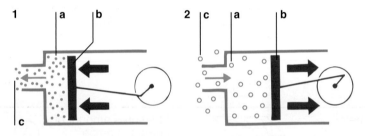

Bicycle pump
1 Sucking air in As the pump handle (**a**) is pulled out, air enters through a small hole at the top and moves past a collapsed flexible washer (**b**) and fills the barrel (**c**).
2 Pumping air out As the pump handle (**a**) is pushed in, the flexible washer (**b**) forms a seal, and air is forced out under pressure through the valve (**d**) into the tire.

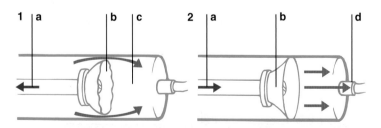

Presses
Hydraulic press
This transfers force via pressure in a liquid. If a 1 lb force is applied to the master cylinder (**1**) with an area of
1 sq in, a pressure of 1 lb per sq in is raised throughout the fluid system (**2**). A 4 lb load on a slave cylinder (**3**) can be moved provided the cylinder area is
4 sq in or above.

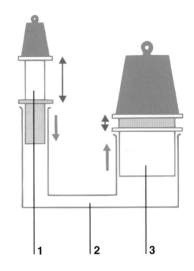

Car jack
In a hydraulic car jack, working the hand pump (**1**) draws oil from a reservoir (**2**) and delivers it under pressure to the cylinder (**3**) which raises the lifting piston (**4**). Valves (**5**) ensure that oil travels in one direction only. A release valve (**6**) lowers the lifting piston.

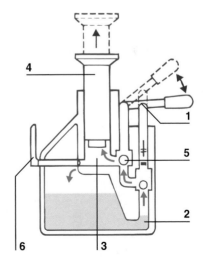

17

Guns

The common components are a barrel and a carriage.

1 Muzzle loading Common until the 19th century.

a A charge of gunpowder is rammed down the barrel, followed sometimes by a wad, and then the cannonball.

b A flame is applied to a touchhole which ignites the powder, propelling the ball out of the barrel.

2 Breech loading 19th–20th century.

a The breech is opened and loaded with a combined cartridge case and shell.

b The propellant explosive is detonated and the shell discharged through a rifled barrel.

3 Recoilless gun 20th century.

The gun is of light construction since recoil-absorbing features are not required. The barrel is open at both ends. The gases from the exploding propellant dissipate in a cleared area behind the gun (**a**).

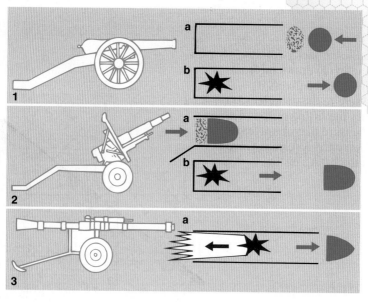

DEVICES USING LIGHT
Optical telescope
A telescope gives a close-up view of a distant object. Most telescopes use lenses, or lenses and mirrors, to produce a real image inside the telescope tube.

Refracting telescope
In a simple astronomical telescope, the convex objective lens (**1**) bends incoming light rays (**2**), producing an image (**3**) which is upside down, viewed through the eyepiece lens. Adding another convex lens (**4**) gives an upright image.

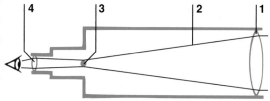

Reflecting telescope
This uses a curved mirror of large diameter. Large mirrors can be made more accurately than large lenses, and are used for higher magnification telescopes. Light entering (**1**) is reflected from the concave primary mirror (**2**) onto a convex secondary mirror (**3**). This reflects light onto two flat mirrors (**4**) which form a real image (**5**) viewed through the eyepiece lens (**6**) at the side of the telescope.

Proposed 98 ft (30 m) diameter mirror for the CELT optical telescope composed of 1,080 hexagonal segments

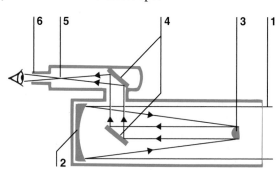

17

Microscope

This works on the same principle as a refracting telescope but with the object very close to the objective lenses, giving a highly magnified view.

A mirror (**1**) reflects light rays (**2**) through a condenser (**3**) which concentrates them. The rays pass through and illuminate the object (**4**). Objective lenses (**5**) form an image which is further enlarged through the eyepiece lenses (**6**). Focusing is achieved by moving the objective lenses nearer to or further away from the object.

See also page 340 for further information

Microscope

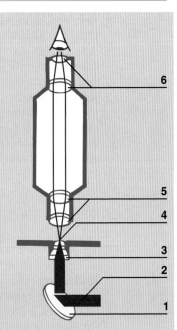

Binoculars

These are essentially two refracting telescopes joined together for use with both eyes, giving a 3-D effect. Light (**1**) passes through the objective lens (**2**), forming an inverted and reversed image. Two prisms (**3**) correct the image before viewing through the eyepiece lenses (**4**).

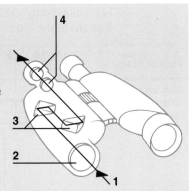

Film camera

A camera is essentially a light-proof box containing a convex lens system which focuses an image onto photographic film at the back of the camera. The single-lens reflex (SLR) camera uses a single set of lenses for both viewing and photographing. Other types of camera have separate sets of lenses for the two functions.

Viewing

Light rays (**1**) pass through the open diaphragm (**2**) and are focused by a convex lens system (**3**) onto a mirror (**4**). This reflects the light onto a focusing screen (**5**) where the image is formed. The inverted and reversed image is corrected by a five-sided prism arrangement (**6**) and then viewed through the viewfinder eyepiece (**7**).

Taking a photograph

When the shutter release is pressed, the mirror (**4**) flips up and the shutter (**8**) moves across, allowing light rays to reach the photographic film behind it.

The amount of light reaching the film is controlled by the size of the aperture in the diaphragm and the length of time the shutter is open. Focusing is achieved by moving the lens system nearer to or further away from the film.

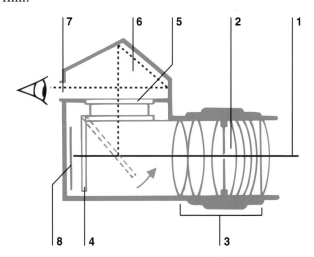

17

Photographic film

Composition Black-and-white photographic film consists of a flexible base of cellulose triacetate (**1**), a light-sensitive emulsion of silver salts (**2**) and a protective gelatin layer (**3**). Color films use different emulsions sensitive to red, blue, and green light.

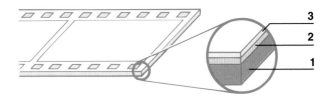

Developing After exposure to light, the film is developed in a chemical solution (**1**). This reduces the silver salts to black metallic silver. The more light originally reaching the film, the deeper the blackening. The developed film, or photographic negative, is then washed (**2**) to stop the development process. Fixing (**3**) dissolves away unreduced silver salts. Washing (**4**) stops any further chemical reaction, and the negative is then dried (**5**).

The negative and printing paper are held together in a frame. Light is passed through the negative to the paper underneath. This exposes the paper forming a latent image which becomes visible after development and chemical treatment to create a print, or photograph.

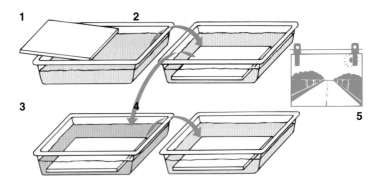

Digital camera

A digital camera has no film. Instead it has an image sensor that converts light into electrical charges. When the shutter button on the camera is fully depressed, the shutter opens allowing light to enter the camera and strike the sensor.

A camera's light sensor is made up of millions of tiny individual elements. Each of these tiny elements responds to the amount of light that falls on it. The amount of light at each element is then measured and converted into a digital value by a microprocessor. This information is sent to the camera's internal memory. The more elements there are on a sensor, the more detailed the final image. The completed image is then transferred to the memory card in the camera.

Pixels

1 This is an image shot on a digital camera. Digital images are made up of thousands of tiny squares called pixels.
2–4 Enlargements of a small area of the image.
5 At an even greater enlargement, individual pixels are visible.

1

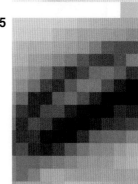

2

3

4

5

COMMUNICATION DEVICES
Radio

Radio is the communication of sound by the transmission of electromagnetic waves in the frequency range 3 kHz to 40,000 MHz (wavelength of 0.4 in to over 0.6 mi).

Radio transmission

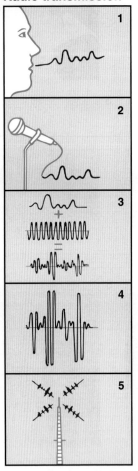

Sound waves are produced by a source (**1**), converted into an electrically equivalent signal by a microphone (**2**), and then imposed on a carrier wave by a modulator (**3**). The resulting signal is then amplified (**4**) and transmitted by an antenna (**5**).

At a receiver, an aerial (**6**) picks up the signal, which is captured by a tuned circuit (**7**). The signal is then demodulated (**8**) to remove the carrier wave and the resulting signal amplified (**9**) and passed to a loudspeaker (**10**) where the electrical signal is reconverted to sound waves.

Radio reception

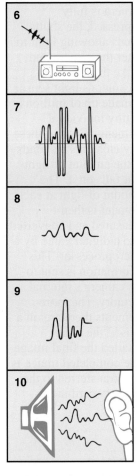

Telephone

In the telephone's mouthpiece (**1**) a carbon microphone (**2**) converts sound waves into a fluctuating electrical current. This passes through wires (**3**) to the earpiece (**4**) of the receiver. The fluctuating current affects a magnetic coil (**5**) which in turn moves a diaphragm (**6**) acting as a loudspeaker to produce audible sounds. The telephone operates as a complete electrical circuit with a power source (**7**).

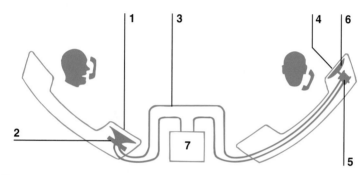

Cellular telephone

A cellular, or cell phone is essentially a sophisticated radio. Cell phone networks are made up of hundreds of small areas, or cells, that cover the country. Each cell is about 10 square miles and has its own base station. All of the cells in an area are controlled by a Mobile Telephone Switching Office (MTSO). Each cell phone has a unique identifying number that it transmits to the nearest base station. The MTSO is able to connect calls made in one cell area to a phone in another cell area.

17

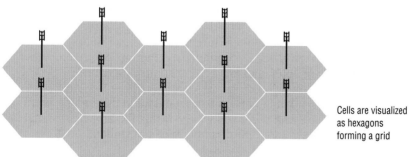

Cells are visualized
as hexagons
forming a grid

Television

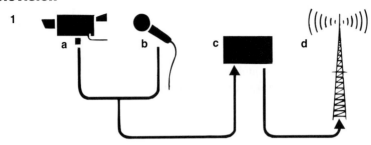

1 In a live broadcast a TV camera (**a**) converts the image into electrically equivalent signals representing the three primary colors. A microphone (**b**) converts sound into an electrical signal. Sound and picture signals are synchronized in a transmitter (**c**) and transmitted through an antenna (**d**).

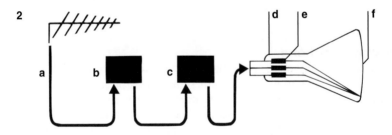

2 At a receiver, the aerial (**a**) picks up the transmission, relays it to a tuned circuit (**b**) in the television, and a decoder (**c**) reconverts the signals into sound and primary color signals. In the picture tube (**d**) three electron guns (**e**) – red, blue, and green – scan rapidly across the screen (**f**). Each dot lights up and fades in turn to produce 625 lines of dots in 1/25 second. The viewer sees a continuously illuminated screen, rather than moving dots of color, and this gives a complete picture.

Digital television is likely to become the standard in the coming years. The main difference with digital television is that the broadcast signal is digital, allowing much more information to be transmitted.

Compact disc

A compact disc is a plastic-coated metal disc (**1**) which has about 3 mi of playing track (**2**) on its underside. CDs play by means of a light beam from a low-powered laser which reads microscopic pits and flat areas on the playing track. The pits and flats form a digital code which is interpreted by the CD player, and then amplified and fed to loudspeakers.

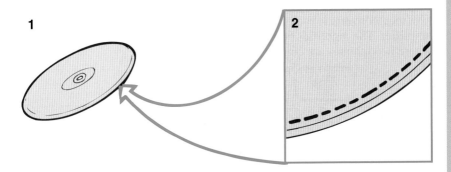

1

2

CD-ROM

This works in the same way as a compact disc, but instead of storing just sound it is used to store many kinds of data for display on a computer screen. A CD-ROM disc can store multimedia information: written text, visual images (both static and moving) and sound, often combined in interactive ways. One disc can hold as much information as a printed encyclopedia. (ROM is explained on page 527.)

DVD player

The drive of a DVD player consists of three components: a drive motor to spin the disc, a laser and lens system to focus on and read the data stored on the disc, and a tracking mechanism to move the laser so the beam can follow the track. The laser focuses on the track of pits and flats. The flat areas reflect light differently to the pits and the lens detects the change in reflectivity. As the disc rotates the laser moves outward and the motor drive spins the disc at a constant speed so that the track travels past the laser and the data comes off the disc at a constant rate.

17

MP3 player

An MP3 player is a device which allows the user to transfer and listen to compressed audio files. The basic parts of an MP3 player are: memory, microprocessor, Digital Sound Processor (DSP), amplifier, and audio port. The player plugs into a computer and transfers files, which are saved in the player's memory. The microprocessor monitors the input and sends directions to the DSP telling it how to process the audio. The DSP then pulls the song data from the memory, decompresses the MP3 file, then converts it back to sound waves and streams them to the amplifier. The amplifier boosts the signal and sends it to the audio port where headphones are connected.

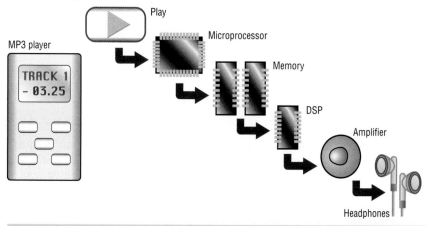

Radar

Radar is short for RAdio Detection And Ranging. Radar has many applications. Air-traffic controllers depend on it to find the positions of aircraft. A radar aerial (**1**) acts as both transmitter and receiver. Radio waves are transmitted (**2**) and reflected back (**3**) from a within-range aircraft. Time taken for return gives distance, and direction of return gives bearing. A second radar aerial (**4**) transmits radio waves (**5**) to a transponder (**6**) on the aircraft. This sends back information (**7**) giving the aircraft's height and identity. Information from the two aerials is combined and displayed on a radar screen.

Tape recorder

Reel-to-reel tapes have largely been replaced by cassette tapes, certainly for domestic use.

1 Recording Sound is picked up by a microphone, converted into an electrical signal, mixed with a steady tone, and fed to an amplifier. The combined signal is passed to the coil of a recording head. This produces a varying magnetic field that aligns particles in a magnetic tape.

2 Playback The tape passes over the playback head and the tape's magnetic field induces a current in the head's coil. The current is sent to an amplifier and then to a loudspeaker to reproduce the original recorded sounds.

Modem

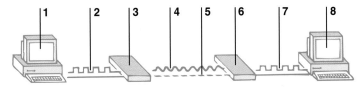

This is short for MOdulator/DEModulator. It allows computers to send data to, or receive data from, a telephone line. A computer (**1**) sends a digital signal (**2**) to a modem (**3**) which converts it to an analog signal (**4**). This is transmitted through a telephone line (**5**) to a second modem (**6**) which reconverts the signal to digital (**7**) for a receiving computer (**8**).

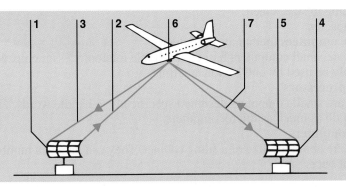

17

COMPUTERS

Computer components

A computer is an electronic information-processing machine. Information is fed in, or input, processed by the computer, and fed out again, or output. Recent massive advances in computer speed, power, and reliability are largely due to silicon technology. The computer's complex circuitry is miniaturized inside silicon chips, wafer-thin silicon crystals with electronic circuits etched onto them (**1**). Within these circuits (**2**) are microscopic switches (**3**) which turn electric currents on and off. The resulting series of electrical pulses (bits) form the messages the computer uses to carry out instructions coded in computer programs.

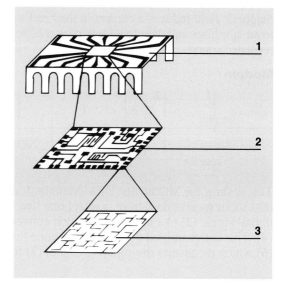

Types of computer

Computers are classified according to size, speed, and capacity.

Microcomputers (personal computers)
These are small computers based on a single microprocessor chip. Most can only be used by one person at a time.

Wordprocessors
These are small computers designed specifically to handle words. They cannot do as much as microcomputers.

Minicomputers
These are about the size of a filing cabinet. They can handle a number of tasks at once.

Mainframe computers
These are large and powerful, and require special
air-conditioned rooms. They can handle hundreds of users at a time.
Supercomputers
These are used in research laboratories. They are very fast, with large
memories.

Hardware
The hardware comprises the parts of a computer system that you can
touch and handle. There are normally four components:
a input devices (to get information into the computer);
b a central processing unit (CPU), with its processor(s) and
memory;
c a backing store of memory;
d output devices (to get information out of the computer).

A typical microcomputer set-up comprises:
1 A keyboard as the input device.
2 The computer itself with a CPU, backing store of memory, and a
  visual display unit (VDU) similar to a television screen.
3 A printer as the output device.

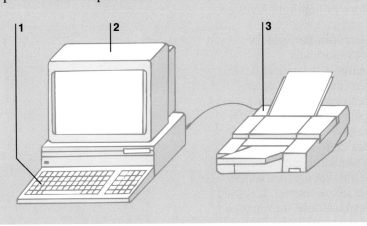

17

Input devices
These include:

1 Keyboard This is similar to a QWERTY typewriter keyboard. It is used for entering words, numbers, and instructions.

2 "Mouse" A ball mounted in a box with sensors detecting its movement. Moving the mouse moves a pointer on the VDU screen. A button on the mouse activates the pointer to trigger commands.

3 Joystick Used particularly in computer games for moving parts or the whole of the VDU screen display. The joystick has a button to trigger commands.

4 Light pen Used with VDUs to draw or highlight items on the screen.

5 Microphone Used for inputting sounds.

6 Scanner An optical device, rather like a photocopier, which copies an image for display on the VDU and for storage.

7 Bar code reader In library use, similar to a light pen. In supermarket use, a sensitive panel in the counter. It is used to read bar code information.

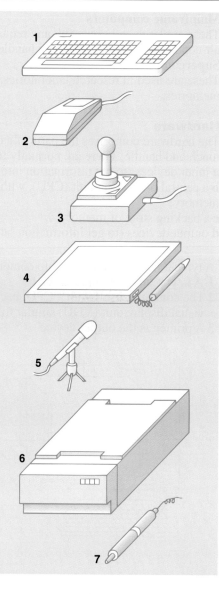

The central processing unit (CPU)
This controls the step-by-step running of the computer by sending electrical signals to various parts of the system. It contains two types of memory. RAM (random-access memory) is a temporary memory which can be altered. Anything stored in RAM is lost when the computer is switched off. ROM (read-only memory) is a permanent memory store. ROM can be read from, but not altered.

Storage devices
Storage capacity is measured in kB (one thousand bytes) or MB (one million bytes). Computer information has been stored and can be stored in a variety of ways:
1 Temporarily in the RAM of the computer
(64 kB–16 GB),
or more permanently:
2 On a cassette tape (less than 250 kB).

3 On a floppy disk (0.25–2 MB) inserted in a disk drive.
4 On a hard disk
(20 GB–500 GB).
5 On a reel-to-reel magnetic tape (10–700 MB).
6 On a CD-RW, a compact disc (500–1000 MB) inserted in a disk drive.
7 On a DVD-RW, a digital video disc (4.7 GB–9.4 GB) inserted in a disk drive.

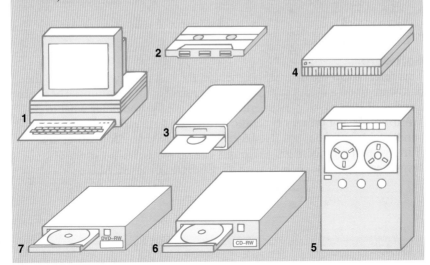

17

Data storage

As hardware capacity has increased, the standard units for measuring data storage have changed, from hard drives measured in megabytes to DVDs measured in gigabytes.

data units

bit(s) = 1 unit		bit(s) = 1 unit	
1	bit	1073741824	gigabit
4	nibble	8000000000	gigabyte
8	byte	8589934592	gigabyte
16	word	$1.09951162778 \times 10^{12}$	terabit
32	double-word	$8.79609302221 \times 10^{12}$	terabyte
64	quadruple-word	8×10^{12}	terabyte
1024	kilobit	$1.12589990684 \times 10^{15}$	petabit
4096	block	$9.00719925474 \times 10^{15}$	petabyte
8000	kilobyte	8×10^{15}	petabyte
8192	kilobyte	$1.15292150461 \times 10^{18}$	exabit
1048576	megabit	$9.22337203685 \times 10^{18}$	exabyte
8388608	megabyte	8×10^{18}	exabyte
8000000	megabyte		

Software

This refers to all the instructions held in the computer which enable the hardware to do a useful job. Software is made up of programs. These are a series of step-by-step instructions which tell the computer what to do. Word-processing programs handle written text, spreadsheet programs handle tables of data, and database programs handle information in a filing system arrangement. Programs can be written in a variety of computer languages such as BASIC, COBOL, or PASCAL.

Output devices
The visual display unit (VDU) can be regarded as an output device. It can be monochrome (usually black and white) or color. It can be low resolution (few dots per sq in) or high resolution (many dots per sq in). Printers produce output onto paper – what is called hard copy:

Inkjet printers These are moderately costly, low-speed printers with reasonable print quality. They squirt ink through a fine nozzle to form characters.

Laser printers These have a higher cost and are moderately fast with reasonable to high print quality. They are similar in principle to a photocopier, but they use a laser beam to cause the powdered ink to stick to the paper.

CONSTRUCTION
Roads
After soil excavation and provision of suitable drainage, the road surface is constructed. The following applies to a main road such as a freeway.

1 Granular sub-base Normally laid on compacted earth and consisting of rolled aggregate 12–24 in thick.

2 Lower road base A 10 in base layer of concrete to provide strength and bind to the sub-base.

3 Upper road base A 3 in layer of rolled macadam (tar and stones).

4 Wearing surface A 1.5 in top layer of rolled asphalt (bitumen). This gives a smooth, flexible road surface.

5 Concrete haunch This finishes off and supports the edge of the road surface.

6 Hard shoulder A thinner section of road surface which provides a breakdown lane.

17

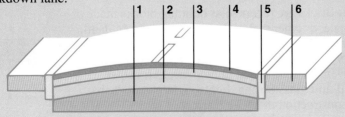

Building construction

1 Wattle and daub Wattle and daub is a construction method of building walls in which vertical wooden stakes, or wattles, are woven with horizontal twigs and branches, then daubed, or plastered, with mud or clay. It is one of the oldest methods of making weather-proof structures. This method was used as fill-in for medieval timber-frame structures in Europe.

2 Timber-frame Timber is used as a frame for buildings, especially houses. A heavy timber sill is constructed on the foundation and on top of this are nailed floor joists. The frame of the house is built upward. The frame was traditionally filled by wattle and daub or bricks. In modern timber-framed houses, the walls are covered in plywood, to which a surface cladding is added.

3 Stone Stone is an important building material. It is used for foundations, walls, supports of piers and bridges, finishing, and decorating structures. Stone can be cut into blocks or slabs of definite, regular shape and size. Stone is a durable building material which is expected to last at least 100 years.

4 Concrete Concrete is fireproof and watertight. It is comparatively easy and cheap to make. When it is first mixed, concrete can be moulded into almost any shape. It quickly hardens to form an extremely strong material. Concrete can be strengthened by adding metal rods or cables. It is used for frames, walls, floors, roofs, and roads.

5 Brick Bricks are rectangular building blocks made of clay, shale, or other materials. Bricks are strong, hard, resistant to fire, and damage from the weather. They are uniform in shape and size and they are fired, or baked in an oven. Mortar is used to hold bricks together.

6 Metal and glass Strong, lightweight materials that allow construction in a wide variety of forms.

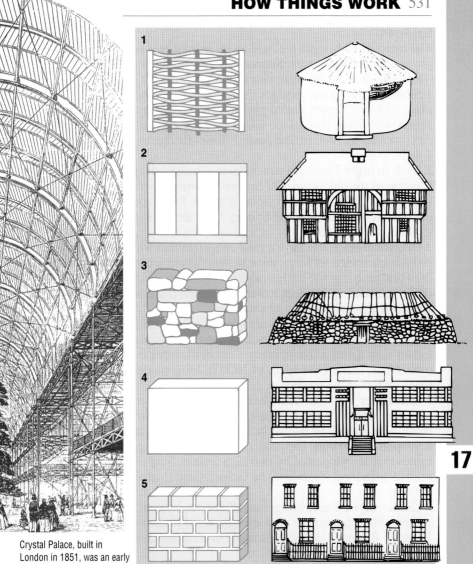

Crystal Palace, built in
London in 1851, was an early
metal and glass structure

17

Bridges

The majority of bridges are held up by at least two supports set in the ground, called abutments. Supports in the middle of a bridge are called piers. The distance between two supports is called a span.

1 Single girder Girder bridges include many road bridges. They are made of single beams, called girders, whose ends rest on piers or abutments. These bridges are used to cross most areas. A span length can reach up to 1000 ft. The Jesse J. Jones Bridge in Houston, Texas has a main span of 755 ft.

2 Arch bridges These are structures in which each span forms an arch. It is one of the oldest types of bridge. The majority of arch bridges have short spans and are made of stone or wood. Long-span bridges are made of concrete or steel, as is the Sydney Harbour Bridge, Australia. This has a main span of 1650 ft.

3 Drawbridges These have a road crossing them which is moved to provide clearance for large ships to pass. There are three types of drawbridge: a bascule bridge (**a**) which tilts upward to open; a lift bridge (**b**) which rises up between towers at each end; and a swing bridge (**c**) which swings sideways to let ships pass.

4 Truss girder Truss bridges are supported by a framework called trusses. The parts of the trusses are arranged in triangles. A truss is lighter than a girder. These bridges are built over canyons, rivers, and other areas. Many have spans of 1000 ft. Most modern bridges have roads on top of the trusses.

5 Cantilever Two individual beams called cantilevers extend from opposite banks of a river and are joined together above the water by a beam. The Forth Rail Bridge in Scotland has two spans of 1710 ft.

6 Suspension bridge The road, or deck, of the bridge hangs from steel cables that are supported by two high towers. Suspension bridges are used to span long distances. The Golden Gate Bridge has a main span of 4200 ft.

7 Cable-stayed These bridges are similar to suspension bridges but the cables which support the road are connected to the towers. The Second Hooghly Bridge, India is an example of a cable-stayed bridge.

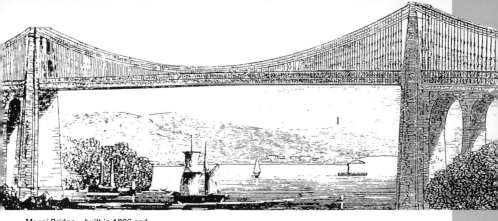

Menai Bridge – built in 1826 and
the first modern suspension bridge

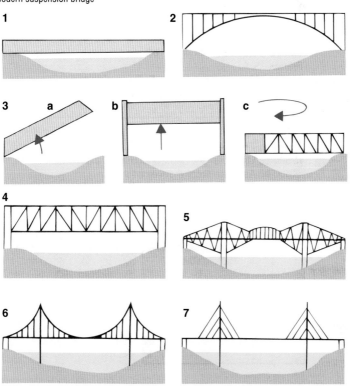

1

2

3   **a**   **b**   **c**

4

5

6

7

17

Venus of
Willendorf

25,000–5000 BC

25,000 BC Use of fire, stone tools, and weapons
20,000 BC Improved stone, wood, and bone tools and weapons
10,000 BC Delicate stone tools, sickles, handsaws, needles, fishing
lines and hooks, boats, canoes, nets, and traps

ARCHITECTURE

20,000 BC		AD 1

Neolithic 7000–1500 BC

8000–6000 BC Catal Hüyük, Turkey

PAINTING AND SCULPTURE

30,000–25,000 BC Venus of Willendorf
15,000–10,000 BC Cave paintings, Lascaux, France
15,000–10,000 BC Clay relief of bison, Le Tuc d'Audobert, France
15,000–10,000 BC Relief horses, Cap Blanc, France
15,000–10,000 BC Carving of bison with turned head, La Madeleine,
France
8000–3000 BC Hunting scene, El Cerro, Spain
6150 BC Painting of landscape with volcano, Catal Hüyük, Turkey
5900 BC Sculpture of seated goddess, Catal Hüyük, Turkey

Cave painting,
Lascaux, France

5000 BC – AD 1

3200 BC Early farmers and cultivators
2500 BC Ur of the Chaldees, a Sumerian city, flourishing
1500 BC Assyrian empire develops
  336 BC Alexander the Great becomes king of Macedon

ARCHITECTURE

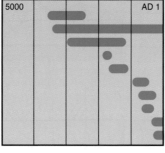

5000		AD 1

Sumerian 3500–2500 BC
Egyptian 3500 BC–AD 480
Minoan 3000–1100 BC
Babylonian 1900–1750 BC
Mycenaean 1500–1100 BC
Assyrian 1000–612 BC
Etruscan 750–c. 200 BC
Greek c. 600–300 BC
Hellenistic 300–30 BC
Roman 300 BC–AD 395

Alexander the
Great

3000s BC White Temple, Uruk
2650 BC First pyramid for King Zhoser, Saqqarah, Egypt
2600–2500 BC Pyramids, Giza, Egypt
2500 BC Stonehenge, England
2000 BC Ur-Nammu's Ziggurat, Ur
1500 BC Knossos, Crete, Greece
1300 BC Lion Gate, Mycenae
742–706 BC Palace of Sargon II, Khorsabad, Iraq
575 BC Ishtar Gate, Babylon
518–460 BC Persepolis, Iran
447–436 BC Parthenon, Athens, Greece
300 BC Tomb of the Reliefs, Cerveteri, Italy
20 BC Pont du Gard, France

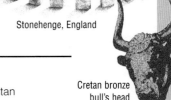

Stonehenge, England

PAINTING AND SCULPTURE

3000 BC Murals, Egypt
2500–2000 BC Statuette of dancer, Mohenjo-Daro, Pakistan
2530 BC Great Sphinx, Giza, Egypt
2113–2096 BC Stele of Ur, Ur
1712 BC Lion Hunt, Mesopotamia
1500 BC Cretan figures cast in bronze, Crete
1500 BC Bull fresco, Knossos, Crete
1365 BC Bust of Nefertiti, Egypt
850 BC Reliefs from the city of Nimrod, Iraq
525 BC Frieze showing battle of gods and giants, Delphi, Greece
500 BC Apollo, Veii, Italy
480 BC Tomb of the Diver (banqueting scenes), Paestum, Italy
450 BC Discobolus by Myron
190 BC Winged Victory of Samothrace
100 BC *Venus de Milo*, Melos
60–50 BC Dionysiac frieze, Villa of the Mysteries, Pompeii, Italy

Cretan bronze
bull's head

MUSIC

2200 BC Egyptian harp
2000 BC Lute known in Mesopotamia
800 BC Assyrian music
657 BC First music school established in Sparta
408 BC Choir forms part of *Orestes* by Euripides

Bust of
Nefertiti

18

THEATER

458 BC *The Oresteia* by Aeschylus
441 BC *Antigone* by Sophocles

413 BC *Electra* by Sophocles
411 BC *Lysistrata* by Aristophanes
166 BC *The Girl from Andros* by Terence

LITERATURE

2345 BC Earliest pyramid texts
2000 BC The Gilgamesh epic, Sumer
800 BC Phoenician alphabet
800 BC *The Iliad* and *The Odyssey* by Homer
590 BC Poetry by Sappho of Lesbos
500 BC Aesop's fables
55 BC *De Oratore* by Cicero
30 BC *The Aeneid* by Virgil

Achilles
dressing
Patroclus's
wounds from
Homer's *Iliad*

AD **1–800**

64 Great fire of Rome
79 Eruption of Vesuvius, destruction of Pompeii and Herculaneum
267 Goths sweep across Asia Minor
610 Prophet Mohammed begins conversion of Arabs to Islam
711 Muslim invasion of Córdoba, Seville, and Toledo
771 Charlemagne becomes sole ruler of the Franks

ARCHITECTURE

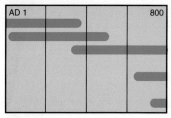

Roman 300 BC – AD 395
Early Christian AD 33–500
Byzantine 330–1453
BRITAIN
Anglo-Saxon c. 650–1100
FRANCE
Carolingian 750–900

72–80 Colosseum, Rome, Italy
118–28 Pantheon, Rome, Italy
200 Teotihuacán, Mexico
212–16 Baths of Caracalla, Rome, Italy
306–16 Porta Nigra, Trier, Germany
432–40 Nave of Santa Maria Maggiore, Rome
532–7 Hagia Sophia, Istanbul, Turkey
540–8 San Vitale, Ravenna, Italy
691 Dome of the Rock, Jerusalem

Porta Nigra, Germany

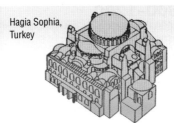

Hagia Sophia, Turkey

Trajan's Column

PAINTING AND SCULPTURE

1–10 Painting from villa at Boscotrecase, Italy
63–9 Paintings from the House of the Vettii, Pompeii, Italy
113 Trajan's Column, Rome, Italy
161–80 Bronze equestrian statue of Marcus Aurelius, Rome
203 Carvings on the Arch of Septimus Severus, Rome
312–15 Carvings on the Arch of Constantine, Rome
422–32 Doors of Santa Sabina, Rome
500 Painting of St. Peter at the Monastery of St. Catherine, Mount Sinai
700 Lindisfarne Gospels, England

MUSIC

390 "Allelujah" hymns established in Christian Church
c. 500 Bone flutes and skin drums in Peru
580 Harps of six and 12 strings played in Europe
700–800 Wind organ introduced in western Europe
790–815 Church organs introduced to Europe from Constantinople

THEATER

c. 25–65 Seneca the Younger writes nine tragedies based on Greek myth
197 *Apologeticus* by Tertullian
c. 290 Roman theater in Verona
c. 300 Records of the earliest religious plays
304 The actor Genesius is martyred during a performance in Rome

LITERATURE

9 *Metamorphoses* by Ovid
48–130 New Testament Gospels
77 *Natural History* compiled by Pliny the Elder
98–128 Satires by Juvenal
105–115 *Parallel Lives* by Plutarch
117 *Annals* by Tacitus
730 *Beowulf*, Anglo-Saxon poem

Greek masks portraying comedy and tragedy

18

Rayonnant-style architecture

800–1200

800 Coronation of Charlemagne as Holy Roman Emperor
1066 Norman conquest of Britain

ARCHITECTURE

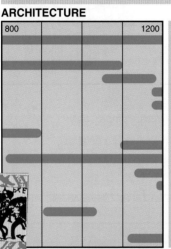

800				1200

Byzantine 330–1453
BRITAIN
Anglo-Saxon c. 650–1100
Norman 1045–1180
Early English 1175–1250
Gothic 1175–1630
FRANCE
Carolingian 750–900
Cistercian 1098–1270
Romanesque c. 800–1200
Gothic 1140–1534
Rayonnant 1194–1400
GERMANY
Ottonian 900–1024
SPAIN
Mudejar 1110–1500

Bayeux Tapestry portraying the Norman conquest of England

1063 San Marco, Venice, Italy
1079–93 Winchester Cathedral, England
1093–1133 Durham Cathedral, England
1150 Wooden stave church, Borgund, Norway
1194–1220 Chartres Cathedral, France

PAINTING AND SCULPTURE

1066–77 Bayeux Tapestry, France
1090–1100 Bronze doors of Santa Zeno, Verona, Italy
1140 *Life of Moses*, St. Denis, Paris, France
1150–60 Winchester Bible, England
1156 Decoration on the royal portal, Chartres Cathedral, France
1178 *Descent from the Cross* by Antelami, Parma Cathedral, Italy
1135 *Three Prophets* by Niccolò, Ferrara Cathedral, Italy

MUSIC

950 Book of Songs, by Abu'l Farad
1175 The Minnesinger create a tradition of German songs inspired by the troubadors

THEATER
900–1000 Miracle plays popular in England

LITERATURE
821 *Life of Charlemagne* (*Vita Caroli Magni*) by Einhard
891 *The Anglo-Saxon Chronicle* begun
c. 1100 *Chanson de Roland*
1180 *Legend of the Holy Grail* by Chrétien de Troyes
1196 *Igor Song* written in Russia

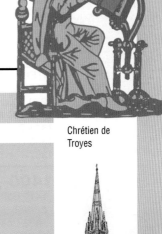

Chrétien de Troyes

1200–1400
1288 Ottoman Empire founded
1347 Black Death

ARCHITECTURE

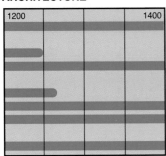

Byzantine 330–1453
BRITAIN
Early English 1175–1250
Gothic 1175–1630
FRANCE
Cistercian 1098–1270
Gothic 1140–1534
Rayonnant 1194–1400
SPAIN
Mudejar 1110–1500

1220–58 Salisbury Cathedral, England
1299–1301 Palazzo Vecchio, Florence, Italy
1309 Ducal Palace, Venice, Italy
1316–64 Palace of the Popes, Avignon, France
1351–1412 Cloisters of Gloucester Cathedral, England
1391 Court of the Lions, Alhambra, Granada, Spain

Salisbury
Cathedral

PAINTING AND SCULPTURE
1210–15 Decoration on the south portal, Chartres Cathedral, France
1225–55 Decoration on the west front, Wells Cathedral, England
1265 Pulpit, Siena Cathedral, Italy
1304 Fresco cycle by Giotto, Padua, Italy
1325–8 *Book of Hours* by Jeanne d'Evreux
1360–80 *Madonna della Rosa* by Pisano
1380 *Nativity* by Giusto de' Menabuoi, Padua

18

The Divine
Comedy

MUSIC
1200–1300 Carmina Burana, songs collected
c. 1250 "Sumer is icumen in", English song
c. 1300 The madrigal emerges in Italy
1388 The recorder (end-blown flute) is first mentioned

THEATER
1320 *Ten Virgin Play* performed at Eisenach, Germany
1367–70 *Piers Plowman* by William Langland

LITERATURE
1205 *Nibelungenlied*, Germany
1270 *Summa Theologica* by Thomas Aquinas
1307 *The Divine Comedy* (*Divina Commedia*) by Dante Alighieri
1351 *The Decameron* by Giovanni Boccaccio
1366 *Canzoniere* by Petrarch
1387 *The Canterbury Tales* by Geoffrey Chaucer

1400–1550

1415 Battle of Agincourt
c. 1455 Gutenberg's Bible printed
1492 Columbus discovers San Salvador
1527 Sack of Rome

ARCHITECTURE

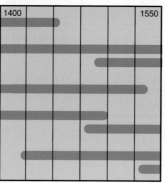

1400				1550

Byzantine 330–1453
BRITAIN
Gothic 1175–1630
Tudor 1485–1558
FRANCE
Gothic 1140–1534
SPAIN
Mudejar 1110–1500
Plateresque 1480–1552
ITALY
Renaissance 1420–1600
Mannerism 1530–1600

Geoffery
Chaucer

Columbus's ship

1419 Foundling Hospital by Brunelleschi, Florence, Italy
1458 Palazzo Pitti, Florence, begun
1503–19 Henry VII's Chapel, Westminster Abbey, London, England
1520 Hampton Court Palace, London, begun

PAINTING AND SCULPTURE
1425–52 *Gates of Paradise* by Ghiberti, Florence
1428 *Annunciation* by Fra Angelico
1434 *Arnolfini Marriage* by Jan van Eyck
1435 *David* by Donatello
1475 *Martyrdom of St. Sebastian* by Antonio Pollaiuolo
1495–7 *The Last Supper* by Leonardo da Vinci
1498–1500 *Pietà* by Michelangelo, St. Peter's Basilica, Vatican City
1501–4 *David* by Michelangelo
1503 *Mona Lisa* by Leonardo da Vinci
1536–41 *Last Judgement* fresco by Michelangelo, Sistine Chapel
1554 *Perseus* by Cellini

Hampton Court
Palace

MUSIC AND OPERA
1523 Keyboard music printed in Italy with right- and left-hand staves
1537 Music conservatories founded for boys in Naples, and for girls in Venice

THEATER AND BALLET
1400–1500 Morality plays develop in France
1490 Ballet develops at Italian courts
1465–1519 *Mankind* and *Everyman* performed in England
1516 *Orlando Furioso* by Ludovico Ariosto

Sir Thomas
Malory

LITERATURE
1424 *La Belle Dame Sans Merci* by Alain Chartier
1435 *Della Pittura* (*On Painting*) by Leon Battista Alberti
1444 *Eurialus and Lucretia* by Aeneas Silvius Piccolomini
1450 Vatican Library revived
1469 *William Tell* legend written
1470 *Le Morte d'Arthur* by Sir Thomas Malory
1492 *La Cárcel de amor* (*The Prison of Love*) by Diego de San Pedro
1503 "The Thrissill and the Rois" by William Dunbar
1516 *Utopia* by Sir Thomas More
1521 Bible translation begun by Martin Luther
1528 *Il libro del cortegiano* by Baldassare Castiglione
1534 *Gargantua* by François Rabelais
1544 *The Heptamaron* by Margeurite of Navarre

François
Rabelais's
Gargantua

18

1550–1650

1558 Coronation of Elizabeth I of England
1618 Thirty Years' War begins
1620 Pilgrim Fathers set sail from Plymouth for the New World
1643 Reign of Louis XIV begins

ARCHITECTURE

King Louis XIV

St. Basil's,
Moscow

1550				1650

BRITAIN
Tudor 1485–1558
Elizabethan 1558–1603
Jacobean 1603–25
Classical-Baroque 1619–1724
FRANCE
Louis XIV 1643–1715
ITALY
Renaissance 1420–1600
Mannerism 1520–1600
Early Baroque 1585–1625
High Baroque 1625–75
NORTH AMERICA
English Colonial 1607–1700
Dutch Colonial 1614–64

1555–60 Cathedral of St. Basil, Moscow, Russia
1567 Villa Rotonda, near Vicenza, Italy, by Andrea Palladio
1588–91 Dome of St. Peter, Rome, Italy
1562–82 The Escorial Palace, Spain, by Juan Bautista de
Toledo and Juan de Herrera
1587–91 The Rialto Bridge, Venice
1619–22 The Banqueting House, London, by Inigo Jones

Dome of
St. Peter,
Rome

The Escorial Palace, Spain

PAINTING AND SCULPTURE
1554 *Venus and Adonis* by Titian
1554–67 *Mars* and *Neptune* by Sansovino
1565 *The Peasant Wedding* by Brueghel the Elder
1591–4 *The Last Supper* by Tintoretto
1597–1601 *The Life of St. Matthew* by Caravaggio
1586 *The Burial of Count Orgaz* by El Greco
1622–5 Medici cycle by Rubens
1625 *Apollo and Daphne* by Bernini
1642 *The Night Watch* by Rembrandt

Michel de Montaigne

MUSIC AND OPERA
1571 Five-part Mass by Palestrina
1575 *Cantiones sacrae* by William Byrd and Thomas Tallis
1580 First mention of "Greensleeves"
1607 *L'Orfeo* by Monteverdi
1627 *Dafne* by Heinrich Schütz
1642 *L'incoronazione di Poppea* by Monteverdi

THEATER AND BALLET
1590 *Tamburlaine the Great* by Christopher Marlowe
1581 *Ballet Comique de la Reine* (the earliest ballet with music) by Baltasar de Beaujoyeux
1600–1 *Hamlet* by William Shakespeare
1621 *Andromeda* by Lope de Vega
1637 *Le Cid* by Corneille
c. 1643 Illustre Théâtre founded in Paris by Molière

Don Quixote by Cervantes

LITERATURE
1578 *Sonets pour Hélène* by Pierre de Ronsard
1580 *Essais* by Michel de Montaigne
1581 *Jerusalem Delivered* (*Gerusalemme Liberata*) by Torquato Tasso
1590–96 *The Faerie Queene* by Edmund Spenser
1605 *Don Quixote* part I by Miguel de Cervantes
1633 Poems by John Donne, published posthumously
1638 *Lycidas* by John Milton

John Donne

18

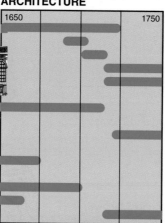

Rococo-style
architecture

1650–1750

1666 Great Fire of London
1672–1725 Peter the Great of Russia

ARCHITECTURE

1650				1750

BRITAIN
Classical–Baroque 1619–1724
William and Mary 1689–1702
Queen Anne 1702–14
Georgian 1714–1820
Palladian 1715–70
FRANCE
Louis XIV 1643–1715
GERMANY
Rococo 1720–60
ITALY
High Baroque 1625–75
NORTH AMERICA
English Colonial 1607–1700
Dutch Colonial 1614–64
Georgian 1714–76

Palais de
Versaille, France

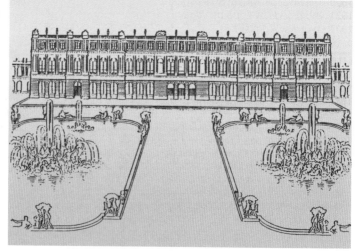

1661–1756 Palais de Versaille by Louis le Vau
1675–1710 St. Paul's Cathedral, London by Christopher Wren
1705–24 Blenheim Palace, Oxfordshire, by Vanbrugh and Hawksmoor
1723–5 The Spanish Steps, Rome by Francesco de Sanctis

PAINTING AND SCULPTURE

1654 *Bathsheba* by Rembrandt van Rijn
1656 *Las Meninas* by Velázquez
1665–68 *The Lacemaker* by Jan Vermeer
1715 *Mezzetin* by Antoine Watteau
1725 *Four Views of Venice* by Antonio Canaletto
1740 *The Triumph of Venus* by François Boucher

Rembrandt

MUSIC AND OPERA

1689 *Dido and Aeneas* by Henry Purcell
1724 *Julius Caesar* (*Giulio Cesare*) by George Frederick Handel
1725 *The Four Seasons* by Antonio Vivaldi
1727 *St. Matthew Passion* by J.S. Bach
1729 *The Beggar's Opera* by John Gay
1737 *Castor et Pollux* by Jean-Philippe Rameau
1742 *Messiah* by George Frederick Handel

Antonio Vivaldi

THEATER AND BALLET

1666 *Le Misanthrope* by Molière
1667 *Andromaque* by Jean Baptiste Racine
1678 *All For Love* by John Dryden
1713 School of Dance established at the Paris Opera
1738 Imperial Ballet School founded in St. Petersburg

Molière

LITERATURE

1660 Samuel Pepys begins his *Diary*
1667–74 *Paradise Lost* by John Milton
1668–94 *Fables* by La Fontaine
1678 *La Princesse de Clèves* by Comtesse de La Fayette
1699 *Télémaque* by Fénelon
1719 *Robinson Crusoe* by Daniel Defoe
1726 *Gulliver's Travels* by Jonathan Swift
1748 *Clarissa* by Samuel Richardson
1749 *Tom Jones* by Henry Fielding

18

Illustration from
Gulliver's Travels

1750–1800

1776 American Declaration of Independence
1789 French Revolution begins

ARCHITECTURE

1750				1800

BRITAIN
Georgian 1714–1820
Neoclassical 1750–1840
Gothic Revival 1750–1900s
FRANCE
Late Renaissance 1715–1830
Louis XV 1715–74
Neoclassical 1750–1870
GERMANY
Rococo 1720–60
Neoclassical 1750–1830
Greek Revival 1788–1830
ITALY
Neoclassical 1750–1870

1748–77 Strawberry Hill, Twickenham, England, by Horace Walpole
1757–90 Panthéon, Paris, by Jacques-Germain Soufflot
1767–75 Royal Crescent, Bath, by John Wood the Younger
1776–78 Teatro della Scala, Milan by Giuseppe Piermarini
1789–93 Brandenburg Gate, Berlin, by Carl Langhans

Francisco Goya

PAINTING AND SCULPTURE

1751 *Exhibition of a Rhinoceros at Venice* by Pietro Longhi
1755 *Madame de Pompadour* by Maurice-Quentin de La Tour
1767 *The Swing* by Jean Fragonard
1773 Self-portrait by Joshua Reynolds
1784 *The Oath of the Horatii* by Jacques-Louis David
1800 *Maja Unclothed* by Francisco Goya

MUSIC AND OPERA

1762 *Orfeo ed Euridice* by Christophe Willibald von Gluck
1786 *The Marriage of Figaro* by Wolfgang Amadeus Mozart
1787 *Eine kleine Nachtmusik* by Mozart
1798 *The Creation* by Franz Joseph Haydn

THEATER AND BALLET

1776 Bolshoi Ballet founded in Moscow
1784 *Le Mariage de Figaro* by Caron de Beaumarchais

Wolfgang
Amadeus Mozart

LITERATURE
1759 *Candide* by Voltaire
1759–67 *Tristram Shandy* by Laurence Sterne
1761 *Julie, ou la Nouvelle Héloïse* by Jean-Jacques Rousseau
1766 *The Vicar of Wakefield* by Oliver Goldsmith
1774 *The Sorrows of Young Werther* by Johann Wolfgang von Goethe
1776–88 *Decline and Fall of the Roman Empire* by Edward Gibbon
1782 *Les Liaisons dangereuses* by Choderlos de Laclos
1786 *Poems, chiefly in the Scottish dialect* by Robert Burns
1798 *Lyrical Ballads* by Wordsworth and Coleridge.

Johann Wolfgang
von Goethe

1800–1850

1804 Napoleon becomes Emperor of France
1837 Accession of Queen Victoria of the United Kingdom

ARCHITECTURE

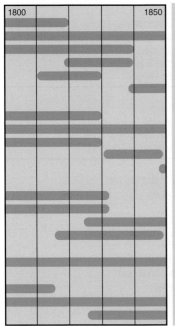

BRITAIN
Georgian 1714–1820
Gothic Revival c. 1750–1900
Neoclassical 1750–1840
Greek Revival c. 1819–40
Regency 1811–30
Victorian 1837–1901
FRANCE
Late Renaissance 1715–1830
Neoclassical 1750–1870
(First) Empire 1800–30
Neo-Renaissance 1830–48
High Neo-Renaissance 1848–70
GERMANY
Neoclassical 1750–1830s
Greek Revival 1788–1830s
Gothic Revival c. 1824–80s
Biedermeier c. 1815–48
ITALY
Neoclassical 1750–1870
UNITED STATES
Post-Colonial c. 1790–1815
Greek Revival 1798–1860
Gothic Revival c. 1825–70

Late Renaissance
architecture

18

Johann von
Schiller

ARCHITECTURE
1806–15 The Admiralty, St. Petersburg, by Andreyan Zakharov
1806–35 L'Arc de Triomphe, Paris, by Jean Chalgrin
1823–47 The British Museum, London, by Robert Smirke
1825 Buckingham Palace, London, by John Nash
1836–41 Law Courts, Lyons, by Louis Baltard
1840–64 Houses of Parliament, London, by Charles Barry

PAINTING
1819 *The Raft of the Medusa* by Théodore Géricault
1821 *The Haywain* by John Constable
1821 Bust of Goethe by Christian Rauch
1830 *Liberty Leading the People* by Eugène Delacroix
1833–6 *La Marseillaise* by François Rude

MUSIC AND OPERA
1800 Symphony No.1 in C Major by Ludwig van Beethoven
1805 *Fidelio* by Beethoven
1808 Symphony No.5 in C Minor by Beethoven
1816 *The Barber of Seville* by Gioacchino Rossini
1819 *"The Trout" Quintet* by Franz Schubert
1830 *Symphonie Fantastique* by Hector Berlioz
1843 *The Flying Dutchman* by Richard Wagner

James
Fenimore
Cooper

THEATER AND BALLET
1804 *Wilhelm Tell* by Johann von Schiller
1808 *Faust* part I by Johann Wolfgang von Goethe
1836 *The Government Inspector* by Nikolai Gogol
1842 *Giselle* by Adolphe Adam first staged in London

LITERATURE
1812–15 Fairy tales by Jacob and Wilhelm Grimm
1813 *Pride and Prejudice* by Jane Austen
1819–24 *Don Juan* by Lord Byron
1818 *Frankenstein* by Mary Shelley
1826 *Last of the Mohicans* by James Fenimore Cooper
1830 *Le rouge et le noir* by Stendhal
1831 *Notre Dame de Paris* by Victor Hugo
1835–72 Fairy tales by Hans Christian Andersen
1837–8 *Oliver Twist* by Charles Dickens
1842 *Dead Souls* by Nikolai Gogol
1844–5 *The Three Musketeers* by Alexandre Dumas
1847 *Wuthering Heights* by Emily Brontë

Alexandre
Dumas

1850–1900

1859–61 Unification of Italy
1861 Outbreak of American Civil War

ARCHITECTURE

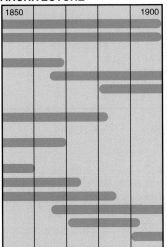

BRITAIN
Gothic Revival c. 1750–1900
Victorian 1830–1900
FRANCE
High Neo-Renaissance 1848–70
Beaux Arts 1865–1913
Art Nouveau 1880s–1914
GERMANY
Gothic Revival c. 1824–80s
ITALY
Neoclassical 1750–1870
NORTH AMERICA
Greek Revival 1798–1860
Gothic Revival c. 1825–70s
Italianate 1850–85
Beaux Arts 1865–1913
Chicago School c. 1871–93
Classical 1890–1943

Art Nouveau
architecture

1861–74 L'Opéra, Paris, by Charles Garnier
1865–71 St. Pancras Station Hotel, London, by George Gilbert Scott
1864–72 Albert Memorial, London, by George Gilbert Scott
1865 The Capitol, Washington DC, completed by Thomas U. Walter
1882–1930 Sagrada Familia, Barcelona by Antonio Gaudí
1887–9 Eiffel Tower, Paris, by Gustave Eiffel
1897–1909 School of Art, Glasgow, by Charles Rennie Mackintosh

PAINTING AND SCULPTURE

1852–4 *Ophelia* by John Millais
1856 *Madame Moitessier* by Jean Auguste Ingres
1859 *The Angelus* by François Millet
1863 *Le Déjeuner sur l'Herbe* by Édouard Manet
1871 *The Dying Centaur* by William Rimmer
1872 *Impression: Sunrise* by Claude Monet

Beaux Arts
architecture

18

Vincent Van
Gogh

1875–7 *Age of Bronze* by Auguste Rodin
1881 *Petite Danseuse de quatorze ans* by Edgar Degas
1889 *Self-portrait with Severed Ear* by Vincent Van Gogh
1893 *The Scream* by Edvard Munch

MUSIC AND OPERA

1853 *La traviata* by Giuseppe Verdi
1861 Piano Concerto No 1 in D Minor by Brahms
1867 *By the Beautiful Blue Danube*, waltz by Johann Strauss
1876 *Der Ring des Nibelungen* by Richard Wagner
1888 *Scheherazade* by Nikolai Rimsky-Korsokov
1894 *L'après-midi d'un faune* by Claude Debussy
1896 *La Bohème* by Giacomo Puccini

THEATER AND BALLET

1860 Imperial Russian Ballet of St. Petersburg (Kirov Ballet)
1867 *Peer Gynt* by Henrik Ibsen
1870 *Coppélia* by Léo Delibes
1877 *Swan Lake* by Peter Tchaikovsky
1890 *Hedda Gabler* by Henrik Ibsen
1891 *The Nutcracker* by Peter Tchaikovsky
1894 *Arms and the Man* by George Bernard Shaw
1895 *The Importance of Being Earnest* by Oscar Wilde
1895 *The Seagull* by Anton Chekhov

Henrik Ibsen

LITERATURE

1857 *Madame Bovary* by Gustave Flaubert
1857 *Les Fleurs du mal* by Charles Baudelaire
1858 *The Song of Hiawatha* by Henry W. Longfellow
1862 *Les Misérables* by Victor Hugo
1863–9 *War and Peace* by Leo Tolstoy
1866 *Crime and Punishment* by Fyodor Dostoevsky
1871 *Middlemarch* by George Eliot
1881 *Portrait of a Lady* by Henry James
1885 *Germinal* by Émile Zola
1891 *Tess of the D'Urbervilles* by Thomas Hardy

Henry James

1900–1945

1914–18 World War I
1917 Russian Revolution
1939–45 World War II

ARCHITECTURE

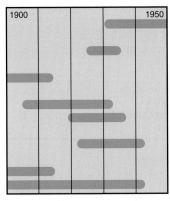

1900				1950

International Modern 1930–
BRITAIN
Art Deco 1925–35
FRANCE
Art Nouveau 1880s–1914
GERMANY
Expressionism 1905–33
Bauhaus 1919–37
ITALY
Fascist 1922–43
NORTH AMERICA
Beaux Arts 1865–1913
Classical 1890–1943

Robie House
by Frank
Lloyd Wright

1905–6 La Samaritaine department store, Paris, by Frantz Jourdain
1909–10 Robie House, Chicago, by Frank Lloyd Wright
1909–11 St. Jude's, Hampstead Garden Suburb, London,
by Edward Lutyens
1909–23 Stockholm City Hall by Ragnar Østberg
1923–5 Tribune Tower, Chicago, by Raymond Hood
1925–6 Bauhaus School of Art, Dessau, by Walter Gropius
1929–31 Empire State Building, New York, by Shreve, Lamb
and Harmon
1936 Impington Village College, Cambridge, by Gropius and Fry

PAINTING AND SCULPTURE
1901 *Madeleine I* by Henri Matisse
1906–7 *Les Desmoiselles d'Avignon* by Pablo Picasso
1908 *Nu Rouge* by Marc Chagall
1909 *The Kiss* by Gustav Klimt
1913 *Unique Forms of Continuity in Space* by Umberto Boccioni
1917 *Seated Girl* by Amedeo Modigliani
1921 *Composition in Red, Yellow, and Blue* by Piet Mondrian
1929 *Reclining Figure* by Henry Moore
1931 *The Persistence of Memory* by Salvador Dalí
1933 *The Human Condition* by René Magritte
1937 *Guernica* by Picasso

18

Empire State
Building

Igor Stravinsky

MUSIC AND OPERA
1901 Piano Concerto No. 2 in C Minor by Sergey Rachmaninoff
1904 *Madama Butterfly* by Giacomo Puccini
1907 March "Pomp and Circumstance" by Edward Elgar
1909–10 Symphony No. 9 in D Major by Gustav Mahler
1911 *Der Rosenkavalier* by Richard Strauss
1922 *Façade* by William Walton
1924 *The Cunning Little Vixen* by Leoš Janáček
1935 *Porgy and Bess* by George Gershwin
1936 *Music for Strings, Percussion, and Celeste* by Béla Bartók
1942 *Lincoln Portrait* by Aaron Copland

THEATER AND BALLET
1904 *The Cherry Orchard* by Anton Chekhov
1910 *The Firebird* by Igor Stravinsky
1913 *The Rite of Spring* by Stravinsky
1921 *Six Characters in Search of an Author* by Luigi Pirandello
1928 *Boléro* by Maurice Ravel
1925 *Hay Fever* by Noël Coward
1938 *Romeo and Juliet* by Sergei Prokofiev
1941 *Mother Courage and her Children* by Bertolt Brecht

LITERATURE
1901 *Buddenbrooks* by Thomas Mann
1908 *A Room with a View* by E.M. Forster
1913–27 *À la recherche du temps perdu* by Marcel Proust
1922 *The Waste Land* by T.S. Eliot
1922 *Ulysses* by James Joyce
1925 *The Trial* by Franz Kafka
1927 *To the Lighthouse* by Virginia Woolf
1928 *Lady Chatterley's Lover* by D.H. Lawrence
1930 *Collected Poems* by Robert Frost
1932 *Brave New World* by Aldous Huxley
1933 *La Condition humaine* by André Malraux
1940 *For Whom the Bell Tolls* by Ernest Hemingway
1942 *L'Étranger* by Albert Camus

Marcel Proust

1945–2005
1950–3 Korean War
1954-75 Vietnam War
1991 Gulf War
1991-95 Bosnian War

ARCHITECTURE

1945				1990s

International Modern 1930–
Brutalism 1950–80
Post Modernism 1980s–
High Tech 1980–

1946–60 Guggenheim Museum, New York, by Frank Lloyd Wright
1948–50 Termini Station, Rome, by Eugénio Montuori
1977 Centre Georges Pompidou, Paris, by Rogers and Piano
1977–8 East Building, National Gallery, Washington DC, by I.M. Pei
1980 Portland Building, Portland, Oregon, USA, by Michael Graves
2004 AOL Time-Warner Center, New York

PAINTING AND SCULPTURE

1947 *Man Pointing* by Alberto Giacometti
1948 *Number One* by Jackson Pollock
1953 *Figure with Meat* by Francis Bacon
1958 *Four Darks on Red* by Mark Rothko
1962 *Marilyn Monroe* by Andy Warhol
2005 *The Gates* by Christo

Francis Poulenc

MUSIC AND OPERA

1945 *Peter Grimes* by Benjamin Britten
1954 *Moses und Aron* by Arnold Schoenberg
1955 *A Midsummer Marriage* by Michael Tippett
1957 *Dialogues des Carmélites* by Francis Poulenc
1971 Mass by Leonard Bernstein
1971 Symphony No.15 in A Major by Dmitri Shostakovich
1981 *Nixon in China* by John Adams
2004 *You Are (Variations)* by Steve Reich

Tennessee
Williams

THEATER AND BALLET

1946 *The Iceman Cometh* by Eugene O'Neill
1947 *A Streetcar Named Desire* by Tennessee Williams
1949 *Death of a Salesman* by Arthur Miller
1954 *Waiting for Godot* by Samuel Beckett
1956 *Look Back in Anger* by John Osborne
1960 *The Birthday Party* by Harold Pinter
1962 *Improvizations* by Aaron Copland
1982 *The Real Thing* by Tom Stoppard
2002 *The Goat, or Who is Sylvia* by Edward Albee
2004 *I Am My Own Wife* by Doug Wright

18

Scene from O'Neill's play
The Iceman Cometh

LITERATURE
1954 *Lord of the Flies* by William Golding
1955 *Lolita* by Vladimir Nabokov
1957 *On the Road* by Jack Kerouac
1962 *One Day in the Life of Ivan Denisovich* by Alexander Solzhenitsyn
1967 *One Hundred Years of Solitude* by Gabriel García Márquez
1988 *The Satanic Verses* by Salman Rushdie
1997 *Harry Potter and the Philosopher's Stone* by J K Rowling
2004 *The Da Vinci Code* by Dan Brown

WESTERN STYLES AND ART MOVEMENTS

Prehistoric Art

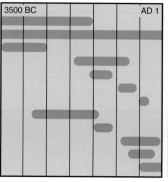

35 000 BC–AD 1
Prehistoric Art 35,000–1500 BC
Egyptian Art 3500 BC–AD 480
Sumerian Art 3500–2500 BC
Babylonian Art 1900–750 BC
Hittite Art 1600–1150 BC
Assyrian 1000–612 BC
Ancient Persian Art 539–330 BC
Minoan Art 2800–1400 BC
Mycenaean Art 1500–1100 BC
Ancient Greek Art 900–30 BC
Etruscan Art 750–200 BC
Roman Art 509 BC–AD 476

Romanesque Art

Gothic Art

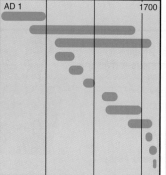

AD 1–1700
Early Christian Art AD 33–500
Byzantine Art 330–1453
Islamic Art c. 600–1630
Celtic Art 600–800
Carolingian Period 750–900
Ottonian Period 900–1024
Romanesque Art 1100–1250
Gothic Art 1140–1500
Renaissance 1420–1600
Mannerism 1530–1600
Baroque 1585–1675
Dutch painting 1650–1675

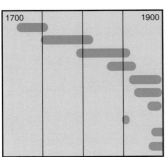

1700–1900
Rococo 1720–60
Neoclassicism 1748–1815
Romanticism 1790–1860
Realism 1830–70
Arts & Crafts Movement 1860–1900
Impressionism 1865–1900
Post-Impressionism 1879–1900
Pre-Raphaelites 1848–60
Symbolism 1886–1914
Art Nouveau 1880–1910

Rococo
architecture

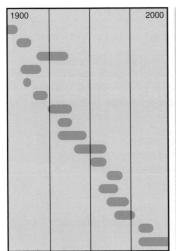

1900–2000
Fauvism 1899–1908
Expressionism 1905–14
Bauhaus 1919–37
Cubism 1908–20
Futurism 1909–14
Dada 1915–24
Surrealism 1924–39
Social Realism 1930s
American Realism 1930–48
Abstract Art 1940s–60
Pop Art 1950s–60s
Op Art 1960s
Color Field Painting 1955–67
Conceptualism 1960s–70s
Photorealism 1960s–70s
Fluxus 1980s
Installation Art 1980s–2000s

Dada

Expressionism

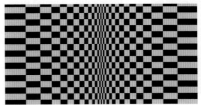

Op Art

18

POPULAR CULTURE

The cinema

1850s Thaumatrope (spinning disc) creates illusion of movement. Zoetrope (revolving disc) involves images on the inside of a disk appearing to move when seen through a slit.

1869 Celluloid replaces glass plates as a way of storing photographic images.

1872 Eadweard Muybridge records movement of animals and humans with sequences of still photographs.

1877–9 Praxihoscope projects sequential pictures onto a screen.

1878–95 Marey explores photographic techniques of recording movement.

1888 William Friese-Green patents a movie camera.

1889 Edison invents 35 mm film.

1890–4 Edison demonstrates kinetograph camera and kinetoscope (personal viewer of picture sequence).

1895 The Lumière brothers project moving images in public performances.

1896 Pathé combines recording discs in synchronization with film projection. Vitascope device used to project images onto a screen.

1902 Georges Méliès annotated movie *A Trip to the Moon* (*Le Voyage dans la Lune*).

1903 First Western, *The Great Train Robbers*.

1906 Kinemacolor (earliest color film) patented.

1908–11 Emile Cohl explores film animation.

1911 Camera records Antarctica Polar expedition.

1912 Eugene Lauste designs system for recording sound on film.

1914–18 Newsreel coverage of World War I.

1915 D.W. Griffith directs *The Birth of a Nation* and introduces the techniques of flashback and fade-out.

1916 D.W. Griffith pioneers camera close-ups in *Intolerance.*

1919 *The Cabinet of Doctor Caligari* uses expressionist art techniques. United Artists Corporation formed.

1922 *Nosferatu* – an early vampire film by F.W. Murnau.

1923 Phonofilm technique produces first sound film.

1924 Kinescope television picture tube patented.

1925 *The Gold Rush* by Charlie Chaplin, a full-length comedy featuring the famous tramp. *Battleship Potemkin* by Sergei Eisenstein, shows significant advances in film editing.

1926 *Napoleon* by Abel Gance makes use of the wide screen.

A Trip to the Moon

Charlie Chaplin

1927 *The Jazz Singer*, the first major talking film.
1928 John Logie Baird transmits television pictures across the Atlantic. *Steamboat Willie* – Walt Disney's first Mickey Mouse cartoon. Fox Films develops synchronized sound and motion film.
1932 Technicolor process developed.
1936 *Triumph of the Will* by Leni Riefenstahl. Cinema as propaganda.
1939 *Gone With The Wind* starring Clarke Gable and Vivien Leigh.
1941 Color television invented by Peter Carl Goldmark. *Citizen Kane*, Orson Welles' first film, gains immediate critical acclaim.
1952 Cinerama (wide screen projections) films produced.
1953 Cinemascope (wide screen projections) films produced. 3D films (three-dimensional projections viewed through colored spectacles) produced.
1956 Video recorder patented by American Ampex Corporation.
1976–7 Films commercially available on video for home viewing.
1977 *Star Wars* by George Lucas. Exemplary use of special effects.
1980 Video cameras produced commercially by Japanese Sony Corporation for personal use.
1982 Steven Spielberg's film *ET* released – the first film to exceed $200 million in box-office receipts.
1993 Steven Spielberg's *Jurassic Park,* using innovative special effects, becomes the most commercially successful film ever.
1995 *Natural Born Killers* renews debate on screen violence. *Toy Story*, the world's first entirely computer-generated film.
1998 *Titanic* wins 11 oscars. It breaks box-office records.
2004 *The Return of the King* by Peter Jackson repeats *Titanic*'s feat and wins 11 oscars.

The Jazz Singer

Popular music

1884 Emile Berliner records "The Lord's Prayer" on cylinder.
1888 First popular artist recording made by pianist Joset Hoffman for Edison.
1892 First million-selling song on sheet music, "After the Ball".
1903 Caruso makes first million-selling record, "On with the Motley".
1914 W.C. Handy records "St. Louis Blues". Irving Berlin's first musical, "Watch Your Step", produced in New York.
1917 First jazz recording, "Darktown Strutters' Ball", by Original Dixieland Jazz Band.
1920 "Dardanella" by Ben Selvin's orchestra – the first million-selling dance record. First blues vocal record by a black artist – "Crazy Blues" by Mamie Smith.

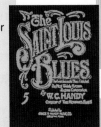

"St. Louis Blues"

18

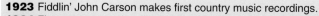

Ella Fitzgerald

Glenn Miller

Chuck Berry

1923 Fiddlin' John Carson makes first country music recordings.

1924 First country music million-selling record – Vernon Dalhart's "The Prisoner's Song".

1927 Al Jolson stars in first talking film, a musical – *The Jazz Singer*.

1928 Al Jolson has first million-seller with "Sonny Boy". Jimmie Rodgers becomes first major country music star with "Blue Yodel".

1930 Mills Brothers' "Tiger Rag" – first black vocal group million-seller.

1935 First production of Gershwin's *Porgy and Bess* in New York.

1937 First million-seller by female group – Andrews Sisters' "Bei mir bist du schön". Bing Crosby's first million-seller – "Sweet Leilani". Tommy Dorsey's first million-seller – swing arrangement of "Marie".

1938 Ella Fitzgerald's first million-seller – "A Tisket, A Tasket". Benny Goodman plays first-ever jazz concert at Carnegie Hall, New York.

1939 Lale Anderson records "Lily Marlene", biggest hit of World War II. Glenn Miller records his signature tune, "In The Mood".

1940 *Billboard* publishes first US singles chart.

1942 Bing Crosby's "White Christmas" – biggest-selling single ever.

1943 Frank Sinatra's first million-seller – "All Or Nothing At All". *Oklahoma!* launches the careers of Richard Rogers and Oscar Hammerstein, who create some of the most popular musicals in history.

1944 Glenn Miller disappears in plane over English Channel. Louis Jordan's first million-seller – "Is You Is or Is You ain't my Baby".

1946 Ink Spots sell a million of both "To Each His Own" and "The Gypsy". Al Jolson's "The Jolson Story" is first million-selling album.

1947 Frankie Laine's first million-seller – "That's My Desire".

1948 Nat "King" Cole's first million-seller – "Nature Boy". Fat's Domino's first million-seller – "The Fat Man". Bluesman John Lee Hooker finds fame with "Boogie Children" and "I'm In The Mood". Jazz guitarist Lonnie Johnson sells a million of "Tomorrow Night".

1949 Gene Autry records "Rudolph the Red-Nosed Reindeer" – second all-time biggest Christmas hit. Hank Williams' first million-seller – "Lovesick Blues".

1950 Roy Brown has early rhythm and blues million-seller with "Hard Luck Blues". Zitherist Anton Karas' instrumental million-seller, "The Third Man".

1951 Johnnie Ray has double-sided million-seller with "Cry/Little White Cloud That Cried". Vera Lynn is first UK artist to top US singles chart, with "Auf Wiedersehen".

1953 Trumpeter Eddie Calvert's million-seller "Oh Mein Papa". Orioles have first "doo-wop" million-seller with "Crying In The Chapel".

1954 Chuck Berry perfects individual performing style.

1955 "Rock Around the Clock" by Bill Haley and the Comets at No. 1.

1956 Elvis records for RCA.

1957 Jerry Lee Lewis storms onto the pop scene with "Whole Lotta Shakin' Goin' On". Composer Leonard Bernstein and lyricist Stephen Sondheim write *West Side Story*, a musical based on William Shakespeare's *Romeo and Juliet*.

1959 *The Sound of Music* – musical by Rogers and Hammerstein.

1960 Motown's first million-seller by the Miracles – "Shop Around".

1961 Chubby Checker sparks "twist fever" across the world.

1962 "Love Me Do" – The Beatles first release, begins worldwide Beatlemania. In US, they take 20 singles to No. 1 in *Billboard* chart.

Elvis

1964 The Rolling Stones hit the US top 40 for the first time.

1965 James Brown achieves international success with his US top-ten million-seller – "Papa's got a Brand New Bag".

1966 Simon and Garfunkel's first US No. 1 – "The Sound of Silence".

1967 Jimi Hendrix first appears in pop charts. Musical *Hair* sparks controversy over its portrayal of rebels against the Vietnam War.

1968 The Doors' biggest hit – "Hello I Love You" – at No. 1 in US.

1969 Woodstock Rock Festival attended by 400,000 people. Led Zeppelin release their first two best-selling LPs.

Jimi Hendrix

1970 Three Dog Night go to No. 1 in the US with Randy Norman's song "Mama Told Me (Not To Come)". Jimi Hendrix dies in London.

1971 Led Zeppelin's fourth album is released. One of the tracks is "Stairway to Heaven," set to become an all-time classic. Composer Andrew Lloyd Webber's *Jesus Christ Superstar* is the first in a string of successful musicals.

1972 Chuck Berry reaches No. 1 in US and UK with "My Ding-A-Ling".

1973 Elton John has his first US No. 1 – "Crocodile Rock".

1974 Queen begin a hugely successful career with their first UK single, "Seven Seas of Rhye". Barbra Streisand has first US No. 1 with "The Way We Were".

Sex Pistols

1975 The Bee Gees become prime movers in the roots of the disco explosion with the release of "Jive Talkin'".

1976 Sex Pistols release "Anarchy in the UK". Punk takes off.

1977 The two most successful recording artists ever die this year – Elvis Presley and Bing Crosby.

1979 Elton John is first solo rock artist to perform in Israel and USSR. Former Sex Pistol Sid Vicious dies in New York from a drug overdose.

1980 John Lennon killed in New York.

1981 Reggae superstar Bob Marley dies from a brain tumor in Miami.

1983 Michael Jackson has three US No. 1s from his album "Thriller."

18

John Lennon

Michael Jackson

1984 Prince achieves worldwide fame with his film "Purple Rain." Madonna has first US No. 1 with "Like a Virgin."
1985 Live Aid concert in aid of the starving in Africa. Whitney Houston releases her album "Whitney Houston." It becomes the best-selling debut album of all time.
1989 Pink Floyd's album "Dark Side of the Moon" reaches 730 weeks in the US charts – a US record.
1990 Opera singers José Carreras, Placido Domingo, and Luciano Pavarotti release popular, best-selling classical album "In Concert" for the football 1990 World Cup Finals.
1991 Michael Jackson signs $890 million recording contract with Sony – the largest recording contract ever.

Olmec sculpture

Ashanti
metalwork

NON-WESTERN ARTS

Major periods of artistic activity are given with examples.

Central and South America

Olmec	1200–100 BC	Giant stone statues
Teotihuaca	100 BC – AD 750	Wall paintings at Teotihuaca
Maya	100–1542	Limestone ziggurats; Tula sculpture
Inca	1100–1530s	Architecture; metalwork; pottery
Aztec	1325–1521	Gold sculpture

India

Indus	c. 3000–1500 BC	Copper and bronzework; fertility figures
Vedic	1500–600 BC	Ajanta cave carvings
Mauryan	322–185 BC	Stone carving
Gupta	c. AD 320–750	Buddhist iconography; Gandhara Art
Mughal	1526–1750	Miniatures; red forts; tombs

Africa

Pharaonic	3000–2000 BC	Pyramids
Nok	200 BC	Ironwork; terracotta
Shona	1000s–1800s	Architecture
Dogon	1400s	Wood carving
Yoruba	1500s	Masks
Ife	1500s–1800s	Bronzework
Ashanti	1600s	Bronzework; gold weights

1992 Freddie Mercury of Queen dies of Aids. "I Will Always Love You" by Whitney Houston is at No. 1 in the US for 14 weeks – a US record.
1994 Woodstock Rock Festival is revived after 25 years. Barbra Streisand goes on a sell-out tour after a 12-year absence.
1995 "Anthology 1", first new Beatles material since 1970, is released.
1997 Elton John's "Candle in the Wind 2", commemorating the death of Diana, Princess of Wales becomes the biggest selling single of all time.
1998 Frank Sinatra dies.
2001 George Harrison dies.
2005 Live 8 concerts watched by 3 billion people, staged to persuade world leaders to cancel the debt of African nations.

Madonna

China

Yangshao	2000–1500 BC	Black and red fired pottery
Shang	1766–1028 BC	Cast bronzework
Qin	256–206 BC	Terracotta army
Han	206 BC – AD 220	Bronze; jade; monuments
Tang	618–907	Landscape painting; Yueh stoneware
Song	960–1278	Landscape painting; celadon stoneware
Ming	1368–1644	Porcelain
Qing	1644–1912	Lacquerwork; porcelain

Japan

Jomon	10,500–250 BC	Pottery
Yayoi	c. 100 BC	Bronzework; pottery
Kofun	c. AD 400	"Keyhole" tombs
Heian	c. 900	Kana script
Ashikaga	1300s	Noh drama; ink painting
Edo	1800s	Color-prints; miniature sculptures; lacquerwork; Shino ware

Southeast Asia

Dong Son	300s BC – AD 1	Bronzework
Sailendra	600–1100	Architecture
Khmer	802–1431	Architecture (Angkor Wat)
Pagan	849–1287	Architecture (Ananda Temple)

18

Shang Dynasty bronzework

CLASSICAL ARCHITECTURE
Features of the front of a temple

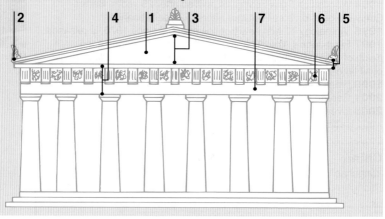

1 Tympanum The triangular space within a pediment
2 Acroterion A pedestal on the apex or sides of a pediment supporting a statue or ornamental figure
3 Pediment A low pitched triangular gable above a façade
4 Entablature The upper part of an order of architecture, comprising the cornice, frieze, and architrave
5 Cornice The upper and protruding part of an entablature
6 Frieze The middle section of an entablature, an ornamental band, either abstract, botanical, or figurative
7 Architrave The lowest of the three divisions of an entablature

Temple of Artemis, Ephesus

Columns
Column structure
1 **Abacus** Flat area at the top of a capital, dividing a column from its entablature
2 **Echinus** A type of moulding
3 **Annulet** A decorative moulded ring or band used in Greek, Romanesque, and Gothic architecture
4 **Capital** The architectural feature at the top of a column
5 **Astragal** Classical moulded band atop a column shaft
6 **Torus** Convex moulding at column base
7 **Scotia** Concave moulding at column base
8 **Dado** Central part of pedestal between the base and cornice
9 **Plinth** Base of column pedestal
10 **Pedestal** The supporting part of a column

Doric column

Classical orders
1 **Doric** No base, a heavy, fluted shaft, and a capital composed of an ovolo moulding under a square abacus
2 **Ionic** The capital is carved to resemble a scroll
3 **Corinthian** The capital is ornately carved to resemble acanthus leaves

Ionic capital

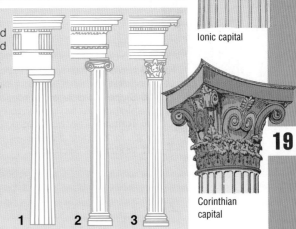

Corinthian capital

19

CHURCHES

Parts of a church 1

1 Aisle The side corridors of the main church. The north aisle is on the left when facing the altar, and the south aisle is on the right

2 Almonry A special room used for the distribution of alms

3 Ambulatory The continuation of the aisle around the choir and behind the altar

4 Chancel The area containing the choir and the altar, originally reserved for the clergy

Cloister (**8**), Toledo, Spain

5a Chapel A small area set aside for private worship

5b Chantry Chapel An endowed chapel in which prayers could be said for the soul of a benefactor

5c Lady Chapel Set at the east end and dedicated to the Virgin Mary

6 Chapterhouse The administrative center

7 Choir The area between the nave and the altar, for use by the choir and clergy

8 Cloister The covered walkway around a courtyard

9 Crossing The central area between the nave, the chancel, and the transept

10 Crypt The area under the main church

11 Presbytery The area around the main altar

12 Sacristy or **Vestry** A room for storing the priests' vestments and sacred vessels. Often also used for meetings, Sunday School, etc.

13 Sanctuary The most sacred part of the chancel, used in the past to provide fugitives from the law with immunity from arrest

14 Nave The main area of the church used by the congregation. It usually has aisles on either side

15 Slype A passageway from cloister to transept or chapterhouse

16 Transept The two areas on either side of the crossing, which form part of the cross-shaped plan of the church

17 Vestry *see* **Sacristy**

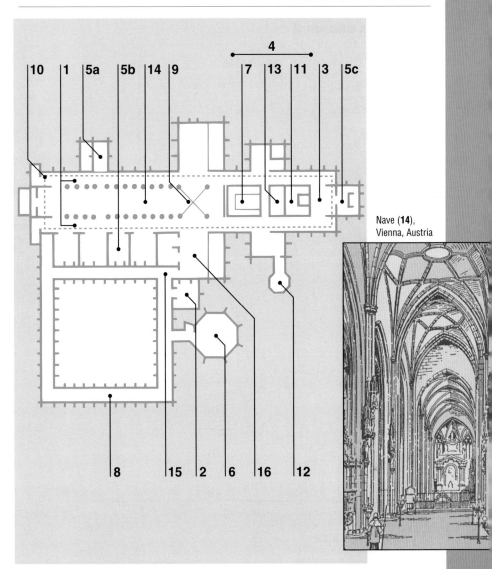

Nave (**14**),
Vienna, Austria

Parts of a church 2

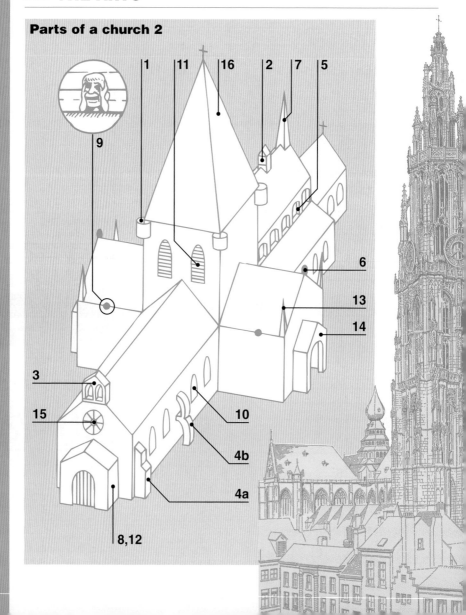

1 Bartizan A small turret projecting from a wall, parapet, or tower

2 Bellcote A bell tower on a roof

3 Bell gable A bell tower mounted on the end of a wall

4a Buttress A masonry support against a wall

4b Flying buttress A support which is arched so that the brace is away from the wall

5 Clerestory A row of windows in the upper part of a wall, above the roof of an aisle

6 Finial An ornament on top of buildings

7 Flèche A small wooden spire

8 Galilee An enclosed porch at the west end of the church

9 Gargoyle A spout carrying water from the roof, usually decorated with a grotesque figure or head

10 Lancet A tall and pointed window

11 Louvre A window opening, in church towers, covered with overlapping boards

12 Narthex A porch at the west end of a church, that is usually at right angles to the nave

13 Pinnacle A small stone spire on top of buttresses, parapets, or roofs

14 Porch An entrance that is covered

15 Rose window A circular window

16 Spire A tall, pointed structure, most commonly found on a tower

Buttress (**4a**)

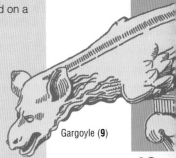

Gargoyle (**9**)

19

Spire (**16**),
Antwerp Cathedral,
Belgium

Brass (**2**)

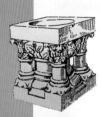

Font (**7**)

Pulpit (**13**)

Parts of a church 3

1 Altar The table at the east end of the church from which acts of worship are conducted. It is divided from the choir by rails

2 Brasses Engraved brass plates attached to tombs. They usually depict the deceased

3 Canopy A small protective hood usually placed over a pulpit or tomb

4 Choir screen The partition, usually of wood, between the choir stalls and the nave of the church

5 Credence A small table or shelf on which is placed the bread and wine used for the communion service

6 Easter Sepulcher A recess in the north chancel to hold the effigy of the risen Christ used during Easter celebrations

7 Font A large, raised, fixed basin containing holy water used for baptisms

8 Funeral A wooden painted shield, or hatchment, bearing the arms of a deceased member of the local gentry

9 Lectern A desk or stand designed to hold a bible or large service book

10 Misericord A ledge, often decorated or carved, projecting from the underside of a hinged seat, built to support a standing person

11 Pew Wooden seating for the congregation

12 Piscina A stone basin with a drain placed near the altar and used for washing the sacred vessels

13 Pulpit An elevated platform, often approached by a flight of steps, from which the congregation is addressed

14 Reredos A decorated screen behind the altar

15 Rood A cross or crucifix placed in the east part of the nave and in front of the choir stalls

16 Roodscreen The support to the rood, often in elaborately carved wood or stone

17 Screen A parclose screen is one around an altar or shrine

18 Sedilia Seats for the clergy, often recessed into the wall

19 Squint A small slit in the wall or pier to enable members of the congregation (originally lepers in a separate room) to have sight of the altar

20 Stall Another name for a pew

21 Stoup Basin of holy water near the church entrance

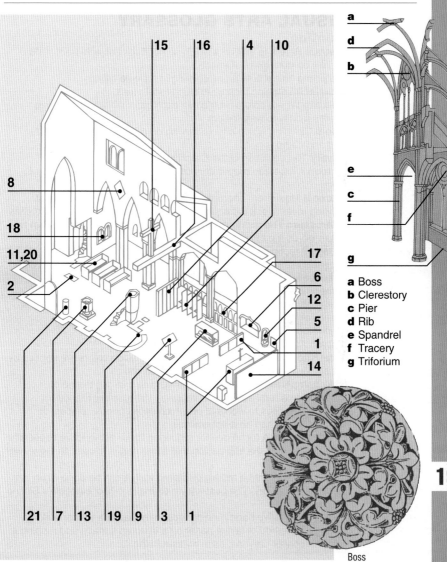

a Boss
b Clerestory
c Pier
d Rib
e Spandrel
f Tracery
g Triforium

19

Boss

VISUAL ARTS GLOSSARY
Painting

abstract Refers to artworks which do not depict objects from nature but rely on pure form for effect

alla prima To execute an oil painting in a single sitting

aquatint An etching technique using tonal areas

bleeding Where colors merge into each other while wet; the term applies mostly to watercolors

bloom Clouding which affects varnish on a picture if left exposed to cold and damp

calvary The depiction of the Crucifixion of Christ

cartoon A full-sized preparatory drawing on paper for a painting or mural

charcoal Made from charred wood, charcoal is among the oldest drawing materials. It is frequently used in making preparatory sketches

chiaroscuro The distribution of light and shade in an image. From two Italian words meaning clear and obscure

collage A technique in which pictures are built up of a variety of materials like paper, fabrics, found objects, etc. It is a method favoured by surrealists

composition The arrangement of the elements in a picture to achieve overall harmony. There are many theories about how to achieve this, but no reliable rules

Foreshortening

Frieze

craquelure The cracks in old varnish or paint

diptych An altarpiece made of two panels

encaustic An ancient painting technique in which colors are applied by hot beeswax and pressed in with a heated iron

fête champêtre/fête galante Paintings with a strong theme of escapism in a rural setting – in vogue in 18th-century France

figurative Applies to works of art which depict people, places, or scenes, rather than abstract designs

foreshortening A technique for rendering linear perspective especially in figures, to give the impression that some part is "closer" to the viewer than the rest

fresco Painting onto a freshly plastered wall. It can be done while the plaster is wet or dry. The best-known example is Michelangelo's Sistine Chapel ceiling

frieze A decorative band running around the top of a wall or building

frottage A method of laying paper on a textured surface and rubbing it with charcoal or crayons, as in brass-rubbing

glaze Painting a layer of transparent color over other colors which have already dried

golden mean A geometrical rule laid down by the Roman architect Vitruvius for ensuring harmonious composition. It states that the division of a line or two-dimensional figure should be such that the proportion of the smaller to the greater is the same as that of the greater to the sum of the two

gouache Opaque watercolors

grisaille Paintings done entirely in shades of grey, which consequently have a sculptural feel to them

grotesque A decorative style making use of animals, foliage, and human forms

hard edge A technique used mostly in abstract painting, in which the elements making up the image are clearly defined

illumination Primarily a medieval art form, involving the elaborate decoration of manuscripts with patterns, miniature paintings, gold leaf, and even precious stones

impasto Heavily applied oil paints which show brush or palette-knife marks

miniatures Small paintings, usually portraits, made for putting in lockets or carrying around. The best examples are British, from the 16th and 17th centuries

minimal art Abstract painting or sculpture which uses simple geometric shapes and primary colors

monochrome Work done using different shades of a single color, as opposed to polychrome (involving many colors)

montage Rather like collage, only involving the use of bits of other pictures, such as photos or drawings

murals Paintings done on walls. A fresco is a kind of mural

op art A style of abstract art which exploits optical illusions, especially those conveying movement

pastoral An idealized depiction of rural life

paysage A depiction of the countryside, a rural landscape

pentimento Traces of a painting which show through a later image painted on top

perspective The technique of rendering the impression of three-dimensional space on a two-dimensional surface. It involves the use of one or two vanishing points

pietà A depiction of the Virgin Mary mourning over the body of Christ

pointillism A technique in which forms are made up of many closely spaced dots of color

Grotesque

Perspective

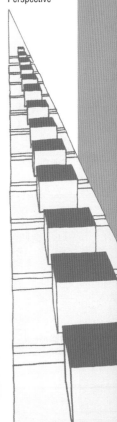

Silhouette

sfumato A very smooth gradation of tone, giving a hazy effect
sgraffito A decorative technique in which the top layer of glaze or pigment is scratched away to reveal the color beneath
silhouette A picture showing a head or figure in profile, often cut from black paper
still life A depiction of a group of inanimate objects like a bowl of fruit
stipple Applying small spots of color with the tip of a brush
tempera Pigment mixed with some substance such as egg yolk, to give a very permanent paint
tint A color
tondo A circular painting or relief
tone The shade or value of a particular color
triptych An altarpiece made of three panels
trompe l'oeil A style of painting which tries to convey objects so realistically that they are mistaken as genuine. From the French, meaning "deceiving the eye"
underpainting The first layer of a picture, which indicates the general design and main areas of light and shade. It must be low in oil content, to allow later layers to dry without cracking
vignette A picture, usually small and decorative, the edges of which fade away softly rather than end in a border or frame
wash A coat of diluted watercolor applied to a background
watercolor Generally, any water-soluble paint

Still life

Sculpture and pottery terms

alabaster Substance used for sculpting that resembles marble
anaglyph A sculpture or carving in low relief
armature A framework to support clay or other modeling material
atlas, telamon A supporting column decoratively carved as a male statue
banker The name given to a sculptor's workbench
basaltware Black pottery that is unglazed
bas-relief, basso rilievo, low relief A type of sculpture in which the form projects slightly, but is not separate from, the background
biscuit, bisque Pottery that is unglazed
bone china Porcelain made of clay mixed with bone ash
calvary A sculpture of the Crucifixion of Christ
cameo A small portrait in low relief, with the projecting form in a different color from the background
cameoware Pottery with a colored background and raised designs in white

Triptych

caryatid A supporting column decoratively carved as a female statue

celadon ware Pottery colored with a pale gray-green glaze

chryselephantine A statue either made of or overlaid with ivory and gold

cire perdue, **lost-wax process** A method by which bronze is cast using a mould formed around a wax pattern, which is then melted and drained away

corbeil A decorative carving resembling a basket of fruit or flowers

crackle ware Pottery exhibiting a network of fine cracks in the glaze

diaglyph A decorative carving with the design cut into it

faience Fine pottery named after Faenza, Italy, decorated with a colorful glaze

gesso Plaster of Paris or gypsum mix used to prepare a painting surface or as a base for low-relief sculpture

intaglio A method of carving in which a design is cut into the material

ironstone Pottery that is hard and white

jasper ware Design of stoneware pottery invented by Josiah Wedgwood, in which a raised white design contrasts with a colored (usually blue) background

maiolica, majolica Pottery that is brightly decorated in 16th-century Italian style

mantle A clay mould formed around a wax model, which is then melted and drained away

maquette, bozzetto A practice model made before a sculpture

mobile A sculpture suspended in midair which has balanced parts that move when pushed or blown

nankeen Pottery, originally imported from Nanking, with a Chinese-style blue and white design

Parian ware White porcelain of fine texture that resembles marble

pietà A sculpture showing the Virgin Mary mourning over the body of Christ

porcelain White, translucent ware made by mixing chine clay and chine stone together to form the body, which is then fired at high temperature.

putto, amorino A sculpture of a small boy, cherub, or Cupid

relief, relievo A type of sculpture in which the form half projects, but is not separate, from the background

restrike Re-use of a sculptor's mould sometime after it was first used

stabile A stationary, hanging abstract construction

stoneware Pottery fired at a high temperature and glazed with salt

terracotta Pottery made of a mix of clay and fine sand that is unglazed

Intaglio decorated goblet

Majolica vase

Porcelain vase

19

MUSICAL NOTATION

Orchestral musical score

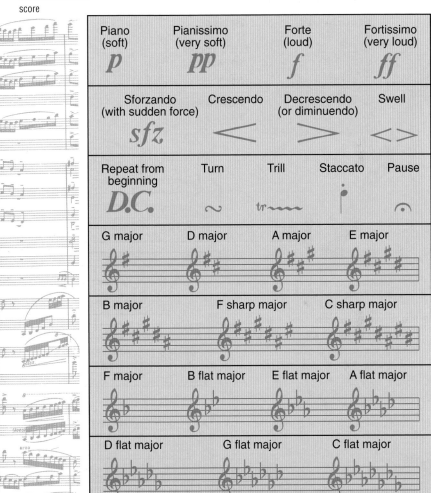

Piano (soft)	Pianissimo (very soft)	Forte (loud)	Fortissimo (very loud)
p	*pp*	*f*	*ff*

Sforzando (with sudden force)	Crescendo	Decrescendo (or diminuendo)	Swell
sfz	<	>	<>

Repeat from beginning	Turn	Trill	Staccato	Pause
D.C.	~	*tr*		

G major   D major   A major   E major

B major   F sharp major   C sharp major

F major   B flat major   E flat major   A flat major

D flat major   G flat major   C flat major

20

COMPARATIVE PITCHES OF INSTRUMENTS

Woodwind
1 Piccolo
2 Flutes
3 Clarinets
4 Oboes
5 Cor anglais
6 Bass clarinet
7 Bassoons
8 Contrabassoon

Brass
9 French horns
10 Trumpets
11 Tenor trombones
12 Tuba

Percussion
13 Timpani

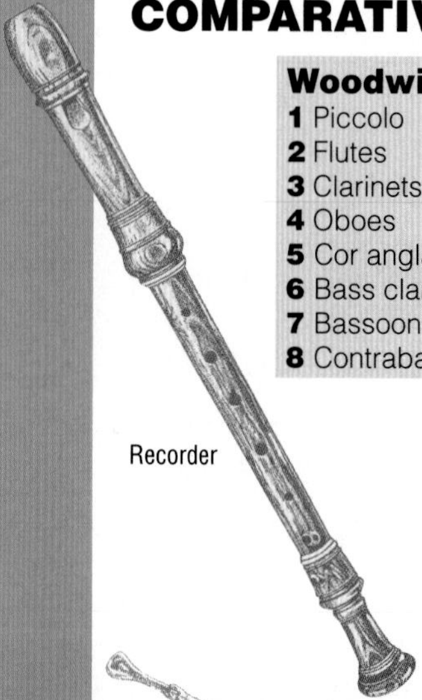

Recorder

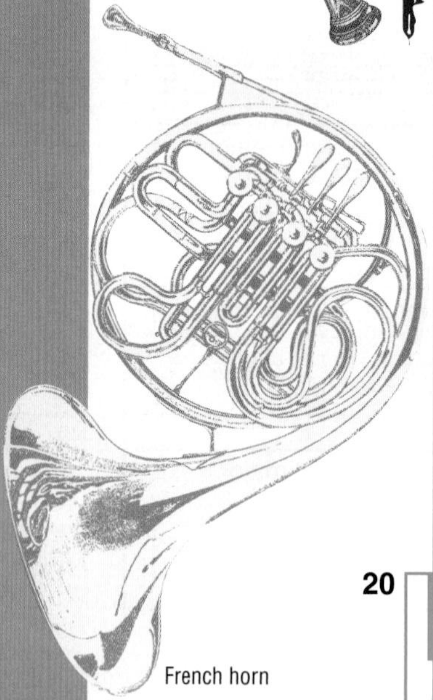

French horn

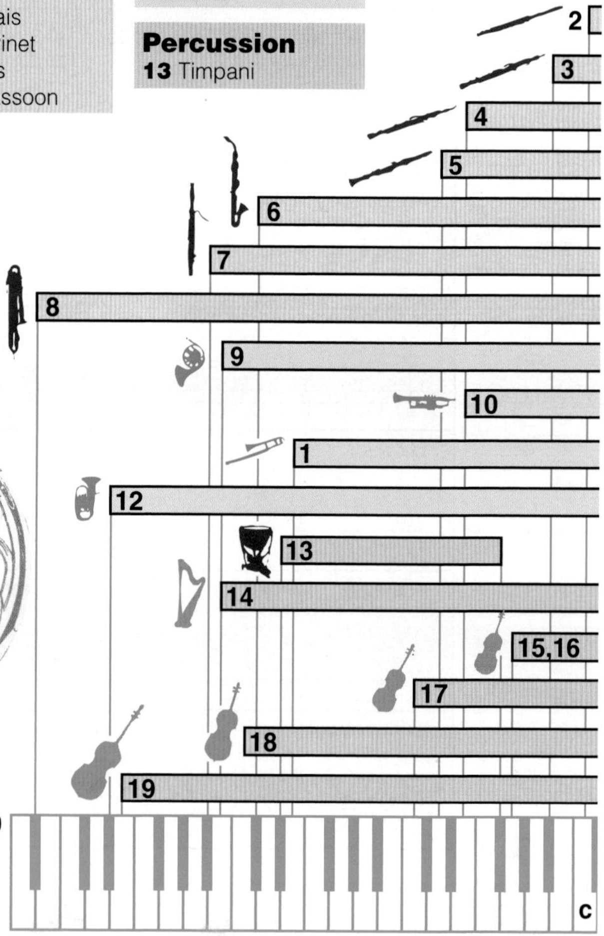

Strings
14 Harp
15 1st violins
16 2nd violins
17 Violas
18 Cellos
19 Double basses
20 Piano

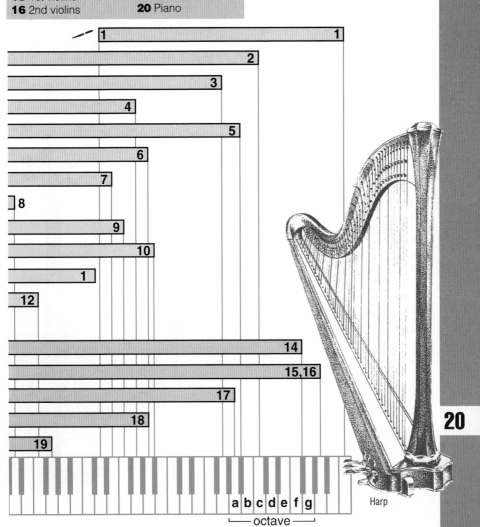

abcdefg

octave

Harp

20

ORCHESTRAL FAMILIES

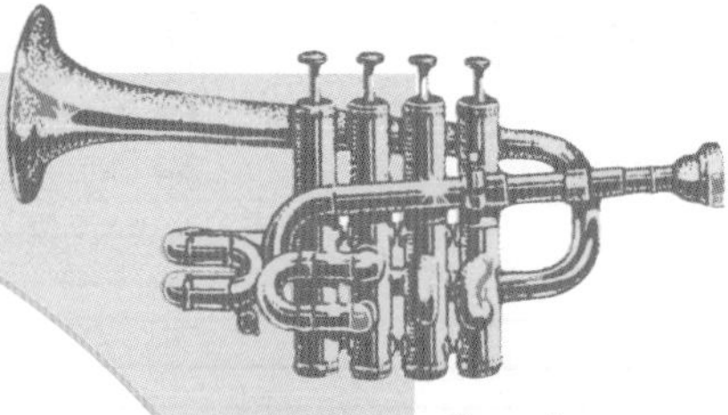

Woodwind
1 Piccolo
2 Flute
3 Oboe
4 Cor anglais
5 Clarinet
6 Bass clarinet
7 Bassoon
8 Contrabassoon

Brass
9 French horn
10 Trumpet
11 Trombone
12 Tuba

Percussion
13 Tam-tam
14 Cymbals
15 Xylophone
16 Glockenspiel
17 Tubular bells
18 Side drum
19 Bass drum
20 Timpani

Strings
21 Harp
22 1st violins
23 2nd violins
24 Violas
25 Cellos
26 Double basses

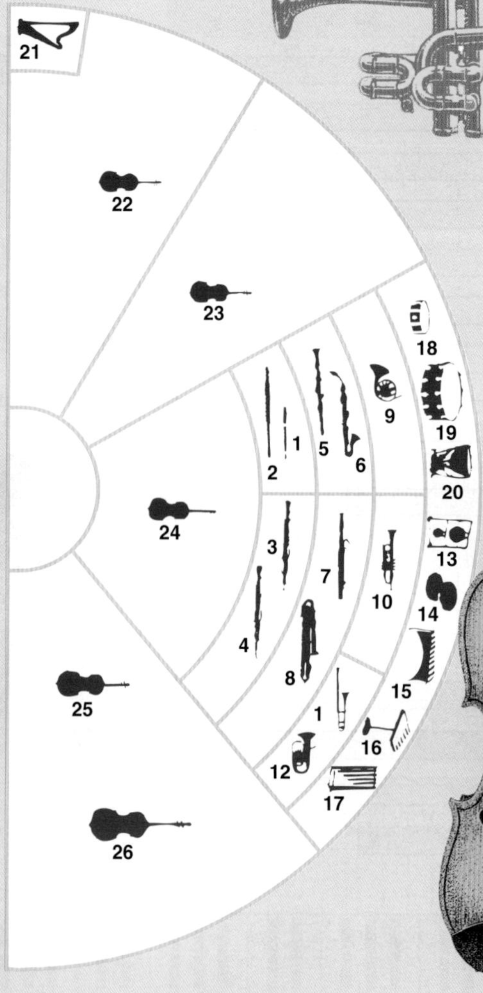

Trumpet –
brass

Violin – strings

Flute – woodwind

GROUPS OF MUSICIANS

The names given to groups made up of specific numbers of musicians are listed below. These groups include either vocalists or instrumentalists, or a combination of both. The instruments used depend on the musical piece being performed.

1 Soloist   **3** Trio   **5** Quintet   **7** Septet
2 Duet   **4** Quartet   **6** Sextet   **8** Octet

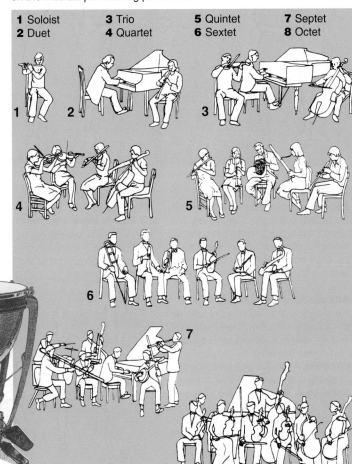

Timpani – percussion

20

BALLET MOVEMENTS

1 The Five Basic Positions
2 Fouetté (A whipped movement) Step executed on point, the working leg whipped out to the side and into the knee with a slight circular movement. Frequently combined with turns as *fouetté en tournant* to which it gives momentum
3 Attitude A pose on one leg with the corresponding arm open to the side or back, the other leg extended back at 90° with the knee bent, corresponding arm raised above the head
4 Pirouette A turn on one foot propelled by a swing of the arm
5 Arabesque A pose as though poised for flight, supported on one leg, the other extended backward and the arms disposed harmoniously, usually with the greatest reach

6 Grande jeté A leap from one foot to the other
7 Pas de deux A sequence, walking or dancing, for two people
8 Cabriole A leap with one leg outstretched, the other leg beating against it

Performing
a fouetté

NATIONAL EMBLEMS

The national flag is the Stars and Stripes, or Star-Spangled Banner. It consists of seven red and six white stripes, representing the original colonies, and 50 white stars representing all the states, on a blue field.

The Great Seal was designed in 1782. It shows the bald eagle, the national bird, with a ribbon in its beak bearing the Latin words "One out of many." In its talons are the arrows of war and the olive branch of peace.

The national motto "In God We Trust" was adopted in 1956. It appeared on coins during the Civil War, and is based on the phrase "In God is our trust," which is featured in the national anthem.

US population 291,049,000 – third most populous country in the world

The National Anthem is the *Star-Spangled Banner*, adopted in 1931. It was written by Francis Scott Key in 1814 during the bombardment of Fort McHenry in Baltimore. The melody was originally called "Anacreon in Heaven," and was suggested by Key's friend, Judge J.H. Nicholson.

US area 3,537,438 sq miles – fourth-largest country in the world

The national bird is the bald eagle, chosen in 1782 because it is the only eagle found exclusively in North America.

The national flower is the rose.

LOCATION

The extreme limits of the contiguous 48 states of the USA are

1 North Lake of the Woods, Minnesota 49° 15' N, 94° 45' W
2 South Key West, Florida 24° 34' N, 81° 48' W
3 East West Quoddy Head, Maine 44° 49' N, 66° 57' W
4 West Cape Alava, Washington 48° 10' N, 124° 45' W

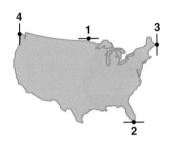

Extreme points including Alaska and Hawaii

1 West Cape Wrangell, Alaska 52° 55' N, 172° 25' E
2 North Point Barrow, Alaska 71° 22' N, 156° 30' W
3 South Ka Lae, Hawaii 18° 58' N, 155° 24' E

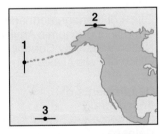

National holidays	
Jan 1	New Year's Day
Monday closest to Jan 15	Martin Luther King Day
Feb 12	Lincoln's Birthday
3rd Monday in Feb	Washington's Birthday
Last Monday in May	Memorial Day
Jul 4	Independence Day
1st Monday in Sep	Labor Day
Monday closest to Oct 12	Columbus Day
Nov 11	Veterans' Day
4th Thursday in Nov	Thanksgiving
Dec 25	Christmas Day

21

THE GOVERNMENT

Government at national level is made up of three branches: the Executive, Legislative, and the Judiciary. Each is generally independent of the others. Checks and balances ensure that no branch exceeds its authority. A written constitution specifies the powers of each branch.

Executive branch

The President is responsible for recommending measures to the Congress, nominating Supreme Court judges and other officials, and exercising the power of veto over Congressional bills. The President is the Commander-in-Chief of the Armed Forces.

The President
Executive Office of the President
White House Office
Office of Management and Budget
Council of Economic Advisers
National Security Council
Office of Policy Development

Office of the US Trade
  Representative
Council on Environmental Quality
Office of Science and Technology
  Policy
Office of Administration
The Vice President

Departments of
Agriculture
Commerce
Defense
Education
Energy
Health and Human Services
Homeland Security

Housing and Urban Development
the Interior
Justice
Labor
State
Transportation
the Treasury
Veterans' Affairs

House of Representatives

Consists of 435 members

Legislative branch

Congress consists of the House of Representatives and the Senate. The 435 Representatives are elected by the states – the size of each state's population determining the number of its Representatives. The Senate is made up of 100 members, two elected by each state. Congress is responsible for handling legislation, ratifying treaties and confirming Presidential appointments.

General Accounting Office
Government Printing Office
Library of Congress
Ofice of Technology Assessment
Congressional Budget Office
Copyright Royalty Tribunal

Judicial branch

The Judiciary is split between the Supreme Court and other federal courts. The Supreme Court is the highest court in the land. Judges of these courts are appointed by the President with the approval of the Senate. They hold office for life.

The Supreme Court
Courts of Appeals
District Courts
Claims Court
Court of Appeals for the Federal
    Circuit
Court of International Trade
Territorial Courts
US Court of Military Appeals
US Tax Court
Administrative Office of the US
    Courts
Federal Judicial Center

The Senate
Consists of 100 members

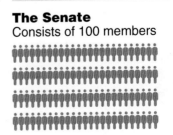

THE PRESIDENTS
Facts in brief
Qualifications

A candidate must be a natural-born US citizen, subject to the jurisdiction of the US at the time of birth, and have lived in the US for at least 14 years.

Term of office

The President holds office for four years and may be re-elected only once.

Removal from office

If he is impeached by a majority vote in the House of Representatives, and tried and convicted by a two-thirds majority in the Senate, the President may be removed from office.

George
Washington

Thomas
Jefferson

Abraham Lincoln

Term in office	President	Party
Apr 1789 – Mar 1797	George Washington 1732–99	F
Mar 1797 – Mar 1801	John Adams 1735–1826	F
Mar 1801 – Mar 1809	Thomas Jefferson 1743–1826	DR
Mar 1809 – Mar 1817	James Madison 1751–1836	DR
Mar 1817 – Mar 1825	James Monroe 1758–1831	DR
Mar 1825 – Mar 1829	John Quincy Adams 1767–1848	DR
Mar 1829 – Mar 1837	Andrew Jackson 1767–1845	D
Mar 1837 – Mar 1841	Martin Van Buren 1782–1862	D
Mar 1841 – Apr 1841	William Henry Harrison 1773–1841	W
Apr 1841 – Mar 1845	John Tyler 1790–1862	W
Mar 1845 – Mar 1849	James K. Polk 1795–1849	D
Mar 1849 – Jul 1850	Zachary Taylor 1784–1850	W
Jul 1850 – Mar 1853	Millard Fillmore 1800–74	W
Mar 1853 – Mar 1857	Franklin Pierce 1804–69	D
Mar 1857 – Mar 1861	James Buchanan 1791–1868	D
Mar 1861 – Apr 1865	Abraham Lincoln 1809–65	R
Apr 1865 – Mar 1869	Andrew Johnson 1808–75	NU*
Mar 1869 – Mar 1877	Ulysses S. Grant 1822–85	R
Mar 1877 – Mar 1881	Rutherford B. Hayes 1822–93	R
Mar 1881 – Sep 1881	James Garfield 1831–81	R

PRESIDENTS 587

Party abbreviations
F – Federalist
DR – Democratic-Republican
D – Democrat
I – Independent
W – Whig
R – Republican
NU – National Union Party
(a Republican–War Democrats coalition)
* Johnson returned to the Democratic
Party 1868

Franklin D.
Roosevelt

Term in office	President	Party
Sep 1881 – Mar 1885	Chester A. Arthur 1829–86	R
Mar 1885 – Mar 1889	Grover Cleveland 1837–1901	D
Mar 1889 – Mar 1893	Benjamin Harrison 1833–1909	R
Mar 1893 – Mar 1897	Grover Cleveland 1837–1908	D
Mar 1897 – Sep 1901	William McKinley 1843–1901	R
Sep 1901 – Mar 1909	Theodore Roosevelt 1858–1919	R
Mar 1909 – Mar 1913	William H. Taft 1857–1930	R
Mar 1913 – Mar 1921	Woodrow Wilson 1856–1924	D
Mar 1921 – Aug 1923	Warren G. Harding 1865–1923	R
Aug 1923 – Mar 1929	Calvin Coolidge 1872–1933	R
Mar 1929 – Mar 1933	Herbert Hoover 1874–1964	R
Mar 1933 – Apr 1945	Franklin D. Roosevelt 1882–1945	D
Apr 1945 – Jan 1953	Harry S. Truman 1884–1972	D
Jan 1953 – Jan 1961	Dwight D. Eisenhower 1890–1969	R
Jan 1961 – Nov 1963	John F. Kennedy 1917–63	D
Nov 1963 – Jan 1969	Lyndon B. Johnson 1908–73	D
Jan 1969 – Aug 1974	Richard M. Nixon 1913–94	R
Aug 1974 – Jan 1977	Gerald R. Ford 1913–	R
Jan 1977 – Jan 1981	Jimmy Carter 1924–	D
Jan 1981 – Jan 1989	Ronald Reagan 1911–2004	R
Jan 1989 – Jan 1993	George Bush 1924–	R
Jan 1993 – Jan 2001	Bill Clinton 1946–	D
Jan 2001 –	George W. Bush 1946–	R

Dwight D.
Eisenhower

John F. Kennedy

21

TIME ZONES

The contiguous 48 states are divided into four time zones: Eastern, Central, Mountain, and Pacific. In each zone the time is an hour earlier than in its eastern neighbor, and an hour later than in its western neighbor.

Time differences

The time difference between Washington DC and the following cities is

1 Eastern time (no difference)

Atlanta, GA	Hartford, CT
Baltimore, MD	Indianapolis, IN
Boston, MA	Miami, FL
Charleston, SC	New York, NY
Cleveland, OH	Philadelphia, PA
Detroit, MI	Wilmington, DE

2 Central time (−1 hour)

Birmingham, AL	Kansas City, MO
Chicago, IL	Memphis, TN
Dallas, TX	New Orleans, LA
Duluth, MN	Omaha, NE
Houston, TX	

3 Mountain time (−2 hours)

Boise, ID	Denver, CO
Butte, MT	Phoenix, AZ
Cheyenne, WY	Tucson, AZ

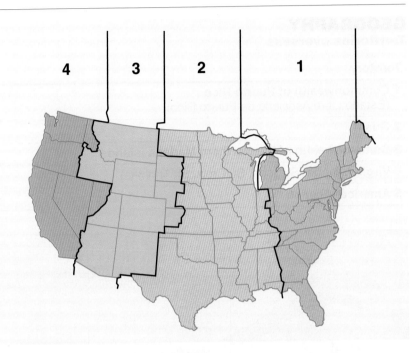

4 Pacific time (–3 hours)

Los Angeles, CA	San Francisco, CA
Reno, NV	Seattle, WA

Other cities (–4 hours)

Fairbanks, AK
Juneau, AK

Other cities (–5 hours)

Honolulu, HI

21

GEOGRAPHY
Territories overseas

Territory
1 Commonwealth of Puerto Rico (Estado Libre Asociado de Puerto Rico)
2 Guam
3 Commonwealth of the Northern Mariana Islands
4 Virgin Islands (St. John, St. Croix, St. Thomas)
5 American Samoa

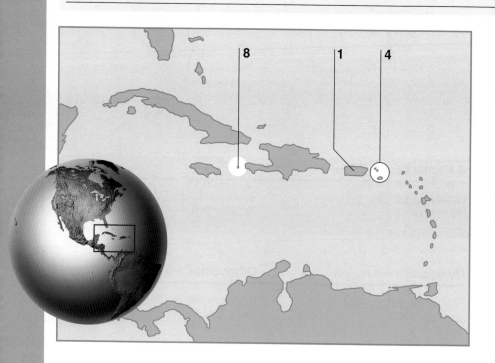

Area (sq mi)	Population 2005 (000s)	Capital
3515	3916	San Juan
209	163	Agana
184	72	Saipan
136	108	Charlotte Amalia
77	65	Pago Pago

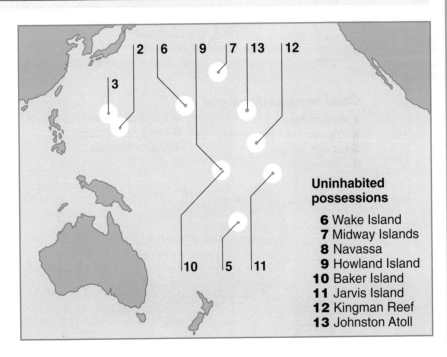

Uninhabited possessions

6 Wake Island
7 Midway Islands
8 Navassa
9 Howland Island
10 Baker Island
11 Jarvis Island
12 Kingman Reef
13 Johnston Atoll

Major land regions (excluding Alaska and Hawaii)

1 Atlantic coastal plain
2 Appalachian Highlands
3 Interior plains
4 Ozark-Ouachita Highlands

5 Rocky Mountain system
6 Intermountain plateaus
7 Western Mountain system

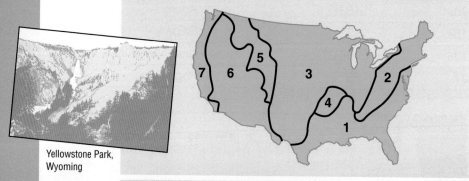

Yellowstone Park, Wyoming

Chief mountain ranges

1 Alaska range
2 Appalachian Mountains
3 Brooks range
4 Cascade range

5 Coastal Mountain system
6 Rocky Mountains
7 Sierra Nevada

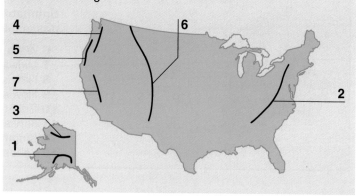

The highest mountains (height in ft)

1 McKinley   20,320   **4** Bona   16,550
2 St. Elias   18,008   **5** Blackburn 16,390
3 Foraker   17,400

Glacier at Mt.
Hayes, Alaska

Major deserts (area in sq mi)

1 Sonoran Desert 70,000   **3** Painted Desert 7500
2 Mojave   15,000   **4** Death Valley   3300

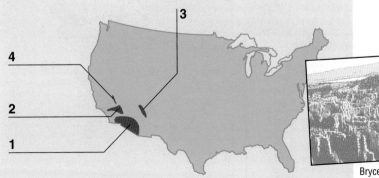

Bryce Canyon,
Utah

21

The longest rivers (length in mi)

1 Mississippi	3710	4 Arkansas	1459
2 Missouri	2540	5 Colorado	1450
3 Rio Grande	1900		

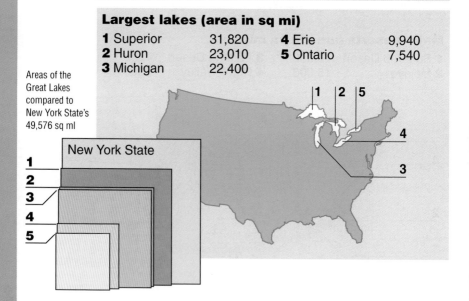

Largest lakes (area in sq mi)

1 Superior	31,820	4 Erie	9,940
2 Huron	23,010	5 Ontario	7,540
3 Michigan	22,400		

Areas of the
Great Lakes
compared to
New York State's
49,576 sq ml

New York State

1
2
3
4
5

POPULATION

The following population "pyramid" shows the structure of the American population, in terms of age and sex, in 2004. It shows, for example, that among people under five there are slightly more boys than girls, while among people over 85, there are more than twice as many women as men.

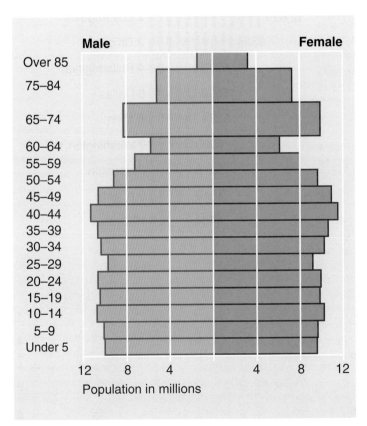

The most populated urban areas (2003, 000s)

The figures refer to metropolitan areas larger than the named city, e.g. New York includes northern New Jersey and Long Island.

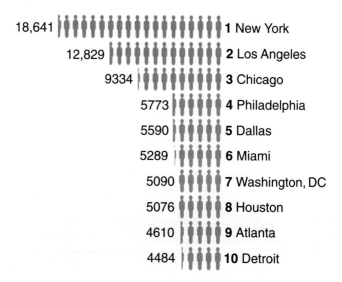

18,641 — **1** New York
12,829 — **2** Los Angeles
9334 — **3** Chicago
5773 — **4** Philadelphia
5590 — **5** Dallas
5289 — **6** Miami
5090 — **7** Washington, DC
5076 — **8** Houston
4610 — **9** Atlanta
4484 — **10** Detroit

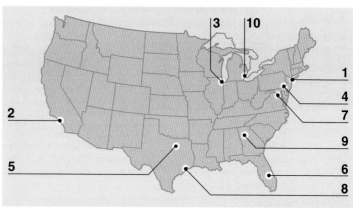

Urban states
States with highest percentage of their populations living in urban areas, 2000.

1 District of Columbia 100 **4** Nevada 91.5
2 California 94.5 **5** Hawaii (not shown) 91.5
3 New Jersey 94.5

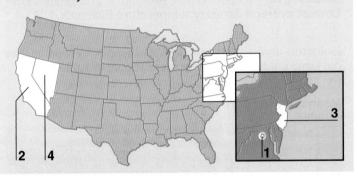

Rural states
States with highest percentage of their populations living in the country, 2000.

1 Vermont 61.8 **4** Mississippi 37.2
2 Maine 59.8 **5** South Dakota 48.1
3 West Virginia 53.9

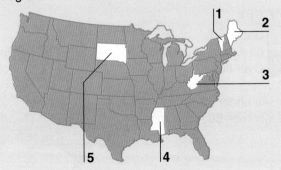

21

CLIMATE
Temperature
Hottest ever Greenland Ranch, Death Valley, CA: 134 °F in July 1913
Highest average July temperature Phoenix, AZ and Las Vegas, NV: 105 °F
Coldest ever Prospect Creek, AK: −80 °F in January 1971
Lowest average January temperature Bismarck, ND: −4 °F

Isotherms are lines on a map which link places experiencing the same temperature. These maps show typical isotherms for January and July.

Mean daily temperature
January (°F)

- 0–10
- 10–30
- 30–50
- Over 50

Alaska 10–30
Hawaii over 30

July (°F)

- Under 60
- 60–80
- Over 80

Alaska under 60
Hawaii over 80

Rainfall
Greatest average annual precipitation Mount Waialeale, Kauai, HI: 460 in.
Lowest average annual precipitation
Las Vegas, NV: 4.19 in.
Most rainfall in 24 hour period Alvin, TX: 43 in. on July 25–26, 1979

The map shows the average annual rainfall across the US. Generally, there is more precipitation in the eastern half of the country, though the highest levels are found in the west.

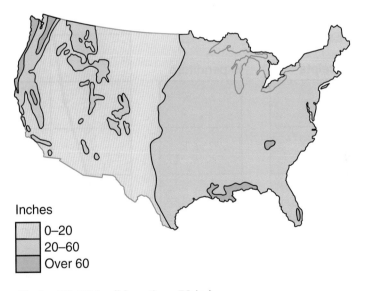

Inches
0–20
20–60
Over 60

Alaska 20–60 in. (More than 50 in.)
Hawaii 20–60 in. (More than 20 in.)

21

NATIONAL FINANCES
Public finance
all figures in $ billions

Year	Receipts	Expenditure	National debt
1980	0.517	0.590	0.909
1990	1.032	1.253	3.206
2000	2.025	1.788	5.628
2004	1.798	2.318	7.486

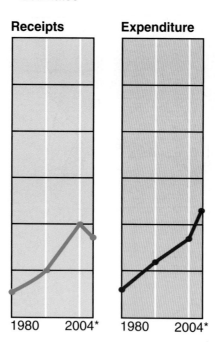

* Estimates

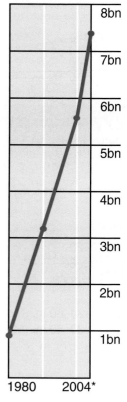

Personal finance
These tables show the consumer price index for various commodities.

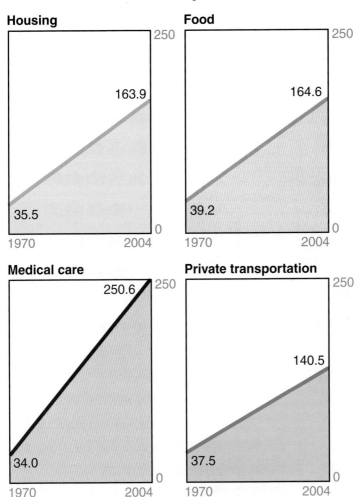

Housing

250

163.9

35.5

1970　　　　　2004

0

Food

250

164.6

39.2

1970　　　　　2004

0

Medical care

250.6　250

34.0

1970　　　　　2004

0

Private transportation

250

140.5

37.5

1970　　　　　2004

0

1982–4 = 100　annual averages of monthly figures

21

AGRICULTURE

Together, these tables show that as the number of farms decreases, the size of farm holdings goes up.

The number of farms in the USA 1940–2002 (000s)

Year	Farms
1940	6300
1950	6000
1960	4500
1970	3800
1980	2400
1990	2100
2000	2200
2002	2100

All figures have been rounded to the nearest 100

The average size of farms 1940–2002 (in acres)

Year	Acres
1940	168
1950	213
1960	297
1970	374
1980	427
1990	460
2000	434
2002	441

Amount of farmland

The ten states with the largest amount of farmland in 2002, in thousands of acres.

1	Texas	129.9	**6**	South Dakota	43.8
2	Montana	59.6	**7**	North Dakota	39.3
3	Kansas	47.2	**8**	Wyoming	34.4
4	Nebraska	45.9	**9**	Oklahoma	33.7
5	New Mexico	44.8	**10**	Iowa	31.7

Farm income

The top ten states in terms of net farm income (2002, $ millions).

1	California	5179	**6**	North Carolina	1661
2	Texas	3686	**7**	Arizona	1462
3	Florida	2667	**8**	Idaho	1256
4	Iowa	1767	**9**	Alabama	1200
5	Georgia	1699	**10**	Nebraska	980

Value of farm real estate (2002, in $ billions)

1	Texas	100.5	**6**	Minnesota	41.8
2	California	96.1	**7**	Ohio	39.6
3	Illinois	66.7	**8**	Indiana	36.3
4	Iowa	64.2	**9**	Wisconsin	35.8
5	Missouri	45.3	**10**	Nebraska	35.7

21

COMPARATIVE DATA

The largest states (area in sq mi)

1 Alaska   591,004
2 Texas   266,807
3 California   158,706
4 Montana   147,046
5 New Mexico   121,593

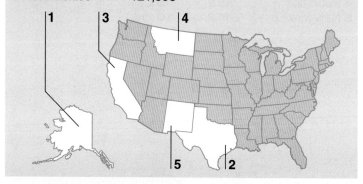

The smallest states (area in sq mi)

1 District of Columbia   69
2 Rhode Island   1212
3 Delaware   2045
4 Connecticut   5018
5 Hawaii   6471

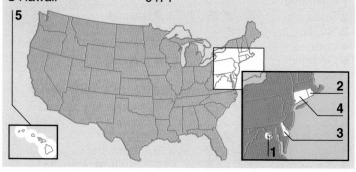

The largest populations (2003, 000s)

1	California	35,484
2	Texas	22,119
3	New York	19,190
4	Florida	17,019
5	Illinois	12,654

The smallest populations (2003, 000s)

1	Wyoming	501
2	District of Columbia	563
3	Vermont	619
4	North Dakota	634
5	Alaska	649

21

The wealthiest states
(2003, per capita income in $)

1 District of Columbia 48,342
2 Connecticut 43,173
3 New Jersey 40,427
4 Massachusetts 39,815
5 New York 36,574

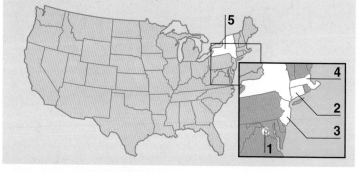

The poorest states
(2003, per capita income in $)

1 Mississippi 23,448
2 Arkansas 24,289
3 West Virginia 24,379
4 New Mexico 25,541
5 Montana 25,920

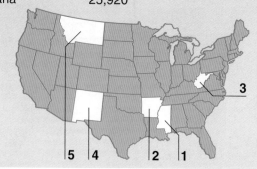

Highest population densities
(2003, people per sq mi)
1 District of Columbia   9,175.6
2 New Jersey   1,164.6
3 Rhode Island   1,029.9
4 Massachusetts   820.6
5 Connecticut   719.0

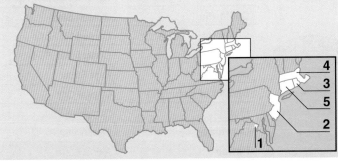

Lowest population densities
(2003, people per sq mi)
1 Alaska   1.1
2 Wyoming   5.2
3 Montana   6.3
4 North Dakota   9.2
5 South Dakota   10.1

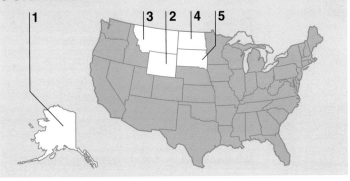

21

Alabama

Delaware

Iowa

Minnesota

EMBLEMS OF THE STATES

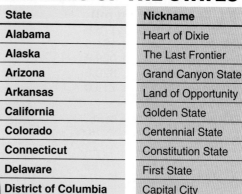

State	Nickname
Alabama	Heart of Dixie
Alaska	The Last Frontier
Arizona	Grand Canyon State
Arkansas	Land of Opportunity
California	Golden State
Colorado	Centennial State
Connecticut	Constitution State
Delaware	First State
District of Columbia	Capital City
Florida	Sunshine State
Georgia	Peach State
Hawaii	Aloha State
Idaho	Gem State
Illinois	Prairie State
Indiana	Hoosier State
Iowa	Hawkeye State
Kansas	Sunflower State
Kentucky	Bluegrass State
Louisiana	Pelican State
Maine	Pine Tree State
Maryland	Old Line State
Massachusetts	Bay State
Michigan	Great Lakes State
Minnesota	North Star State

Capital	Flower	Motto
Montgomery	Camellia	We Dare Defend Our Rights
Juneau	Forget-Me-Not	North to the Future
Phoenix	Saguaro flower	God Enriches
Little Rock	Apple blossom	The People Rule
Sacramento	Golden poppy	I Have Found It
Denver	Blue columbine	Nothing Without Providence
Hartford	Mountain laurel	He Who Transplanted Still Sustains
Dover	Peach blossom	Liberty and Independence
Washington	American beauty rose	Justice For All
Tallahassee	Orange blossom	In God We Trust
Atlanta	Cherokee rose	Wisdom, Justice, and Moderation
Honolulu	Yellow hibiscus	The Life of the Land Is Perpetuated In Righteousness
Boise	Syringa	It Is Perpetual
Springfield	Native violet	State Sovereignty – National Union
Indianapolis	Peony	Crossroads of America
Des Moines	Wild rose	Our Liberties We Prize and Our Right We Will Maintain
Topeka	Sunflower	To The Stars Through Difficulties
Frankfort	Goldenrod	United We Stand, Divided We Fall
Baton Rouge	Magnolia	Union, Justice, and Confidence
Augusta	Pine cone and tassel	I Direct
Annapolis	Black-eyed Susan	Manly Deeds, Womanly Words
Boston	Mayflower	By The Sword We Seek Peace, But Peace Only Under Liberty
Lansing	Apple blossom	If You Seek a Pleasant Peninsula, Look About You
St. Paul	Showy lady slipper	Star of the North

Mississippi

New Mexico

Rhode Island

Wyoming

State	Nickname
Mississippi	Magnolia State
Missouri	Show Me State
Montana	Treasure State
Nebraska	Cornhusker State
Nevada	Sagebrush State
New Hampshire	Granite State
New Jersey	Garden State
New Mexico	Land of Enchantment
New York	Empire State
North Carolina	Tar Heel State
North Dakota	Peace Garden State
Ohio	Buckeye State
Oklahoma	Sooner State
Oregon	Beaver State
Pennsylvania	Keystone State
Rhode Island	Little Rhody
South Carolina	Palmetto State
South Dakota	Coyote State
Tennessee	Volunteer State
Texas	Lone Star State
Utah	Beehive State
Vermont	Green Mountain State
Virginia	Old Dominion
Washington	Evergreen State
West Virginia	Mountain State
Wisconsin	Badger State
Wyoming	Equality State

Capital	Flower	Motto
Jackson	Magnolia	By Valor and Arms
Jefferson City	Hawthorn	The Welfare of the People Shall Be the Supreme Law
Helena	Bitterroot	Gold and Silver
Lincoln	Goldenrod	Equality Before the Law
Carson City	Sagebrush	All For Our Country
Concord	Purple lilac	Live Free or Die
Trenton	Purple violet	Liberty and Prosperity
Santa Fé	Yucca	It Grows as It Goes
Albany	Rose	Ever Upward
Raleigh	Dogwood	To Be Rather Than To Seem
Bismarck	Wild prairie rose	Liberty and Union, Now and Forever, One and Inseparable
Columbus	Scarlet carnation	With God, All Things Are Possible
Oklahoma City	Mistletoe	Labor Conquers All Things
Salem	Oregon grape	The Union
Harrisburg	Mountain laurel	Virtue, Liberty and Independence
Providence	Violet	Hope
Columbia	Yellow jessamine	While I Breathe, I Hope
Pierre	Pasque flower	Under God, The People Rule
Nashville	Iris	Agriculture and Commerce
Austin	Bluebonnet	Friendship
Salt Lake City	Sego lily	Industry
Montpelier	Red clover	Freedom and Unity
Richmond	Flowering dogwood	Thus Always To Tyrants
Olympia	Western rhododendron	By and By
Charleston	Big rhododendron	Mountaineers Are Always Free
Madison	Wood violet	Forward
Cheyenne	Indian paintbrush	Equal Rights

21

THE STATES AND THE UNION

The table shows the states which constitute the Union, the date they joined, and their rank. The original 13 colonies which signed the Declaration of Independence in 1776 are highlighted in red. The District of Columbia, which is treated as a state in many respects (see pp. 604–9), is not recognized as a member of the union.

State	Joined	Rank	State	Joined	Rank
Alabama	Dec 14, 1819	22	Nebraska	Mar 1, 1867	37
Alaska	Jan 3, 1959	49	Nevada	Oct 31, 1864	36
Arizona	Feb 14, 1912	48	New Hampshire	Jun 21, 1788	9
Arkansas	Jun 15, 1836	25	New Jersey	Dec 18, 1787	3
California	Sep 9, 1850	31	New Mexico	Jan 6, 1912	47
Colorado	Aug 1, 1876	38	New York	Jul 26, 1788	11
Connecticut	Jan 9, 1788	5	N. Carolina	Nov 21, 1789	12
Delaware	Dec 7, 1787	1	N. Dakota	Nov 2, 1889	39
Florida	Mar 3, 1845	27	Ohio	Mar 1, 1803	17
Georgia	Jan 2, 1788	4	Oklahoma	Nov 16, 1907	46
Hawaii	Aug 21, 1959	50	Oregon	Feb 14, 1859	33
Idaho	Jul 3, 1890	43	Pennsylvania	Dec 12, 1787	2
Illinois	Dec 3, 1818	21	Rhode Island	May 29, 1790	13
Indiana	Dec 11, 1816	19	S. Carolina	May 23, 1788	8
Iowa	Dec 28, 1846	29	S. Dakota	Nov 2, 1889	40
Kansas	Jan 29, 1861	34	Tennessee	Jun 1, 1796	16
Kentucky	Jun 1, 1792	15	Texas	Dec 29, 1845	28
Louisiana	Apr 30, 1812	18	Utah	Jan 4, 1896	45
Maine	Mar 15, 1820	23	Vermont	Mar 4, 1791	14
Maryland	Apr 28, 1788	7	Virginia	Jun 25, 1788	10
Massachusetts	Feb 6, 1788	6	Washington	Nov 11, 1889	42
Michigan	Jan 26, 1837	26	W. Virginia	Jun 20, 1863	35
Minnesota	May 11, 1858	32	Wisconsin	May 29, 1848	30
Mississippi	Dec 10, 1817	20	Wyoming	Jul 10, 1890	44
Missouri	Aug 10, 1821	24			
Montana	Nov 8, 1889	41			

X

Y

Z